Trustees for Nature

A Memoir

Dr Arthur Edward Smith CBE MA
Portrait by Bill Bates 1998

Trustees for Nature

A Memoir

by

Ted Smith CBE

What would the world be, once bereft
Of wet and of wildness? Let them be left,
O let them be left, wildness and wet;
Long live the weeds and the wilderness yet.
Hopkins

Published by

Lincolnshire Wildlife Trust
Nature Conservation from the Humber to the Wash

Banovallum House, Manor House Street, Horncastle, Lincs LN9 5HF

2007

ISBN 978-0-9538270-2-2

Typeset by Susan Curtis
Picture research by Barrie Wilkinson
Editing and design by David Robinson

Cover:
Gibraltar Point 1996
(Barrie Wilkinson)

Printed by Cupit Print, The Ropewalk, 23 Louth Road, Horncastle, Lincolnshire LN9 5ED

To Mary, Alison and Helen
and to the memory of Peter

Grass of Parnassus by Mary Smith

Contents

Foreword   8

Preface   9

Part I In The Beginning

Chapter 1   11
A Discovery – Scenes from Childhood – Town and Country –
Schooldays – Leeds 1938-1946 – Lincolnshire Landscapes –
Norfolk 1947 – Return of the Native – 1948 Annus Mirabilis

Part II Lincolnshire: The Making of the Trust

Chapter 2 The Trust is Launched – Building the Organisation   35
Chapter 3 Family Matters 1950s   43
Chapter 4 Gibraltar Point: The First 25 Years   53
Creating the Nature Reserve – The First Local Nature Reserve
in England – The Reserve Under Threat – The Bird Observatory –
Managing the Reserve – Interpreting the Reserve and its Wildlife –
Promoting Research and Education

Chapter 5 Nature Reserves: A Salvage Operation   95
Selecting the Sites – The First Acquisitions 1950 -1960

Chapter 6 Saltfleetby-Theddlethorpe Dunes   105
Establishing the Nature Reserve – Nature Reserve or Caravan Camps -
National Nature Reserve Status

Chapter 7 Conservation on the Humber   119
Pits and Reedbeds – The Humber Wildfowl Refuge and Read's Island

Chapter 8 Nature in Retreat   129
Robert's Field – Waddingham Common – Manton Common –
Messingham Heath – Saltmarshes – Woodlands

Chapter 9 In the Path of the Juggernaut   159
A New Agricultural Revolution – Meadows – Roadside Verges and
Hedgerows – The Incident on Tetford Hill – The Protected Road
Verge Scheme – Rivers and Streams – Toxic Chemicals and Wildlife –
Postscript

Chapter 10 1958 -1973 Growing Pains   189
The Volunteer Force: Central organisation and Area Groups,
Managing the Nature Reserves, Promotion and Publicity;
Local Authority Relationships – Financing Development and Staffing –
Changes in Local Government – Moving House – A Personal Footnote

Chapter 11 The Expanding Estate 1960 – 1975   207
Survey and Selection of Nature Reserves – Management Planning –
New Nature Reserves: Coastlands, Woodlands, Chalk Grasslands,
Limestone Grasslands, Other Grasslands, Heathland and Bog, Wetlands

Part III Nationwide: The Trusts' Movement Develops

Chapter12 Wider Horizons   241
The National Context – Promoting New Trusts – Developing a
Partnership – The Cambridge 'Declaration' – A Proposal to SPNR –
A Council for Nature: Solution or Diversion? – Back to the SPNR –
The Regional Liaison Committee – The First County Trusts' Conference

Chapter 13 The Trusts' Movement Expands 1960-1970   261
Launching New Trusts – Financial Assistance to Trusts – The Trusts
in SPNR – Administering the Society in the 1960s – External
Relationships: The Council for Nature, The Nature Conservancy,
The RSPB, The Forestry Commission, The National Trust;
The RSPBNR? A Merger Too Far

Chapter 14 Re-structuring the SPNR   283
Constitution, Governance and Administration – Committee Structure
and Implications: Education, Promotion and Public Relations:
A Magazine for the Trusts, A Trusts' Reserves Handbook, Conferences,
Nature Trails, A Sales Business – Conservation Policy Practice and
Achievement: A Biological Sites Recording Scheme, Wildlife Legislation,
Rivers and Streams, Nature Conservation and Agriculture – The Future
of the Nature Conservancy

Chapter 15 Nature Reserves: The Changing Role of the SPNR   303
Funding the Nature Reserves – The Carnegie UK Trust –
The Countryside Commission – Local Authorities – The Nature
Conservancy Council – Time To Go

Part IV The Conservancy Years

Chapter 16   317

Part V The Lincolnshire Trust up to Now in Outline

Chapter 17   323
Constitution and Administration: Governance, Personnel, Membership
and Area Groups, Wildlife Watch, Staffing, A New Home for the Trust
in Banovallum House 1993 – Biodiversity, Land Use and Planning –
Nature Reserves Acquisition and Management: Selection Criteria,
Management Issues, Funding for Acquistion and Management –
Habitat Representation: Coastlands, Woodlands, Chalk and Limestone
Grassland, Other Grasslands, Heathland and Bog, Wetlands,
The Urban Environment – The Future for Nature Reserves –
Education and Promotion – Financing the Organisation

Part VI Home at Pyewipes

Chapter 18 Family, Home and Garden   369
The Smith Girls – And Mary – Garden and Wildlife –As For Me

Epilogue – Past and Future   381

Foreword

How did it happen that, during the last fifty years, people who care for the British countryside – for its birds and its plants, its butterflies and its badgers – are no longer regarded as slightly eccentric specialists with private concerns of little interest to the public at large, but have become a unified group with a powerful voice both in local and national government and with wide support from all sections of society? This book is written by one of those who brought about that transformation.

Like so many naturalists, Ted Smith began his working life in a quite different profession – as an English teacher and an adult education tutor. But it soon became clear to his naturalist friends that in addition to his expertise in the field he had particular skills as an organiser and an inspirer. He understood, to a degree that verged on the magical, the diplomacies needed to coordinate and energise organisations. He could convince people who were under the impression that they disagreed with one another that, on the contrary, they wholeheartedly shared the same opinions. He could even persuade some to take on responsibilities that they did not seek and to believe that they enjoyed doing so.

Naturalists, by their very character, are devoted to their native heaths. Ted's patch is Lincolnshire and his pioneering labours on its behalf led to the establishment of England's first statutory Local Nature Reserve and later its first statutory Wildfowl Refuge. He battled to outlaw the use of lethal chemical insecticides by those seeking to intensify agriculture. He fought to save his county's ancient species-rich meadows and heaths and to halt the felling of native woodlands and their replacement by plantations of conifers.

Other people, meanwhile, elsewhere in the country were waging similar campaigns and Ted and a few others soon realised that their separate and often differing voices would have to unite if they were to make themselves properly heard. That was no easy task. So often national organisations begin singly and centrally and then extend outwards. This country's nature conservation movement grew in exactly the opposite way – springing up separately in numerous places and extending inwards to try and establish a co-ordinating centre. Each element was proudly, fiercely and understandably independent and anything or anybody that attempted to diminish that independence was likely to be resisted.

Ted Smith, quiet, unobtrusive, diplomatic, but with steely determination, was one of the key figures in dealing with these problems. Having been a founding father in the Lincolnshire Trust, he took on national responsibilities. He devised ways of helping counties that did not have a Naturalists Trust to set one up, until eventually no part of the country was left un-represented and he established the framework for them all to meet and hammer out common policies.

The following pages will be of absorbing interest to those who care about the British countryside for in them one of the front-line fighters for its conservation reveals how so many of the crucial battles were won.

David Attenborough

Preface

These recollections have been set down over several years. Initially my intention was simply to leave a record for the archives, but encouragement and advice from friends persuaded me that there is a story worth publishing. I knew where to start, but nature conservation is a constantly unfolding process responding and adapting to changing circumstances. It was therefore more difficult to decide where to stop, especially in relation to the Lincolnshire Trust in which I have continued to be active to the present day. As I explain at the beginning of Chapter 17, I had originally decided that my account of the Trust should cover its first thirty or so years, up to about 1980, but in view of the many developments and changes taking place in the conservation scene I have added a further chapter briefly describing the Trust's progress into the new century. For the national association I determined that my account should conclude with my retirement as General Secretary of what is now the Royal Society of Wildlife Trusts at the end of 1978, although I continued as a Special Adviser and a member of the Executive Committee and Council for some time afterwards.

My story is as much about people as it is about wildlife. I have referred to many of them individually, especially those pioneers whose voluntary dedication brought the Lincolnshire Trust and all the other Trusts and their national association into being and set them on the road to success. I am proud and privileged to have known and worked with many of them and counted them among my friends. To all those and to many others not individually identified I am deeply indebted for support and collaboration.

More specifically I have received much help and advice in the preparation of this Memoir. No-one has done greater service to the cause of nature conservation worldwide than Sir David Attenborough, and I am especially grateful for his generous Foreword. Dr John Sheail of the Centre for Ecology and Hydrology at Monks Wood, himself a distinguished historian of the nature conservation movement, has given me help and encouragement in developing the Memoir for publication. My fellow officers in the Lincolnshire Trust and its Director have made helpful comments on the text, and have considered it of sufficient value to recommend to the Board of Trustees that it be published by the Trust.

David Robinson, my friend and colleague of fifty years in adult education and in the Lincolnshire Trust, has generously devoted his editorial skill and experience to the preparation of the Memoir for publication including the selection and presentation of the illustrations. Barrie Wilkinson has given invaluable help in the search for photographs and in their preparation for printing. I am grateful for permission from several people to use their photographs, and I am especially fortunate to have been able to draw on the wealth of material from Geoff Trinder and Barrie Wilkinson.

Susan Curtis has typed the text through many changes and amendments with patience and understanding, and tolerance of my poor handwriting. I am indebted to her for her interest and dedication.

Mary has given me unfailing support and co-operation in all that I have done in nature conservation. I dedicate the Memoir to her and to our children with love and admiration.

BARRIE WILKINSON

DAVID ROBINSON

MARY SMITH

FRED CLIFT

Top left: *Harvesting on Croftmarsh from Gibraltar Road*

Top right: *'Gaudy new houses' on Aylmer Avenue*

Ruined Gibraltar House

Coastguard Station

Sea buckthorn

Steeping River Estuary

10

Part I

In The Beginning

– 1 –

Home is where one starts from Eliot

THE BIKE wheels churned deep into the soft sandy track. It was hard going, and after a while I gave up and walked the rest of the way. On the right, fields of wheat, potatoes and sugar beet stretched away towards the low rim of hills in the distance. The wheat was ripening to harvest under a cloudless August sky. A horse-drawn reaper-binder was already at work in one of the fields, the blades clattering noisily as the sheaves slithered off the rack. On the other side of the track close-mown golf links had given way to sandhills partially covered with a silvery leaved shrub which I later knew as sea buckthorn. Three gaudy new houses on a road recently cut into the dunes struck an incongruous note. Was this the start, I wondered, of the kind of holiday development which was already transforming much of the Lincolnshire coast to the north of Skegness. On the right again the red-pantiled roofs of a farmhouse and farm buildings showed up among elms and sycamores as the track veered into a hollow through the dunes. Another few hundred yards and I topped a steep bank to see the place called Gibraltar Point.

The estuary of a little river curved away through saltmarshes where patches of purple sea lavender and silvery sea wormwood caught the eye amidst the sober greens of sea purslane and couch-grass. An old rowing boat lay on the muddy bank. Beyond the river mudflats wet from the morning tide glistened in the sun. A distant cloud of birds rose and fell like gnats in tight formation. Away to the east a long way off over a sandy beach was the sea, waves breaking over sandbanks, and beyond the sea the low hills and woods of another shore.

Near at hand on the seabank was a ruined house, a long low building with the remains of a pantiled roof sagging precariously. A little further on the track ended at another building in dark brick, slate-roofed, high gabled, with a tower on the south side pierced with narrow little windows, all of it enclosed within an old brick wall. Out there at the end of the line of dunes surrounded by saltmarshes it seemed strange and lonely and yet somehow an indispensable element of the scene. I went on to explore the place and its birds in detail, but that first and lasting impression was of space and distance, a fusion of land and sea and sky.

Scenes from Childhood

In a sense that is where I begin this history: on the sea bank at Gibraltar Point on that far off August day in 1937, but 'home is where one starts from', so I must go back still further. I had come from home that morning cycling the fourteen miles from Alford where I was born two years after the end of the Great War, 'the war to end wars'. I was a late child; my sister had preceded me by ten years. My father was a versatile chap. He had left school at fourteen, but being of an enquiring mind had continued his education by night school courses and reading. He came from a long line of local rural craftsmen. His grandfather was a blacksmith; his father was the head cooper at the Alford brewery of Soulby, Son & Winch, now alas long since defunct. So, apprenticed and qualified as a plumber, he had set up in business on his marriage in 1906, but to supplement the living he soon acquired a small grocer and bakers business. He prepared the dough for bread in the evening, rose at six in the morning, baked the day's supply for the shop and then went off to his work as a plumber. My mother meantime managed the shop which often stayed open until nine or ten at night. Numerous cousins from my mother's family were brought in to assist in the shop and with the baker's round which involved pushing a truck laden with loaves in all weathers round the town and out to the hamlet of Farlesthorpe three miles away.

It was an unusual combination – baker, grocer and plumber – but my parents kept it up for more than forty years, working long hours, contented in their way but earning only a modest living and enjoying few luxuries. In all those years they took only one real holiday together: a memorable journey on the Rhine in 1936 when Hitler was already firmly in power in Germany. There were some poor families in Alford in the 1920s and 30s and the grocery business suffered a good deal from minor debts. My father was generous and easy going, more tolerant of the bad payers than my mother who took a less charitable view. It was an issue which caused more family friction than any other that I remember.

My mother's family had been a large one: two brothers and five sisters. Both maternal grandparents had died before I was born. Like my father's side they were from local Marshland stock, my grandmother from families with interesting names of Scandinavian origin like Pinney and Starmer, the latter meaning a sedgy mere, star being the popular name of the once common fen sedge *Cladium mariscus* used for ridge thatching. Three of the sisters had died prematurely from tuberculosis and one brother had been killed on the Somme in 1916. My childhood was punctuated by anniversaries of deaths, pathetically and infallibly remembered.

Our house and our domestic life were, I suppose, somewhat spartan by modern standards. There were few modern conveniences or comforts. There was a radio, but very few books of any kind. A children's encyclopaedia bought for me one Christmas was a prized possession, the natural history sections especially being frequently consulted. The shop, facing South Street, had been a pub, the Cross Keys, before my parents bought it. The store rooms were still called the bar and the cellar. The all-purpose living room was behind the shop; off that was the pantry, dark and cool, I remember, with a large stone jar or pipkin to hold the water. For many people in the days before the mains were laid, water had to be fetched from an elevated tank along the road which was supplied from a borehole, but we had our own well, the water being drawn by a pump in the yard with a creaking wooden handle. Beyond the living room was a kind of scullery, a part of it in the early days open to the sky, with a large soft water tank to collect precious rain water from the roof for washing. Then came the bakehouse with a big wooden trough for the dough and an old baking oven with a heavy iron door and a fire hole at the side. The loaves were extracted from trays on a peel, a flat shovel with a long wooden handle, and lined up in rows on a table. The smell of newly baked bread was one of my cherished childhood memories. On Good Friday the living room table was also brought into service and when I came downstairs there were already seemingly endless rows of hot cross buns. People were coming to the bakehouse door by seven o'clock to buy them for breakfast. My father also made a very popular brand of traditional Lincolnshire plum bread, particularly delicious with cheese. His currant squares, liberally stuffed with juicy raisins and currants soaked in treacle and enclosed in flaky pastry, were also much in demand.

A passage led beside the oven to a wash-house equipped with a copper heated by a coal fire underneath, a mangle and a dolly tub in which the clothes were pummelled with a three legged wooden posher. Monday was wash day of course, rigidly so, like spring cleaning and all other routine tasks. Outside across a narrow passage was a building called the warehouse, another place of smells, this time of corn - wheat, oats and barley meal – which we sold as pig and chicken food. They were kept in a row of big wooden bins with heavy hinged lids. Next was a yard with the pump, an open ash pit and a privy emptied at regular intervals by the night-soil cart. Beyond that was the plumbing part of the establishment, a yard full of heavy coils of lead pipe and stacks of galvanised pipes and a great heap of 'waste', disposed of periodically to the local scrap merchant. The workshop was a two-storey building with a pigeon cote in the gable end, although we never kept pigeons there. It had all the paraphernalia of the plumber's trade of sixty to seventy years ago, an untidy, chaotic, fascinating place where as a child I was allowed only on strict conditions of behaviour. The only mementoes of the workshop that remain to us are my father's folding boxwood ruler with brass hinges, and a rather battered straight-sided pewter mug - a relict no doubt of the Cross Keys – in which he had kept oil! At the side of the workshop was a ramshackle lean-to in which we kept at various times both pigs and chickens. The pig was still a prized member of most households in the town in those days, fed cheaply on scraps and potatoes and barley meal. 'Putting the pig away' was a great ceremony in which various relations were engaged to assist. Pieces of 'fry' and other delicacies had to be allocated to friends and relations in a discreetly ordained order of priority. To miss out anyone with legitimate expectation was to risk giving mortal offence! Flitches of salted bacon and strings of dried sausages hung for months from ceiling hooks.

Finally in this long narrow site were the greenhouse and the garden. My father was a keen chrysanthemum grower, those hugely double, in-curved blooms so heavy that they had to be staked. They seemed to me strangely unreal, scarcely recognisable as flowers. The garden was small and unambitious, predictably the same year after year: chrysanthemums, gladioli, a large rhubarb bed, a decaying cucumber frame, an American pillar rose covering an ugly galvanised fence, and a lone, heavily pollarded sycamore from which we hung the occasional coconut won at the November fair to feed the tits. My interest in rock plants obviously began at quite an early age because I tried at one time to enliven the garden by constructing a small rockery, but it was a pathetic affair. We also had an allotment on the edge of the town; I liked to go there because there was a large bed of lavender next to our plot and in summer this attracted many butterflies in which I developed an early interest. There was also a secluded little reed-fringed clay pit at the edge of the allotments where I first saw, or rather heard, a kingfisher. It was the sound of a fish being battered to death before being swallowed that first drew my attention to the bird.

Our house was at the south end of a terraced row which my parents owned. It was built of putty coloured local brick from the nearby Farlesthorpe brickyard, and roofed in Welsh slate, the common building materials of Alford after the railway came in 1848. On the opposite side of South Street was the beck (now filled in) in which the local children caught sticklebacks, and where in later years, when my interest in birds developed, grey wagtails regularly in winter and kingfishers occasionally used to delight me. A few yards upstream the beck flowed under a bridge where three roads met, a place known as the Pinfold where in the distant past stray animals had been impounded. The bridge parapet was a solid block of Millstone Grit cold and rough to the touch with grey crystals of felspar and glistening grains of quartz. It was a rock which I came to know well as a sombre building stone in my years in Leeds. The Pinfold was a popular meeting place in the evenings for children and in summer for old men, the Alford 'Parliament' as it was popularly known.

My bedroom looked out over grass fields – the Little Field of pre-Enclosure days and still known by that title in the 1920s. Several small farms survived in the town in the 20s and 30s – one of them owned by my maternal uncle – and these fields were grazed by a few cows which were taken home to milk in the afternoons. The lower parts often flooded in winter when they attracted snipe, and in icy weather provided marvellous slides. The big overgrown hedges with substantial thorn trees which separated the long rectangular Enclosure fields, were made for climbing, a favourite children's pastime in which you were judged by the height to which you had the nerve to go. Once in a particularly daring escapade I slipped and tore a pair of new short trousers from top to bottom. Clutching the pieces together I crept home fearful of my mother's wrath. For once, bless her, she had to laugh.

The house was on a corner. The southern side of the property was bounded by 'The Lane', originally Enderby's Lane – after a 19th century publican at the Cross Keys – but rather grandiosely renamed Finsbury Street. At the corner stood a large smooth grey-blue boulder put there to prevent carts from grazing the brickwork. Later I knew it to be a bluestone, an erratic ice-carried boulder brought perhaps from the Bluestone Heath up on the Wolds. It became a kind of symbol of durability for me and I often look even now as I pass to see that it is still there. The lane, free of traffic, except the occasional cart or van, was a children's playground. There was a scatter of houses interspersed with gardens and orchards along it - one of them belonging to my grandparents - and at the top a meadow full of flowers. The summer butterflies there still remain in my memory. In the mid-1930s it became the site for a new secondary modern school. The lane itself is now crammed with bungalows, almost unrecognisable from what it was in my childhood.

Most of the houses in the lane were roofed with pantiles, ideal for nesting swifts. As a small boy I often lay awake on summer evenings listening to them screaming over the rooftops, the mysterious birds of my childhood. In one of the little cottages in a row lived an old man called 'Taggy' Lambert - most of the older characters in the town were known by nicknames descriptive of their stature or behaviour or trade, or some memorable incident in their lives. 'Taggy' was one of a dying race of people who earned a precarious living off the land. He gathered and sold in their seasons mushrooms (of which he made ketchup), blackberries, and samphire from the coast, and he had the large lavender beds in the allotments. July and August would see him selling bunches of lavender to the holiday-makers at Mablethorpe, a precursor of today's popular dried flower trade. Swifts nested under the eaves of his cottage and, knowing my interest in birds, he would stop me in the street on a day in early May with the news "t'owd devlins are back". The coming and going of the devil's birds were the boundary markers of his summer. My other memory of him is standing with my school class at the War Memorial on chilly Armistice Days and hearing in the vicar's quavering tones the names of three of his sons killed in the Great War. The war indeed cast a long shadow over the 1920s and new storm clouds were gathering over Europe by the early 30s.

Town and Country

Alford in the inter-war years was the epitome of the sleepy little country town, more country almost than town. Its 2000 inhabitants were packed into a small compass, the well-to-do professionals and retired farmers mainly in Church Street and the tree-lined East End; the poor concentrated near the town centre in rows of terraced houses – Mount Pleasant, Ranters Row, Gashouse Lane. These 'slums' were demolished in the mid 1930s and the occupants moved out to the southern edge of the town into ugly new Council houses. Our end of the town, South Street, was socially somewhere in between. There were a few larger houses occupied by tradesmen mainly of a non-conformist and Liberal persuasion. Nearly all the houses had a well-tended garden, and whilst few people, whether workmen or retired farmworkers, had any spare cash, most of them managed with thrift and dignity. Many older social and domestic customs and observances still survived, and dialect speech was still common. I am proud that I can still speak in broad Lincolnshire, and use irreplaceable dialect words and phrases of Danish origin.

Alford stood at the junction of three farming regions then clearly distinctive: the Wolds, sheep and barley country; the Middle Marsh, an area of mixed husbandry; and the Outmarsh then predominantly grazing pasture. Alford's Tuesday cattle market and November Bull Fair still flourished. The town had three working windmills, including the tall and elegant town centre mill affectionately known as the 'high-waisted lady'. The station on the Grimsby-Peterborough railway line was on the outskirts of the town, for me a place of reluctant departures and welcome home-comings in early student days. The motor car was still a comparative rarity in my boyhood years, and we could safely run hoop races round the main streets on summer evenings. Much of the traffic was still horse-drawn: the farm carts and wagons, the carriers' and tradesmens' vans, the station dray which distributed goods brought in by train, and the town council's – Alford was then an Urban District – 'dilly cart' still doing its nightly rounds. When the station dray became a motorised van the same driver exchanged reins for steering wheel, but he continued to drive at the same pace as he had always done with the horse! I have an over-riding impression of a slower, quieter world. The contrast with today's noisy traffic in and through the town never escapes me.

Many of the small engineering and manufacturing industries which had flourished in the late 19th and early 20th centuries had disappeared by the 1920s and the population had fallen steeply from the high point of nearly 3,000 in the 1890s. There were nonetheless still two blacksmiths, a wheelwright, a tinsmith and a saddler, and a firm of millwrights which still continues and is said to be the only specialist firm of its kind left in the country. There was also a tannery in the middle of the town, not very popular on account of the smell! By far the largest employer was the brewery of Soulby Sons and Winch producing what would now no doubt be described as 'real ale'. The workforce coming and going on their bikes and the shift buzzer were among the most familiar sights and sounds of the town. Like many local breweries it eventually succumbed to competition from the big companies and closed in 1953. The tall maltkiln, now a gaunt ruin, is still a dominant feature of the town skyline.

As a service and social centre for the surrounding countryside Alford was still flourishing in the 1930s. There were many clubs and societies catering for a variety of recreational and cultural interests, but, unfortunately for me, the Naturalists' Society which had been active up to the turn of the century had long since become defunct. There were no less than seven pubs – there had been more before the First World War - and a cinema where for a couple of hours on thick pile carpets and plush chairs we left reality behind to watch the stars of the silent and early talking films: comic geniuses like Charlie Chaplin and Laurel and Hardy, and glamorous actresses with unlikely names like Greta Garbo and Myrna Loy. The cinema, I remember, was crowded (it seated 150) for the first 'talkie' to be shown there. That the film arrived late and the projection broke down twice during the showing didn't matter: we all agreed that it was a momentous event!

Religious divisions still made their mark in society. The church people were fairly predictable: the gentlefolk, the professionals, the 'superior' tradesmen, the retired farmers and others for whom church going was the hallmark of Tory respectability. The church of local greenstone - part Decorated, part Perpendicular, its proportions ruined by a squat outer north aisle added in the 1867 restoration – stands prominently near the market place on a mound which might be of pre-Christian origin. Nineteenth century non-conformist schisms were readily apparent: the Wesleyans, the better off and more conservative element, in a large chapel of rustic mid-Victorian inelegance; the Primitive Methodists (the 'Prims'), the radicals of the non-conformist movement, associated with the agricultural workers' union and the rising Labour Party, in a gaunt and austere building in South Street; and the Free Methodists, a small group somewhere in between the other two. My parents had no strong religious persuasions, but in my childhood we sometimes attended the Free Methodist chapel largely, I believe, because the daughter of its superintendent, a venerable, white-bearded smallholder, was my mother's best friend. I remember spontaneous and unnerving alleluia-type interjections from the congregation and the occasional sinner publicly declaring his repentance, not always, I suspect, for the first time! Those and the yellow gas lamps and the hard benches are my dim memories of Sunday night services there.

I was sent to the Wesleyan Sunday School, but was banished in disgrace when I refused to sign a teetotal pledge! My parents, although almost teetotal themselves, supported my right to self-determination. One memory of that Sunday School was of a teacher who had fought in the Boer War and told us exciting tales of his exploits. Our family was Liberal in politics, but the Horncastle Division had become a safe Conservative seat and few people were prepared to declare their political allegiance.

In my early teens I went to stay occasionally in summer holidays with friends of my parents in north London, being taken most memorably to museums, the zoo and that vast white elephant the Alexandra Palace. It was, I believe, at one of the museums where in the early 30s I saw on a flickering screen experimental television transmission. Otherwise summer treats consisted of day visits to the seaside - occasionally by charabanc to Skeggy (Skegness). Once on a visit to Mablethorpe my mother and I picnicked on the sandhills. Near to us a brightly coloured little bird with black head and a reddish breast was feeding young in a nest deep in a bush. To my distress two youths began to search for the nest, but perhaps because we watched disapprovingly soon gave up and the parents resumed their feeding. Much later I realised the birds were stonechats which until the mid-1930s nested in several places along the Lincolnshire sandhills. That incident occurred when I was six or seven years old. I remember too from that early age distinguishing between the blue, great and coal tits which came to the coconuts which we hung in the garden. And I remember being fascinated by the comings and goings of the blue tits which nested each year in a tiny cavity in the brickwork on the front of the shop. Most of the local boys went 'nesting' in the spring. Once I was persuaded to accept an egg from a hedgerow nest - probably a greenfinch's – but that night I was so stricken with remorse that I got up at first light in the morning and returned the egg to the nest. I never went even looking for nests again.

Another bird which made an early impression on me was the rook. With four rookeries, including one in South Street, they were - and still are – an indispensable element of the Alford townscape. There is something reassuring about rooks. They reflect a sense of stable community and tradition which used to characterise village and small town society. I have retained a great affection for them.

Schooldays

Early schooldays in infants and Church of England boys' schools in antiquated 19th century buildings leave very few memories. At the age of eleven I went to Alford Grammar School as a fee-payer, scholarships being few and far between in those days. There were only sixty-six boys and the range of subjects was very limited, especially in science which consisted only of chemistry. There was no biology and the only encouragement my natural history interest received from the school was from a teacher of French who took a few of us on local expeditions and once youth hostelling to the Peak District in September when I saw dippers for the first time and that lovely flower the grass-of-Parnassus which I long remembered.

Whence my interest in birds originated I know not. It certainly did not come from my family and was not shared by any boyhood friends. In fact I knew no-one else who was seriously interested until I went to university. By my early teens the interest was well developed and I acquired, probably as a birthday or Christmas present, the two volumes of T A Coward's *British Birds* with their much reduced Thorburn illustrations. These were aesthetically pleasing but of limited use for identification. The modern field guide was still in the future, and Coward's excellent little books were the most effective available. My general natural history reading was restricted by the paucity of such books in the school library, but I remember being fascinated by the descriptive writing of the French naturalist J H Fabre. The greatest influence on my development as a naturalist, however, was undoubtedly the *Natural History of Selborne*, and I sought to capture some of the originality and freshness of Gilbert White's observations. For a time I kept a diary, but I never sustained it for very long, and later as pressures of work increased – no excuse really – even my note taking became meagre and spasmodic. In that sense, I suppose, I failed one of the basic tests of a good naturalist.

Armed with a pair of cheap binoculars - also no doubt a present since there was little pocket money – my countryside excursions assumed a new purpose. On the southern edge of Alford lies the Well Vale estate which consisted at that time of several thousand acres of farmland and woods. The early Georgian mansion is set in a beautiful landscaped park with two lakes created by damming a little stream which rises from the chalk in the upper park. From there a narrow valley stretches up into the Wolds for more than a mile. The Vale, as it is known, was planted up in the mid-18th century and many old trees survived in the 1930s. The estate was heavily keepered, but there were some public footpaths and I had permission to wander within limits. Birds were abundant and I especially remember the flocks of hawfinches which I watched in winter on the hornbeams in the Vale, marvelling that even their stout beaks could open such hard seeds. Since that time hawfinches have become very scarce in Lincolnshire and I have not seen one here for many years. Another memorable event at Well was my first smew, a magnificent drake, on the upper lake. It was Christmas day and I spent so long watching the bird that I disgraced myself by being late for the family dinner!

One of my school friends lived in a rambling 17th century manor house at Tothill close to an enormous earthwork, the motte of a mediaeval castle. It was another of my favourite places. There the Great Eau – a little river in spite of its name - meandered through rushy pastures which often flooded in winter. There were reed buntings, and probably more nesting snipe in a mile or so of that valley than in the whole of Lincolnshire today. I found their 'drumming' one of the most fascinating of all bird sounds. There was Tothill Wood nearby as well, a fine oak-ash wood with well-managed rides, and home to red squirrels, silver-washed fritillary butterflies and a great variety of birds.

Queen Elizabeth's Grammar School was housed in late Victorian buildings near the edge of the town, almost surrounded by fields. From the windows of the 5th and 6th form rooms overlooking a lawn and a shrubbery, spotted flycatchers provided a welcome distraction in the summer term. My school career was uneventful. I kept myself near the top of the form in most subjects, except maths, by painstaking work, but the competition was not great. To organised games I applied the same diligence as I did to learning, justifying my place as an undistinguished member of school cricket, football and hockey teams. By 1937 when I reached the 6th form, pupil numbers had increased, but there was only a handful of boys in the 6th where I studied English, French and History. There was little opportunity to meet local girls at the same stage of school careers. They had to travel to grammar school in Louth. Compared with today's youths we were in any case a bunch of innocents. Most of us were awkward with girls, but there was one 'Flash Harry', I remember, who in the 6th form came to school occasionally driving his father's car and was reputed to have got a girl 'into trouble'! There were also a few – but only a few – who smoked surreptitiously even on school grounds.

I made holiday expeditions with a school friend in the 6th form years. A strenuous walking tour in the Lake District introduced me to the beauties of lakes and mountains at a time when I was just beginning to appreciate Wordsworth and the other Lake poets. Another time we explored the gentler delights of Cotswold lanes, villages and churches. On both occasions we used youth hostels which were still relatively new. They were usually fairly spartan, and washing up and cleaning help was expected, but for those reasons they generated a camaraderie which is hard to recapture. Those expeditions were important to me. They introduced me to new landscapes and gave me a feel for the diversity of English countryside. I was pleased too that I was able to experience such places before the post-war expansion of towns and villages and whilst they were still relatively free of traffic and tourists.

University applications took me to Sheffield and Leeds. Both universities offered me places, but I chose Leeds largely because three or four others from the school had gone there previously. We were not considered by the headmaster – an Oxford man – to be good enough material for Oxbridge! As for subjects, it was generally assumed that you would select the one in which you achieved the highest exam marks – in my case French. There was a similar assumption that you would become a teacher; the local education authority grant indeed carried some obligation to that effect.

Leeds 1938 - 1946

The beginning of my second year at university coincided with the outbreak of the Second World War, an eventuality which even for a teenager had overshadowed the previous three or four years. Involvement in running the local ARP post lent a certain excitement to the first few weeks of the war, but that soon disappeared when university term started in early October. Every generation of students has to make the adjustment from school to university. I do not suppose it was any more difficult in 1938/9 than it is today, but life in Leeds, especially in war-time with blackout and other restrictions, was something of a shock to a country boy from a cloistered background. The transition for me was made more painful by difficulties with French studies and the growing realisation that I had chosen the wrong subject. At the beginning of the spring term I was faced with a critical decision. I must try to switch to English or consider giving up a university career. The Professor of English Literature was amenable to a change, but the Language Professor, Bruce Dickins, was initially forbidding. When he learned that I came from Lincolnshire, however, his attitude softened – he was himself a Lincolnshire man - and he agreed to accept me. Although he published little, Bruce Dickins was a man of great scholarship with a wide-ranging interest in the fields of language, history, archaeology and architecture. He went on from Leeds to become Professor of Anglo-Saxon at Cambridge. My own cultural interests owe much to his influence and teaching.

Of the remainder of my University career I shall say little. I was no brilliant scholar, but by hard work and application obtained a First Class Honours degree and went on to gain an MA with Distinction by a study of Offa of Mercia, that great but shadowy figure who dominated 8th century England. The experience and discipline of research and the organisation of a thesis proved to be of long-term value to me. I then spent a further year obtaining a Diploma of Education which my local authority grant required me to do, but which I fear was not a very profitable expenditure of time, except that some of my teaching practice was done at Leeds Grammar School where I subsequently joined the staff.

I was able to complete five years of study and begin my teaching career throughout the war because, although called up for active service in 1942, I was assessed as unfit as a result of a severe bout of jaundice that year and a suspected heart condition; and although summoned for medical examination every six months the assessment remained unchanged throughout.

In 1944 I was appointed acting Senior English Master at Leeds Grammar School, a direct grant school, with a thousand or more pupils. Because of staff shortages due to the war I found myself in charge of 6th form English studies, two 5th forms taking School Certificate and the form of 3A of my own. In addition I was expected to produce a Shakespeare play each year, an arduous but very satisfying assignment. It was very much a deep-end experience and very hard-going - much more so than the kind of administrative job I might have been given in the Services. During this time I continued to live in Devonshire Hall, the University Hall of Residence, as Deputy Warden, an arrangement which on the whole I found congenial.

In spite of its war-time drabness, life in Leeds was not without its compensations, especially as my confidence grew. In the Northern Philharmonic Society concerts at the Town Hall I discovered the delights of classical music. My interest in architecture, stimulated by Bruce Dickins, was further encouraged by an old history master at the Grammar School who had retired about the time of my appointment. We made expeditions together by train to look at some of Yorkshire's fine churches and ruined abbeys. Then there were occasional weekend excursions into Wharfedale and beyond. Apart from the school visits to Derbyshire and the Lake District in school days, those were my first real encounters with mountain streams and their birds, with valley oak woods and wood warblers, with upland pastures and curlew, snipe and globeflowers, with heather moors and red grouse. Once I went as far as Ingleton to hear corncrakes which still occurred there in the 1940s, and to discover limestone pavements and the lovely purple saxifrage high up on the mountain. There was another unexpected compensation of the war-time blackout in Leeds: I learned the map of the night sky. Cassiopeia and Pegasus, Taurus and Leo, the Gemini, the Northern Cross, Sirius and 'Great Orion sloping slowly to the west' became as familiar to me as landmarks. It is knowledge that has given me a lifetime's pleasure and satisfaction and one which I passed on to my children.

I gradually made contact with other naturalists through a natural history society which met at the City Museum. William Bennett, one of the pioneer bird photographers, kept a small private hotel where I was always welcome; and with A G Parsons, a Cornishman who worked at the hospital, I visited Fairburn Ings and other birdwatching sites. There was a young museum assistant whose name I have forgotten, who was killed on active service later in the war; and there was Peter Stocks, an art student of my own age with whom I struck up a close friendship. Destined, I believe, to be a bird artist of considerable renown, he too was killed while serving as a pilot in the RAF. Of all my contemporaries who perished in the war, Peter's loss I felt more keenly perhaps than any other. I still cherish a few of his drawings and his last poignant letter written a few weeks before he died.

Above: Cross Keys on South Street, Alford about 1905 and the Smith shop in the late 1930s with my mother and cousin at the door.

Left: My parents in their seventies.

Queen Elizabeth's Grammar School, Alford, 1930s.

Grammar School Hockey XI 1937 with Headmaster H.J.H. Dyer. I am on the left of the front row.

The English School University of Leeds, 1941. Professor Bruce Dickins is seated centre.

TED SMITH

*The southern Wolds from Harrington Hill towards
the Bluestone Heath ridge.*

Lincolnshire Landscapes

The landscaped park at Well Vale near Alford.

TED SMITH

Somersby - Tennyson's birthplace - in early spring.

TED SMITH

GEOFF TRINDER

The silver-washed fritillary once common in the broad-leaved woods of the boulder clay Middle Marsh.

Elms on the road to Well before Dutch elm disease.

TED SMITH

A herdsman's cottage in the Outmarsh painted around 1890 by Stella Sharpley.

An 'island' hamlet church - St. Andrew, Hannah - in the Outmarsh.

Old ridge and furrow pasture in the Outmarsh at Saltfleetby.

There were university friends too. I remember walking on the Sussex Downs with a kindred spirit, a farmer's son from the Yorkshire Wolds with whom I subsequently lost touch. Much of the downland had already been lost to wartime ploughing but there were still extensive tracts of it, enough to convey the character and atmosphere described by W H Hudson, H J Massingham and other writers. I remember on the fringes of the beechwoods around Findon hearing for the first time the lovely flutey song of the woodlark. And there was another walking holiday in Easter holidays with a school teacher colleague in 1946, this time in the Malverns and the Welsh borders - Housman country. The 'blue remembered hills', the half-timbered black and white villages, historic towns like Ludlow, churches full of architectural interest, orchards and little rivers, and that great monument Offa's Dyke familiar to me from my study of Offa: these, and the sense of deep, quiet country made a lasting impression on me.

By late 1944 victory in the war seemed to be assured, and, with the prospect of a return to party politics after wartime coalition, I was drawn into activity with the Leeds Young Liberals of which by the time of the 1945 election I had become chairman. Involvement in practical politics in this way and in the Students' Union was useful experience for a later role in eco-politics! The outcome of the 1945 election was a severe setback to the hopes of a Liberal revival, hope which indeed remained in suspense for the next forty years. The new Labour administration of 1945, however, proved to be a great reforming government which significantly advanced the cause of nature conservation by the National Parks and Access to the Countryside Act of 1949 and by the creation of the Nature Conservancy.

Lincolnshire Landscapes

Landscape plotted and pieced – fold, fallow and plough Hopkins

My links with home and Lincolnshire never weakened throughout my years in Leeds. I was back there as soon as term was over or work permitted. There were no less than five railway routes which I could take from Leeds to Alford in those days. My favourite was via Lincoln where I could break my journey to see my friend Tom Baker, the curator of the City and County Museum and honorary secretary of the Lincolnshire Naturalists' Union. Ideas about post-war nature conservation in Lincolnshire were sown in those discussions. The great cathedral frequently drew me up the hill to marvel at its gothic splendour and the fascinating details of its carvings. From Lincoln I usually went on the Witham Valley line to Boston, looking out for herons and great crested grebes on the river; and then on the Grimsby line to Alford. Once I changed at Bardney on that exciting line through the heart of the Wolds to Louth which was closed in 1951. What a tragedy it was that the track was not retained as a public footpath.

Gibraltar Point was in military occupation throughout the war, but with a police permit I was able to watch autumn migrants along the coast at Huttoft and Anderby. A large military camp in the park at Well put another of my favourite haunts out of bounds, but I explored the countryside elsewhere on foot and by bicycle. The landscapes of Wold, Marsh and Fen were taking on a new meaning for me as I learned more of their human and natural history, their place-names and their buildings. Rawnsley's *Highways and Byways in Lincolnshire* was a constant companion. Like others in that charming, nostalgic series, it was written in the pre-motor car era when byways and even highways were quieter, and when the life of the countryside proceeded at a more tranquil pace. The Outmarsh, that tract of flat country immediately inland from the sea, was still largely pastoral as it had always been, a landscape of ancient pastures grazed in summer by stocky Lincoln Red cattle. There were nesting lapwings in nearly every field and vast flocks of them with golden plovers in winter; reed-fringed dykes with arrowhead and flowering rush; scattered villages largely untouched by bungaloid sprawl, some of them on outcrops of boulder clay mounds revealing their island origins; crumbling sandstone churches half hidden in clumps of trees; and the occasional herdsman's cottage out in the fields surrounded by a big thorn hedge for shelter from the wind off the North Sea. I have an evocative little watercolour of just such a cottage painted around 1890 by Louth artist Stella Sharpley.

Further inland, the Middle Marsh on the hummocky boulder clay was classic Enclosure countryside of mixed farming, of stock and crop, with small fields of plough, fallow and pasture and flower-rich meadows; of well kept hedgerows, copses and ponds; of winter stackyards, those great hard weather refuges for birds; of scattered farmsteads and compact villages, and market towns like Alford, Spilsby and Louth along the Wold edge. Windmills - all tower mills by that time - were a prominent feature. Little tree-lined roads criss-crossed the landscape with many a right-angle bend betraying their origin as open field trackways.

No doubt because of the intractable nature of the boulder clay soils the Middle Marsh was well wooded country with many ancient fragments and some large blocks of broad-leaved woodland, their centuries old coppice-with-standard system already far in decline by the 1940s. Most of the woods were jealously guarded and heavily keepered, but there were a few which I knew it was safe to enter. There I found such treasures as the butterfly orchid, elegant and deliciously fragrant, and the strangely fascinating herb Paris. Red squirrels were still quite common. Once as a boy I had climbed up to what I thought was a magpie's nest but as I got within touching distance it 'exploded' and several young squirrels scattered around in the branches. Trying to distinguish between the songs of blackcap and garden warbler was an annual exercise never completely mastered until years later, and it was a long time before I could connect with the song of the lesser whitethroat, that unwarbler-like rattle coming from big hedges. But perhaps the most memorable creature of the woods was the magnificent silver-washed fritillary butterfly. I remember exactly where I stood beside an old oak tree in Greenfield Wood when I saw one for the first time. There it was gliding majestically along the ride and alighting within arms length of me on a bramble spray. That particular wood was clear-felled in the 1940s and re-planted with conifers, and later housed some kind of leisure complex. It is unrecognisable now and the fritillary, like all of its kind, has been extinct in Lincolnshire for thirty years or more.

In all the time that I have lived in Lincolnshire the low rim of the Wolds, often darkly etched against magnificent sunsets, has formed my western horizon. These rolling chalk hills seldom exceed 300 feet but they command spacious vistas of Marsh and Fen and distant sea. Tennyson had known and loved them in his youth at Somersby. The view from Harrington Hill one October morning in 1833 reflected his mood of grief and melancholy following the sudden death of his friend Arthur Hallam.

Calm and still light on yon great plain
That sweeps with all its autumn bowers,
And crowded farms and lessening towers,
To mingle with the bounding main.

Already in the long summer holidays of schooldays I had cycled the quiet dusty hill roads with their wide flowery verges. From that ancient ridgeway, the Bluestone Heath Road, one sees the changing vistas of Marshland and distant sea with the great cloudscapes of the Lincolnshire sky overhead. From there it was not difficult to reconstruct in imagination the open downland of pre-enclosure days with its great bustards and stone curlews, with red kites and buzzards in the sky and miles of flower-studded turf. Neolithic and Bronze Age barrows; mounds and hollows of deserted mediaeval village sites patterned in the grass of remote valleys; and tiny churches in isolated hamlets are all evidence of changing human use of the land and its resources. I became particularly attracted to the flowers of the chalk – knapweed and scabious, salad burnet, rockrose and felwort, and orchids - pyramidal and spotted, twayblade and bee, the latter especially an annual delight to find. Old chalkpits were some of the most interesting places. Overgrown, heavily shaded access tracks opened magically into sunlit places of flowers and bees and butterflies.

The Fens were further away and at that time less familiar, but in war-time summer holidays I went church visiting there by bicycle, using the train to return. From Wainfleet to Boston, Boston to Spalding, and Spalding to Kings Lynn are some of the finest parish churches in England, testimony to the mediaeval wealth and prosperity of the Fenland. From Spalding there is Early English at its most intimate at Weston; the great perpendicular spire at Moulton; Gedney with its long series of windows riding high like a galleon, and Long Sutton with its magnificent lead spire and impressive Norman nave. My excursions were usually in August when the Fenland is at its best: the vast distances, the crops ripening to harvest and the great skies piled high with billowy cumulous clouds. The tree-girt villages seemed like oases in the hot and dusty landscape. Motoring now, as I sometimes do, on the lorry-packed A17, I marvel that only sixty years ago I could cycle safely on the same road encountering little traffic.

Our feelings about nature, about places and landscapes are shaped by personal experiences; they are coloured too by the sensibilities of others expressed in painting, poetry and prose. That was certainly true in my case as the scope of my reading widened. Of poets, Tennyson was particularly important to me. He had lived at Somersby for the first 28 years of his life - perhaps the most creative years - and his descriptions of Wold and Marsh landscapes, though imbued with his own feelings, reflect what is still their essential character. And no poet had a more observant eye for nature down to the finest detail. When later I became a university tutor in Lincolnshire, courses on Tennyson were an essential part of my repertoire. There were many others, of course, who influenced my feelings about nature: the pure simplicity of Dorothy Wordsworth in her Journals; the almost mystic vision of Gerard Manley Hopkins; the earthiness of John Clare, to mention but three.

For the naturalist the publication during the war years of *The Handbook of British Birds*, and the first of the New Naturalist series, Ford's *Butterflies* in 1955, were exciting landmarks. And W G Hoskins' *The Making of the English Landscape* in

1955 was a seminal work of great significance in understanding the way in which man and nature had interacted to shape the landscape. Even earlier my university colleague Maurice Barley had explored a similar theme in *Lincolnshire and the Fens* to which I made some minor contribution. Joan Thirsk's impressive agrarian history of Lincolnshire *English Peasant Farming* (1957) confirmed in historical perspective the distinctive pattern of farming which had shaped the landscapes of the county's varied regions of Marsh and Fen, Upland and Clayland.

Norfolk 1947

By 1946 I was becoming restive. Staff at Leeds Grammar School who had been away on service were returning, and my post as Senior English master was – understandably – reclaimed by its former occupant. Besides, after eight years I had had enough of a great city and longed to be back in the country. I was successful in my first attempt to secure a new job – at the Grammar School in North Walsham in north-east Norfolk, the Paston School. I left Leeds with little regret and I have never been back there. Nevertheless my university studies had not only made a scholar of me, but had stimulated my appreciation of literature and widened my sense of place and history, and so incidentally prepared me for my eventual career in adult education. School teaching was hard work. Some aspects of it I enjoyed and I think I was moderately successful. But I never regarded it as a life-time job although I didn't know at that time what else I could do except go back home and be a plumber!

North Walsham and rural Norfolk was a stark contrast to life in Leeds. To begin with, pupils' standards of achievement were much lower, but the boys were friendly and easy-going, and teaching there presented no great problems for me. Other aspects of the school unfortunately did. It had a small boarding establishment and, although I had rejected the offer of living in as a house-master, I accepted the offer of temporary accommodation in the boarding house, only to find myself trapped there for one of the worst winters of the century. I had started in the spring term of 1947. The first couple of weeks were idyllic – mild and sunny and I was back in the country – but on 27 January it began to snow and for six weeks thereafter we were virtually imprisoned. Road and rail communications were blocked for most of the time and the school was closed for long periods. My room on the third floor of the 18th century schoolhouse was cold and draughty with only a small coal fire. My rural idyll was somewhat shattered. Eventually in the summer term I escaped from the boarding house and found lodgings.

For the rest of that year in spare moments I enjoyed the north Norfolk countryside. Rural Norfolk was a backwater in many ways in the late 1940s; there were still many horses at work in the fields, and little traffic on country roads. Another bachelor colleague had a little sports car and we travelled to Cromer and Sheringham; looked at splendid churches like Salle and Worstead, and we went occasionally to Norwich, a fine city with which my connections were to be renewed many years later. The paintings of the Norwich School in the Castle Museum were a particular attraction.

I was also able to visit Hickling Broad, the Norfolk Naturalists' Trust's premier reserve. The NNT was still an isolated phenomenon, the only County Trust to be formed in the inter-war years. It had already been instrumental in saving several important Norfolk sites in addition to Hickling – Cley Marshes and Scolt Head on the north coast, and Thetford and Weeting Heaths in the Breckland. It was very much an old style nature protection body in the rural landowner tradition – its wardens even in 1947 were still called 'keepers' – and its reserves were very private; for non-members to gain access to them was not easy. Making friends with the keepers was perhaps the most effective way and that is what I did. But of course I was impressed by the marvellous places the Trust had acquired. Hickling Broad was as yet untouched by pollution and recreational pressures. From a punt you could watch eels and shoals of fish in the clear shallow water. The reedbeds were alive with reed warblers, and I had my first sight of marsh harriers and the magnificent swallowtail butterflies, but the winter before had taken heavy toll of the bearded tits and bitterns and I looked in vain for those that summer.

Return of the Native
In June 1947 the post of Resident Tutor in Lindsey in the Department of Adult Education at Nottingham University was advertised. The Resident Tutor would be required to have his own teaching programme and to organise and supervise classes over the whole of the southern half of the old county of Lindsey. He would be required to live in the area. The job seemed too good to be true. In spite of the fact that I had been at the Paston School little more than six months, here was an opportunity I could not afford to miss. It would take me into a different and more congenial kind of teaching and it would take me back to my native county. But I had no experience of adult education and I did not expect even to get an interview. No-one was more surprised therefore than I was when I was called for interview and offered the job. I had to serve out another term at North Walsham, but in January 1948 I started my duties as Resident Tutor using my parents' house in Alford as my base.

Knowing that I should need my own transport for the University post I purchased my first car, having passed a driving test ten years earlier. There were still no new cars on the market in 1947 – at least of the kind I could afford - so I got a second-hand Morris 8 EAU 616 (odd that I can remember that registration number when I have difficulty in memorising the current one) of about 1936 vintage with goodness knows how many miles on the clock. The price, as I remember, was £370, a year's salary in 1947. It broke down every few hundred miles; spares were scarce and the costs of repairs were painful. There was one other comparatively minor drawback: the roof leaked, so it was necessary to wear a mac with a hood when it rained! Nonetheless it was my first car. It gave me a new dimension of independence, and I remember it with a certain nostalgic affection.

At this point I must go back a few years to my involvement in Lincolnshire natural history and the affairs of the Naturalists' Union. I had joined the Union in 1938 whilst still at school, but without transport and few immediate contacts, to say nothing of examination pressures, it was difficult to attend meetings. In 1939, however, being home from University for the summer break, I accepted Tom Baker's invitation to organise the Union's August field meeting in the Wolds at Haugham Pastures where there were interesting chalk pits – planted with conifers shortly afterwards – and at Tetford Hill, one of the classic Wold sites which figures later in these memoirs. Since my interest in natural history had been entirely self-generated, and since I had known scarcely anyone who shared my enthusiasm, meeting a group of other naturalists at that meeting – all of them, I imagine, older than I was and appearing to me much, much older than perhaps most of them really were – was a formidable occasion. It was a warm, sunny August day. The chalk flowers and the butterflies of late summer were at their best, the highlight of the day being the commas, then just recolonising Lincolnshire after a long absence. For a few hours the war clouds gathering over Europe were forgotten, but the storm was to break even sooner than we feared. That was in fact the last Union field meeting to be held for nearly two years.

After its ineffectual years and lost opportunities of the 1930s, the Society for the Promotion of Nature Reserves had been drawn into the programme of planning for post-war reconstruction. The Nature Reserves Investigation Committee which it set up in 1944 had appointed county sub-committees to prepare lists of potential nature reserves. The Union was asked to appoint a Sub-Committee for Lincolnshire, and I was invited to join it, although I was at that time still living in Leeds and home only for school holidays. We drew up our list entirely on the basis of existing knowledge of sites; it was war-time and there was little opportunity for new survey work.

When the report of the NRIC appeared in 1946 it was disappointing to find that no Lincolnshire site had been selected for possible National Nature Reserve status; it was even more disappointing that the Society for the Promotion of Nature Reserves (SPNR) gave no encouragement to the County Sub-Committees to remain in being. Nevertheless, several members of the Lincolnshire Sub-Committee, including Tom Baker and me, decided that the momentum for nature conservation achieved by our work should be sustained; and the LNU was persuaded to set up a Committee, the Nature Reserves and Wildlife Conservation Committee, for that purpose. Although there was still in 1946 no immediate prospect of my permanent return to Lincolnshire I was invited to become Honorary Secretary of the Committee. It quickly became apparent, however, that a committee of a county natural history society was totally inadequate for the ambitious conservation programme which it had set itself: no less than securing the protection by the most appropriate means - including purchase if necessary - of all the sites on the NRIC Sub-Committee list, as well as mounting a new survey to discover others worthy of protection. The formation of a Naturalists' Trust in Yorkshire in 1946 and my own experience of the work of the Norfolk Trust stimulated proposals to set up a Trust for Lincolnshire. My return to the County in January 1948 was the determining factor, and Tom Baker and I, with the advice of Sir Francis Hill, then the Senior Partner at Lincoln solicitors Andrew & Co, soon began to prepare the ground. The first problem was to persuade a somewhat suspicious LNU to agree to the setting up of a separate, fully autonomous body. We rejected suggestions that the Union might re-constitute itself as a Trust, but it was eventually agreed that the Union should be entitled to appoint six members of the Council of the governing body of the Trust. Otherwise the Memorandum and Articles were adopted from the Norfolk model, although by 1948 they already appeared somewhat archaic.

When the NRIC Committee was set up by the Union my first thoughts were for the future of Gibraltar Point. I have no record of my first post-war visit there, but it must have been some time in the summer of 1946. War-time use had left its mark on the place. Derelict army buildings disfigured the Spit beyond the Coastguard House, barbed wire and anti-tank defences littered the beach, and the home close at Sykes Farm was lined with army Nissen huts, some of them already occupied by squatters. But the old magic was still there: the same sense of space; the same blend of dune and marsh, of sea and sky; there were waders on the shore and migrants in the buckthorns. After the desolate war years the place seemed to be a symbol of a brighter future.

Under the aegis of the Union Committee and with the support of Tom Baker and Reginald Wood Powell, an active member of the Committee, I had drawn up a set of proposals for the County Council to designate their Gibraltar Point property as a nature reserve in order to conserve its wildlife and natural features and to promote education, research and public interest.

The Lincolnshire Naturalists' Trust had an unremarkable birth: no fanfare, no public meeting, the barest of press notices. The ten signatories of the Memorandum and Articles met in the City library in Lincoln for the signing ceremony on 2 November 1948 and formal incorporation followed on 2 December, the official birthday. I established the first registered office at my parents' house, 43 South Street, Alford, where I was then living. What attracted the attention of the press was the Gibraltar Point nature reserve agreement between the Trust and the County Council sealed just a week later. To be entrusted with the management of a large coastal reserve with open access was an auspicious but challenging start for the new Trust and one which set it initially on a very different course from that of its two predecessor Trusts in Norfolk and Yorkshire.

1948 Annus Mirabilis

I had met up in 1946 with fellow ornithologist Lenten Ottaway. Like me he had lived near the Lincolnshire coast most of his life and was aware of its importance for migrants. The concept of the bird observatory for observation and ringing on the lines of the Skokholm and Isle of May examples from the mid-thirties was soon revived after the war. Gibraltar Point seemed an ideal site for such an observatory, and in order to find out what would be involved, Lenten and I made a visit to Skokholm in May 1948. Having read Ronald Lockley's description of the island and the account of his adventurous life and pioneering bird studies there in the 1930s, I was full of eager anticipation. The Observatory, which Lockley had started, had been taken over by the Field Studies Council and linked to the new Field Centre on the mainland at Dale Fort of which John Barrett had just become the first warden. Lockley's farmhouse on Skokholm had been converted into a hostel for a few visitors with Peter Conder in charge. My association with Peter resumed in later years when he became first the Reserves Officer and then the Director of the RSPB.

It was my first experience of an island alive with nesting seabirds. The sheer numbers of auks and kittiwakes on the cliff ledges and their incessant clamour; the puffins sitting outside their burrows every bit as comic as I had imagined; the constantly changing rafts of birds on the sea; the gannets from Grassholm spectacular in their diving: it was overwhelmingly exciting. And the background was an island of flowers: on the cliff tops mounds of thrift and sea campion in pink and white, and delicate vernal squills in pale blue; and unexpectedly over large tracts of the island sheets of bluebells in the deepest purple-blue. After dark the strange calls of Manx shearwaters and storm petrels, as they came in to relieve their partners on the nest, added to the excitement.

For all these things it would have been a memorable visit, but there was something else equally unexpected and like Thomas Hardy returning from Lyonesse I came back 'with magic in my eyes'. Mary Goddard had been to Skokholm the previous summer to study the flora, and, hearing of the wonders of the island in spring, had decided to pay a second visit during her Whitsun holiday from her teaching post in a London Special School. Mary and I found we had much in common in addition to a love of nature. I had aspirations to make a garden, but Mary was already a skilled and knowledgeable practitioner. She had secured an RHS diploma in school and cottage gardening and received a handsome medal as the top student of the year. There were similarities too in our family background: a country childhood and hardworking, thrifty parents. Mary's father was a self-employed architect and estate agent; to supplement family income her mother kept the village Post Office. A heart condition – which eventually stabilised - had interrupted Mary's education. She missed the opportunity to go to university, but trained as a teacher at Salisbury Training College starting work in 1936 in a newly opened secondary school at Whitton in Middlesex, and moving to special school teaching in Isleworth in 1944. As a night-time air raid warden during the war she experienced the London blitz at first-hand. Weekend visits home helped maintain an allotment and assist her mother in coping with her ailing father who was suffering from Parkinson's Disease.

Her home was the village of Finchampstead in Berkshire at the point where that county meets both Hampshire and Surrey. It was a different landscape from mine, softer and sheltered with patches of heath and pinewoods. Agriculture was a much less significant influence both environmentally and socially. Rural society was more genteel; the proximity of the Royal Military College at Camberley made it a favourite retirement area.

Mary's natural history interests were stimulated by a summer course at Exeter University in 1946. The following year she spent a camping holiday on the Pembrokeshire coast. An overnight visit to Skomer determined her to go to Skokholm the following year. She had indeed planned a series of island visits. She did go to Lundy later that summer, but that was the last island visit on her own.

After that idyllic week on Skokholm Mary came to Lincolnshire for a weekend in June. I proposed to her then, appropriately at Gibraltar Point, and we were married at her parents' home in Finchamstead in Berkshire on 4 June 1949. We set up house at 51 West Street Alford, an end terrace house with four bedrooms, one of which we converted into an office for my university work and for the Trust whose registered office plate was proudly displayed by the front door.

1948 had indeed proved to be my *annus mirabilis*: I had returned to my native county, I had met my future wife, and the Trust had been launched.

Peter Conder ringing sea birds on Skokholm, assisted by Mary, 1948.

Skokholm Bird Observatory, 1948.

Wood sandpiper and black tern by Peter Stocks, 1939.

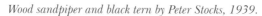

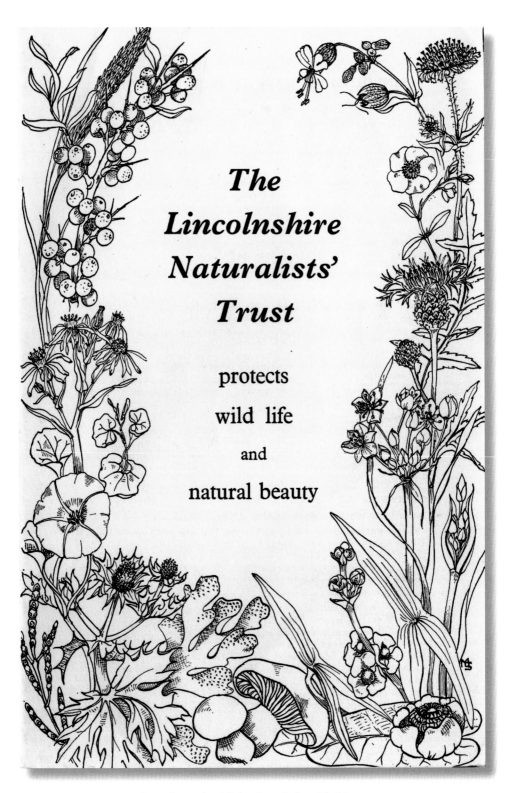

**The
Lincolnshire
Naturalists'
Trust**

protects

wild life

and

natural beauty

An early membership brochure designed by Mary.

Part II

Lincolnshire: The Making of the Trust

– 2 –

The Lincolnshire Naturalists' Trust

THE TRUST'S first office in our spare bedroom consisted of a desk inherited from my father-in-law, a filing cabinet in the shape of a cardboard box, a telephone and a cumbersome old typewriter – the property of my university department – on which I rather laboriously learned to type though never really getting beyond the two or three finger stage. The Gibraltar Point negotiations, the establishment of the bird observatory and the preparations to launch the Trust had occupied much of the time I could spare from my new university duties during 1948. But where did we go from there? There was no manual to tell one how to run a county trust. Of the only other two in existence Yorkshire was as new to the business as we were, and after more than twenty years of splendid isolation Norfolk preferred to stay that way and offered no support or advice.

We had plenty of ideas for putting conservation into practice: creating nature reserves, promoting awareness through education and so on, but first there was the less glamorous but equally demanding job of building an organisation by attracting members and funds and active volunteer involvement. We accordingly made our first appeal for members in a modest little brochure in May 1949 and by the end of that year we had 119 Ordinary Members (at 10/-) and 10 Life Members (at £10). The total income for the year was £82 of which we spent £64, leaving a surplus of £18! It was a very small beginning, and the Annual Report for 1949 warned that "a considerable expansion of membership will be necessary during 1950 if the Trust is to fulfil the aims it has set itself".

It was only with hindsight in later years that I realised how crucial those first few years were to the Trust's future development. It was a fragile creation, and after the initial success of Gibraltar Point, we could easily have stagnated or faltered through failure to increase and broaden our support across the county. But at the time the energy and enthusiasm of youth knew no such qualms. Mary was just as dedicated to making a success of the venture as I was. Lenten Ottaway was devoted to the bird observatory which was already attracting helpers. Of the members of the first Council of the Trust, Tom Baker's wisdom and experience and practical support in Lincoln were invaluable. He served for the first eleven years as Honorary Treasurer, and remained a member of Council until 1989. Tom spent a lifetime in the service of Lincoln City Council becoming Director of the Libraries, Museum and Art Gallery. Whilst he was pre-eminently an archaeologist and local historian - for services to which he was appointed OBE – he made a tremendous contribution to natural history and nature conservation. In addition to his service to the Trust, he was the Honorary Secretary of the LNU from 1933 to 1960 and Editor of the Transactions until 1966. Courteous, warm-hearted and highly organised, he was a man of great vision and understanding of man's relationship to the natural world.

The first President was T H Court, retired schoolmaster, a lepidopterist and specialised collector of butterflies. He was somewhat austere and humourless, but he became devoted to the Trust and its objectives and left a generous legacy to it and to the SPNR. R Wood Powell, a Lincoln dentist and the first Vice-President, was an enthusiastic supporter who worked quietly behind the scenes to promote the Trust and its causes. I owed much to his encouragement. Dr Raymond Hull, a senior scientist with the British Sugar Corporation, was a leading authority on the causes and control of Virus Yellows disease in sugar beet. He later became Chairman of the Executive Committee of the Trust from 1953 to 1960. He was a very cautious man who did not, I believe, share all my ambitions for the Trust and was anxious to keep it out of controversy at a time of increasing agricultural intensification. Arnold Roebuck, a genial and experienced agricultural zoologist, had been consulted by the Government's Wildlife Conservation Special Committee about sites in Lincolnshire and elsewhere in the East Midlands. He could have been more influential in Trust affairs, but he lived outside the county, and being also near the end of his working career, his connections with Lincolnshire were becoming somewhat tenuous.

The most distinguished member of the first Council was undoubtedly Sir Francis Hill, our solicitor. He is perhaps best known now as the historian and benefactor of Lincoln, his native city, but he was also an outstanding leader of local government in Lincoln and on the national scene, and he was for many years President of the Council and subsequently Chancellor of the University of Nottingham. His services as Honorary Legal Adviser and his wise counsels in wider fields of public relations were of great value in those formative years of the Trust. He played a particularly important part in the establishment and defence of the Gibraltar Point nature reserve and in the development of relationships between the Trust, the County Council and Skegness Urban District Council, and the University of Nottingham.

Eric Scorer was another outstanding character among the first members of the Council. A man of wide interests and immense energy, he had recently retired after many years as Clerk of Lindsey Council where he had, among other achievements, conceived and piloted the Lindsey Sandhills Act of 1932, a unique piece of pioneering conservation and planning legislation. Like Francis Hill he was not a naturalist, but he saw the Trust as an important contributor to the cultural life and heritage of the county. His experience and lively personality were a great asset in those first few years. He was also the first in a long line of retired senior officers of Lindsey – and later Lincolnshire County Council – to play an important role in the Trust. His successor Herbert Copland also served on the Council after retirement. Copland's successor Walter Lane became President of the Trust soon after he took early retirement in 1974. His deputy Richard Pepler was for many years the Trust's Deputy Chairman and constitutional adviser. The current Honorary Treasurer of the Trust Bob Prentice was the Treasurer and then the Chief Executive of Lincolnshire County Council. Tom Twigg, the Trust's Honorary Land Agent, had been Land Agent to Lindsey and then Lincolnshire County Council; whilst Derek Golicher, the current Convenor of the Education Team, was first the Council's Field Studies Tutor and later an Inspector in the Education Department. The experience which all of these brought to the Trust over the years has contributed significantly to its success.

In an attempt to solicit their interest and support, we invited all three Lincolnshire County Councils to nominate a member for election to the first Council of the Trust. Holland did not respond, but the other two selected what they apparently thought to be the 'right' person. So Kesteven nominated Captain J S Reeve, a tall, gangling country squire with genuine Dundreary whiskers whose main credential seemed to be that he had amassed a very large collection of birds' eggs! Lindsey nominated Colonel S V Hotchkin, a landowner and sportsman. Whether he had any real interest I never discovered, but he did little more in any case than attend the initial meeting. He was later replaced by Colonel Oliver Sutton Nelthorpe, another landowner, who played an active role and was President from 1951 to 1963. Another landowner and County Alderman, Sir Weston Cracroft Amcotts, became President in 1966 following his retirement as Chairman of Lindsey County Council. His wisdom and experience were a great asset at a crucial time in the Trust's development. We tried to maintain links with the landowning and farming communities by such appointments to Council, and through the Patrons who also included large landowners. Most notable of these was the Earl of Ancaster, the highly respected Lord Lieutenant of Lincolnshire and owner of the historic Grimsthorpe estate. As Patron from 1953 until his death in 1983 he maintained a close interest in the Trust's welfare and achievements.

The Naturalists' Union's initial appointments were not particularly inspired. Some of them, like the eminent Nottingham geologist Professor H H Swinnerton, proved to be ephemeral, although the later appointment of Professor C G C Chesters, Professor of Botany, strengthened the connection with the University. Dr R W Butcher, marine biologist and botanist, also served on the Council for several years in the 1950s. A somewhat eccentric character, he was the author of a monumental 2-volume *Illustrated British Flora* for which my wife drew some of the plates.

The more permanent Union appointment, who continued later as an elected member, was Miss Joan Gibbons, the leading county botanist. Born in the Edwardian era, when the study of wildflowers was a common pastime among ladies of means, she became an expert field botanist entirely self-taught. Her knowledge of the Lincolnshire flora was unrivalled and was of great value to the Trust in discovering and assessing sites of interest. Her recording 'system', however, was highly disorganised, not quite the back of envelope variety but not much better. Although she brought some order into it in preparing her *Flora of Lincolnshire* (1975), the latter was unfortunately based on an obscure and cumbersome system of natural divisions devised in the early years of the century by the Reverend Adrian Woodruffe-Peacock. Her attitude to the Trust and its aims was ambivalent, seeming sometimes quite irrational. Having urged us to save the Scotton Common site from development, for example, she pleaded with me at the last minute to call off the negotiation because she feared the publicity would lead to the reserve being stripped of its flowers by vandals. She represented, albeit in a somewhat extreme form, the confused attitude of many older naturalists to conservation: the recognition of the need to save wild places and their treasures on the one hand, but the fear on the other that they would be overwhelmed or even destroyed by popularity. It was perhaps understandable but increasingly unrealistic. The world had changed, and conservation, to have any chance of success, had to win widespread support and understanding.

Among the early members of the Trust there were, of course, many naturalists – many of those also members of the Naturalists' Union – but a rapidly increasing number came from outside the ranks of traditional naturalists, people who were simply concerned about the natural environment. It was a trend which we were keen to encourage and one which soon distinguished the Trust – and later others of its kind – from natural history societies.

The Council was supportive and helpful, but apart from Tom Baker and, in legal matters Sir Francis Hill, they made little contribution to the affairs of the Trust between meetings. My adult education work, although giving a certain amount of timetable flexibility, was very demanding and I was still finding my way in a relatively new job. Typing Trust letters and reports was laborious. Looking now at the faded carbon copies I am appalled at the amount of time which they consumed. Mary and I packed and despatched annual reports and other communications to members almost unaided for the first two or three years. But the kind of help I needed most of all was someone whom I could consult on a regular basis and who would also take on some aspects of the growing volume of business. In that respect I was in fact very lucky.

In the summer of 1949 Dick Cornwallis made contact with the Trust through the Gibraltar Point bird observatory and within a few months he had agreed to become the Assistant Honorary Secretary. It was a post which he held through all the Trust's formative years. He was briefly President in 1964 and 1965, and Chairman from then until his untimely death in 1969. So for nearly twenty years Dick and I worked in close association and friendship to carry the Trust forward. A rebel against the aristocratic traditions in which he was brought up, he had come to Lincolnshire to farm during the war, the leader of a group of pacifists. A natural leader of great ability he commanded respect and affection in all the spheres in which he moved. He made great contributions to agriculture in Lincolnshire – he was the County Chairman of the National Farmers' Union in 1964 and 1965 – as well as to conservation through his work not only for the Trust but for the LNU, the SPNR, the RSPB, the BTO, and the Nature Conservancy on all of which he served. He was an ornithologist of national repute. His understanding of the impact of modern farming on wildlife - the subject of several outstanding papers – was of particular value to the Trust in a period of intensifying agriculture. His contribution to the Trust's development was immense. Without his wisdom, constant support and encouragement my own mission would have proved infinitely more difficult and my involvement in the national scene well nigh impossible. I have never ceased to regret his loss at the early age of fifty-three.

*Dick
Cornwallis*

*Tom
Baker
OBE*

Eric Scorer OBE

Sir Francis Hill CBE

*Sir Weston
Cracroft Amcotts*

Earl of Ancaster

Miss Joan Gibbons

Arnold Roebuck

NATURE CONSERVATION IN LINCOLNSHIRE
1950
THE SECOND ANNUAL REPORT
OF THE
LINCOLNSHIRE NATURALISTS' TRUST LTD.

Building the Organisation

During 1949 I addressed meetings on the Trust at Louth, Lincoln and Grimsby. A well attended meeting in Lincoln in November, organised in association with the Lincolnshire Naturalists' Union and the RSPB, was addressed by Philip Brown, the Society's Director of Sanctuaries, who had been stationed at RAF Northcotes during the war and had carried out his pioneering studies of reed warblers there. He returned to Lincoln in November 1951 to show films of the RSPB's recently acquired nature reserves at Minsmere and Havergate Island, the forerunners of many splendid sanctuaries. Brown, who became the Secretary of the RSPB in 1952, was well disposed to the prospect of county trusts. He envisaged little danger of competition, especially since he saw the RSPB as exclusively concerned with birds at a national level. Although about to undergo rapid expansion, the Society at that time was still a relatively small organisation with a membership of around 10,000. Although he left the RSPB in 1963 under something of a cloud he helped to lay the foundation of its later development especially through the purchase of the headquarters at Sandy in 1961 which replaced the inadequate offices in Eccleston Square in London.

We brought another well-known ornithologist to lecture at the first annual meeting in April 1950. W B Alexander had been the first Director of the Edward Grey Institute of Field Ornithology at Oxford, and in 1950 was the chairman of the British Bird Observatories' Committee of the British Trust for Ornithology in which capacity he had already visited Gibraltar Point, as described elsewhere. His lecture on the Observatories was followed by films of some of them, including Gibraltar Point, taken by Clifford Holt, one of the Leicestershire and Rutland Ornithological Society members who had begun to visit the Point. That first annual meeting was attended by 45 members out of 129. (45 incidentally was more than the average number attending annual meetings in the 2000-2005 period when the membership had increased to over 20,000!). More than 100 members and guests were present at the lecture and film show which followed the business meeting. A similar number heard Phyllis Barclay-Smith, Secretary of the British Section of the International Bird Protection Committee, speak on the Conservation of Wildfowl after the second AGM in April 1951. And when Peter Scott came to Lincoln to speak on 'Wild Geese in the Canadian Arctic' in May of that year we attracted an audience of nearly 500! Scott was already a popular personality as the son of a national hero, as a wartime naval commander, and as an artist of evocative wildfowl and wilderness scenes. He had special links already with the county. It was at the lighthouse at the mouth of the Nene where he started his wildfowl collection in the 1930s, and incidentally began a lifelong friendship with Boston surgeon Rick Pilcher who became one of the leading personalities in the Trust. In the early 1950s Scott - who had founded the Severn Wildfowl Trust in 1946 - had begun to visit Croft Marsh each autumn to catch and ring pink-footed geese in pursuance of his study of their populations and migrations.

Throughout the 1950s we continued to organise meetings in Lincoln, many of them in association with the LNU. The attendance was seldom less than 100, and in January 1955 more than 200 came to hear popular ornithologist James Fisher speak about The Fulmar. An exhibition of the work of the Trust prepared for the annual meeting in 1953 was subsequently shown in Scunthorpe and Boston and at Gibraltar Point. The first indoor meeting outside Lincoln took place in Louth in March 1955 when J K Yeates, ornithologist and bird photographer, gave an illustrated talk about Iceland. Held in association with the Louth Naturalists', Antiquarian and Literary Society it too attracted more than 200 people. The popularity of all those meetings was evidence of a growing interest in the natural world. Colour television with its now familiar high quality natural history programmes had scarcely begun to make its mark in the 1950s, and the new films which speakers brought with them were undoubtedly a major attraction.

Membership numbers advanced steadily if not spectacularly in the 1950s. By the end of 1955 they had reached 430, and at the end of the first ten years in 1959 stood at 540. Realising the importance of keeping members well informed and involved we had from the outset issued periodical bulletins about the progress of the Trust and about general problems of nature conservation. These were simple duplicated affairs containing news from the reserves and other conservation work, announcements, appeals for help and subscription renewals, and developments on the national scene. From one or two pages they had expanded up to ten pages by the time they were replaced by printed newsletters in 1965.

The news bulletins and newsletters became an essential means of communicating with members, but neither they nor the centrally organised meetings, however well attended, were an adequate means of involving members actively in the Trust's work.

The need for local help in managing reserves – evident from the start at Gibraltar Point and Friskney Decoy Wood – and the local support which they immediately generated at places like Scotton and Linwood pointed towards some devolution of the Trust's administration and activities, especially necessary in a county as vast as Lincolnshire. We had wardens and helpers for the reserves, but we also felt the need for groups to cover a wider range of interests such as the recruitment of members, the organisation of activities, publicity and land planning issues as well as reserve management. In July 1953, therefore, the Council decided that regional committees should be appointed, although it was not until July of the following year that the first of these – for North-West Lindsey – was set up. Others for Holland and South Kesteven and for East Lindsey followed in 1955.

The functions of those committees were somewhat tentatively defined as providing local management for established reserves, watching other sites of interest, organising surveying and monitoring, arranging local meetings, and generally stimulating interest in the Trust in their areas. Their creation was timely and they gave several valuable members an active role in the Trust – David Robinson, for example, who eventually became the Trust's long-serving Honorary Secretary, began his active involvement through the East Lindsey Committee. Marson Peet, who was to succeed Tom Baker as the Honorary Treasurer of the Trust in 1959, was the first Secretary of the Holland and South Kesteven Committee. In the longer term, however, the regional concept proved to be flawed. The areas were far too large to be adequately covered and the interest of the committees still tended to focus down on particular reserves. In 1959, therefore, as part of a major reorganisation of the administration of the Trust, the regional committees were replaced by committees for each reserve or group of reserves, although something of the regional pattern was preserved by the appointment of regional officers whose duties as volunteers foreshadowed in many respects the much later appointment of staff to act as regional wardens.

– 3 –

Family Matters 1950s

W E HAD spent a brief honeymoon in north Norfolk, travelling the length of that splendid coast road from Hunstanton to Sheringham with its changing vistas of sea, sand-dunes and saltmarshes on the one hand, and on the other its heathlands overlooking the sea and little valleys running up into the hills. It was still quiet and relatively traffic free in 1949, much as Lilias Rider Haggard described it in the 1930s in her delightful *Norfolk Notebook*. We went out to see the terns on Scolt Head; we walked the shingle beach at Cley and admired the horned poppies and the sea kale; we listened to woodlarks and nightjars on Salthouse Heath; we stopped to look at red-backed shrikes perched on the telephone wires every few miles; and we watched the fulmars gliding stiff-winged along the cliff-top at Weybourne.

Post-war austerity was still the order of the day in 1949 and travel abroad was out of the question. In any case we were anxious to settle into our new home and begin to shape our life together. 51 West Street, Alford was the end house of a terrace of four. The front room had been a music shop and we never replaced the large shop window, partly for reasons of costs and partly because we seldom used the room. The back of the long, narrow house was quieter and more intimate. Mary soon laid out the little garden enclosed by a tall wooden fence, and we began the collection of plants which was to become a lifetime's pleasure. The copper from the old outside wash-house made a little pond, and, in spite of the enclosing fences, soon attracted frogs and newts whilst toads mysteriously turned up in the cellar, presumably having fallen through the grating on the pavement outside. A cricket lived in a crack in the hearth bricks in the parlour, its 'song' a homely, reassuring sound which very few people experience these days. One other animal visitor in that first year was a ginger kitten which turned up on the doorstep one day in a very dirty and dishevelled condition. I was used to cats and fond of them, but Mary had had dogs and was initially uncertain about cats. However, we agreed to keep the little waif, and he was the first of an unbroken line of cats which have been an integral feature of our household ever since. Most of them have been well-fed, neutered toms, too idle to be much of a menace to garden birds. Each has had his own personality and is fondly remembered.

A settled home life and opportunities to botanise in the field enabled Mary to develop her skill as a botanical and wildlife artist. She illustrated most of the Trust's early reports and recruitment literature, and produced illustrations and diagrams for exhibitions and meetings and for interpretation purposes at the Gibraltar Point bird observatory and field station and elsewhere. Her work, much admired by Trust members and visitors to reserves and meetings, led to an invitation from Dr Roger Butcher, then a member of the Trust Council, to provide illustrations for his ambitious 2-volume *Illustrated British Flora*. Over several years in the 1950s Mary drew some 120 plates, mainly of the orchids and some of the *Compositae*, detailed work, which involved drawing parts of the plant and the seeds as well as the whole. It was a demanding and sometimes frustrating task. To ensure a representative specimen Butcher himself provided most of the plants which arrived often unexpectedly in a variety of old tins, sometimes in a near moribund condition. In spite of a warning to avoid a few days when our third child was expected, the military orchid, a rare and precious specimen, arrived in an advanced state of decay on the day of the birth! As Helen and the illustration in the *Flora* demonstrate, both the plant and the baby received the necessary attention! It was nevertheless very satisfying for Mary to contribute to a highly regarded work – it was published in 1961. The pity was that through delay in publication and lack of promotion it never gained the popularity already enjoyed by the better known *Flora of the British* Isles by Clapham, Tutin and Warburg, the separate illustrations for which were being drawn at the same time as those for Butcher's work. Mary received further invitations to provide illustrations for Floras, but in the time available from home, family, garden and social work, she preferred to develop her artistic talents in other ways. She continued to provide illustrations for the Trust, however, for many years.

I had to learn my job in adult education by experience. Tutoring adults I found was very different from teaching in schools. There were no formal means of assessing the results by exams, but enhancing people's appreciation and understanding of literature, their local environment and the natural world was even more rewarding than good exam results. I was responsible for a large area consisting of approximately the southern half of the old division of Lindsey where I aimed to sustain a programme of at least thirty classes in a wide variety of subjects for which suitable tutors had to be found. In a scattered rural area that was not always an easy task. Most of the classes were provided for WEA branches and groups, and I worked closely with the Association's Tutor Organiser for the area. My own teaching programme consisted of four or five classes with an emphasis at that time on three-year courses, a type which became increasingly difficult to promote. The main 'term' extended from September to April, and with my own teaching and visiting other classes I was usually occupied five evenings every week, travelling around my extensive patch in all weathers. In the summer I organised a number of one-day and weekend schools - some of them at Gibraltar Point as the field-station there developed - and one or two weeks were occupied by Summer Schools. It was an exacting and challenging job, but it allowed a degree of flexibility to develop other related interests. At a time when university teaching was becoming increasingly specialised, liberal adult education provided a rare opportunity to contribute to the cultural and community life of one's region. I was fortunate indeed to be involved in it. What I was able to do in developing field studies and research at Gibraltar Point and in building up the Trust would have been extremely difficult in any other job. Once the facilities of the old coastguard house at the Point became available in 1959 my Department agreed with the Trust to allow me to act as the Director of Studies, although they made no concessions on the rest of my programme!

Science had not traditionally been an adult education subject, and indeed there was no scientist on the Department staff when I was appointed and not for several years afterwards. Early in my career I began to take courses in local studies – for which I had some academic qualification – and after a few years, and rather tentatively, I embarked on natural history courses on the basis of my knowledge and experience as a naturalist. In spite of my lack of an academic background in the subject the Department encouraged me and, somewhat to my embarrassment, I became a kind of unofficial adviser on the life and earth sciences. So here again the post, uniquely perhaps, enabled me to deploy my broad environmental knowledge and interests in teaching in a field which was assuming increasing social and scientific importance as the environment became a major issue. The Trust also benefited, incidentally, from this process: the nuclei of two or three of its later area groups originated in the membership of my classes, and several of its leading activists in the 1950s and 60s emerged from them.

One benefit of all this was the opportunities afforded to me to spend more time at Gibraltar Point than was ever possible in later years. There was, in the first place, the excitement of discovering more about its flora and fauna. Mary contributed an article for the first field station report in 1949 on the vegetation of the various habitats of the reserve, and her illustrated 'Shrubs of the Sandhills' article was published in the journal *Country-Side* in July 1949. She also joined me in becoming a very competent bird ringer. We could even at times rush off there at short notice to see something special. I remember Dick Cornwallis, who was staying there at the time, telephoning me one autumn morning to say that they had just trapped a yellow-browed warbler and there was a great grey shrike sitting on top of the trap! In less than an hour I had seen them both! It was the time too when we were exploring other exciting places in Lincolnshire for the survey of sites described elsewhere.

Halcyon days – which these seemed to be – are usually short-lived and these were no exception. Midway through her first pregnancy in 1951 Mary had been unwell for a few days. There seemed to be no cause for anxiety and we attached little significance to it. We realised later that it was almost certainly an attack of Rubella to which, having had it previously, she had thought herself immune. A near miscarriage during a short holiday at Ingleton in the Yorkshire Dales was rather more ominous; but the child, a boy Peter, was born apparently healthy just after Christmas that year. Within a few weeks, however, it became evident that the child was sick. He cried a great deal, slept fitfully and was increasingly difficult to feed. Unfortunately our doctor seemed to take little notice of the symptoms, conveying rather the impression that as inexperienced parents we were making an unnecessary fuss. In the end it was the more perceptive district nurse who insisted that something be done. The child was taken to the County Hospital in Lincoln where his condition deteriorated rapidly and he died within a few days. The post mortem revealed a congenital heart malformation. It was a traumatic experience which left us both emotionally and physically exhausted.

We decided straight away that a change of doctor was essential and we went to another fairly new partner in the practice, Bill Lapage, who became a lifetime friend. Bill was a caring and compassionate doctor, an ardent supporter of environmental and social causes, and for many years a popular County Councillor, one of the great characters I have known. There was, he said to us, only one thing to be done: have another child as soon as possible. A repetition of the tragedy was unlikely. First though we needed to recuperate and restore Mary's confidence. Fortunately my main teaching season in 1952 was almost over and the summer lay ahead of us. A holiday in the South-West coupled with a visit to Mary's mother at Finchampstead – her father had died in 1950 - helped the restoration process and the will to begin again. Alison, a fine healthy baby, was born at home on a lovely spring day, it was Palm Sunday 4 April 1954. We both rejoiced, and Helen followed on 18 June 1956, a mid-summer child. By that time Mary was almost 40 and we decided with some reluctance that our family was complete.

Meantime the death of my father in November 1955 brought new grief and new problems. To rural craftsmen like him retirement was almost an unknown concept, and in any case there was no great accumulation of capital to draw on in spite of a lifetime of hard work. He had slowed down somewhat in the previous couple of years leaving more to my cousin who had been his assistant since leaving school. When finally he became ill terminal cancer was diagnosed and mercifully he died within a few weeks. The baking and grocery business had been relinquished a few years earlier and I had pressed him to build a bungalow on land adjoining his property which he had purchased. He was reluctant to move, however, and they continued to live in the inconvenient old house behind the shop which had been let. Building the bungalow was now the solution to rehousing my mother, but it was necessary also to ensure an adequate regular income for her. I also felt a strong obligation to my cousin to sustain the business until he was able to take it over. Settling my father's somewhat neglected business affairs, moreover, proved to be a long and tedious process. My mother lived on in failing health and mind until 1965 after which I was thankful to be able to transfer the business to my cousin whose two sons still run it successfully under my father's name. It had become an onerous extra burden at a time when demands of family, profession and voluntary work were all growing apace.

We had never regarded the Alford house as more than a starter home, and by 1954 we had begun to search the area for a house in a village with enough land to satisfy our gardening ambitions. In the village of Willoughby, which we often passed through on our way to and from Gibraltar Point, was an old house on a corner which always attracted us. Its small, warm brown bricks and tumbling in the gables dated it to the mid-18th century. Local red pantiles had long since replaced its original thatch. Leaded windows were a more recent replacement but also seemed to be in harmony with its character. There was an air of neglect about it, but it had lost nothing of its simple, unassuming dignity. It had been for many years the village shop, the insertion of a large shop window marring the original symmetry of the frontage. To the east of the house a range of early 19th century brick and pantile outbuildings had housed a butcher's shop, slaughter-house, stable, cart-shed and pigsty. Old metal signs for Quaker Oats, Park Drive cigarettes, Fry's chocolate and others still covered the walls. Once a place of lively activity, a focal point of the village, it had fallen into dilapidation from which, we felt, it cried out to be rescued. It was occupied by an elderly brother and sister who had given up the business some years previously. They were the last of a long line of Thorndykes to have lived there.

Behind the house was a small paddock and an orchard bounded by a lane which ran from the main road corner to Covells, an old farmhouse reputedly the birthplace of Captain John Smith, the founder of the State of Virginia. The old part of the village is grouped around three and half sides of a square in the centre of which is old pasture where earthworks are evidence of former settlement. Our house stands at the north-west corner; the church with its 14th century brick-patched Spilsby sandstone tower and the former rectory at the opposite corner. The pub is at the south-west, and the spring – there were once several – at the north-east. Originally, no doubt, the springs created a swampy area covered in willows from which the village got its name. The central pasture - now the village green – is bordered by trees, Church Lane having some fine beeches. There was a rookery in the rectory trees; tawny owls nested regularly in the ivy-covered ash trees at Covells, and there were swallows in our cart-shed.

On the opposite side of the corner was the village school, and a quarter of a mile along the road the station on the main Grimsby-Peterborough-Kings Cross line, a junction for the coast loop line to Mablethorpe and Louth. The presence of the railway had pulled the village out in that direction especially since the building of a large dairy near the station in the 1930s. The road through the village, although on a main route from Alford to Skegness, was still relatively quiet in the 1950s. Traffic was light and three railway level crossings were a deterrent to Skegness-bound vehicles which tended to take the alternative route over the Wolds.

The site indeed had all the qualities we were seeking, and, since there seemed little prospect of the house coming onto the market, we tried to persuade the Thorndykes to sell us a part of the paddock on which we could build. The sister was willing, but her brother was understandably reluctant – I should have felt just the same. Then a strange thing happened. One snowy night in December 1954 she died suddenly of a heart attack, and her brother, seeking help from neighbours, also collapsed and died. We subsequently negotiated the purchase of the house, the paddock and the orchard from the family executors for £1150. By today's values that sounds a ridiculous sum, but in 1955 it represented a reasonable market price for an old house in dilapidated condition.

That condition became fully apparent once we were able to carry out a closer internal inspection. The inside of the house had to be virtually gutted and the space rearranged to incorporate a wash-house and loft with no previous access to the rest of the house. The reversal of the stairs eliminated the door at the front in favour of a side entrance. That and the replacement of the shop frontage enabled the symmetry of the windows to be restored. The roof at the back had been raised a few years earlier – regretfully disfiguring some of the tumbling in the gable – and it was necessary to replace the old pantiles at the front. The new ones were of the right design, but much darker in colour. I was initially disappointed with them, but they have mellowed with green and yellow lichen growth.

One room, partly the old shop, had to be devoted to a study since home continued to be my work base. We also had to have a Trust office, a problem solved by the conversion of the old butcher's shop in the range of outbuildings, the rest of which made a garden shed, garage and wood store. The restoration work extended spasmodically over many months, and there was still much to complete when we moved in one March day in 1957. It was another of those landmark moments in life: a new home in the country in which to bring up a young family; a base for developing both my professional work and the Trust; an opportunity to create a garden, and not least to be part of a small community in which Mary soon became closely involved.

There was one small but not unimportant problem which exercised us: what to call the house – there was no existing name, it had just been 'the shop'. Facetiously we considered 'Park Drive' since we had a ready-made sign! Seriously we decided on 'Pyewipes' the old Marshland name for the lapwing which then still nested in the field at the back.

We soon got to work on plans for the garden. There was some advantage in starting with an undeveloped site, but it was clear that we should have to proceed in phases and to begin by planting boundary and internal hedges to give shelter from the north-east winds – in that direction there is no land over 200 feet between us and the Urals! A vegetable plot was a priority, and so was the view from the living room and kitchen windows. That was created by a long lawn with shrub and herbaceous borders enclosed by a beech hedge on one side and a wall of old brick, which I was fortunate to obtain, on the other. At the end of the lawn in front of a rectangular pond we built a brick shelter, replaced later by a larger summerhouse. In the north-east corner we planted a little wood with oak, ash, birch and rowan and an understorey of hazel, guelder rose and sallow to be coppiced at regular intervals. Finally, after a few years, we developed the last pieces: a larger pond and border, a raised bed of acid soil, and a shrub border edged with a low box hedge. The old orchard already had spring carpets of snowdrops and daffodils. The existing front garden was dull and formal and we replaced it with a type of more exuberant cottage garden crowded with flowers, and with a low terrace and stone troughs planted with alpines. Such troughs could simply be begged from local farms at that time. We made the maximum use of the house and outbuilding walls for climbers and tender shrubs needing shelter, especially on the south-facing front aspect. The garden thus fell into a series of compartments which, as the hedges grew up, created a small element of surprise and expectation. This design was the result mainly of the necessity of phasing, but we were influenced too by the example of Hidcote – one of the first National Trust gardens which we visited – where Lawrence Johnston had created a mosaic of gardens each with its own distinctive character. Over the years we have collected a great variety of bulbs, herbaceous plants, shrubs and trees to create year-round interest. Attracting wildlife was a major objective: nest sites and sources of food for birds; flowers for butterflies, bees and other insects; water for frogs, toads, newts, and dragonflies and other pond life. It was fascinating to watch the colonisation process as the garden developed and matured. In all its aspects and at all seasons it has given us immense mutual pleasure; it has made us many friends and we have shared it with others whenever possible, opening it for the Trust and for local events. It expresses perhaps something of our philosophy and characters.

Willoughby is a Middlemarsh village – it used to be known as Willoughby-in-the-Marsh – but the edge of the Wolds, an ancient cliff line, is only a mile away to the west. For Lincolnshire it is a well-wooded area with the large block of Willoughby and Welton Woods and Claxby Hoplands – the latter to become a Trust nature reserve in 1964 - where I had heard my first nightingale back in the

1930s. Just beyond Hoplands is the Mill Hill chalkpit, the 'hill' being a Bronze Age burial mound and the site of a wooden post mill long gone and forgotten. The quarry also became a Trust reserve, but in 1956 it was still being worked for road stone. Knowing the caretaker we frequently went there to find bee orchids and other treasures. In the valley below the pit a spring issues from the base of a chalk cliff to form a pool by the road side. In its clear cold water under stones studded with caddis cases lives a rare flatworm *Crenobia alpina*, an ice age relict. 'Claxby Water' as they called it, was always popular with our children. After a long journey it signified we were nearly home! We often stopped there to look for spotted flycatchers in summer, and grey wagtails in winter; and once we watched a water rail stalking along the far bank apparently oblivious of our presence. One winter afternoon as we passed in fading light a tiny silver flash caught my eye. We stopped to look and there was a dipper plunging into the water no doubt to catch freshwater shrimps. What I had seen was the blinking of the white eyelid as the bird cleaned its eye after immersion. Such small incidents stay in the mind. It gives me great satisfaction that 'Claxby Water', a little gem of a place, is also now under Trust management like Hoplands and Mill Hill.

Before the Second World War there had been four small farms in Willoughby, but by the time we arrived they had all been engrossed by the two large ones of the Manor and the Grange. Although for a time both of them kept stock there was little old pasture and even fewer meadows left. Almost the only one of the latter that eventually survived was acquired by the Trust as a nature reserve in 1976. Changes in land holding and agricultural practices had already begun to reduce the labour force, a trend which continued to accelerate. In 1956, however, most people in the village were still dependent on agriculture or had some connection with it. That was to change drastically over the next thirty years.

Claxby Spring ('Claxby Water').

Nottingham University Adult Education Department summer field course,
Beinn Eighe National Nature Reserve, Wester Ross, 1959

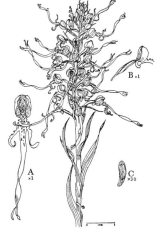

Above: Thorndyke's shop and range of
outbuildings in Willoughby c. 1910.

Below: 'Pyewipes' after restoration
and conversion 1957.

The Lincolnshire Naturalists' Trust office
(1957-1965) was at the left end
of the range of outbuildings.

Lizard orchid drawn by Mary Smith
from R W Butcher's
'A New Illustrated British Flora' 1961.

NATURE CONSERVATION IN LINCOLNSHIRE

1953

THE FIFTH ANNUAL REPORT

OF THE

LINCOLNSHIRE NATURALISTS' TRUST, LTD.

Gibraltar Point c. 1951

– 4 –

Gibraltar Point: The First 25 Years

THE negotiations with Lindsey County Council to establish a nature reserve at Gibraltar Point had a favourable wind from the outset. The place had narrowly escaped being developed as a new seaside resort in the early 1930s. The three bungalows which I had seen on my first visit there in 1937 were the first of an intended 800, and it was only the financial collapse of the speculative building company, the Tennyson Glen Estate Company, that prevented the development. Lindsey County Council had promoted an Act of Parliament, the Lindsey CC Sandhills Act, in 1932 to enable them to control development of the coastal sandhills and to acquire them if necessary. In 1937 the Council used those powers to purchase (at a cost of £12,000) 190 acres of the Gibraltar Point sandhills with the intention of maintaining them as 'a public open space and wild bird sanctuary'.

The Sandhills Act was a unique pioneering effort in coastal protection and the Council was particularly proud of its achievement. By 1948 the Council's sandhills estate was a major asset, some of it, like the model caravan camp at Ingoldmells, a useful source of income. It was controlled by an active sub-committee whose members included some influential councillors, most of them well disposed to our proposals. The negotiations were also helped by the senior officers responsible. Eric Scorer, the dynamic Clerk who had been primarily responsible for the Sandhills Act, had just retired (he was shortly to join the Trust Council) and been succeeded by his Deputy, Herbert Copland. Copland was a much more cautious man and, partly for that reason perhaps, well trusted by councillors, but he was basically sympathetic to our aims and, after retirement, he too served on the Trust Council. His Deputy, Richard Pepler, was a planning specialist and went on later to play a major role in the development of the Trust as its Deputy Chairman. Another key figure was one of the chief clerks in the Clerk's Department, B C (always known as 'Jack') Duddles. His responsibilities covered a multitude of county council functions from Quarter Sessions administration to diseases of animals. He also serviced the Sandhills Subcommittee and was in effect the manager of the Sandhills Estate, a job which he clearly enjoyed. Many of his weekends were spent on the coast attending to estate matters. The concrete posts which he had erected to define the County Council's properties still survive in places. For seventeen years until his retirement he was my most immediate day-to-day contact with the County Council on Gibraltar Point affairs. I could not have wished for anyone more congenial or more helpful; his advice and guidance were invaluable.

I was a comparative stranger to the County Council in 1948, but Tom Baker, as a senior officer of Lincoln Corporation, Sir Francis Hill and Reginald Wood Powell were acquainted with many of the councillors and senior officers with whom we were involved. Their association with the embryonic Trust helped to give the credibility needed to persuade the Council to consider our Gibraltar Point proposals. These were first set out in a memorandum 'Gibraltar Point as a Nature Reserve' submitted to the County Council by the Nature Reserves and Wildlife Conservation Committee of the Lincolnshire Naturalists' Union, the precursor of the Trust. As a result of discussions with County Council representatives at Gibraltar Point in July 1948, I prepared a set of practical proposals for the establishment and administration of a reserve which were then presented to the Council.

The popular concept of a nature reserve at that time was of a place not designed to encourage visitors, an impression which I had certainly received in trying to see some of the Norfolk reserves during my sojourn there in 1947. We knew that Gibraltar Point had to be different. It would for the most part be open to the public, and management would have to reconcile that with the conservation of the wildlife and natural features which people would come to see, study and enjoy. I was in any case much influenced by the new approach to nature conservation and the function of nature reserves set out in the report of the Wildlife Conservation Special Committee, the famous Cmd.7122, and in Sir Arthur Tansley's stimulating little book *Our Heritage of Wild Nature* published in 1945. Where appropriate, the Committee recommended, reserves should not only function as sanctuaries and 'reservoirs' for plants and animals, but should also serve as outdoor laboratories and living museums, places for study, research and the enjoyment of nature.

So, in our proposals to establish a nature reserve at Gibraltar Point, we set out three main aims: to promote the conservation of wildlife, to encourage scientific study and research in the natural sciences, and to secure the amenities of the area for public enjoyment. By means of notices and other publicity we proposed that visitors be asked to respect the natural features and wildlife of the area which would be interpreted by displays and by voluntary wardens. The County Council would delegate day-to-day management to the Trust whose responsibilities were defined in a detailed Scheme of Management. The Trust also undertook to provide facilities for field study and research, initially by adapting wherever possible remaining wartime army buildings – the adaptation of the bird observatory laboratory was already under way. That the Trust took that undertaking very seriously is evident from the fact that at only their second meeting on 29 October 1949 the Council resolved to establish a field centre in the reserve and appointed a subcommittee to consider the type of building needed and the means of funding its construction. In July 1950 the Council considered a plan for a small centre prepared voluntarily by architect Warren Neil. Unfortunately nothing came of these early attempts to provide a purpose-built centre and the plan in question does not seem to have survived.

The proposals for the reserve were accepted by the County Council who sealed the agreement on 10 December 1948. The Trust had come into being eight days earlier. The agreement, which covered the whole of the County Council's property at Gibraltar Point, provided for the establishment of a Joint Advisory Committee to oversee and advise on its implementation. At its first meeting on 24 September 1949 the Committee recommended the County Council to expand the reserve by the acquisition of adjoining areas, notably the seventy acres at the southern end on which the old coastguard house stood (although the building itself was subject to a private lease until 1958); the land to the north between the reserve and the golf links, and the adjoining foreshore. The Council was successful in acquiring the first area and in securing leases of the foreshore, but the other area, belonging to the Measures family, did not become available until 1997 when it was acquired by the Trust.

The new reserve, conceived in the spirit of those post-war reports on nature conservation, and believed to be the first to be created by a statutory/voluntary body partnership, attracted a good deal of publicity in the local and national press. Both *The Times* and the *Manchester Guardian* carried descriptions of it. 'Lindsey Leads the Way in Plan for Wildlife Reserve' was a typical local headline. "Every resident of the county who has at heart the preservation of its natural beauties and the development of its cultural values will join us in congratulating the Lindsey County Council on its far-sighted and enlightened action" was the complimentary editorial comment of *The Lincoln Rutland and Stamford Mercury* which had a wide circulation in south Lincolnshire. The press found the bird observatory and the mysteries of migration which it was designed to help unravel, a particularly fascinating subject. 'German gadget aids Lincs Naturalists' was a *Grimsby Evening Telegraph* headline description of the observatory's Heligoland trap. It was 1949 and things German perhaps still aroused a certain suspicious curiosity! The Trust's work at Gibraltar Point received particularly extensive coverage in the *Skegness News*. Its editor, Stanley Major, had been a devotee of Gibraltar Point for many years. Once satisfied of the Trust's intentions he became a firm and valued supporter.

The establishment of the reserve was also welcomed by the newly created Nature Conservancy which came into being in March 1949. Later that year I was invited by the Director General, Cyril Diver, to attend a meeting of his Council at their temporary headquarters in Victoria Street to describe what we were doing at Gibraltar Point. Most of the original members of the Nature Conservancy were present, but to my great regret the Chairman, Professor Sir Arthur Tansley, had had to leave before I arrived. Tansley retired in 1952 and died in 1955, so I missed the opportunity to meet the 'father' of nature conservation in Britain. Writing a few years later in his book *Britain's Nature Reserves* Max Nicholson, who succeeded Diver as Director-General in 1952, had this to say about the Gibraltar Point Reserve:

> It is encouraging to observe that all this pioneering activity has been carried through without the necessity for any national organisation to lend more than background encouragement and support. Such initiative on the spot helps not only to extend but to diversify and enrich the common fund of experience about ecological field studies and Nature Reserve management.

The publicity and warm reception accorded the reserve certainly provided an excellent start for the Trust. It also stood us in good stead when the new reserve unexpectedly came under serious threat in 1952. The Trust was indeed fortunate in having to cut its teeth on a reserve where it was in partnership with local authorities, and where it had to satisfy the needs of people and enlist their support to conserve a place of outstanding natural interest and beauty. It was this kind of experience perhaps which equipped it to take a leading role in the development of the county trusts' movement in the next twenty years.

The First Local Nature Reserve in England

The National Parks and Access to the Countryside Act (1949) gave County and District Councils the same powers as the Nature Conservancy to declare nature reserves provided they first consulted the Conservancy. It was an early recommendation of the Gibraltar Point Joint Advisory Committee that the County Council make such a statutory declaration. The Council accordingly approached the Conservancy and the matter was discussed in August 1950 when Diver accompanied by two of his Council members, Professor Alfred Steers and Max Nicholson, visited Gibraltar Point and met the Chairman and Clerk of the County Council and officers of the Trust. The Conservancy representatives seemed to be quite satisfied that the reserve qualified for declaration, and Diver undertook to seek the approval of his Council and to provide a form of words for this. There followed, however, a long period of procrastination on the part of the Nature Conservancy. More than a year later – in November 1951 - the Trust Council instructed me to write to Diver about the delay, but it was not until 1952 that he produced a form of declaration for the County Council to use. 'Technical difficulties' was the reason given for the delay, but I suspect there was an even more unsatisfactory motive. The Nature Conservancy had made a faltering start and criticism was mounting over lack of action. Had they given prompt approval to the Gibraltar Point declaration it would have been the first to be made under the 1949 Act. For that to have been done by a mere local authority would have been a further blow to the sagging reputation of the Conservancy at that time. Significantly, the latter gave the go-ahead to Lindsey County Council as soon as the first small batch of national nature reserves had been declared. As it was Gibraltar Point was still the first local authority reserve to be declared in England, on 1 August 1952.

There remained to the north at Seacroft some 200 acres of sand-dunes belonging to Skegness Urban District Council which it was clearly desirable to include in the reserve. On the recommendation of the Joint Advisory Committee in 1952 the Clerk of the County Council asked the UDC to consider bringing this area within the reserve by making its own statutory declaration if it so desired.

The UDC's first reaction was to reject the suggestion on a majority vote in spite of a strong plea from Councillor Cedric Fry, a local industrialist and member of the Trust Council. Fear that they would lose control of the property, which some still saw as having development potential, was the main reason for refusal. However, they agreed to meet representatives of the County Council and the Trust for further discussion. It was clearly necessary to persuade them that inclusion of their property within the reserve would not only be valuable for education and research (including research into coastal processes), but that in the long term the existence of an unspoilt stretch of coast on its southern flank would be a considerable asset for Skegness. With the help of Sir Francis Hill we mustered a formidable team to present our case: not only senior County Councillors and their Clerk and the President and officers of the Trust, but also the Vice-Chancellor and three professors from the University of Nottingham whose students were already using Gibraltar Point for student training and research. The UDC representatives were clearly taken aback by the strength of our representation. "It was", said Councillor Dutton of the UDC, "a distinguished gathering". He had been the leading opponent of the original proposal but as a result of the meeting he subsequently moved that the Council make a declaration of their property and collaborate with the County Council and the Trust in the management of the whole reserve.

Unfortunately, having taken the decision, the Council encountered an unforeseen problem. The 1949 Act gave declaration powers to local authorities only for land within their own boundaries; the Seacroft dunes although owned by the UDC lay in the parish of Croft. The UDC refused to allow the County Council to act for it, but made a non-statutory declaration in exactly the same form and procedure. That served quite adequately until the property passed to the East Lindsey District Council in 1974. The actions of the County and Urban District Councils had thus brought more than 1,000 acres of dune, marsh and shore into protection.

Reporting on a visit to the reserve in August 1953 Iolo Williams, the distinguished countryside correspondent of *The Times*, was able to write in an extensive article in that newspaper on 3 August:

> Clearly Gibraltar Point, with the Steeping River (which begins life as the brook about which Tennyson wrote) flowing to sea to the south, and its dunes, slacks, and saltmarshes northwards, is a place to give great pleasure and interest both to the professional or amateur naturalist and to the more contemplative and observant member of the public at large. It is all the more pleasant to find such a peaceful spot only 3 miles from the noise and vast illuminated fun-fairs of Skegness. Great credit is due to the County Council, the Urban District Council, the Lincolnshire Naturalists' Trust, and all those who are doing their best to ensure the survival and effectiveness of this admirable reserve.

The Reserve Under Threat

When that was written, however, a situation had arisen which threatened the very existence of the new reserve. Sykes Farm, the buildings of which I had noticed among the elm trees on my first visit to the Point in 1937, had been requisitioned for army use during the war. The farmhouse was still unoccupied when it was burnt down one night in September 1947, possibly by an incendiary target indicator dropped by an aircraft using the Wainfleet bombing range. In front of the house was a lawn shaded by a weeping wych elm, and an orchard in the shelter of the sea bank; behind it the farmyard which contained a fine range of buildings: the three-bay cart shed (one bay had already been demolished) with barn above dating from about 1820 when the farm was built; another large barn of later date, and a crew yard surrounded by a brick wall. To the south of the house and the farmyard lay an old grass paddock where the farm horses used to graze. Army huts had been constructed around the edges of the field and in 1952 one of them was still occupied by a family of squatters. Early in that year we learned that a Mr W G Moore proposed to take a lease of the field from the owner

Mr G E Hyams with a view to re-opening the property as a caravan site which, it was claimed, it had been before the material date in 1937 defined in the Town & Country Planning Act of 1947. The County Council as the planning authority determined that the development would require an application under the Act. Mr Moore appealed against that decision and a Public Inquiry was held in Skegness on 11 November 1952. Witnesses were called on both sides. The County Council did not deny that some tents and one or two old bus bodies had occasionally been occupied on a small part of the field prior to 1937, but they contested that this was of such casual and sporadic occurrence that it was materially different from the use now proposed. However, the Council failed to convince the Minister who, in a decision announced in January 1953, ruled in favour of the appellant. The decision was on a technical interpretation of the Act, but the effect was to give Mr Moore the right to develop the whole of the six acre field as a caravan site.

The decision caused widespread consternation and dismay. All that had been achieved in the previous four years was put in jeopardy. We had, of course, gladly accepted that the nature reserve would be open to the public, but to have up to 300 people living virtually on the site in a large caravan camp with its own shop and recreational facilities was a completely different proposition. Our judgement – and it was overwhelmingly supported – was that the reserve as we knew it could not survive the impact of such a development.

At the Public Inquiry in November we had had to stand by helplessly. Now it was time for action. First it was necessary to convey our views to the County Council. Accordingly, at the Council's invitation, a deputation from the Trust consisting of the President Colonel Nelthorpe, Sir Francis Hill, Professor C G C Chesters of Nottingham University and myself attended a joint meeting of the County Council's Planning Committee and Sandhills Sub-committee on 5 February 1953. We emphasised the irreplaceable scientific and amenity values of the reserve which the County Council had established, and explained in detail the Trust's view that a caravan camp on the site proposed would make effective maintenance of the reserve and the conduct of research impossible. The County Council had also been in consultation with the Nature Conservancy and were assured of their support for any action to safeguard the reserve. On the recommendation of its committees the County Council resolved on 20 February that the field in question should be managed as part of the nature reserve; that an agreement to this effect be sought with the owner and occupier of the field, but that if no such agreement could be secured a Compulsory Purchase Order for the acquisition of the field be made.

The negotiations between the Council and the owner and occupier of the site failed and the Council made a Compulsory Order under Sections 18 and 21 of the National Parks and Access to the Countryside Act (1949). It was a bold move on the Council's part, but Max Nicholson, by then the Director General of the Nature Conservancy, was astonished when he realised that the Council had used the 1949 Act powers rather than those available to them under the Town & Country Planning Act of 1947. The Nature Conservancy and the National Parks Commission had both given assurances to the government that they would use compulsory powers under the 1949 Act only with the express authority of Ministers. The Sykes Farm Order in fact remains, as far as I am aware, the only contested Compulsory Order ever made under the 1949 Act. It was submitted to the Minister of Housing and Local Government for confirmation and a Public

Inquiry was fixed for 28 July 1953.

The Trust's next task was to muster as much support as possible from other local and national organisations and from the general public. Our policy of welcoming people to the reserve for study and for enjoyment of nature now paid handsome dividends. I wrote to all those natural history and ornithological societies whose members had visited the reserve in the previous four years or who had other associations with it. Thirteen societies from Lincolnshire, Bedfordshire, Cambridge, Leicestershire, Northamptonshire, Nottinghamshire and Yorkshire submitted written evidence in support of the County Council. National non-governmental bodies who did likewise were the Amateur Entomologists' Society, the International Committee for Bird Protection, the Royal Society for the Protection of Birds, the British Trust for Ornithology and the Society for the Promotion of Nature Reserves. Some of those bodies and a number of others authorised me to represent them at the Inquiry. All this was very encouraging. Ironically the only organisation which refused to give support was our neighbour across the Wash, the Norfolk Naturalists' Trust. From the Trust's secretary, Miss Connie Gay, I received a bleak reply to the effect that they knew nothing of "Jamaica (sic) Point" and could not comment. So much for the Trust which should have been the pioneering leader of a new movement!

The Inquiry was held in Skegness Town Hall, and perhaps because it was the first Order of its kind, the Ministry appointed one of its senior inspectors, Mr E Fitzgibbon, to conduct it. A well-known barrister, Mr H Marnham, appeared for the appellant, and the County Council's case was ably conducted by the Deputy Clerk, Richard Pepler. Evidence for the Council was given by its Clerk, Herbert Copland, and its Planning Officer, Robert Stirling. They concentrated on the Council's coastal planning policies which made ample provision for caravan sites elsewhere, and on its efforts to retain Gibraltar Point as an undeveloped area and to promote the nature reserve and its educational and scientific aims. The Council's case was powerfully supported. Spilsby Rural District Council and Skegness Urban District Council both objected to the proposed development, and the Deputy Clerk of the latter authority handed to the Inspector a petition signed by 669 Skegness residents expressing the view that it was in the best interests of Skegness that Gibraltar Point remain in a quiet natural condition. "The Nature Reserve", the petition continued "is obviously a place of national importance and many local people and visitors have derived interest and pleasure from it". Nicholson sent the Conservancy's Administrative Secretary, P H Cooper, to make a supporting statement. Another powerful ally was the Lincolnshire River Board whose clerk, Geoffrey Phillipo, expressed great alarm at the damaging effect which the occupants of a caravan camp would have on the fragile sand dunes of Gibraltar Point which form an important sea defence on the southern flank of Skegness. With the floods of 31 January/1 February of that year still fresh in mind this was a cogent message. Scientific evidence – particularly on the importance of the reserve for birds – was presented on behalf of the British Trust for Ornithology and the Royal Society for the Protection of Birds by W B Alexander, former director of the Edward Gray Institute at Oxford and then chairman of the BTO's Bird Observatories Committee. Professor C G C Chesters, Professor of Botany at the University of Nottingham, described the vegetation cover of Gibraltar Point and reinforced the River Board's concern about the danger of erosion by excessive use.

As I was called to give evidence for the Trust – and for some twenty other bodies – and to face cross-examination, I recalled Max Nicholson's warning that naturalists involved in conservation would have to become 'eco-politicians'. My purpose was to describe first the wildlife of the reserve and its local and national importance; and then the aims of the reserve in conservation and in promoting education, research and the appreciation of nature. The County Council's far-sighted action and determination, I said, had set a valuable example and it would be a serious setback to conservation throughout the country if this was to be thwarted by the proposed development. There was one particularly tricky issue with which I had to deal: to differentiate between the effect of day visitors to the open reserve and the presence of people living on a caravan camp on the edge of it. Inevitably Counsel for the appellant pressed me hard on that. He also tried to make capital out of the disturbance allegedly caused by the RAF bombing range on Wainfleet Sands. Overall he had a difficult task. He was able to make little impression on the witnesses supporting the County Council, and his client, Mr Moore, was feeble and inconsistent under cross-examination. His frustration showed at times especially in his attempts to belittle and even ridicule the values of nature conservation and scientific studies in the field. He might have had a stronger point, however, in his final submission that the 1949 Act was the wrong instrument to use in this case and in his contention that the Minister had no power to confirm the Compulsory Purchase Order.

It was late afternoon when the Inquiry finished. The Inspector announced his intention of visiting the site and suggested that two or three representatives of both parties should accompany him after a meal. Richard Pepler and I attended for the County Council and the Trust. It was a tranquil summer evening at Gibraltar Point. The sea lavender was at its best, purple carpets of it on either side of the South Marsh Road as we crossed to the shore. On the headland at that time, at the base of what later developed into the Spit, we had erected a hide. On the incoming tide we watched the waders flighting in to roost on the higher sandbars. The Inspector, who proved to be a knowledgeable ornithologist, became very absorbed in watching and identifying the various species. Only Mr Moore's solicitor had accompanied us thus far and he soon made his excuses and left. He can have heard little to encourage him. We stayed on until the setting sun illuminated the white cliffs of Hunstanton, and away to the north-east the Lynn Well lightship began to flash its guiding beam. It was twilight when I drove home. The adrenaline which had sustained me throughout the day had drained away and I was exhausted. It had though been an interesting and in many ways satisfying experience.

It was mid-December before we received the Minister's decision. He confirmed the County Council's Order without modification. The Minister, incidentally, was Harold MacMillan. I had a soft spot for 'Super Mac' thereafter although he probably had little to do personally with the Gibraltar Point decision. The County Council's enlightened and determined policy was rewarded. The future of the nature reserve was assured and we could go ahead confidently with our plans for management and development. It was also a landmark for the Trust in other ways. We had taken a leading role in a major battle for nature conservation, one of the first of the post-war period. It had attracted tremendous support, much more than we had anticipated. It had earned the Trust new respect and had boosted confidence in our purposes. It was well summed up by the Nature Conservancy in their annual report for 1953-4: "Here again strong and far-sighted local initiative was vindicated by the depth and breadth of support for the Reserve, and for the idea of conservation which it expresses".

There was one unfinished piece of business stemming from the Public Inquiry. It had been the County Council's intention to apply the Compulsory Purchase Order not only to the field, but also to the adjoining farmhouse and farmyard site. Unfortunately the latter was accidentally omitted from the map defining the area to be acquired under the Order. There was some excuse for this because the Order was made only three days after the East Coast floods of 31 January/1 February 1953. County Council officers were overwhelmed in dealing with the consequences. In normal circumstances I might have been asked to check the map; as it was there was no such opportunity and by the time I was able to point out the error it was too late to amend it. They had also omitted the roadside bank, thereby depriving the Council of access to the site, a fact which the appellant's Counsel was quick to point out. After the decision the owner agreed to include the roadside bank in the sale, but he adamantly refused to sell the farmhouse and farmyard site. Apart from an arrangement which he made with the adjoining farm estate to use it for pheasant feeding, it remained for the next twenty-five years neglected and unguarded. One of the barns was demolished, tiles were stolen and the remaining buildings deteriorated still further. More seriously, it carried permission to re-develop the house and there was also the possibility that attempts might be made to develop the farm buildings for dwelling purposes; there were even suggestions of a hotel. The threat which it potentially posed to the reserve therefore was not insignificant. In October 1977 the owner - by this time Mrs H Jeffries, the daughter of the previous owner - advertised the site for sale with re-building permission. A buyer was forthcoming but when he failed to complete the purchase we decided that, costly though it would be, the Trust should purchase the site. £12,000 was a lot of money to find from our own slender resources, but the purchase further safeguarded the reserve from building development and it has proved over the years to have been an excellent investment.

There was one other small property matter which arose in the 1950s. Between the second and third bungalow built by the Tennyson Glen Estate Company in the west dunes in the early 1930s on what they named Aylmer Avenue there was left for some reason a vacant plot. In view of their determined policy of protecting the new nature reserve it came as something of a surprise that in 1955 the County Council decided to offer the plot for sale. Whilst planning policies should have safeguarded it against development, the Trust decided to avoid any such risk by purchasing the plot itself. Following the appointment in 1972 of a warden for the field station and the provision of accommodation on site, the Joint Advisory Committee recommended in its development plan for the reserve that a bungalow be built on the vacant plot in Aylmer Avenue to house the nature reserve warden. Planning permission was sought and obtained on the grounds that this was necessary for the management of the reserve. The County Council then re-purchased the land from the Trust, built the bungalow and let it to the Trust. It has been occupied by the reserve warden ever since.

GIBRALTAR POINT RESERVE

WILD LIFE ON COAST OF LINCOLNSHIRE

BY OUR SPECIAL CORRESPONDENT

Details are published, from time to time, of National Nature Reserves "declared" by the Nature Conservancy under the National Parks and Access to the Countryside Act of 1949. That Act, however, also provided for the creation of other nature reserves by local authorities, and one such has, in fact, come into existence.

This is the Lindsey County Council's reserve at Gibraltar Point, which is now just a year old, and remains, so far, the only area of the kind belonging to any county council.

Opening paragraphs of a report in The Times, 3 August 1953, with photograph above of the flooded saltings at high tide.

FRED CLIFT

Public Inquiry on Future of Nature Reserve

---o---

EMINENT AUTHORITIES GIVE EVIDENCE ON THREAT PRESENTED BY PROPOSED CARAVAN CAMP

---o---

UNIQUE FEATURES OF GIBRALTAR POINT AREA

---o---

COUNTY COUNCIL SEEKS CONFIRMATION OF COMPULSORY PURCHASE ORDER

Headlines of a report in the Skegness News, 29 July 1953.

BARRIE WILKINSON

Ruins of Sykes Farm barns and cartsheds.

Oystercatchers

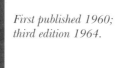

THE BIRD
IN THE HAND

R. K. CORNWALLIS and A. E. SMITH

BRITISH TRUST FOR ORNITHOLOGY
FIELD GUIDE NUMBER SIX
THREE SHILLINGS

First published 1960;
third edition 1964.

Gibraltar Point in Winter

GRIMSBY EVENING TELEGRAPH

Heligoland bird trap, 1950.

Lenten Ottaway in the ringing laboratory, 1950.

Logo used on first Bird Observatory Report 1949.

Bird Observatory with Frank Bean, volunteer warden, 1949.

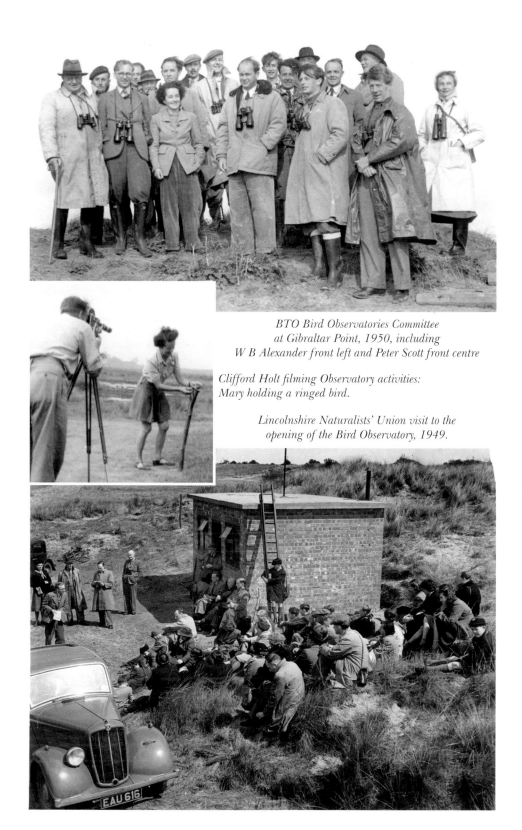

*BTO Bird Observatories Committee
at Gibraltar Point, 1950, including
W B Alexander front left and Peter Scott front centre*

*Clifford Holt filming Observatory activities:
Mary holding a ringed bird.*

*Lincolnshire Naturalists' Union visit to the
opening of the Bird Observatory, 1949.*

The Bird Observatory

To begin with, in 1949 and 1950, much of the time that I could spare from my new professional duties went into the establishment and running of the Gibraltar Point reserve. The promotion of education, research and public interest was one of the principal objectives of the reserve identified in our management agreement with the County Council. For these purposes the bird observatory provided an initial focal point of activity and interest. We built the first Heligoland trap on the headland in the winter of 1948/49, and renovated the little brick building which the army had conveniently left nearby. It was doorless and windowless when we first found it, but Lenten Ottaway and I slept there occasionally in the autumn of 1948, rising at first light to watch migration before others joined us to work on the building and the trap. I still remember those early September mornings: the mist drifting from the shore as the sun rose over the sea; the distant hills and woods of Norfolk in dim silhouette; skylarks and meadow pipits everywhere, and soon after dawn the coastal passage of swallows and martins, many thousands an hour on good days; on fine mornings of spring tides thousands of waders in close-knit flocks – oystercatchers, knots and bar-tailed godwits, dunlins and others – flying in to sit out the high tide on the sandspits and foredunes. And all that usually with no-one else in sight. I have seen it all so often again, but then it was a fresh experience of birds and early morning, of the excitement and complexity and mystery of migration.

Already in that first autumn we saw a fascinating pattern of migratory movement which became familiar in the years that followed. Low pressure and south-westerly winds brought early morning passage in late August and September of hirundines, larks, pipits and finches. Anticyclonic conditions over the near continent with winds from an easterly quarter often brought dramatic 'falls' of migrants which had been 'drifted' over the North Sea. Pied flycatchers, redstarts, whinchats and various warblers were characteristic 'drift' migrants, and with them the occasional rare vagrant from the far east of Europe. I saw my first red-breasted flycatcher and bluethroat in that September of 1949. Later, in October, similar weather conditions brought large falls of blackbirds - more than 1,000 in three days towards the end of the month - redwings, fieldfares and goldcrests, and with them a great grey shrike and a tiny yellow-browed warbler all the way from the Siberian taiga. Those were – and still are – exciting days if you are fortunate enough to be there. Sometimes migrants arrived overnight and in the morning the dune bushes would be full of birds: hungry thrushes in October eagerly devouring berries, and the thin voices of the goldcrests a constant reminder that these tiny five gram scraps of feathers really had made the long and hazardous crossing of the North Sea. I never cease to wonder at it. Sometimes an influx took place in the afternoon. The 1949 Bird Observatory report records, for example, that on 12 September as the wind backed north-east and freshened to Force four there were few birds about till 6 o'clock in the evening, but then quite suddenly the reserve was full of them many appearing tired and still there the following day. There were few robins in autumn 1949, but two years later in 1951 there was a massive immigration of them beginning in the middle of the day on 1 October and continuing until nightfall and again on the following day. On the first evening it was estimated that more than 500 were present in the reserve. Robins being solitary in winter it was strange to hear a dozen or more 'ticking' in every bush as the light faded. It was equally exciting, of course, to receive the first ringing recoveries and to discover, for example, that blackbirds being trapped and ringed at the observatory on autumn passage originated from a wide area of north-west Europe from Norway and the Baltic to the Low Countries; and that pied flycatchers made their autumn journeys through France, Spain and Portugal to winter as far away as the Central African Republic.

Our activities at the observatory soon attracted the curiosity of several local people from Skegness who were used to visiting the Point. Among these were Phillip and Douglas Lill, owners of the Skegness cast stone works, the first of whom kept a boat in the Haven; Ken Green, a garage proprietor in Drummond Road; Jack Chambers, a banana warehouseman and distributor, the owner of a huge pair of old naval binoculars for which he built himself a unipod out of bits of metal found on the beach (hence his nickname 'Unipod Jack'); and Frank Bean, a local builder who did sterling work in constructing the trap and repairing the building. He is commemorated by 'Bean's Hole', the pool at the junction of the South Marsh road and the sleeper track into which he accidentally drove his little van one foggy November afternoon. Later, in retirement, there was Jack Palmer, a Probation Officer; Bob French, the Skegness Postmaster, and Fred Clift, shop manager and amateur photographer whose splendid pictures provide an invaluable record of the reserve in its early days. We were also much assisted by Wilf Holland who had acted as a kind of caretaker for the County Council. Having been born in Gibraltar House, the ruins of which I had seen on my first visit, he had known the place intimately all his life and was a mine of helpful information. A friendly, courteous man he was a familiar figure bringing visitors from Skegness for a sedate ride to Gibraltar Point in his landau. These and other local supporters, some of whom were members of my long-running natural history class in Skegness, formed in due course an invaluable nucleus of a task force and local liaison group which played an important pioneering role in the establishment first of the bird observatory and then of the nature reserve. They were typical of the broad cross-section of society which the Trust began to attract wherever it developed a focus of activity. It was the observatory too which attracted Dick Cornwallis to the Trust. I first met him there one day in the summer of 1949. It was the beginning of a twenty year friendship and working partnership which will loom large in the following chapters.

The successful launch of the bird observatory was due in large measure to the enthusiastic devotion of Lenten Ottaway. Lenten was an excellent field ornithologist and a meticulous notetaker, an accomplishment which I never managed to cultivate. A bachelor at that time, he had inherited from his father a small watch repairing and jewellery business, and although tied largely to shop hours he devoted most of his spare time including weekends to the observatory taking responsibility for the supervision of the ringing operation and record keeping. His knowledge and geniality soon endeared him to all the early visitors who came to man the observatory and assist in the management of the reserve. When he married and moved to Louth in 1952 he switched his attention to the Trust's recently established Saltfleetby-Theddlethorpe Dunes reserve where he became the first honorary warden. Later he was appointed the first volunteer regional officer for East Lindsey, one of several such early appointments. A good companion, a man of great modesty and generosity he was one of the outstanding pioneers who helped to build the Trust from the outset.

Birdwatching was just beginning to gain popularity among the young, and we soon had a bird observatory 'boy', Dennis Hill, who went on to become a professional scientist and university professor. Barrie Wilkinson, who followed on in the early 1950s, was more diffident initially, but became totally dedicated to Gibraltar Point and to the Trust in which he was destined to play a leading role for the rest of the century and beyond.

The observatory started operations unobtrusively on 11 April 1949, but a ceremonial inauguration took place later that month when a joint Trust-Naturalists' Union field meeting was held at the Point. As soon as the observatory was functioning we applied for recognition by the British Trust for Ornithology which had set up a Bird Observatories Committee under the chairmanship of W B Alexander who had been the first Director of the Edward Gray Institute at Oxford. Gibraltar Point was almost unknown outside Lincolnshire and the application came as a surprise to the ornithological establishment.

'W.B', as he was affectionately known, came to inspect the observatory in June 1949, and although he confessed that he had had to consult a map to see where Gibraltar Point was, he wrote - following a second visit in autumn – in a Foreword to the first (1949) Field Station and Bird Observatory Report: "I have had the pleasure of two visits, and Gibraltar Point is to me no longer a mere name on the map, but a fascinating bit of wild coastal country associated in my mind with views of interesting and rare birds and the sight of flocks travelling along the dunes impelled by the mysterious impulse of migration". In September 1949 Lenten, Mary and I attended our first meeting of the Bird Observatories Committee in Edinburgh which included a visit to the Isle of May. George Waterston, who was then planning his ambitious new observatory on Fair Isle, was one of the hosts at that meeting. In autumn 1950 the Committee met in Skegness and visited Gibraltar Point. Over twenty representatives and guests from six observatories attended the meeting, including Ronald Lockley of Skokholm fame, and Peter Scott who had recently set up the Severn Wildfowl Trust at Slimbridge and who returned to Skegness soon afterwards with a team to trap and ring pink-footed geese on Croft Marsh, an annual event for several years.

In addition to providing a focus for local and amateur interest and support for the nature reserve and the Trust, the bird observatory attracted regional and national attention to Gibraltar Point from ornithologists and conservationists. Natural history and ornithological societies and bird clubs from the Midlands and many individuals came to hear about the work of recording and to see a demonstration of ringing techniques. Foremost among these was the Leicestershire and Rutland Ornithological Society whose Honorary Secretary, Ronald Hickling, eventually became for many years the Chairman of the Gibraltar Point Observatory Committee. More importantly, it was Hickling's experience of the work of the Trust that encouraged him to promote the formation of a similar trust in Leicestershire which became in 1956 the fourth county trust. In the first full year of the observatory, 1950, there were more than 600 visitors, and, in spite of the rudimentary accommodation, 35 ornithologists manned the observatory throughout the spring and autumn seasons, some of them like Harold Hems, a Sheffield schoolteacher, and Richard Alison, an old pupil of mine at Leeds Grammar School, staying for several weeks each year. Another of those attracted to Gibraltar Point in the early 50s was Marson Peet then living in Oakham. When he moved into Lincolnshire in 1952 he soon played a leading role in the Trust's affairs, notably as Honorary Treasurer from 1959 to 1974 and later as a tireless botanical recorder.

The 1950s and 60s were the heyday of bird observatories and Gibraltar Point was very much at the forefront of the movement. The first BTO manual on ringing and ancilliary techniques *The Bird in the Hand*, written by Dick Cornwallis and me and published in 1960 was based on our experience at the Gibraltar Point observatory. The later acquisition of more adequate accommodation in the Old Coastguard House enabled us to co-operate with the British Trust for Ornithology in pioneering training courses for ringers, and in June 1965 the late Kenneth Williamson of the BTO conducted the first 'crash' Common Birds Census in the reserve. The results, published in British Birds under the title of *A Bird Community of Accreting Sand-dunes and Saltmarsh* provided an invaluable base-line for all subsequent CBC work in the reserve.

By the 1970s the ringing functions of many observatories were in decline as a result of the increasing use of the more mobile mist net. The importance of the Gibraltar Point observatory has faded somewhat – although regular observations and ringing continue there – but in those first twenty years it made a significant contribution to knowledge of migration and to the development of the nature reserve and the Trust generally.

Managing the Reserve

In the early 1950s there seemed to be little need for active management of the vegetation of the reserve. New dunes were accreting rapidly beyond the main eastern ridge, and a high sandbar extended southwards from the headland where in 1950 we erected the first bird hide for the observation of waders at their high tide roost. This sandbar also became the main nesting site for little terns and ringed plovers as visitor pressure on the beach opposite the main access increased. The Spit, as it became known, sheltered the mudflats to the west so encouraging the development of new saltmarsh. Vegetation was slow to become established on the Spit itself, however, and it was not until the 1970s that dune grasses and other plant colonists had taken a firm hold. By that time a new ridge had developed to the east and the distal end of the Spit was beginning to decay. Further north dune formation was proceeding rapidly and one of our early concerns was the damage to new dunes being caused by motor vehicles penetrating into the reserve from the Seacroft end. Barriers erected by Skegness UDC in 1960 were initially broken down, but with persistence the menace was largely overcome, although it has recurred in recent years through irresponsible behaviour by owners of four-wheel drive vehicles and trial bikes.

One of the features of the Skegness section of the reserve is the so-called Seacroft 'lagoon'. This is a wide saltmarsh slack which extends across the northern boundary of the reserve and which is accessible from Seacroft Esplanade. A wide beach and dunes had formed in front of it, but it was regularly flooded at high spring tides through a tortuous creek at its southern extremity. In the late 1940s the Urban District Council Surveyor made a crude attempt to block the creek by filling it with sand with a view to using the dried-out floor of the lagoon for some kind of visitor attraction or development – an open-air zoo was one somewhat bizarre suggestion. Predictably the sea soon broke through again, but the outflow of tidal water was impeded and the salinity of the standing water increased and for

69

many years retarded the growth of saltmarsh vegetation. In creating their section of the nature reserve in 1952 the UDC accepted our management proposals to refrain from interference with the natural development of the coastline and so gain a better understanding of the process. The temptation to use the lagoon did not entirely go away, however, and in 1962 the UDC Clerk – prompted perhaps by a special interest group – inquired what attitude the Trust would take to the development of the lagoon for dinghy sailing. That would first have involved major works to dam and deepen the lagoon and would subsequently have attracted large numbers of sightseers. It would have been disastrous for the reserve and its wildlife and our response was a firm rebuttal of the idea. We heard nothing further of it and I believe the Clerk was relieved not to have to pursue it.

At the Gibraltar Point end of the reserve the first management requirement in 1949 was to prevent vehicular access to the east dunes along the Mill Pond and South Marsh Roads constructed by the army during the Second World War. The County Council appreciated the necessity of this and readily agreed to the installation of gates at the western end coupled with the designation of parking areas beside the public road which over the years have been expanded and improved.

Both western and eastern dune ranges bore the scars of army occupation. Wartime buildings south of the Old Coastguard House and in the east dunes were demolished, but the former NAAFI building by the road side north of the sea bank was left, becoming eventually the headquarters of the Skegness Sailing Club. That building and huts round the perimeter of Sykes farm paddock were occupied after 1947 by families of squatters, the last of whom hung on until the 1953 flood forced them to leave. After the County Council acquired the field in 1953 the huts were demolished, though the concrete foundations are still in evidence. Most of the wartime pillboxes on the eastern dunes were retained as accretion markers and as nest sites for swallows.

Trust volunteers played their part in clearing up the wartime debris. With hindsight we would also have done well to try to eliminate the rosebay willowherb brought in and encouraged by military activity on the east dunes. It spread rapidly in the 1950s and 60s and much effort has gone in to trying to control it in the last few years. We also became concerned - unnecessarily as it turned out – about another invasive plant, the cord grass *Spartina townsendii*. This had apparently been introduced in the vicinity of Gibraltar Point in the early 1940s in an attempt to hasten the stabilisation of mudflats for reclamation purposes. By the early 1950s it had begun to colonise the New Marsh in the reserve which was developing in the shelter of the Spit. To our alarm it had also appeared among the sea lavender beds on the Old Saltmarsh. Fearing that it might dominate that also, we called in the newly formed Conservation Corps under the formidable Brigadier Armstrong to dig it out and burn it. We need not have worried. It made little headway on the Old Marsh, and after becoming dominant for a few years on the New Marsh it died back and allowed the normal vegetation succession to take over.

Myxomatosis decimated the high rabbit populations in the reserve in the mid 1950s with dramatic consequences for vegetation. Sea buckthorn - the tender young shoots of which were eaten by rabbits - spread rapidly covering large areas of open dune grassland both in dune hollows and on ridges. Whilst this provided the best example of sea buckthorn habitat in Britain - Gibraltar Point became the classic site for its study – and was a rich breeding habitat for several bird species, it eliminated much of the open grassland favoured by butterflies and other invertebrates, including insects like the magnificent hunting wasp *Ammophilla sabulosa* which we used to watch carrying caterpillar prey to its pre-prepared hole on a bare patch of sand. Along with other insects this sand wasp declined as bare sand and blow-outs were colonised by vegetation. In the absence of rabbit grazing grasses also became ranker to the detriment of smaller, low-growing plants like bird's-foot trefoil and storksbill, the food of butterflies and other insects. The disappearance of the brown argus butterfly for more than thirty years may be attributable to that.

By the early 1960s action was considered necessary to retain grassland areas on the older western dunes, and we acquired our first tractor and bush hog with the aid of an early grant from the Nature Conservancy for the purpose. Since then annual mowing of areas formerly covered by sea buckthorn on both east and west dunes has restored and maintained open grassland, a process enhanced in recent years by sheep grazing in selected areas. It has also improved floristic diversity. It was not so easy to restrict the spread of sea buckthorn on to outer dune ridges, and the succession to climax scrub, especially in the northern part of the reserve, is today more abrupt than it used to be with consequent reduction of intermediate stages.

A dramatic example of a simple management regime, sustained over 20 years, can be seen in the patch of grassland opposite the sailing club's headquarters. Noting a few cowslip plants there in the early 1970s the Trust's field officer at that time, Barrie Wilkinson, decided to mow and rake the litter in autumn each year. Today the area carries abundant cowslip, pyramidal orchid and other plants including meadow saxifrage hitherto unknown on the reserve. 'Barrie's plot' has become one of the show pieces of Gibraltar Point.

Reconciling access and use of the reserve with conservation of its various habitats and their wildlife was a principal objective of management and one that assumed increasing importance as the number of visitors and educational users grew throughout the 1950s and 60s. The visitor survey of 1965/68, which I describe in the next section, was designed to help us in managing access for that purpose. We had already realised, however, that one of the essential requirements was a carefully designed network of pathways which would enable people to see the reserve but which would confine and absorb much of the pressure. This was especially important in more sensitive areas. The two principal access routes to the shore from the new roadside parking places were the Mill Pond track from the north car park and the South Marsh road from the main park at the end of the public road. Where they crossed the marsh both had been made up with hardcore by the Army during the war, but where they crossed the west and the wide eastern dunes they were simply unmade paths. There, within a few years, the pressure of feet had worn away the vegetation and created ever widening gulleys where the wind added to the erosion. The difficulty of walking on the soft sand encouraged people to try to find alternative routes, so causing exactly the kind of damage and disturbance which we had sought to avoid.

At that time large numbers of railway sleepers were becoming available in Lincolnshire from lines being taken out of use. They could be bought quite cheaply and the Joint Advisory Committee agreed in 1965 that the County Council should acquire sufficient of them to make a track through the dunes on the South Marsh

71

route, a distance of some 400 yards. The Trust offered to find most of the labour for that purpose, and within a couple of years the track had been completed and enclosed in a chestnut paling fence. It was a great success. It straightway stopped the erosion problem, it encouraged people to stay on the track, and it provided an excellent transect for demonstration purposes through the dune grassland on the ridges and sea buckthorn and other scrub in the main hollow. A similar track was laid on the Mill Pond route in 1973 with a flight of steps leading to a viewpoint on Mill Hill, the highest point of the reserve. That work was also carried out by voluntary work parties, mainly of boys from Skegness Grammar School and Police cadets on an exercise. When a similar path erosion problem developed in the dune hollow between the Mill Pond and South Marsh routes we made a hardcore track which served its purpose equally well providing a good walking surface now largely grassed over.

In 1973/4 the rough chalk surface of the South Marsh road which had become difficult to walk on was given a tarmac surface. There were some objections that such a surface would be out of keeping with the natural saltmarsh through which the track passes. In fact it blended in better than before and it stopped the erosion of vegetation at the edges where people had sought to find easier walking.

These early improvements successfully achieved the purposes for which they were designed. They were among the first of their kind to be carried out on any coastal nature reserve in the country and they attracted a great deal of appreciative comment from visitors and interest from other reserve managers. The sleeper track eventually wore out and was replaced in the 1990s by a smooth surface of crushed stone which provides excellent access and has blended in equally well. The slopes have been regraded for wheelchair access, and a viewing point has been provided overlooking the shore.

The acquisition by the County Council of the home paddock of Sykes Farm by compulsory order in 1953 and its inclusion in the reserve posed an interesting management problem. The options of trying to improve the floristically impoverished grassland or planting it with woodland were carefully considered, and the latter course was chosen. Apart from the old trees around the farmyard there was no tall tree cover anywhere in or near the reserve at that time and it was felt that the creation of three acres of woodland cover would be especially valuable for migrant birds, and so it has proved to be. The original composition of trees, which was much influenced by the County Council's tree officer who carried out the planting in the mid-1960s, was far from ideal, but it has been modified and improved over the years by thinning conifers and replacing sycamore and dead elm with more ash, birch and alder. The plantation – further improved by the creation of a pond in an open meadow area – now forms a valuable element in the habitat variety of the reserve, not only for migrant birds, but for breeding species not previously present and for insects such as dragonflies and butterflies which take advantage of the sheltered, sunny rides.

There was an external development which had a considerable effect on the reserve both visually and environmentally, greater perhaps than we appreciated at the time. In 1966 the owner of land across the river to the west of the reserve undertook the reclamation of 120 acres of adjoining saltmarsh. That involved the construction of a new bank beside the river opposite the Field Station. The view to the west was henceforth restricted by the bank; the long term ecological effect on the reserve of the loss of the adjoining mature saltmarsh was more complex and more serious. I shall discuss the environmental consequences of saltmarsh reclamation in The Wash generally in a later chapter, but regrettable though we found it, neither the Trust nor the Nature Conservancy in the mid-1960s had the necessary scientific information or the resources to mount a successful challenge to reclamation of that kind. That state of affairs, however, was to change dramatically over the next ten years.

The northern end of the Old Saltmarsh in the reserve had been enclosed by a bank, known as Bulldog Bank, towards the end of the 19th Century. It served as a flood defence barrier limiting the incursion of tidal water, and provided grazing for sheep and cattle. Grazing had ceased, however, well before the Second World War, and in 1949 when we made a preliminary survey, the area had developed a varied damp meadow flora including cowslip, cuckooflower, adder's-tongue and several orchids - green-winged, common spotted, pyramidal, bee and twayblade. There were also a number of freshwater pools with interesting marginal vegetation and good amphibian and invertebrate populations.

In the great flood of 31 January 1953 Bulldog Bank was breached in several places and the whole of the area beyond was inundated. Salt water remained for several weeks and killed almost all the vegetation. The bank was repaired, but on three occasions in the following fifteen years it was again overtopped by tidal water and further damage was done to the freshwater marsh. Heightening the bank was the only way to prevent that happening again, and in 1971 we persuaded the then Lincolnshire River Authority to adopt it as the sea defence line, offering at the same time to make a contribution to strengthening it. The height was raised in 1972, and the bank was completely rebuilt in 1981.

Once that work was completed we turned our attention again to a project planned during the 1960s to create a large body of freshwater in the area north of the bank. Hope that the Royal Engineers would undertake the excavation as a training exercise had come to nothing, but then one day in early January 1972 Walter Lane, the Clerk of the County Council, called me to say that the Council could find £2,000 for the work provided it could be committed in that financial year. Rapid action enabled tenders to be obtained and a contract signed within the time limit, and within a few months a 2½ acre mere with three small islands had been excavated and a substantial brick hide with access from the Mill Pond road had been built into the bank. In the early part of 1974 the mere was extended by another 1½ acres, and the spoil banks along the northern and eastern edges lowered to blend more naturally with the grassland areas beyond.

Frogs and toads were both pairing in the Mere before the excavator had finished, and various invertebrates were soon present in numbers. Water crowfoot was in flower by the first summer and that most persistent invader of shallow water near the sea, the sea clubrush - which we have had to control periodically over the years – quickly put in an appearance. The Mere proved immediately attractive to birds: migrant waders, ducks in autumn and winter, herons and kingfishers, and finches and other passerines coming to drink and feed on the banks. The hide proved equally attractive to human visitors, several hundreds of them using it in the first year. To see the birds – even common ones – at close quarters without them being aware of one's presence was a new and delightful experience for many people. The Mere quickly matured and became one of the most popular features of the reserve. It also stimulated plans to create more fresh and brackish wetland habitats.

From the outset one of our main management concerns was the protection of the nesting shorebirds: little terns, ringed plovers and oystercatchers. The little terns, those most gracefully elegant of all our small seabirds, were particularly vulnerable to disturbance and damage to eggs and chicks by the increasing numbers of people frequenting the shore in the post-war years. It was that which led to the extinction of many of their colonies around the coasts of England and Wales and put them onto the endangered list. During the war years when the beach at Gibraltar Point was mined the colony had increased and spread northwards, but by the early 1950s numbers had declined to between 10 and 15 pairs which were concentrated largely on the sandspit at the southern end where they remained for the next forty years until the spit had developed into a vegetated dune unsuitable for nest sites.

We organised a voluntary wardening rota for weekends, and posted notices – including the pictorial boards I refer to elsewhere – asking people to avoid the nesting area and to keep dogs under control as they were supposed to do under the bylaws. To reinforce those measures the Joint Advisory Committee for the reserve agreed in 1965 that the main nesting area should be wired off during the breeding season. In spite of our efforts, however, the colony teetered on the brink of extinction. In 1964 it was virtually deserted after damage and disturbance during the Whitsun holiday weekend. In 1969 only two young fledged and the situation was little better in the following four or five seasons. In 1975 only five pairs nested and failed to rear any young. Drastic action was clearly needed to save the colony, and in 1976 we applied to the World Wildlife Fund for a grant to employ a seasonal warden to guard and study the nesting area on the spit. We were very fortunate to attract Dr Kevin Woodbridge, an experienced ornithologist with Lincolnshire connections, looking for a seasonal job with birds before going into general practice. Deeply tanned with a long bushy beard Woodbridge was a striking personality who later became well known in Scotland as an ornithologist and as a doctor in remote island communities. With a tent at the base of the spit and with the help of volunteers he was able to mount a 24 hour watch over the colony thereby soon discovering that a dozen or more foxes were regularly foraging in the nesting area. After almost all the first nests had been predated a double-strand electric wire fence was erected around the perimeter. That and some other fox control measures was a turning point in the fortunes of the colony. Ten young fledged that year, the highest total for eight years. Equally important was the fact that we learned a great deal more about the behaviour of the birds and the methods of protecting them, knowledge which was used to good effect in the following years when a seasonal shorebird warden became a regular member of the nature reserve staff. Two of those - Dave Bromwich, the Trust's present Assistant Director (Nature Reserves) and Kevin Wilson, the present Gibraltar Point Site Manager – began their association with the Trust in that seasonal capacity. The tern colony, like most others, has fluctuated in numbers and breeding success since that time, but it has survived in viable numbers (40 pairs and 30 fledged young in 2006) and so has the ringed plover population. To have saved them from almost certain extinction must be one of the Trust's most notable achievements.

The management of Gibraltar Point and its developing facilities would have been task enough alone for the new Trust. It was made possible by the tremendous

'Sleeper' Track across the East Dunes, 1966.

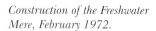

Construction of the Freshwater Mere, February 1972.

Strip Saltings

East Dunes

Bulldog Bank

'Sleeper' Track

Mere

West Dunes

Saltmarsh

ancient creek

Sykes Farm

Field Station

Car park

Steeping River

Oblique air view of Gibraltar Point 1972.

Film-maker Robin Crane photographing little terns.

Demonstrating a 'Take Care! Nesting Shore Birds' picture board by Len and Betty Watkinson to Max Nicholson (left) and Lord Hurcomb, 1960.

First shorebird wardens Dr Kevin Woodbridge and Eric Blood, 1976.

76

volunteer input, by the support of the County Council and by the understanding attitude of my University Department which enabled me to devote more than just spare time to it, although the University was a beneficiary of it by the provision of field study opportunities. By 1958, however, and with the acquisition of the Old Coastguard House as a residential field station, it became evident that a full-time warden to supplement voluntary effort was essential.

The Trust offered to meet half the cost of employing a warden, and the Joint Advisory Committee, which was strongly committed to the reserve and its facilities, recommended that the County Council should contribute the remainder and provide the warden's accommodation by converting the building constructed by the army within the curtilage of the coastguard house. That recommendation was accepted by the Council. We accordingly launched an appeal for £1,000 to enable the Trust to meet our share of the cost over the first five years of the appointment. We produced a simple but effective brochure illustrated with an evocative photograph of dunes and flooded saltings by Skegness amateur photographer and devoted Trust member Fred Clift. The text likewise sought to evoke the appeal of the reserve at all seasons.

The appeal raised some £500 from members, a reasonable total in 1959/60 values from a membership of about the same number. In addition the SPNR made a generous grant of £100 a year for four years. Although somewhat short of the £1,000 target we decided after consultation with the County Council to go ahead with the appointment and we placed advertisements in autumn 1960.

There were very few people at that time with experience of wardening a nature reserve or country park, and whilst there were a good many applicants for our post only two or three were worth serious consideration. An enthusiastic young naturalist named Ray Collier was an attractive candidate (he later became a chief warden of the Nature Conservancy and was seconded to the Trust as our first Conservation Officer from 1971 to 1976), but we chose Arthur Lodge, a mechanic by training, a fitter and air gunner in the RAF during the war and subsequently a smallholder and rural postman in the Cleveland Hills. He had a general interest in natural history and had been associated for twenty years with the Scout movement. For a new post with an important public relations role he seemed to offer 'a safe pair of hands', a quality which appealed particularly to the County Council representatives on the selection board who included the Clerk Walter Lane.

Lodge took up his appointment on 1 March 1961. His presence and day-to-day supervision certainly eased the problems of managing the reserve and the field station although he had no direct responsibility for the latter. For the next twelve years until his retirement he remained a conscientious caretaker. Ironically though, public relations, one of the main reasons for appointing him, proved not to be one of his strengths. By the time he left in 1973 a new breed of nature reserve warden, qualified and trained, was coming onto the job market.

Interpreting the Reserve and Its Wildlife
The popular interpretation of nature and natural features was – like field studies – a little known technique in this country in the 1950s, but the more advanced ideas in practice in the USA were beginning to filter through. We encouraged visitors to see the work of the bird observatory in the early years. We used diagrams,

maps and photographic displays to illustrate bird biology and migration. By the mid-50s we had attracted a small group of naturalists to help in the running of the reserve, and through guided walks we were able to introduce many people to the plants of the dunes and saltmarshes, to animals like the cinnabar moths with their warning coloration, to the hunting wasps and the creatures of the shore. Two members of this group, Len and Betty Watkinson, were specially skilled and ingenious at pictorial illustration, and produced several colourful and arresting picture boards to convey warnings about such dangers as treading on the eggs and chicks of shore nesting birds – a large foot descending on four 'frozen' chicks; uncontrolled dogs – a ferocious hound chasing a bird; the menace of fires, and so on. Illustrations of two of these appeared in the extensive report on Gibraltar Point in the Report of the Nature Conservancy for the year ended 30 September 1960.

Interpretation techniques received further stimulus from the 'Countryside in 1970' Conferences which began in 1960. The first nature trail in Britain – another American import – had been mounted by the Berkshire, Buckinghamshire and Oxfordshire Trust (BBONT) in 1962, and we published a trail guide for Gibraltar Point in 1963. With increasing numbers of private cars and growing interest in wildlife and the countryside, visitor numbers by the early 60s had already reached 150,000 a year. To meet the demand for information and reinforce the conservation message, the Joint Advisory Committee proposed to the County Council the construction of an Information Centre on the main car-park.

The Council accepted the proposal with enthusiasm and the building, designed by the County Architect, was opened by Peter (later Sir Peter) Scott on 9 May 1963 in the presence of local authority leaders and a large gathering of Trust members and local supporters. The building had windows on all sides with displays showing features of the reserve through all seasons of the year. Exhibits were designed and constructed in-house, largely by the Trust's Honorary Publicity Officer, Len Watkinson. It was, I believe, the first such centre on a nature reserve in England. Copies of the nature trail were available at the Centre - more than 1,200 were sold in the first year - and volunteers were on hand there at weekends to provide first-hand information.

After fifteen years the Trust had gained much experience in the task of reconciling educational use and public enjoyment of the reserve with the conservation of its wildlife and natural features. Increasing pressures on use, however, demanded more knowledge of the numbers, motivations and expectations of visitors and users and their impact on the reserve and its more vulnerable plants and animals like the nesting shore birds. No detailed study of that kind had been made on any nature reserve in this country, and the Nature Conservancy responded sympathetically to our proposal to conduct one at Gibraltar Point and offered a modest level of funding for the purpose. The obvious person to conduct the survey was Barrie Wilkinson, the principal voluntary warden who had been an active volunteer at the reserve and bird observatory from schooldays and who was now back in Skegness after four years in the RAF. From his own work at the bird observatory and from what he had learned at my natural history classes in Skegness and from university scientists and others visiting the nature reserve, Barrie had become not only an experienced ornithologist, but a proficient all-round naturalist also. He was in addition well endowed with common sense, tact and a pleasant personality. Eager to work full-time in conservation, he readily agreed to undertake the survey on a two-year contract (later extended to three years) and began work in April 1965. He gathered information about the numbers of visitors, their times of visiting, where they went in the reserve, what they liked to see and discover, and their reactions to our nature trail and information centre. He conducted experiments in protecting nesting shore birds and on the effects of trampling on sand-dune vegetation. His report in 1968 formed the basis for much of the subsequent development of visitor facilities and habitat management in the reserve. It also, incidentally, marked the beginning of Barrie's thirty-seven years of dedicated service on the staff of the Trust as Field Officer and from 1988 as the Nature Reserves Manager until his retirement in June 2002.

The little Information Centre served its purpose well for several years, but visitor numbers rose sharply through the 1960s, and – as the visitor survey showed – more adequate facilities were needed. The provision of a new and much larger visitor centre was in fact hastened by another development: local government reorganisation which threatened the future of Lindsey County Council. Anxious to see a further major development in providing for education and public interest the County Council, at Walter Lane's initiative, secured financial support from the Countryside Commission and the Carnegie UK Trust, and work began in 1973 on a new centre adjoining the field station and facing the main car park. Designed by the County Architect, it had roof-to-ground windows on three sides and commanded spacious views over the reserve to the Lincolnshire Wolds on the west, and to the Norfolk coast over the Wash on the east. The main exhibition hall incorporated a small shop, and the other part of the building was equipped as a classroom and lecture room for day visiting parties. Ideally perhaps the building should have been designed to fit the interpretative displays, but the time scale did not allow for that. Had we not seized that opportunity it is unlikely that the Centre would have been built, at least for several more years. As it was, it was not completed before Lindsey County Council went out of existence in March 1974. The ceremonial opening, hosted by the new Lincolnshire County Council and the Trust, was performed by David (later Sir David) Attenborough on 17 October 1974.

The exhibition, designed and executed through the museum and art gallery service for Yorkshire and Humberside by Richard Swanick Limited, was generally regarded as successful, but the heavy furniture was out of keeping with the light and spacious building, and it was replaced in 1983 when the building was extended and altered to accommodate a new exhibition designed by Robin Wade Design Associates. The new display presented the reserve and its habitats through the medium of a panoramic painting in seven sections, each of which was related to text and illustrations produced in a sketch book style. These illustrations by the gifted artist Crispin Fisher were picked out as one of his finest works in the obituary notice of him in *The Times* on his premature death in 1987. The costs of the re-fitting were met by the Trust from voluntary sources assisted by financial aid from Lincolnshire County Council, East Lindsey District Council and the Countryside Commission. This exhibition, with some further improvements in 1995, wore extremely well and was very popular. On re-opening the centre at a ceremony on 18 August 1983, Lord Barber, Chairman of the Countryside Commission, paid tribute to the pioneering work of Gibraltar Point in developing this kind of interpretation facility on a nature reserve.

Promoting Research and Education

Opportunities which the nature reserve offered for many kinds of field studies and research soon aroused the interest of the Geography, Botany and Zoology Departments of the University of Nottingham, an interest which I was able to promote through my position in the Adult Education Department. It was also fortunate that the Trust's solicitor, Sir Francis Hill, was at that time President of the University Council and was thus able to foster co-operation between the Trust and the University at a high level. That co-operation was greatly strengthened by a conference in June 1950 between the Officers of the Trust and the Vice-Chancellor of the University and the Heads of the above-mentioned departments. In the same year I organised a summer school of adult students to study the physiography and vegetation of the nature reserve under the direction of the Professor of Botany, Professor C G C Chesters, whose account of the work was published in the Field Station Report for 1950. Detailed mapping of the dunes and foreshore was also started in that year by Dr Cuchlaine King and Frank Barnes of the Geography Department, thus initiating the association between that Department and Gibraltar Point which continued virtually unbroken for fifty years. Dr (later Professor) King went on to become an international authority on coasts and beaches. Her work at Gibraltar Point assumed new significance after the disastrous flood of 1953. She and Frank Barnes gave evidence to the Waverley Committee which examined the cause of the flood disaster and considered measures to safeguard life and property against a possible recurrence. Her advice was also sought by the Lincolnshire River Board and by local authorities with sea defence responsibilities, another fact which enhanced the value of the field station in the eyes of official bodies. Engineers from such bodies were among those who attended a University extra-mural summer school which I organised at Pilgrim College Boston and Gibraltar Point in the summer of 1953 on Coastal Erosion and Accretion again under the direction of Professor Chesters. Participation as an undergraduate in the University Geography Department's survey work at Gibraltar first brought David Robinson into contact with the Trust. As noted earlier, he went on eventually to play a leading role in the organisation including serving as Honorary Secretary for more than thirty-seven years.

In 1952 Dr May Young of the Zoology Department held the first of many courses for her students. Her preliminary account of the invertebrate fauna of the inter-tidal zone was published in the Gibraltar Point Report for 1952. A number of individual research projects were also carried out in the reserve in the 1950s by university staff and post-graduate students. They included studies of the fungal flora, notably the microfungi of muds and soils by Doctor G J F Pugh whose work was published in several papers in scientific journals. For the study of sea buckthorn Gibraltar Point became the *locus classicus*. Much of the research for the biological flora of the plant, published in the *Journal of Ecology* in 1962, was carried out in the reserve by Dr M C Pearson and his student J A Rogers. The university research and training, which were such an important feature of the programme of the field station throughout the 1950s and 60s, were also greatly facilitated by the acquisition of more adequate accommodation after 1960.

The reserve also attracted amateur naturalists in addition to ornithologists. My wife Mary was responsible for the initial vegetation survey published in the 1949 Report. Local specialists E C Riggall and G W Whatmough contributed records for several years on beetles and spiders respectively, and O M White, a

Nottingham naturalist, worked on Diptera. R E M Pilcher had been recording Lepidoptera at Gibraltar Point since the 1920s and became closely involved with the work of the field station and of the Trust generally. Ectoparasites were collected for identification as part of the bird observatory routine, and we encouraged all ornithologists and others to record butterflies, moths, dragonflies and other orders.

The development of ornithological and other studies and research in the early years exceeded our expectations, and we were encouraged to publish an annual report containing an account of migration and a detailed list of birds recorded together with records of other animals and the survey papers referred to above. The reports published, from 1949 to 1953, show that by the mid 50s Gibraltar Point was already one of the most intensively studied nature reserves in Britain. For those of us involved it was certainly an exciting time of exploration and discovery. After 1953 increasing costs and the Trust's need for funds elsewhere made further publication of an annual report impossible. The bird observatory report was published thereafter as part of the Lincolnshire Bird Report, but it is satisfying that since 1989 the Gibraltar Point staff have been able to resume publication of a separate annual report of the reserve and its natural history.

The lack of on-site accommodation in those early years was a major drawback to the promotion of field studies and research. The little brick bird observatory building could accommodate only two or three people in cramped and rudimentary conditions. The Trust Council's ambitious proposal in 1952/3 to build a field studies centre – for which architectural plans were actually prepared – had foundered for lack of funding and preoccupation with the caravan camp threat in 1952. We made a modest advance about that time, however, by acquiring (for £46) an ancient caravan (originally a Nottingham bus body) from an old sailor, Fred Grunill, who had somehow managed to live there through the war years. 'Fred's Place', as it became known, stood beside what is now the main car-park. It too was exceedingly cramped and water had to be transported from Skegness in milk churns, but the students in particular enjoyed it and it typified the pioneering spirit of the whole enterprise. Even more spartan as a dormitory was the old gun emplacement, now the Wash Viewpoint, acquired in the mid 50s from Phillip Lill after whom it was known for many years as 'Lill's Hut'. It also became jocularly known as 'the spacious brick building' which is how I described it to Dr May Young when she first made an inquiry about student accommodation!

In 1958 the Old Coastguard House, situated on land which the County Council had acquired five years earlier, became available, and the Council immediately assigned it on a 21-year lease to the Trust for use as a field station at a rent of £52 p.a. The house with its observation tower and curtilage wall was built in 1859 when the dune ridge on which it is situated still fronted the sea. After the coastguard station closed in 1923 it had become a holiday residence and a new room was added on the east side. The Army had used it during the war and had heightened the tower for observation purposes. Whilst the accommodation was initially very limited (it was supplemented occasionally by tents on the lawn), it was a great advance on what we had had before and it offered new prospects for expansion of education and training. It also gave a much needed base for the administration of the reserve, and a part of the outbuildings erected by the Army was converted into a flat for a warden-caretaker. The response to our appeal for funds (including £500 from the Nature Conservancy and £250 from the Lindsey

Village Welfare Fund (which had accumulated largely from the sale of rose hips to make syrup during the last war) to convert the building into a field station enabled us to provide a mains water supply, to equip a small laboratory and convert the other part of the outbuildings into a students' dormitory. There was also some dormitory accommodation inside the house in two of the three small rooms situated in the space now occupied by the dining-room. Domestic furniture and furnishings and kitchen equipment were largely donated by members. The whole conversion operation was in fact carried out on a shoe-string, but we had taken a great step forward and there was an immediate increase in use by universities, colleges, schools and amateur naturalists and their organisations.

The promotion of education, as well as research and public enjoyment, was one of the main objectives in our original proposals to the County Council. Field study teaching in schools was in its infancy in the 1950s and there were few teachers with relevant experience. This was gradually remedied by the teaching of the science of ecology which was flourishing in several of our universities in the 1940s and 50s, and by the formation in 1943 of the Field Studies Council and the establishment of its various field centres. The alliance between professional ecologically orientated biologists and amateur naturalists – locally as well as nationally - was in large measure responsible for the development of the nature conservation movement and that in turn stimulated the growth of fieldwork in the life and earth sciences. Environmental education featured prominently in the series of influential 'Countryside in 1970' conferences in 1963, 1965 and 1970. As part of the proceedings a special conference on education was held in March 1965 at the University of Keele at which I read a paper on 'The Role of County Conservation Trusts in Education'. A study group of that conference produced a valuable guide to field biology entitled *Science out of Doors*.

As a result of all this we began to attract pioneering teachers to use the reserve and the field station, and to build up knowledge of techniques especially applicable to the place. Notable among such teachers was Wilfred Bullock, the biology master at Repton school, who brought his 6th formers for a field study course over several years in the 1960s. Another early user of the field station was Don Wright, then Head of Biology, Science and Environmental Studies at Kesteven College of Education. Like several other such pioneer users he went on to play a leading role in the Trust, eventually becoming Chairman in 1999. At about the same time Brian Tear, another biology teacher also destined to occupy senior offices in the Trust, was drawn to the organisation by its educational plans and programmes at Gibraltar Point and elsewhere. Since there were only fifteen places available in the station, school use was largely confined to 6th forms who came from schools in Lincolnshire, the East Midlands and even further afield. School use at lower levels continued as day visits until residential accommodation was further expanded.

I was also able to develop natural history studies for adult students as part of my Resident Tutor duties, and I took immediate advantage of the coastguard house to organise residential courses. The first one, on 'Flowers of the Coast' taken by Dr Max Walters of the Botany Department of Cambridge University, took place within a few months of our acquisition of the house. It was the beginning of a 40-year association between the University of Nottingham's Adult Education Department and Gibraltar Point which brought thousands of students on weekend and longer courses to learn about the geology, geomorphology and natural history of the place. Topics have included sand-dune and saltmarsh formation, pebbles on the beach, life on the seashore, plants of dunes and marshes, birds and their migrations, and many aspects of the invertebrate fauna. The field station was also used by adult students as a base for wider studies of the Lincolnshire Wolds, Marsh and coastline.

The research and educational programme of the field station attracted widespread notice and commendation. A paper on the educational use of nature reserves prepared by an officer of the Nature Conservancy in 1962 described the Gibraltar Point educational project as the most advanced of its kind in the country, the activities being comparable in many respects to those of some of the American Centres. Many overseas visitors came in the 1960s – from the USA, Israel, Australia, Spain and Germany among others – to observe and discuss our education and research work and its relationship to the management of the reserve.

The availability of accommodation and facilities in the coastguard house had been an immediate stimulus to educational use. Already in 1960 the field station was continuously occupied from July to October, whilst in the following year the volume of activity more than doubled, most of the increase being in university extra-mural and school use. The former included a week's summer course in Ecology, five weekend courses, and an important one-day course on Coastal Geomorphology sponsored by the Lincolnshire River Board at which Professor King described her research work on the Lincolnshire coastline. In September that year there was a conference of biology and geography teachers in grammar schools in Lindsey and Lincoln to discuss the use and potential of the field station and nature reserve for field studies. Other successful courses that year were a week's training course for bird observatory workers sponsored by the British Trust for Ornithology, and a summer course for the junior section of the LNU. The number of residential student days was well over 900 and the number of day visitors in organised parties over 700.

1962 was another busy year. There were weekend and one-day courses for teachers; the university extra-mural department held a residential summer course; the LNU a week for the junior section, and the BTO a two-week training course for bird observatory workers. There was a further increase in the number of school parties especially those making day visits. In two weeks in July, for example, parties came from six schools in Lincolnshire, Nottinghamshire and Derbyshire. There were several teachers who made individual contributions to research and field study methods. Notable among them was London geography teacher Ken Maggs who produced detailed maps of the reserve based on previous surveys and aerial photographs. They were widely used for a variety of purposes.

The Adult Education Department's Field Studies Summer Courses were a specially notable part of the programme throughout the 60s and 70s. In the early 60s I collaborated in running such courses with two experienced part-time tutors, Wilfred Bullock whom I have already mentioned, and R H (Bert) Hall, a Nottinghamshire teacher and botanist of national repute. A wide range of survey and study of the flora and fauna of the reserve and its hinterland was covered in those courses including distribution and mapping of the vegetation, population and ecological studies of particular animals, and surveys of habitats within the reserve such as the Mill Pond, and of Marsh drains and disused chalk pits inland. The high quality of much of this student work can be judged from the reports which we produced for wider distribution for several years. The summer course tradition continued strongly when David Robinson joined me as WEA Tutor Organiser in Lindsey in 1965, and after 1975 when he replaced me as the university Resident Tutor in adult education. The enthusiasm and camaraderie of those courses are among my happiest memories of my years in adult education.

The further growth of research and education, however, was restricted by two factors: the inadequacy of accommodation and facilities and, in the case of schools and teachers, organisation and on-site guidance for fieldwork. To overcome the first of those limitations the Joint Advisory Committee for the reserve at a meeting in October 1962 recommended the County Council to provide additional accommodation and laboratory space for up to thirty people, and the Council subsequently approved an expenditure of £12,000 for that purpose. The proposal was enthusiastically supported in the Council – a member who expressed reservations about the cost found himself in a minority of one! Its success owed much to the influence of the Clerk, Walter Lane, who had taken a close interest in the work of the Trust at Gibraltar Point and elsewhere since his appointment in 1957.

Although approved at the end of 1962 the new buildings were not ready for use until the 1965 season by which time the need for them was even more apparent. Designed by the County Architect, they consisted of a dormitory block, a large laboratory and small advanced laboratory for a research worker; a classroom mainly for day parties; an additional common room, enlarged dining-room and kitchen space. Of single storey, they were arranged around the existing buildings of which the coastguard house tower formed a central feature. The walls were slate hung and the whole building was designed to harmonise with its setting of dune and saltmarsh. The Trust undertook to furnish and equip the new buildings, to pay additional rent (making £102 p.a altogether) and to be responsible for internal upkeep and maintenance and the payment of rates.

The availability of expanded facilities now made it even more important to address the other limiting factor: the need for expert teaching assistance and supervision of school use. Up to that time in my capacity as Honorary Secretary of the Trust I had been responsible for all the field station bookings and general administration. I had given whatever advice I could to new groups often meeting them on arrival. From 1960 the presence of the nature reserve warden was a great help, but the volume of school use in particular was rapidly outstripping the Trust's capacity to deal adequately with it.

In an attempt to alleviate the supervision problem my university department had offered in 1964 to allow me to discharge the task as part of my duties as Resident Tutor in Lindsey. This acknowledgement by the university of the importance of the field station was warmly welcomed by the Trust and the County Council and it was agreed that I should be designated Director of the field station. This move was in effect a formal recognition of an existing situation and, welcome though it was, it was not accompanied by any corresponding reduction in my normal university duties nor did it contribute significantly to a solution of the problem of school use. That had to be found elsewhere.

The appointment by Local Education Authorities of specialist tutors and advisers in biological and geographical field studies had been strongly recommended by the Keele Conference on Education to which I have already referred. With the full support of the Joint Advisory Committee we therefore suggested to the County Council in 1965 that such an appointment would provide a solution to one of our main problems at Gibraltar Point and would also be of immense assistance to schools throughout the County in developing field studies. The tutor would have a base at the field station where he/she would help to plan residential and day visits for schools, give specialised teaching, provide classroom material and arrange training courses for teachers. He/she would fulfil some of those functions at other nature reserves in the county where educational use would be acceptable; would help the Trust in surveying and developing potential new outdoor study areas, and encourage schools to develop their own nature reserves. In addition to close liaison and co-operation with the Trust he would make contact with the Forestry Commission and with other landowners and users. Our suggestions were well received by the recently appointed Director of Education, George Cooke. His recommendation to the Education Committee to make the appointment was also readily agreed.

The County Council's intention to involve the Trust in the process was demonstrated by the invitation to me (I was at that time also a member of the Lindsey Education Committee representing university education) to sit on the appointing panel, and to Dick Cornwallis, the Trust's Chairman, to attend as an observer. Out of a strong field of candidates we appointed Derek Golicher, a biology teacher with special interest in field studies. He started in 1967 and his presence, together with the availability of the new field station facilities, soon generated a further expansion of field station use not only by schools from Lincolnshire, Derbyshire (to whom Lindsey extended the field study tutor's services) and elsewhere, but also use by universities including Nottingham, Leicester, Manchester and Imperial London, and by colleges of education including Kesteven, Nottinghamshire and Doncaster. An educational nature trail for schools accompanied by a workbook was introduced. It placed great emphasis on encouraging children to discover for themselves, and it proved so popular that many schools outside Lindsey asked to use it. The field studies tutor was also able to regulate the frequency and timing of visits, to assist in their planning and ensure that conservation requirements in the reserve were respected. Whilst his work soon extended throughout the county his input at Gibraltar Point remained for many years a crucial factor in the success of the field station. He brought to it professional organisation and discipline and real dedication. He established excellent relations with the Trust (which he continued to serve voluntarily after retirement) and we always looked on him as a colleague.

The appointment was, I believe, the first of its kind made by a Local Education Authority in this country. So in this, as in many other fields of conservation and education, Lindsey was an enlightened pioneer giving a lead to others. So successful was the field studies tutor in promoting use of the field station – there were more than 5000 residential student days in 1969 – that the County Council decided to further expand the accommodation block and to build a house for a warden in parallel with the construction of the new visitor centre which I have already described. Golicher's success also persuaded the County Council to broaden the scope and status of the post and re-designate it as Adviser for Countryside Studies, and to appoint an assistant. The Trust was again fully consulted about the changes.

All these developments generated renewed interest in the Gibraltar Point project. In June 1972 the Under-Secretary of State at the Department of

Education and Science, Mr W Van Straubenzee, spent some $2^{1}/_{2}$ hours at the reserve and field station to see the educational results of collaboration between the Trust, Lindsey County Council as the Local Education Authority, and the University of Nottingham's Department of Adult Education together with the East Midland district of the WEA. Representatives of all four bodies were present. The Minister was clearly impressed with all that had been achieved at Gibraltar Point, a view which he subsequently expressed in a letter to the Chairman of the Trust following his visit. In the following month of that year members of the Nature Conservancy's Committee for England – of which I was the current Chairman - with the Director and other senior staff visited the reserve and field station as part of a two-day tour of Lincolnshire. They took particular interest in the measures being taken by the Trust to ensure that increasing access and use remained compatible with conservation requirements.

Another distinguished visitor to the reserve at that time was the young Prince of Wales who came on a private and informal visit in July 1971 whilst he was on a course at the RAF College at Cranwell. It was evident from the keen interest he showed in our management problems and methods that wildlife and environment were to become one of his principal concerns.

In the earliest few years of operating the field station we expected residential groups to be self-catering, but by the mid-1960s we were providing catering by employing cooks for the main summer season. There were at that time a number of young women willing to spend several months cooking at bird observatories and field centres. They enjoyed the company and the opportunity in leisure moments to watch birds and pursue other natural history interests. However, the expansion of the facilities, including kitchen and dining room, and the development of more intensive use of the field station after 1970 necessitated a catering appointment of a more permanent nature.

Meantime the provision of a house on the site enabled the Trust to appoint a warden specifically for the administration and management of the field station, and George Evans took up this new post in April 1972. An ornithologist of national repute and an all-round naturalist he came to the Trust after six years as resident warden of Bardsey Bird and Field Observatory.

We had come a long way from the little bird observatory building in 1948, from 'Fred's place' and 'the spacious brick building'. We could say with pride and justification in the March newsletter of 1974 that we had "one of the finest multi-purpose field centres in the British Isles". The enlightened policies of Lindsey County Council and the remarkable partnership between the Council and the Trust had no parallel at that time in the field of nature conservation and education. It has rarely if ever been surpassed since then. A seasoned commentator in the *Grimsby Evening Telegraph* of 23 October 1974 expressed it thus:

> *Gibraltar Point indeed was a splendid pioneering effort in the way of nature reserves; the County has indeed shown the way in conservation matters again and again; and the new centre is indeed a fine new facility. But may I perhaps be permitted to remind everyone that next to the naturalists themselves, it was the old, and now defunct, Lindsey County Council which deserved most of the credit for the enlightened policies which made Gibraltar Point, and many similar efforts, possible. The beginning of it all was some forty years ago, when Lindsey's private Sandhills Act gave it a control of the foreshore that*

no other county had. It was just in time to fight off the spoliation which everywhere seemed inevitable. Let the present Lincolnshire Council preen itself it if wishes, so long as it follows the same policies. But let us not forget the succession of councillors and officers at Lindsey, who over the years followed such enlightened courses of action in these matters.

By the time David (later Sir David) Attenborough opened the new visitor centre and expanded field station on 17 October 1974 Lindsey had indeed been replaced by a new Lincolnshire County Council, although unfortunately this no longer covered the whole of the historic county. The opening ceremony was attended by the Lord Lieutenant of Lincolnshire and Patron of the Trust the Earl of Ancaster; Sir John Cripps the Chairman of the Countryside Commission which had contributed substantially to the costs of the visitor centre; the Chairman of Lincolnshire County Council Mr Hedley Lewis; member and officer representatives from District Councils and from the Trust whose new President Walter Lane, former Clerk of Lindsey County Council, thanked David and all those individuals and organisations who had contributed to the success of the project.

The opening of the new centre and field station marked the beginning of a new chapter in the development of the nature reserve and its facilities for education and public enjoyment of its wildlife. It was a happy coincidence that the Trust was also celebrating its 25th Anniversary in that year. For me it was another satisfying landmark. The appointment of a field station warden, my own move from Honorary Secretary to Chairman of the Trust and my retirement from my University post in 1974 had changed the nature of my involvement at Gibraltar Point, although it had in no way diminished my dedication to it.

Informal visit by the Prince of Wales in July 1971, with David Robinson (left), myself and Walter Lane (right).

*Peter Scott opening the Information Centre in
1963 jokes about his socks, with Trust Chairman
Dick Cornwallis (left) and Chairman of Lindsey
County Council and later Trust President
Sir Weston Cracroft Amcotts (centre).*

*Sand Dunes
display*

*First Warden Arthur Lodge at the
Information Centre.*

*Countryside Award
1970*

'Fred's Place' with Nottingham University zoology students in 1952. The cans were for drinking water which had to be brought from Skegness

The old coastguard station became the Field Station in 1959. Extra tent accommodation was provided in the first few years.

BARRIE WILKINSON

Residential (left) and teaching (right) developments in 1960s and 1970s.

MARTIN CURRY

Derek Golicher teaches about saltmarsh plants.

Betty Watkinson (centre front) with her young naturalists course 1960.

TED SMITH

First Nottingham University Adult Education Department weekend course, on Flowers of the Coast with tutor Dr Max Walters (seated centre left), 1959.

Pond-dipping on a University Summer School 1962.

BARRIE WILKINSON

Dr May Young and Nottingham University zoology students investigating fauna of the muddy inter-tidal zone, 1966.

Dr Cuchlaine King and Nottingham University geography students surveying the Spit, 1968.

Identifying finds on an adult education Pebbles on the Beach course with tutor Philip Doughty (right).

Mr W Van Straubenzee Minister at the Department of Education and Science (with hands behind his back) at the shore end of the sleeper track, June 1972.

LINCOLNSHIRE TRUST
for Nature Conservation

GIBRALTAR POINT
VISITOR CENTRE

opened by

DAVID ATTENBOROUGH CBE

17th October 1974

Lincolnshire County Council

David Attenborough (right) opened the Visitor Centre in October 1974 during the Trust's Silver Jubilee. Left of the plaque is Lord Ancaster, Patron of the Trust.

Part of the original display in the Visitor Centre.

TED SMITH

Scotton Common, 1960.

GEOFF TRINDER

*National Conservation Corps clearing
scrub, 1961 - but it was a losing battle.*

TED SMITH

*Marsh
gentian.*

*Bog
asphodel.*

Scrub had encroached on all except a narrow area of the open heath by 1985.

GEOFF TRINDER

– 5 –

Nature Reserves: A Salvage Operation

These fragments I have shored against my ruins Eliot

IN CREATING the Trust we had been motivated primarily by the need to protect special places in Lincolnshire against damaging development which in the 1940s was perceived largely in terms of urban and industrial growth, of conifer afforestation, and of recreational demand on the coast. The destruction of Freshney Bog near Grimsby – one of the four Lincolnshire sites on SPNR's (Rothschild's) 1916 list of sites of national importance – by municipal refuse tipping, and the 1930s threats to the Saltfleetby dunes and to Gibraltar Point, another Rothschild site, were ominous portents of things to come. The heaths of Scotton and Laughton Commons – also a Rothschild site – and other heathlands in the county had been largely blanketed with conifers by 1940. The Second World War had also seen large-scale felling of ancient broad-leaved woods and their conversion to conifers, a process which reached its most intensive phase about the time of the Trust's formation. The Trust in fact was too late on the scene to have any hope of saving woods of outstanding natural history interest like Newball in the Central Vale lime woods, and Greenfield and Mother Woods in the Middle Marsh.

There were thus compelling reasons to launch the Trust in 1948, but even so we failed to foresee what was to prove the greatest threat of all to Lincolnshire's wildlife and wild places: a new agricultural revolution. We were not alone in that failure. The recommendations of the Scott Report on land use in 1942 were based on the assumption that agriculture, whilst sustaining its greater wartime efficiency, would continue in much the same pattern as before, and that land reclamation and ploughing up of old grasslands would cease once the war was over. Even that far-sighted document, the report of the Wildlife Conservation Special Committee (Cmd.7122) in 1947 showed little recognition of what was to happen to the lowland countryside of Britain in the next three decades. Its Vice-Chairman, Sir Arthur Tansley, the leading ecologist of his day, wrote in 1945: "It is scarcely probable that the extension of agriculture will go much further, for the limits of profitable agricultural land must have been reached in most places".

There was so much to do in those first two years of the Trust that it was perhaps as well that we were not immediately aware of the mountainous tasks that lay ahead in that direction.

Selecting the Sites

We were well aware that successful conservation depended on adequate knowledge and information – in the first place about sites of wildlife importance. The new Nature Conservancy, created at about the same time as the Trust, had been charged with the formidable task of preparing Schedules of Sites of Special Scientific Interest (SSSIs) for notification to local planning authorities as required by Section 23 of the National Parks and Access to the Countryside Act 1949. Having no regional organisation at the outset, the Conservancy sought the help of the Trust in identifying SSSIs in Lincolnshire. This was information we also needed, and Dick Cornwallis and I set about the task of surveying sites using the list prepared by the NRIC Sub-Committee in 1944 and information which had become available since that time.

Our report, a substantial document, was completed within a year and submitted to the Nature Conservancy early in 1951. The 24 sites we selected included examples of all the main Lincolnshire habitats which contained many of the County's rarer plants and animals. There was a supplementary list of sites which it was recommended should be kept under review and safeguarded by the Trust "as far as may be practicable". Each site was briefly described, its notable species mentioned, and its main conservation values identified. The report, however, was more than just a description and evaluation. Ownership of the land, its condition and possible threats to it were all described, and recommendations were made to secure its conservation by the involvement of landowners, local authorities, the Nature Conservancy and the Trust. The introduction to the report concluded: "Any scheme of conservation must in the long run depend for its success on an enlightened public opinion which the Lincolnshire Naturalists' Trust is trying to foster". That was a statement which we would take for granted today, but in 1951 it was a novel concept.

The survey, in which Mary was also actively involved, was an enjoyable task. It helped to cement my friendship and working relationship with Dick – the idea of our book on Lincolnshire's birds was conceived during those excursions. We learned a great deal about the County's natural history and its conservation needs and problems. We became acutely conscious of what had already gone and the consequences of further losses.

Until the middle of the 18th century Lincolnshire had been a half wild county, its fens undrained or only partially re-claimed; its chalk and limestone hills still clothed in great tracts of open downland; its glacial sand and gravel areas – in the north-west and on the Fen edge especially – covered in heather and other heathland vegetation; its coasts remote and unfrequented. The impact of the first agricultural revolution on these landscapes was dramatic. By 1830 the natural fenland had disappeared without trace, and, apart from a few fragments, so had the downlands. The heathlands survived into the present century, but most of them were smothered under conifer plantations in the 1920s and 1930s. Elsewhere many of the ancient deciduous woodlands – already severely eroded in the mid-19th century years of Victorian high farming – were converted to conifers in the years after the Second World War. With the coming of the railways and even more so of the motor car, the coast was invaded by the holidaymaker and much of the sand-dune stretch was developed for recreational purposes.

This was the situation which emerged from our survey in 1950. As we wrote in the introduction: "Lincolnshire is so intensively cultivated that few wild places remain, although these include interesting and important habitats". And we issued a warning: "The few places which remain in a natural or semi-natural state, therefore, are of vital importance and those selected for this list represent the minimum necessary to ensure adequate conservation of the County's flora and fauna. The loss of almost any one of them would be irreparable". That warning was amply justified by the events of the following twenty years.

Several of the sites we surveyed – and we visited all but four of those on the list - were subsequently destroyed despite SSSI designation. Two of them were of outstanding and irreplaceable value: Waddingham Common and much of the Manton – Twigmoor – Messingham area of wet heath and open sand-dunes. Of these I shall write more later. Although we included Freshney Bog it was already virtually destroyed (the present nature reserve is not on the original site). Freiston Shore which was selected as an example of Wash saltmarsh was reclaimed in the 1970s. Much of Skellingthorpe Wood had already been converted to conifers by 1950, but the surviving deciduous core was still the main stronghold of the chequered skipper butterfly and the last site in the County for the marsh fritillary. By the 1960s, however, its interest too had largely gone. The fragment of Stapleford Moor which we listed was hemmed in by conifers and within twenty years had become unrecognisable. Ironically, we deliberately omitted from our list the Robert's Field site at Holywell on the Kesteven limestone, believing that the Nature Conservancy's proposal to schedule it and surrounding areas as a National Nature Reserve would afford it adequate protection. We were to be sadly disillusioned.

We may have had fears for the future of some of these doomed sites, but when we saw them in that spring and summer of 1950 the wealth of their wildlife was a delight and is still keen in the memory. Linwood Warren, for example, one of the heathland remnants, still had two species of sundew, marsh gentian and pearl-bordered fritillary, and nightjars nested there and at Scotton Common where butterwort and black bog-rush could still be found. Most of these species are now extinct or exceedingly rare in the county. There were nesting curlew and redshank and snipe on Manton Common where hundreds of marsh gentians displayed their elegant blue trumpets in August; there were woodlarks on the hillside of the oolite ridge there, and wheatears on the sand-dunes of Manton Warren at the top, the finest inland dune system in eastern England after the war-time destruction of the Lakenheath dunes in Norfolk. The grass-of-Parnassus at Waddingham Common, the last in Lincolnshire, delighted us with the intricate beauty of its flowers – I remembered it from my schooldays visit to Derbyshire. Chequered skippers, another species destined for extinction, still flew like tiny fragments of sunlight and shadow along the ride at Skellingthorpe Wood, although we never saw the marsh fritillary there. It had gone two or three years before as the glade with devil's-bit scabious, its larval food plant, became overgrown. Most of these and other species we had expected to find; they had been known to several generations of naturalists. But there were new discoveries. I remember in particular the excitement of finding the first little ringed plover's nest to be recorded in the County at the Tattershall-Woodhall gravel pits, a site now quite overgrown.

More than a third of the sites on our list or large parts of them were to be destroyed or changed beyond recognition in the years that lay ahead. Even some of those which survived were to suffer from neglect and from damaging external effects, in particular the lowering of water tables from more intensive land drainage and abstraction and the growth of adjoining forestry plantations. I suspect that their wildlife – butterflies, for example – may also have suffered more than is recognised from pesticides and pollution.

Our survey was based on information available at that time. Since then new sites have been discovered, and changes in land use, particularly in agriculture, have created a new scarcity value in habitats like herb-rich meadows which in 1950 were still relatively abundant, so much so that none appeared in the first SSSI schedules.

Those first SSSI schedules for Lincolnshire (then in three administrative counties and two county boroughs) published by the Nature Conservancy towards the end of 1951 included 25 of the 31 sites recommended in our own report. The Trust's contribution to the schedules was generously acknowledged. The Lindsey Planning Committee was quick to accept the SSSI designations and announced its intention to consult the Trust as well as the Nature Conservancy on any development proposals likely to affect them. The Kesteven Committee followed suit soon afterwards. The list of SSSIs also served as the Trust's initial policy on nature reserve acquisition priorities to which we then turned our attention.

The First Acquisitions 1950 - 1960

Whilst much of our energy and resources in those early years had to be devoted to the defence and development of the Gibraltar Point reserve, we began straightway to investigate the possibilities of safeguarding those other sites on our 1951 list which seemed to be most immediately under threat. One of these was a forty acre remnant of **Scotton and Laughton Commons** which had been, until 1920, the largest and richest areas of Coversand heathland and bog in Lincolnshire. Their wildlife was legendary: breeding hen harriers until the mid 19th century; stone curlews and blackcock into the 20th; silver-studded blue butterflies until the 1940s; all three species of sundew, and grass-of-Parnassus, to mention but a few of their former treasures. This splendid wilderness became an early target for afforestation by the Forestry Commission in search of cheap, low-grade agricultural land. Its conservation interest, recognised in the SPNR's 1916 list was ignored, and large-scale planting began in early the 1920s. By 1950 little of the open heathland remained. What had not been covered with conifers had been ploughed and cultivated during the war; whilst along many of the roads there had been ribbon development rash of bungalows and small chicken farms.

Over forty acres of SSSI on the eastern margin of the Commons had miraculously escaped. A tract of low-lying wet heath it was dominated by ling and cross-leaved heath and purple moorgrass. Thousands of spikes of the star-like yellow flowers of bog asphodel studded the heath in June, soon followed by the slender, azure trumpets of the marsh gentian. Glistening rosettes of sundew hid beneath overhanging heather, and there were patches of heath spotted orchid and meadow thistle. Nesting curlews still trilled in courtship flight over the heath, and nightjars churred from the birches in the woodland fringe. The silver-studded blue butterfly had already gone, but the grayling was still there deceiving the observer with its cryptic colouring.

By 1953 the future of this small remnant was also in the balance, and, had we not acted to acquire it then, it would almost certainly have become just another block of featureless plantation or a string of scruffy chicken farms. The owner of three-quarters of the site had some sympathy with our cause and agreed to sell, though not below its then market value of £400. Compared with today's land values that seems a ludicrously small price for thirty acres (in 1997 we paid £30,000 for twenty acres of adjoining land!), but the Trust's total income for 1953 was only £203 and there was less than that available in the Nature Reserves Fund. Without a generous grant from the SPNR – to which I refer in a later chapter – we could not have undertaken the purchase. We were then confronted with another problem: how to manage forty acres (we acquired the other ten acres in the next year or so) of wet heathland being invaded by birch, oak and pine. We had no relevant first-hand experience within the Trust, so we invited a young Cambridge botanist, Dr Max Walters, to come and advise us. His report formed the basis of a management plan which served us well for many years. Max Walters' visit to Scotton Common – like Ronald Hickling's to Gibraltar Point – had wider consequences for the County Trusts' movement as I shall describe in a later chapter.

As at Gibraltar Point, the new reserve soon attracted the kind of local interest and support which was to become an encouraging feature of all new reserve acquisitions. A vegetation survey was completed within a year and an enthusiastic voluntary reserve manager, Frank Norris, and several assistants were quickly forthcoming. Leading county entomologist Joe Duddington was closely associated with the reserve from the outset and was responsible for much of the invertebrate recording over the following forty years. The management of land for conservation evidently provided an exciting challenge and a new focus of interest for naturalists and others. Scotton Common, like all the other heathland and peatland sites, proved indeed to be a daunting and perennial challenge, sometimes a heartbreaking as well as a backbreaking one. The general lowering of the water table, the growth of the adjoining conifer plantation planted in the mid-1940s by the Forestry Commission; the intensification of arable cultivation in the area, all contributed to a drying-out process on the reserve which in turn encouraged the speedier colonisation by birch and pine which we sought to control with hand tools. We had long recognised that grazing provides the only long-term solution to that problem, but it was not until the 1990s that we were able to find the resources to carry out a massive clearance of scrub and woodland, to fence the reserve and introduce Hebridean sheep.

As the first property we actually bought there was for me something special about Scotton Common. It was not, however, the first of our freehold reserves. In 1950 the **Decoy Wood at Friskney**, the most famous of the old East Fen decoys, had been given to the Trust. It was - and still is – a fascinating place, this isolated little wood in the now arable Fens. The decoy pool and pipes were still discernible and we cleared and excavated parts of them with the intention of restoring the decoy for ringing wildfowl, an aspiration which was never realised and was perhaps never a practical proposition. These decoys were an important element in the economy of the old Fenland and there is still a sense of the past about the place where the Skeltons, perhaps the most famous family of Fenland decoymen, plied their trade. Until the drainage of the East Fen in the early 19th century its five decoys were sending 30,000 ducks a year to the London markets, and our reserve – known locally as the New Decoy – had been the most productive of them. Part of the wood had been planted with exotics when the decoy finally went out of use in the 1880s, but much of it carries pine, birch, rowan and ancient coppiced alders, the kind of semi-natural woodland which may well have been characteristic of the Fenland margins before drainage. The bird population was rich and varied and there were large badger setts in the old spoil heaps around the pond. Here too we soon attracted local interest and help, and a working group was quickly formed to manage the reserve. In some respects the Decoy Wood has deteriorated over the years. More intensive land drainage has accelerated shrinkage of the peat and many of the older trees have collapsed in severe gales and heavy snowfalls.

Curiously, it was the management of the Decoy Wood that provoked the first controversy in the Trust. The threat to the trees was already apparent in 1955 and, having taken specialist advice, the Council adopted a plan to part fell and replant the wood in two stages. This resulted in a members' resolution at the next Annual Meeting that the wood be left in 'an undisturbed natural state'. Whilst this may have been somewhat unrealistic, it was a healthy sign of member interest and concern, and the plan was in fact substantially modified in consequence. As more reserves were acquired this, the first of our freehold properties, faded into comparative obscurity.

Our success in acquiring Scotton Common encouraged us to widen the search for more reserves, especially in the threatened heathlands. This led us to **Linwood Warren**, one of the most popular sites with naturalists in the County since the late 19th century. Like Scotton Common, Linwood Warren on the southern fringes of the Coversands of north-west Lincolnshire, was a remnant of once extensive heathlands. Afforestation had largely destroyed the heath to the north and north-east of the Warren. On the higher boulder clay on its southern flank the fine coppice-with-standard Legsby Wood was in process of being clear-felled by the Forestry Commission when we opened negotiations for the purchase of the Warren. The wood was re-planted with a mixture of conifers and broad-leaves, but most of the latter were deliberately killed off by aerial spraying in the 1960s, a Commission practice which aroused a national outcry and was eventually abandoned.

The danger that the Warren might also fall to afforestation or recreational development lent urgency to our efforts to safeguard it. Since it lay less than three miles from Dick Cornwallis' farm at Bleasby Grange, he had a particular concern for it, and he and Thomas Court, the Trust's first President who also lived nearby in Market Rasen, were largely responsible for negotiating its acquisition. It belonged to a consortium who had acquired it with a view to expanding the golf course on the opposite side of Legsby Road. A few years after they sold it to us they asked if they could buy it back. Golf no doubt had proved more popular than envisaged in 1956! The price for the thirty-seven acres was £1,000 and once again the SPNR came to our assistance with a grant of half the cost. To raise some of the balance we launched our first appeal through a modest little brochure.

While the causes were similar, the problem of the falling water table was even greater than that at Scotton. The felling of Legsby Wood deprived the Warren of shelter; a more intensive drainage system and the rapid growth of conifers soon dried up much of the run-off water from the woodland area. In an attempt to mitigate the problem we constructed an elaborate system of irrigation channels to take whatever water became available from the upper boundary ditch to the low-lying parts of the reserve. A large pond was created behind the main dam. This work was done in the summer of 1961 by the recently formed Conservation

Corps of the Council for Nature under its indefatigable organiser, Brigadier E F E Armstrong. The 'Brig', as he was affectionately known, had got the Corps away to a good start. This was one of his early tasks and he brought to it his rare ability to organise with military precision, and to motivate young people to work on conservation management projects. For a few years the irrigation system worked well, but the drying out process went on inexorably and the water supply became increasingly spasmodic. As at Scotton, the falling water table encouraged the invasion of pine and birch and the area of open heath shrank. As a result perhaps, nightjars which had been a feature of the reserve, ceased to nest, and marsh gentian and sundews disappeared, the former in the mid-1960s, the latter in the drought summer of 1976.

Linwood had other management problems. The main tract of heather on the higher heath had been ploughed up to grow potatoes during the Second World War and had reverted to a dense, tussocky cover of wavy hair-grass, very attractive to look at but totally dominating and excluding heather regeneration. In 1984 we fenced part of the heath along with the West End meadow, and grazed it with sheep. Within two or three years the tussocks were dead and heather had begun to re-establish. Twenty years earlier the West End meadow had been the scene of one of the Trust's earliest grazing and mowing experiments conducted through a contract from the Nature Conservancy. Since then resources available through English Nature's Reserves Enhancement Scheme and other sources have enabled scrub clearance and fencing to be carried out in the remainder of the reserve which is now also grazed by the Trust's Hebridean sheep.

As at Scotton, much has been lost at Linwood over the years – the sundews and gentians, the nightjars and the red squirrels - but it remains a place of quiet beauty with its open heath set in a frame of old pines and birch-oak woodland. And, like Scotton, it is still, in spite of losses, one of the richest Trust reserves in its plant and animal variety. It remains a place near to my heart and I am sure that Dick, whose memorial stone stands near the entrance, would still approve its dedication to him.

Enquiries about sites on our 1951 list yielded more results in 1956. In the far north-west, in the Isle of Axholme, that precious piece of Lincolnshire beyond the Trent, a few fen and bog relicts of the great Humberhead marshes had survived. **Epworth and Haxey Turbaries** had been allocated in the Enclosure Awards for parishioners to dig turves for fuel. Peat digging had ceased by the middle of the 19th century, and woodland had colonised most of the open fen and raised-bog habitats of the Turbaries. They remained nevertheless places of great ecological and historical interest, different from almost anything else in Lincolnshire. Only there did the once abundant fen sedge, *Cladium mariscus*, survive – it had been widely used in the Fens for ridge thatching and other purposes. Bog rosemary and the large heath butterfly reached the southern limits of their range in eastern England at Epworth, and there were fine specimens of the royal fern at Haxey.

Whilst once having had common rights the Turbaries had remained the freehold property of the Lords of the Manors of Epworth and Haxey, and by the 1950s the lordships were in the hands of the Public Trustee. He was anxious to be rid of these properties which were to him only a liability. Sir Francis Hill, the Trust's solicitor, negotiated the acquisition of the two Turbaries (about 115 acres altogether) for the sum of £85 having told the Public Trustee that for a bog he regarded the deal as expensive! Technically, the purchase was of the Lordships of the Manors with which went the ownership of the properties. Epworth Turbary was a well defined 82 acres. Haxey, however, had been divided up and one or more cottages built on part of it, perhaps as a result of the establishment of squatters' rights in the past. The Trust's 1958 acquisition comprised the main block and a smaller detached area known as Haxey Carr, a total of some 36 acres. The two Parish Councils concerned raised no objection to the transfer of the properties to the Trust, although some forty years later the Haxey Council disputed the Trust's title.

They were exciting acquisitions but, like Scotton and Linwood, they presented formidable problems of management. For one thing, they had come to be regarded as a kind of no-man's land, places for casual refuse tipping and poaching. Birch and oak invasion was far advanced and the lowering of the water table in the area further encouraged it. Little more than a tenth of Epworth remained as open fen and bog, and the position at Haxey was even worse. There was another problem: we had virtually no members in the Isle at that time. When I first went there in the early 1950s it seemed remote and isolated. In the villages older houses built in warm Trent brick contrasted with large nonconformist chapels - this is Wesley country - and with the somewhat stark Board Schools of the 1880s. There was also a marked contrast in houses between the richer peat areas and the poor sand lands where some people were evidently still living near the bone. At that time there had been little influx of population from south Yorkshire which has since changed much of the character of the Isle. People seemed fiercely independent and suspicious of outsiders. Although we made it plain straightway that we did not wish to restrict public access to the Turbaries and that we would seek good relations with neighbours, it took a good many years, especially at Haxey, before we won a measure of understanding and respect for the reserves.

We were assisted initially by the unexpected appearance on the scene of a couple of benefactors in the shape of two elderly doctors in practice in Haxey, Dr Dyson and Dr Margaret Green. They were very much part of the local scene and they both had their share of Isle of Axholme eccentricity. But they were both very public spirited and had bought several small woods to protect them from being felled in an area where woodland was scarce. In 1957 they offered Bird's Wood and Whin Covert and in 1961 Langholme Wood as gifts to the Trust subject to their retaining a life interest including shooting rights – they were both keen shots. Bird's Wood was a birch-oak wood regenerated on sandy heath on which heather-covered fragments survived. Whin Covert was a rather dull birch wood on peat which we transferred to the Nottinghamshire Trust in whose county it lies when that body came into being. Langholme Wood – its original eighteen acres extended to twenty-eight by a later acquisition – was the most interesting of the three. A pleasant birch-oak wood it had developed on sandy heathland and abandoned farmland. Open patches of heath survived and have since been expanded. So within four years we acquired in the Isle almost twice as much freehold property as we held in total elsewhere. We also acquired more management problems and, in spite of valiant efforts by two or three Scunthorpe members - notably Joe Duddington and Frank Brazier, another great stalwart – it was not until we attracted more support in the Isle itself that we were able to do anything substantially effective about them; or for that matter to give attention to the even more remote and extensive bog relict of Crowle Moors in the far north-west of the Isle.

*Decoyman
George Skelton.*

Friskney Decoy Wood isolated in the East Fen.

*Linwood Warren was one of the last strongholds
of the red squirrel in Lincolnshire.*

*The effect of
grazing (left)
on the wavy
hair-grass.*

Rimac Building Estate and the first wooden huts and tents in the dunes, 1930.

Natterjack toad.

Marsh helleborine.

Where the 'Garden City' would have been at Rimac.

– 6 –

Saltfleetby - Theddlethorpe Dunes

L INCOLNSHIRE'S coastline is an outstanding international wildlife asset, and after our success in helping to safeguard Gibraltar Point we turned to the problems of protecting the other largely undeveloped stretch of sand-dune coast to the north of Mablethorpe. A single line of high dunes extends from Mablethorpe North End to Sea Lane at Theddlethorpe, but northwards from there a new ridge has developed seawards enclosing an extensive freshwater slack. The old high dunes were probably formed before the 14th century when the little river with the big name, the Great Eau, was diverted from its natural estuary in the vicinity of the present Rimac access (the name is derived from a Prussian ship wrecked on this coast in the 19th century) and canalised into Saltfleet Haven in an unsuccessful attempt to keep the port from silting up. These dunes are thus much older than those at Gibraltar Point and have a richer flora, whilst the freshwater slack is a rare feature on the Lincolnshire coast and an uncommon one anywhere in the east of England.

Like Gibraltar Point, this coast had been threatened with sporadic caravan and bungalow development in the 1920s and 30s. At Rimac more than a hundred plots had been sold for building and a network of rough roads laid out. There is a poignant reminder of this in the diaries of the Louth botanist, Miss C D Marsden, who visited the site in 1928.

> *June 7. It is grievous to think that Rimac has been sold to a syndicate formed with a view to erecting a Garden City, where now is a sanctuary for birds and flowers.*
> *July 17. I paid my last visit to Rimac before the building of the Garden City begins. Already teas and refreshments can be had at Rimac House. The caretaker walks about with a hideous plan of the estate, all divided up into little bits – several have been sold and apparently the wildfowls' home on the marsh is to be made into a lake and a row of bungalows, in front of it facing the sea. Will any of our treasured plants survive?*

Lindsey County Council had included the sandhills from Mablethorpe to Saltfleet in its 1932 Sandhills Bill with the intention of controlling that kind of development, but then a quite unexpected event put an end to it in the form of acquisition of the area by the Air Ministry for use as a bombing and firing range. As a result, apart from the building of targets and access roads, it remained largely untouched until after the War. Lenten Ottaway and I visited Rimac several times in the late 1940s and early 50s, and in 1955 after a wet winter when the marsh was flooded Lenten discovered or rather re-discovered the natterjack toad. This fascinating creature – first described as a British animal by Sir Joseph Banks from the Fen edge sand and gravel country near his home at Revesby Abbey in Lincolnshire - had been recorded from Saltfleetby in 1886 and again in 1910 when it was also present at Gibraltar Point. It had apparently not been recorded again until we saw it at Rimac in 1955.

There was much else of interest and beauty. There were pyramidal and bee orchids among the colourful flowers of the dune grassland, and the rare sand-dune form of the lesser meadow rue with its dainty leaves; kingcups brightened the marsh in spring, and yellow flags and lesser spearwort extended the yellow theme into summer. The rabbit cropped edges of the marsh and the shallow pools had rare and locally scarce plants like marsh pea, greater water-parsnip, marsh helleborine, lesser water-plantain, lesser skullcap, felwort, marsh arrowgrass and bog pimpernel. Marsh orchids were a special feature though in nothing like the abundance in which they occurred later in the 1970s and 80s. The pools were full of aquatic creatures. The water spiders carrying their silvery air bubbles to replenish their underwater shelters were a particular fascination. Out on the shore carpets of thrift and sea lavender brought colour to the saltmarsh from spring to high summer.

By 1950 RAF activity was concentrated on the bombing ranges out on the extensive sand and mudflats, and the dunes and marsh were not merely neglected but had become a kind of no-man's land abused by casual refuse tipping – some of it by the RAF themselves - by unauthorised shooting, motorcycle scrambling and commercial moss collecting. In an attempt to rescue the area from these practices I contacted the Ministry's Land Agent, and in 1956 we obtained a licence which enabled us to manage 170 acres of dunes and freshwater marsh. By 1960 the area had been extended to north and south to cover 320 acres. As elsewhere, local support from Louth and district members and from a number of local people was immediately forthcoming. Voluntary wardens - led by Lenten who by that time was living in Louth - were appointed and within a year or so the dunes had been cleared of refuse, vehicular access was controlled and measures to stabilise eroded dunes were initiated. A substantial hut was erected to serve as a wardens' base and tool store. Survey and recording was started and included a valuable geographical survey undertaken by David Robinson then a schoolmaster in Grimsby and later to become the Trust's long-serving Honorary Secretary.

The Trust's action in establishing the reserve not only saved the area from further degradation; without it, as events were soon to prove, it is highly unlikely that the present National Nature Reserve would have come into existence.

The Saltfleetby-Theddlethorpe coast was one of the sites recommended for protection in the 1945 report of the Lincolnshire NRIC sub-committee and also in the report which the Trust prepared for the Nature Conservancy in 1951. As a result it was included in the first schedule of SSSIs notified by the Nature

Conservancy in 1951 to the planning authority Lincolnshire County Council. That designation was confirmed and the scheduled area extended in 1960.

The County Development Plan in 1953 had recognised the need to encourage the holiday industry on the coast by allocating land for large-scale holiday camping in the most suitable areas (by 1961 such allocation for more than 13 750 caravans and 1 700 chalets had been approved), whilst using development control to restrain holiday camping in other areas. The plan made no specific proposals in respect of the Mablethorpe to Saltfleet coastline, but in view of increasing pressures for development, the County Council decided early in 1961 that in the review of the Development Plan they would adopt a more positive conservation policy by designating particular stretches of the coast as 'Coastal Conservation Areas'. "These are areas," they stated, "which are still substantially undeveloped; which are to be preserved from general building or large scale holiday camping development; and in which, subject to the protection of agricultural, scientific and natural history interest, any development is generally to be directed to meet the needs of daily visitors to the coast in search of rest and recreation". One such Area was the whole stretch of coast from Theddlethorpe to Humberston Fitties.

We had kept the County Council closely informed of our negotiations with the Air Ministry to establish the Saltfleetby-Theddlethorpe reserve, and when I heard from the Ministry's Works Department Engineer in February 1959 that the Ministry was considering selling some of their property at Saltfleetby and Theddlethorpe I at once got in touch with the Clerk of the County Council and with the Director-General of the Nature Conservancy reiterating a suggestion which we had made informally two or three years earlier that the County Council should seek to establish the whole of the SSSI as a statutory Local Nature Reserve. The County Council decided in March 1960 to take such action and the Clerk approached the Air Ministry to ask if they would give the Council the first opportunity to acquire the sandhills if they decided to sell them or, should they not be in a position to sell, if they would give the Council a lease with an option to purchase or, at least, enter into an agreement with the Council to enable the area to be declared as a Local Nature Reserve. The Council's proposal met with the full approval and support of the Nature Conservancy, and they too entered into negotiations with the Air Ministry who then took another four years to reach a final decision about the release of their sandhills property. Meantime the negotiations were overtaken by events.

Nature Reserve or Caravan Camps

Throughout the 1950s pressure for holiday caravan development on the coast was increasing, and in June 1958 the County Planning Officer consulted the Trust about an application to develop a caravan camp at Theddlethorpe St Helen on a site adjoining the sandhills to the south of what was at that time the southern boundary of the Trust's reserve. The application was subsequently refused by Louth Rural District Council acting with planning control powers delegated to them by the County Council. One of the reasons for refusal was that "the Local Planning Authority had determined upon a policy of preserving the coastline at Theddlethorpe and further north in its natural state". An appeal against refusal was dismissed by the Minister after a Public Inquiry, one of three grounds for dismissal being that: "It is not desirable to have a caravan camping ground adjoining an Air Ministry bombing range and near to a Nature Conservancy (sic) reserve". However, that was not the end of the matter because the applicant appealed against an Order requiring discontinuance of the site for caravans. His claim that there was an existing right for such use was upheld by Alford Magistrates in September 1960, and he later claimed user rights over a further area.

A Discontinuance Order and Enforcement Notice was then served by the County Council and these were the subject of another Public Inquiry held at Louth on 7 November 1961. The Minister's decision, announced on 3 April 1962, confirmed the Order and Notice with the exception of one small area which the County Council subsequently took additional steps to discontinue. The Minister's reasons were substantially the same as those which he gave for dismissing the 1959 appeal. One of them was that holiday camping use of the appeal site would detract materially from the quiet, rural atmosphere of this virtually unspoilt area and from the value and amenities of the adjacent nature reserve which by that time had been expanded. The Minister moreover confirmed his general agreement with the planning authority's policy – clearly stated by the Deputy County Planning Officer at both Inquiries – of seeking to preserve this unspoilt section of the Lincolnshire coast from large-scale holiday camping and to contain such development in areas allocated for that purpose in the Development Plan.

At both these Inquiries I gave evidence for the Trust in support of the County Council, and it was particularly encouraging that on both occasions the Minister specifically mentioned the proximity of the nature reserve as a reason for upholding the Council's case. At the 1961 Inquiry the County Council were also supported by the Nature Conservancy and the Lincolnshire branch of CPRE. At the 1959 Inquiry Mr F Fowler Senior, a member of Louth RDC and Chairman of one of its Committees, supported the County Council's refusal to give planning permission and put in a petition giving similar support signed by forty six local residents.

The only other caravan site on the Saltfleetby-Theddlethorpe stretch of coast was at Sea View Farm, Saltfleetby St Clement. This was a site of approximately 2½ acres, permission for which was granted in 1948 before the County Council became the local planning authority. On 29 August 1957, Louth RDC acting under their delegated powers gave unconditional permission for the erection of a shop on this site, and in the following year they gave permission for the erection of a recreation building. On 7 January 1959 they gave permission for an extension of the site which more than doubled its existing size to 132 caravans, a decision confirmed on 9 March 1960, together with a further small extension. At the same time they gave permission for the erection of ten chalets. In March and April 1961, they gave further permission for an extension to the clubhouse, for the erection of a bungalow and of a second shop.

The extension to the camping site of 9 March 1960 came to my notice from a reference in a local newspaper which mentioned only the smaller extension which amounted to only about a third of an acre. Neither the Trust nor the Nature Conservancy had been consulted about this or any of the other applications mentioned above and, believing it to be totally inconsistent with the Council's policies, I mentioned it to Robert Stirling, the County Planning Officer, when I saw him on 20 April 1960. He was immediately concerned, said that he had no knowledge of the matter and undertook to make immediate enquiries. However, I heard nothing further about it until preparations had been made for the second Public Inquiry on the Theddlethorpe case described above. At that Inquiry the barrister acting for the County Council admitted that permissions had during the previous two years been granted to extend the Saltfleetby site, and Mr Dickenson, the Deputy County Planning Officer, declared that those were bad decisions and that he would recommend that the Saltfleetby site should also be discontinued.

On 1 December 1961 the County Planning Officer wrote formally to seek the Trust's observations on the possibility of discontinuing the Saltfleetby camp which his Committee then had under consideration. In my reply I reminded him of the evidence I had given at the two Theddlethorpe Inquiries in support of the County Council's conservation policy for this stretch of coast. The Sea View camp, I pointed out, was in an even more critical position being closer to the richest and most vulnerable part of the nature reserve. The Trust, I was authorised to say, would support any action the County Council might take to secure its discontinuance. In the meantime I had checked on the position relating to planning permissions on the site and had discovered the facts stated above. I had already written a confidential letter to the Planning Officer about that on 11 December, but, having received neither acknowledgement nor reply from him, I wrote personally to Walter Lane, the Clerk of the County Council. I pointed out to him, as I had done to Stirling, that throughout the time when the County Council was seeking to discontinue the Theddlethorpe site and were clearly stating their policy for this whole stretch of coast – a policy which had been upheld by the Minister - permissions were being given extending and consolidating the Saltfleetby site against which the same case could be made.

The Trust was then invited to attend a meeting on 1 February 1962 of the Eastern Area Sub-Committee of the County Planning Committee and representatives of Louth RDC. In explaining that the Planning Committee were considering the possibility of making a Discontinuance Order for the Sea View site the Planning Officer did not admit that mistaken or unfortunate decisions had been made nor that the Trust and the Nature Conservancy had not been consulted about the applications. When I was invited to give the Trust's views, therefore, I had the somewhat difficult task of pointing out the inconsistencies of the Sea View decisions and the failure of the agreed consultative procedure, whilst re-stating the Trust's case for preventing development on this stretch of coast and pointing out that this policy adopted by the planning authority had already won the support of the Minister.

The RDC representatives were non-committal, but the Chairman of the County Planning Committee and the members present were clearly deeply concerned at what had happened, and the Chairman and two of the members expressed their regrets to me after the meeting and said they were determined that the mistakes should be put right. Subsequently on 25 May the Committee approved that a Discontinuance Order in respect of the Sea View caravan site and a Revocation Order in respect of the permission for chalets be made. Those orders were subsequently approved unanimously by the County Council. An appeal against the Orders was made by the site owner and a Public Inquiry was arranged. Louth RDC announced their intention of opposing the Orders and of supporting the appellant who was also promised support from Saltfleet and Saltfleetby Parish Councils. In addition to the Trust, the County Council was assured of the support of the Nature Conservancy, the National Parks Commission, the Council for Nature, CPRE and its Lincolnshire branch.

In July the County Council issued a statement describing the aims of their coastal policy of giving positive encouragement to the holiday industry, whilst protecting the amenities and natural interest of the Coastal Conservation Areas. The statement referred to the success of the Gibraltar Point reserve and confirmed that the County Council would assist the Trust in the development of a complementary reserve at Saltfleetby and Theddlethorpe. Attached to this was a statement which had been sent to the Minister of Housing and Local Government setting out the County Council's reasons for seeking his approval for the closure of the Sea View camp.

At the same time the Trust issued its own statement explaining its support for the County Council's coastal conservation policy in general and the discontinuance of the Sea View camp in particular. The County Council's intention aroused a great deal of hostility in the two Parish Councils, and the Trust was a particular target of attack, some of it vituperative and grossly ill-informed. Among several allegations were that the Trust was just a clique seeking only a selfish advantage, that it was responsible for persuading the County Council to make the Order and that we wished to keep people off the dunes entirely. In consequence the President of the Trust, Dick Cornwallis, sent a brief letter to the *Louth Standard* and the *Grimsby Evening Telegraph* refuting allegations and setting the record straight. The situation was not helped by the intervention of Sir Cyril Osborne, the vociferous Member of Parliament for Louth, who made pronouncements to the press without briefing himself about the facts and having heard only one side of the case. Later having seen the Deputy Clerk of the County Council and having received some correspondence from a constituent who was a member of the Trust, he modified his attitude and said that he recognised the strength of the County Council's case. He did indeed become a member of the Trust at the time, feeling no doubt that it was safer to have a foot in both camps!

The Sea View Inquiry took place at Louth on 21, 22 and 23 November. Donald Bain QC appeared for the County Council, Geoffrey Lane QC for the appellant, and Anthony Goodall for the Trust. Lane was at that time making a reputation which led him eventually to become Lord Chief Justice. Appreciating no doubt the strength of the County Council's case on planning grounds, which had already received the approval of the Minister in the Theddlethorpe case, he concentrated on the hardship to the site owner and the owners of the chalets. He tried to show that the Order was the result of a conspiracy in which the Trust had exercised improper influence on the County Council. It soon became clear from the County Planning Officer's evidence that it was in fact the result of a cock-up, but Lane persisted. Stirling was franker this time: the permissions given by Louth RDC to expand the Sea View Camp had been made on the recommendation of his Divisional Planning Officer and in Stirling's view were a mistake. He had known nothing about them, but accepted responsibility. In mitigation though he said that his Divisional Officer was "exceptionally overloaded with work". With only one assistant he was dealing with some 2,000 applications in a year, and the occasional failure to refer to headquarters was inevitable. Lane made the most of it, behaving as if it was a criminal trial with all the histrionics of a flamboyant prosecutor: the accusing finger, the pregnant silence, the climactic question. Pursuing the conspiracy theme he questioned Stirling about his connections with the Trust of which Stirling readily admitted to being just an ordinary member. Then he produced what he evidently thought to be a trump card: "Mr Walter Lane, the Clerk of the County Council, he's a member of the Trust, isn't he?".

I immediately instructed our own Counsel to say that that was not so, but Lane insisted that we produce a register of members, and he had one of his staff go through it from A to Z in search of his name-sake. At the end of the day's proceedings he apologised to the Inspector for his mistake.

The Nature Conservancy's Regional Officer, Bruce Forman, who gave evidence for the County Council was subjected to particularly harsh cross-examination; and Professor Alfred Steers, the most eminent physical geographer of his day, who appeared for the Nature Conservancy and the National Parks Commission, did not fare much better. Steer's main role was to explain the coastal conservation policies which the two agencies were promoting and which they wished to see applied to the Saltfleetby-Theddlethorpe coast.

Several camp occupants and local tradesmen as well as the site owner appeared for the Objectors, and the Clerk of Louth RDC, Gilbert Pitt, called the Chairman of his Council and representatives of local Parish Councils. Understandably perhaps, Pitt objected to the County Council seeking to overturn his own Council's planning decisions, but he was principally concerned that the RDC should have its share of the profitable caravan industry. He agreed that there should be "some measure of conservation" in planning, but he attacked what he called the County Council's "policy of sterilisation" of the coast.

My evidence for the Trust was not called until the third day, and whilst I was determined not to be browbeaten by Lane, the expectation was still somewhat daunting and I slept little the night before. My statement described the aims and objectives of the Trust; the particular natural features and values of the Saltfleetby-Theddlethorpe reserve, and our management policies for it including the provision of opportunities for education, research and quiet enjoyment. I refuted the accusation that the Trust was pursuing "the selfish interests of a few people". Wild nature was an invaluable and irreplaceable natural resource increasingly appreciated as a source of new knowledge and inspiration. The coast was a specially valuable feature of Britain's and Lincolnshire's natural heritage, and whilst much of it had been allocated for holiday development it was essential that the best unspoilt stretches should be protected. Gibraltar Point had already demonstrated the value and popularity of a nature reserve and the Saltfleetby-Theddlethorpe reserve was essentially complementary to it.

Lane was still intent on pursuing his conspiracy theme. He opened his cross-examination of me with what I suppose was a loud aside: "Now perhaps we've got to the nigger at the bottom of the wood pile". It was a menacing start, but he was unable to make much impression on my evidence. We learned later that he had tried but failed to find a renegade biologist or naturalist to counter our evidence, so he had obtained *The Oxford Book of Wild Flowers* and his series of questions about the species in my evidence were tedious to such an extent that the Inspector at one point asked him if the questioning was really necessary. I think Lane seriously overplayed his hand. The Inspector Mr W E Berridge was not concerned with witch hunting.

There was no intrigue. The Trust had never suggested that the County Council make a Discontinuance Order for the camp, but had we not brought to the attention of the Council that the Sea View planning approvals were a serious breach of their declared coastal policy it is highly probable that no action would have been taken to rectify the mistake. It was obvious throughout that the County Planning Officer, whilst acknowledging the mistakes, would have preferred to leave matters as they were. All honour then to the members of the Planning Committee and to the Clerk of the County Council for their courageous action.

The Minister's decision was announced in the middle of March 1963. He accepted his Inspector's recommendation to confirm the Revocation of Planning Permission and Discontinuance Orders. The Inspector in his report said that on hardship grounds he had much sympathy with the objectors and he welcomed the County Council's undertaking to compensate the owner, to help him seek an alternative site, and to delay the effective date of the Orders. Nevertheless, he continued, financial expediency should not be allowed to override soundly based planning principles, and he recommended confirmation of the Orders for the following reasons:

    a) The camp appears as an isolated and inappropriate intrusion into an otherwise unspoiled coastal landscape.

    b) The location of the site is ill considered and fortuitous as the occupants of the site cannot enjoy the normal amenities of the foreshore and sea, few communal facilities are available nearby and the site adjoins a bombing range.

    c) The use of the site by caravanners must in some degree detract from the integrity and scientific value of the adjacent areas leased by the Lincolnshire Naturalists' Trust and notified under Section 23 of the National Parks and Access to the Countryside Act.

With compensation and the site owner set up in a guesthouse elsewhere, the field was acquired by the County Council, cleared of caravans and eventually sold to the Trust. It is now the Sea View Meadow, a rich grassland reserve and the classic site in Britain for the rare Marsh moth *Athetis palustris*.

The Inquiries had been time-consuming and exhausting, and I breathed a sigh of relief when it was all over. There were many congratulations, including from Max Nicholson and Sir Francis Hill, and it had been a consoling coincidence that shortly before the Sea View Inquiry I had received intimation that I was to be awarded the OBE 'for work in promoting the establishment of nature reserves in Lincolnshire and elsewhere'. However, the bitterness engendered locally by the last Inquiry took many years to subside and we had a good deal of resentment and ill-will to overcome. But that was a small price to pay for the hard-won protection of this splendid piece of coastland. Like that at Gibraltar Point ten years earlier the successful defence of the Saltfleetby-Theddlethorpe reserve was a nationally significant achievement in the slow process of establishing nature conservation as a vitally important form of land use.

National Nature Reserve Status

The County Council had continued during this time to press the Air Ministry on the question of establishing a statutory nature reserve at the Saltfleetby-Theddlethorpe Dunes, reminding them that, in the event of disposal, the Council had a strong claim to be offered the land, having foregone its intention to control its use under the Sandhills Act in the early 1930s in favour of the Air Ministry. The Nature Conservancy was also in touch with the Ministry to support the County Council's case for a statutory reserve, and I also drew attention to the fact that the Trust had occupied the land as tenant for eight years and rescued it at considerable cost from falling into an even more parlous condition.

However, when the Air Ministry finally reached a decision to dispose of most of the dune land they were faced with a serious dilemma. Under the 'Crichel Down policy' the Ministry felt bound to offer the land back to the previous owners, but the dunes at Rimac had been sold off in small parcels to more than a hundred owners for caravan and chalet sites in the 1920s and early 30s. To trace even a proportion of those and prove their titles after more than thirty years would have been a virtually insuperable task. There was, however, a possibility that with special Ministerial approval the land could be transferred to another government department or agency, by-passing the Crichel Down procedure. The Trust was keen to acquire the land on which it had established a nature reserve, but it seemed increasingly unlikely that it would be given the opportunity. Since the County Council's prospects of acquiring it also seemed remote, the Trust's Executive Committee decided that the best solution was to persuade the Nature Conservancy to seek the transfer of the land from the Air Ministry. That, we believed, should be accompanied by the appointment of an officer in Lincolnshire to have special responsibility for Saltfleetby-Theddlethorpe, but also to assist and advise the County Council and the Trust on other matters. I accordingly wrote to the Clerk of the Council on 20 June 1963 putting forward our proposals and advancing three principal reasons for it: first, the undoubted national importance of the Saltfleetby-Theddlethorpe Dunes; secondly, the desirability that the Nature Conservancy should contribute financially to the management of the reserve after the County Council and the Trust had defended it at considerable cost, and thirdly, to secure the Conservancy's help and advice for nature conservation in Lincolnshire as a whole. A joint management committee of the three bodies should be established for the reserve with a consultative committee representing wider local interests. The Trust would continue to occupy those parts of the Dunes to be retained by the Air Ministry.

The County Council agreed with our suggestion which was further supported by a conference in July 1964 between the County Council, Louth RDC, the Nature Conservancy and the Trust. The Nature Conservancy then regraded the Dunes as a proposed National Nature Reserve and continued intergovernmental negotiations to acquire it. There followed another eighteen months of official dithering with numerous memos passing between the Conservancy, the Air Ministry, the Office of the Minister of Science and the Treasury. One senior official was moved to ask about one such memo why such a vast amount of paper was needed about such a minor matter! In the end Ministers agreed to the transfer and an NNR was declared in November 1968.

There was one other minor consequence of the creation of the Saltfleetby-Theddlethorpe Dunes NNR which became something of a conservation issue in the years that followed. When consulted about the announcement of the new reserve in October 1968 the County Council and the Trust pointed out to the Nature Conservancy the invidious distinction which the word 'National' would create between Saltfleetby-Theddlethorpe and Gibraltar Point which in the Nature Conservancy's terms was a 'Local' reserve having been designated by a Local Authority. Neither term, observed the Clerk of the County Council in a letter to the Nature Conservancy, had any statutory validity, but 'National' would be interpreted by the general public to indicate greater importance than 'Local' whereas on a scientific and conservation assessment the opposite was probably true in the two cases in question. The Nature Conservancy's rather feeble response was that, whilst they had to use the term 'National' for Saltfleetby-Theddlethorpe to bring it into line with other reserves which they managed, they would refrain from using the term 'Local' in respect of Gibraltar Point, referring to it simply as a nature reserve. The Conservancy was in fact already becoming aware of the problem in the context of a comprehensive review of sites of national conservation importance which they had just initiated and which developed into the massive Nature Conservation Review published in 1977. As a result of that, the successor body, the Nature Conservancy Council, eventually agreed to the principle of according national status and title to reserves of national quality managed by other bodies to approved standards. One of the first to receive that accolade was Gibraltar Point but that was not until 1984 and after frequent representations by the Trust.

In 1965 in anticipation of the NNR declaration the Conservancy appointed their first Warden Naturalist for Lincolnshire, Martin Ball, who took up residence in the former caravan camp bungalow at Sea View leased to the Conservancy by the County Council. The Conservancy also announced their intention to appoint a Warden for the new National Nature Reserve in due course. Until that could be done they entered into an arrangement with the Trust to pay for the services of Barrie Wilkinson on a part-time basis. That very opportunely enabled the Trust to appoint Barrie as Field Officer at the end of his three-year study of access and use of the Gibraltar Point reserve. Apart from occasional disputes about rights-of-way and familiar complaints about foxes, the Saltfleetby-Theddlethorpe Dunes reserve now entered a more tranquil and constructive phase.

Marsh orchids in the dune slack.

114

'Ratepayers face bill for thousands'–Planning officer

LINDSEY'S County Planning Officer, Mr. R. L. Stirling, said at a public inquiry in Louth yesterday that in his view Louth R.D.C. made a mistake when it decided to allow extensions to the Sea View caravan camp at Saltfleetby St. Clement.

Grimsby Evening Telegraph, 22 November 1962.

Warning notices and the bombing range target in the background, 1970.

DAVID ROBINSON

Northern part of the Saltfleetby-Theddlethorpe Dunes NNR, 1990s.

GRAHAM WEAVER

115

My OBE in 1963 was 'for work in promoting the establishment of nature reserves in Lincolnshire and elsewhere'. At Buckingham Palace with Mary, Alison (right) and Helen.

The view south from Zion Hill in the 1960s, with the volunteer warden's hut bottom left.

New pond and flooded freshwater slack beyond.

Barrie Wilkinson, the Trust's first paid Warden at the Saltfleetby - Theddlethorpe reserve.

Zion Hill was once the highest ancient sand-dune on the Lincolnshire coast.

The flooded and reed-fringed former clay pits on the South Humber bank, those in the foreground now the Trust's Far Ings National Nature Reserve. (1985).

Westfield Lakes with remaining buildings on the site of the former cement works, c. 1955.

118

– 7 –

Conservation on the Humber

L INCOLNSHIRE is fortunate in embracing two great estuaries, the Wash and the Humber. The latter also demanded our early attention, initially for two reasons: one because of its importance for wildfowl and waders, and in particular as a main wintering area for pink-footed geese which required some degree of protection from shooting pressures; the other because of the chain of lakes and reedbeds which adjoined the estuary from New Holland in the east to Barton-on-Humber in the west. These lakes were the legacy of the brick and tile manufacturing industry which had flourished here for over two hundred years, but which had gradually faded out in the 20th century. More recently further pits had been excavated for clay for the cement industry which had also used chalk from the nearby Wolds which overlook the river. These lakes and reedbeds formed the most extensive freshwater wetland habitats in Lincolnshire and by the 1950s had been colonised by up to six pairs of bitterns. The pits, however, were already under pressure. Barton UDC's application to tip refuse in a pit on Far Ings Lane, a bittern nesting site, was approved in 1955 by the Lindsey Planning Committee in spite of its SSSI designation in the first schedule in 1951. The Trust had strongly objected, and when I wrote subsequently to the Planning Officer to question the decision he explained rather lamely that there appeared to be discrepancies between the SSSI schedule maps and those in the later county development plan. He asked me to meet his Assistant Planning Officer to check the maps. Earlier, in 1954, I wrote to the Planning Officer to express the Trust's concern about another Barton UDC scheme for draining and infilling a number of the clay pits. Fortunately, apart from the one just described, they did not proceed with the scheme. Recreational use was another potential form of competition for the pits, and whilst the days of more sophisticated and more disturbing sports like water skiing were still some way off, fishing was rapidly regaining its pre-war popularity as transport opportunities increased.

The few hundred members of the Trust in the early 1950s were thinly spread, especially in the north, but we had attracted the support of an enterprising farmer at Goxhill, Jack Hargreaves, one of a group of naturalists in the area who had been associated with the British Naturalists' Association rather than the Lincolnshire Naturalists' Union with which they had little contact. Foreseeing the growth of demand for water-based recreation, Hargreaves was particularly anxious that the Trust should seek to safeguard the pits to the west of Barton known generally as Westfield Lakes. Partly as a result of his interest and local knowledge, I had written as early as May 1950 to Sir George Earle, Chairman of G & T Earle, the cement manufacturers who still owned some of the pits in question. I explained the wildlife interest of the pits and reedbeds and expressed the hope that the Trust might be able to acquire one or more of them when they came up for disposal. His reply was encouraging. The Company would do all it could to safeguard the wildlife on their property which he thought they would want to get rid of in due course. The mention of bitterns prompted him to recount this little story.

"I have only seen a bittern once in my life, and I, unfortunately, shot it, but this was close to Ninevah 25 years ago. In the Old Testament there was a prophecy by someone who did not like the way of people of Ninevah who said that cormorants and bitterns should nest within its walls. I also shot a cormorant within its walls".

In my reply I recalled another appropriate prophecy which I believe to be in Isaiah and refers to Babylon: "I will also make it a possession for the bittern, and pools of water".

Sir George passed me on to the Company Director at Hull, Mr Keeble, who told me in a letter in March 1955 that they were examining the possibility of going over the pits a second time for more clay, but that he would advise me when any of the pits became available for disposal. I subsequently made a further appeal to Sir George hoping that he might use his influence in our favour, but he was then on the point of retiring and was not as forthcoming as on the first occasion. Mr Keeble unfortunately failed to inform us when they decided to sell the Westfield Lakes site and we discovered too late that they had been sold to a Mr Barratt who was living in the gaunt and partly derelict block of buildings which had housed some of the old cement works staff. Barratt was reputed to be a retired South Yorkshire miner who had acquired the pits for the fishing. In discussion with us he indicated his willingness to consider an offer for the property. Although the Trust had no funds for purchase, Hargreaves was confident that he would be able to raise money locally so, having carried out a survey and valuation, we made an offer to Barratt. His first reaction was favourable, but later he came back to seek a higher price. We made an improved offer, but when he repeated the process we were forced to give up the attempt. We also made contact with the sympathetic tenant of Ness Farm, Mr Grimoldby, whose land included the large Ness Pit and its surrounding grassland and scrub, but we reluctantly had to concede that there was little we could effectively achieve at that time to safeguard the pits at least until more local support was available. It was in fact to be another twenty years before new opportunities arose for the Trust to acquire parts of the clay pits, and by that time the Westfield Lakes buildings had been converted into an hotel with a caravan site; Ness End Farm was a ruin, the bitterns had gone, but bearded tits had arrived and we had a very active Area Group based on Barton.

The Humber Wildfowl Refuge and Read's Island

The other Humberside issue in which we became closely involved in the 1950s was the creation of the Humber Wildfowl Refuge, the first to be established in Britain under the provisions of the 1954 Protection of Birds Act. National interest in wildfowl and their conservation had been stimulated in the early 1950s by the research and ringing activity conducted by Peter Scott through his newly formed Severn Wildfowl Trust, and by the International Committee for Bird Preservation whose secretary in Britain was my old friend, the redoubtable Phyllis Barclay-Smith. Wild geese in particular have a popular romantic appeal - which had been stimulated by Scott's own evocative paintings – and discussions leading up to the 1954 Act had created further interest in their protection. More specifically, however, it was concern with the welfare of the pink-footed geese wintering on the Humber which set in motion the campaign for a statutory refuge. In the early 1950s several thousand pinkfeet spent the early part of the winter on the Humber, feeding by day on the stubbles of the Lincolnshire and Yorkshire Wolds and roosting on sandbanks in the estuary from Whitton Sand to Read's Island. The popularity of wildfowling had increased dramatically after the end of the Second World War, and geese were subjected to increasing persecution and disturbance, particularly on their roosts.

By 1950 the situation on the Humber was causing grave concern. The number of shooters was increasing year by year and some were actually digging barrels into the mud from which they shot at the geese as they came in to roost. Duck punts and motor boats were also being used, as were decoys and calls on the feeding grounds. There were particular allegations of excessive shooting and disturbance on Read's Island which was tenanted from the Humber Conservancy Board by Mr (later Sir) Joseph Nickerson and Mr F R Davy. The Island was of special importance at that time for geese, being the only roost in the estuary not subject to tidal flooding at high springs. Whatever the causes there was certainly convincing evidence of a serious decline in the pinkfeet wintering on the Humber. Numbers in excess of 20,000 in the 1930s had been reduced to a maximum of 7,000 by 1950 and only 2-3,000 by the winter of 1952/3.

Growing public concern about the future of the geese on Humberside found dramatic expression in a campaign led by two local farmers, J H (John) Davey of Thornton Abbey and J F D (Jack) Hargreaves of Goxhill – a member of the Trust Council - to persuade landowners and tenants to ban the use of decoys and other unsporting methods of shooting geese on their land. Davey, a fierce and uncompromising campaigner who sometimes found it difficult to appreciate the constraints which representation of an organisation like the Trust imposes, published a pamphlet 'Save Our Wild Geese', and no fewer than 512 landowners and farmers signed a Wild Geese Conservation Contract.

In October 1952 on the instruction of the Trust Council I wrote to Max Nicholson, who had recently become Director-General of the Nature Conservancy, asking that the Conservancy should seek and support means of protecting the Humber geese from excessive persecution, if possible by the establishment of a sanctuary. I suggested in particular that the Conservancy should first approach the owners of Reads Island, the Humber Conservancy Board, and ask them to put a 'No Shooting' clause into any new lease of the Island; and if their present tenants were unwilling to accept that, to let the grazing on the Island to others who would agree not to shoot there at all. We knew there would be no difficulty in finding alternative tenants, and Hargreaves gave me his personal guarantee to protect the Conservancy Board against any financial loss which might result from exclusion of shooting. We had learned that the current lease was about to expire, but it transpired unfortunately that the tenants had a further five-year option, including shooting rights, which they intended to exercise. The Conservancy

Board, according to its Secretary, was therefore powerless to prevent shooting on the Island before 1958.

In view of this Nicholson asked the Board to interview the tenants and "to press them as to what firm quantitative undertakings they were willing to give to carry out their assurance (given to the Board) that they are prepared to shoot the property in a reasonable manner and to 'preserve the fowl so far as they can'". His proposal that I should represent the Conservancy at such an interview was endorsed by the England and Wales Committee.

The Secretary of the Board, whose sympathy seemed to lie with the tenants, convened a conference of interested parties in Hull at short notice on 19 March 1953. Joseph Nickerson was indisposed and did not attend, but his co-tenant Fred Davy was accompanied by seven supporters including Nickerson's brother, and J W Johnson, the National President of the Wildfowlers' Association. Dick Cornwallis, the Trust's Assistant Honorary Secretary, accompanied me; John Davey, Jack Hargreaves and Dr J Thompson, another Trust member who had been active in the anti-decoy campaign, were also present; and so was Dr V Walsh, Chairman of the Hull and East Riding Wildfowlers' Association. The meeting was chaired by the Chairman of the Conservancy Board with three of his members and two senior officials in attendance.

The tenants' case had been thoroughly organised, a fact attested by the presence of Davy's solicitor, and they had obviously solicited the support of the Wildfowlers' Association. The atmosphere was initially tense and confrontational. At the Chairman's invitation I led with a brief statement referring to the decline in wildfowl numbers in recent years – Dick Cornwallis and John Davey later substantiated it in greater detail – and explaining our basic purpose of ensuring the future of wild geese on the Humber by securing protection for them on their feeding and roosting grounds. To that end we asked if the tenants of Read's Island were willing to relinquish their shooting rights so that a sanctuary including the Island could be established.

Davy and his friends, who were very much on the defensive, then spent one and a half hours putting their case, disputing our figures and claiming that their bags were very modest, that the geese had to be controlled in the interests of the grassland on the Island (after claiming that few ever went on to it!), and generally adopting an attitude of injured innocence. Johnson, the Wildfowlers' President, made a somewhat pompous statement in their support in which he questioned my own credentials for representing the Nature Conservancy.

Whilst the meeting produced no apparent change in attitudes and positions, we had clearly succeeded in putting pressure on the tenants who declared themselves willing to consider some limitation on their shooting activities by agreement with the Nature Conservancy, and to co-operate in any measures to control shooting from boats around the Island. Davy offered to meet us to discuss such matters, and, with a renewed mandate from Nicholson, Dick and I, accompanied this time by the recently elected President of the Trust, Colonel Oliver Sutton Nelthorpe, met Davy and Nickerson at Brigg on 31 August 1953.

After the Hull meeting we had established a reasonable rapport with Davy and with Peter Dennis, one of his supporters at the meeting – both subsequently became Life Members of the Trust – but at the Brigg meeting Nickerson, who straightway launched into a defence of their sportsmanship, was clearly the dominant partner and, as I reported to Nicholson, we found him somewhat aggressive and domineering. They were obviously very anxious to secure an option from the Conservancy Board of a further renewal of their lease from 1958 with shooting rights, and they realised that to achieve this they would have to make some concessions in the form of limitations of their shooting, although at that stage they would only undertake not to shoot otherwise than they had done, and to accept further restrictions should the goose population on the Humber decline below the 1952 level.

They then sought direct talks with Nicholson, and after seeing him in London, arranged for him, Peter Scott and Lord Hurcomb, to visit Reads Island in February 1954 (Dick and I had been there with Davy the previous December). The day before the visit the three of them held discussions with Dick, Jack Hargreaves and me in Skegness. We had in no way modified our view that ideally Read's Island should be a sanctuary area within the proposed Humber Wildfowl Refuge, but Nickerson and Davy had a secure lease until 1958, and to oppose a further renewal of shooting rights after that would rule out any agreement with them to limit shooting in the meantime. Moreover we could not even then be sure that the Humber Conservancy Board would refuse to give them such a lease. Reluctantly, therefore, we agreed that Nicholson should seek an agreement restricting the number of shoots to eight a season, and a bag limit on geese. Even with these concessions the tenants were slow to agree, and Nickerson's prevarication on the matter at the meeting to establish the Refuge on 15 January 1955, caused Nicholson to renew his threat to oppose a further lease of the Island to them from 1958.

In the end, after three years of negotiation we achieved only an informal agreement between the tenants and the Nature Conservancy of which the former took very little notice. And any pressure which the Nature Conservancy had been able to exercise through the Humber Conservancy Board disappeared in 1956 when Nickerson purchased Read's Island from the Board. Though he gave the Nature Conservancy an undertaking "not to alter the management of the shooting in any way from the existing agreed arrangements", within five years (in 1961) he advertised the Reads Island shooting in the American periodical *Field and Stream* with the heading 'No Bag Limit'. When it was called to his attention with considerable indignation by Frank Mason, the Honorary Secretary of the Refuge Committee, Nicholson made an immediate enquiry, reminding Nickerson of the terms of the agreement set out in his letter of 11 March 1955. In a decidedly lame reply Nickerson blamed "an over-zealous" PA for the wording of the advert and asked for a copy of the agreement letter which, he said, he had mislaid!

The protracted negotiations with Nickerson and Davy had tended to obscure and had certainly delayed progress in achieving the second purpose for which the Trust had approached the Nature Conservancy in 1952, namely the establishment of a statutory Humber Wildfowl Refuge under the 1954 Bird Protection Act. The need to get on with that, persuaded us in the end to abandon attempts to bring Reads Island within the sanctuary.

The Wildfowlers' organisations were initially suspicions about the intentions of the Nature Conservancy and the Trust. The Humber was particularly hallowed ground for them: it was where their national association had been founded in 1908 by Stanley Duncan. Although initially appearing to support the Read's Island tenants, informal contacts showed that the local clubs on both sides of the river, whilst stoutly defending the practice of shooting from the shore, shared our concern about the use of decoys and about shooting on feeding and roosting grounds. I believe that the stand we took over Reads Island did no harm to our relations with them and may indeed have enhanced our credibility.

Nicholson accordingly convened and chaired a meeting on 15 January 1955 at the offices of the Humber Conservancy Board in Hull to discuss the general conservation of wildfowl on the Humber and the specific proposal to establish a sanctuary. There was an impressive representation of interests: the Conservancy Board, the Wildfowl Trust, the Wildfowlers' Association of Great Britain and Ireland and three local Wildfowlers' Clubs, the Yorkshire Naturalists' Union (though not at that stage the Yorkshire Trust), the Lincolnshire Trust represented by Dick and myself, and Messrs Nickerson and Davy. The distinguished American conservationist and authority on wildfowl, Professor Gustave Swanson of Cornell University, who was visiting Britain, attended as an observer. In his opening remarks Nicholson emphasised the pioneering nature of the meeting. The proposal for a sanctuary was the first of its kind and could set an important example of co-operation for other parts of Britain. He then invited discussion on the proposals which had been set out in a memorandum from the Nature Conservancy circulated in advance of the meeting. The wildfowlers' representatives quickly took the initiative, proposing that instead of attempting to demarcate as refuges sandbanks which were continually shifting – as the Nature Conservancy's memorandum had done - the sanctuary should embrace the whole of the Humber between the Faxfleet/Trent Falls line and a line drawn from Brough Haven to Whitton Ness, excluding the Lincolnshire and Yorkshire banks and a fringe 100 yards below the bank or 100 yards outside any shore vegetation whichever was the lower. Within the sanctuary all unauthorised access should be prohibited. This was in fact our own original proposal except that we had included Read's Island. There was general agreement to it, but Joseph Nickerson gratuitously – and I suspect somewhat triumphantly – emphasised that Read's Island would be outside the sanctuary. He then demanded to know if anyone had any complaints about his sporting conduct! He also asked that the 100 yard fringe for shooting should apply also to Read's Island, an unnecessary request – as Dr Storey of WAGBI and I pointed out – since the Island was not to be in the sanctuary. His request may have been calculated to give added legitimacy to his shooting practices. Once again I sensed little sympathy for him from the wildfowlers.

The scheme made provision for a local advisory committee from the three local Wildfowlers' Clubs, the Yorkshire Naturalists' Union and – this time – the Yorkshire Trust and the Lincolnshire Trust, with the tenants of Read's Island as observers. It was agreed that a seasonal warden would be required, and Nicholson undertook to put this forward for grant-aid from the Nature Conservancy. He further undertook to place the recommendations before the Home Office Advisory Committee on the Protection of Birds with a view to obtaining an Order to establish a statutory refuge for a three-year experimental period.

The meeting had taken place in private, but a press release was subsequently issued outlining the agreed scheme. It was the first time wildfowling and conservation bodies had worked constructively and amicably together on such a project, and the media was perhaps disappointed that it had not resulted in a headline confrontation! The agreement would have been much more difficult if not impossible without Max Nicholson's diplomatic skills as a negotiator and conciliator.

Nicholson convened another meeting on 1 October 1955 to report the implementation of the Sanctuary Order and to formally constitute the Committee. It was generally agreed that a wildfowler should take the chair for the first year and the vice-chairman should be a naturalist, the position to be reversed the following year. With the appointment as Chairman of Trevor Field, the Chairman of the Hull and East Riding Wildfowlers' Association, the first formal meeting of the Committee then got under way later that afternoon. Dick and I could not attend either of those meetings, but I was appointed Vice-Chairman in my absence, and a wildfowler, Frank Mason, was appointed Honorary Secretary, an office in which he enjoyed the confidence of all parties and which he held for the next fourteen years. The meeting discussed practical issues concerned with wardening the Refuge and the duties of the warden who would be paid by the Nature Conservancy but would be directly responsible to the Honorary Secretary and the Committee. A press notice giving an account of the proceedings was issued immediately after the meeting.

The Refuge was now up and running and the Committee began to meet at regular twice-yearly intervals. At the end of the first year I reluctantly declined the chairmanship because of my increasing workload and, although the wildfowlers were anxious that a naturalist should succeed Trevor Field, he was unanimously re-elected. In fact he was so well respected by both sides that he continued to serve as Chairman for another twenty-two years! For the first three years Dick and I attended the meetings fairly regularly, but by 1958 pressures on both of us were growing. The Trust was expanding and we were becoming increasingly involved in national affairs, especially in my case as the Honorary Secretary of the new Naturalists' Trusts' Committee of the SPNR. The Refuge Committee was functioning well and, having put a lot of effort into establishing it, we decided that we would have to accord it lower priority in our own programmes. Unfortunately we found it difficult to interest other Trust members in serving on it with any consistency. Dick continued longer than I did, and Rick Pilcher, with his unrivalled experience of wildfowl as shooter and conservationist, represented us for a number of years in the 1970s. After that our representation became spasmodic, and even when our Barton-on-Humber Area Group was formed in 1972 they could arouse little enthusiasm for it. This was partly perhaps because so much of the wildfowl interest and activity was concentrated on the Yorkshire side - had Reads Island been in it the situation would almost certainly have been different. Another reason perhaps was the fact that geese numbers on the Humber began a steady decline in the 1960s and by the early 70s were reduced to a few hundred. One of the main reasons for this – as at Croft Marsh – was almost certainly the changes in agricultural crops and cropping practices which provided less food for the geese than hitherto.

The Refuge continued to serve a valuable purpose in regulating shooting and protecting ducks and waders, but inevitably some of its original purpose and importance was lost, and to some extent overtaken by new conservation legislation and eventually by such designations as Ramsar and Special Protection Area. Brian Pashby of the Yorkshire Naturalists' Union, who succeeded Frank Mason as Honorary Secretary of the Refuge Committee, wrote an excellent account of the administration and the birds of the Refuge in a Presidential Address to the YNU completed shortly before his untimely death in 1991.

The creation of the Refuge and the bringing together of wildfowlers and naturalists had been an important pioneering exercise in Britain, and we had been proud to be associated with it. It had also provided us with valuable experience in negotiation even if at times this had been tedious and frustrating. It had also brought me into closer contact with Max Nicholson and with the Nature Conservancy to whose England Committee I was appointed in 1956.

As for Read's Island itself, Nickerson subsequently three times tried to sell it: in 1963 for £100,000; in 1969 when he offered it to this Trust (and I believe also to the RSPB) for a similar sum, offering to pay 25% of the costs himself; and again in 1969 by public auction at Brigg when he withdrew it when the bidding stopped at £32,500. The reserve price on that occasion was rumoured to be £50,000 according to *The Grimsby Evening Telegraph*. The Island continued to be an SSSI of great ornithological value, and during the 1970s there was contact between the Trust through David Robinson, the Honorary Secretary, and Nickerson's son Robert about the possibility of some kind of nature reserve status for the Island. At one stage these contacts seemed to be mildly encouraging, but in a letter of 11 November 1976 Robert Nickerson finally quashed the idea: "Our objective now", he wrote, "is to retain facilities for the use of the family and their guests, not to make it into a public place". During this time the sea walls on the Island were suffering severe erosion, and in 1987 the Trust's Viking Volunteers helped to make emergency repairs to seal a breach. A further enquiry about the future of the Island by Stuart Crooks, the Trust's Conservator, in 1989, brought a negative response from the Nickersons' resident Land Agent. Further initially promising contacts were made by Crooks in 1995 with the Agent of the Joseph Nickerson Trustees – Sir Joseph had died in 1990 – but unknown to the Trust the RSPB was also negotiating for a lease of the Island. This they obtained, but then entered into an agreement with the Trust for a joint management scheme, although it was never effectively implemented.

GEOFF TRINDER

Bittern

Pinkfeet geese

*Read's Island
from the Wolds
above South Ferriby,
1985.*

*With Robert
Nickerson (left) on
the eroding north side
of Read's Island,
1972.*

1963

Duke of Burgundy fritillary.

DAVE VANDOME

*Remnant of grassland after
planting with spruce, 1988.*

Felling the spruce, 1996.

BARRIE WILKINSON

TED SMITH

Robert's Field

BARRIE WILKINSON

Spreading green hay, 1997.

Grassland restored, 2006.

BARRIE WILKINSON

– 8 –

Nature in Retreat

After-comers cannot guess the beauty been Hopkins

B Y THE mid 1960s the Trust had made notable progress in establishing nature reserves. Gibraltar Point had been secured; the threat to the Saltfleetby-Theddlethorpe coast had been successfully beaten off; some of the best wet heathland remnants from Linwood Warren to Epworth Turbary had been acquired. During the same time, however, there had also been serious losses, the consequence of intensive land use pressures from agriculture, forestry and mineral extraction. They exposed both the frustrating ineffectiveness of the original SSSI provision, and the scandal of an agricultural policy which not only took little or no account of nature conservation or other environmental considerations, but which actually rewarded people for destroying part of the country's natural heritage. The story of these losses was replicated in the 1950s, 60s and 70s in many parts of Britain. We lost battles in those years but by fighting them we helped to ensure that more enlightened policies and practices eventually prevailed. I describe some notable examples in Lincolnshire.

Robert's Field

The Wildlife Conservation Special Committee had proposed a large NNR covering the Holywell and Pickworth Woods straddling the Lincolnshire and Rutland border, but since the Forestry Commission was already in occupation of most of the woodland, the proposed NNR was whittled down to two isolated pieces: a small patch of limestone grassland known as Holywell Mound; and an area astride the Holywell-Pickworth road, the Lincolnshire Gate Scrubs. On one side of the road was Hewitt's Gorse, a patch of mainly hawthorn scrub with some large oaks; on the other an area of about twelve acres of rough limestone grassland known as Robert's Field.

In view of its proposed NNR status we had deliberately omitted Robert's Field from our 1951 report to the Nature Conservancy on areas of scientific interest in Lincolnshire. Visits in the 1950s, however, left us in no doubt of its conservation value. One such visit paid in company with that great naturalist Rick Pilcher stands out in my memory. It was a sunny morning in late May. Butterflies were

129

on the wing in great profusion, among them four which were to become extinct in Lincolnshire: marbled white, chequered skipper, pearl-bordered and silver-washed fritillaries. Duke of Burgundy was there too, then in its only known Lincolnshire locality. In all twenty-five species were recorded in Robert's Field (and there may have been others), making it the richest butterfly site in the county. It is a sobering thought that this one site in the 1950s held almost as many butterfly species as now occur in the whole of Lincolnshire. Summer visits also revealed a rich limestone flora – pyramidal orchid, clustered bellflower, rockrose, felwort and many others.

The site had appeared in the original 1951 SSSI schedule for Kesteven as a proposed National Nature Reserve, but by 1954 we were becoming very concerned at the Nature Conservancy's inaction and apparent lack of interest in it, especially since it was reported that the Forestry Commission might take it over for afforestation. I raised the matter with Max Nicholson, the Director-General of the Nature Conservancy, in the middle of 1954, suggesting that if the NC no longer intended to try to acquire the site as an NNR, it should move out of the way and leave the Trust to negotiate with the landowner. Later that year the site was removed from the NC's list of PNNRs but retained on the revised SSSI schedule. The Trust was not officially notified of that, however, until 1 July 1955 when the NC sought the Trust's views on a Forestry Commission proposal to plant the whole of the site under a scheme covering all the Holywell estate. In view of the subsequent attitude of the owners, the Mountjoy-Fanes, it is doubtful if the Trust could have persuaded them to sell or lease it, but in any case it was then too late and we had to try to salvage what we could of the grassland interest of the site from the afforestation proposal. We were not helped in this by ignorance and further indecision on the part of the NC about the real conservation value of the site. This became painfully obvious when I pressed them for the reasons why they had retained it in the PNNR list for so long. All they could do was to quote a note from Professor Tutin, the Professor of Botany at Leicester University, expressing the hope that "means can be found to preserve the area as a whole .... to regenerate naturally". There was no suggestion that the succession should be controlled - as it had been up to that time by rabbits - in the interests of the grassland flora, and the ecological richness of the site was totally ignored.

Miss Julia Laptain, the NC's Regional Officer based in Nottingham, paid her first visit to the site in July 1955. Having been somewhat dismissive about it previously, she subsequently submitted a report to her headquarters enthusing about the grassland interest: "probably the last remaining piece of unkempt calcicolous grassland in southern Lincolnshire. Its loss would seem irreparable, and it is a very definite habitat type and offers as much to the entomologists as to the botanists". She recommended that the whole twelve acres should be preserved in its entirety as an example of a limestone grassland flora. However, if afforestation had to be accepted she hoped that only half the area would be sacrificed. Her recommendation was apparently ignored. G N Sale, the Conservancy's Woodlands Officer, whom I knew well, told me in a letter of 23 January 1956 that NC were not prepared to ask the Forestry Commission to refrain from planting. His administrative and scientific colleagues, he said, wanted the Forestry Commission "to manage the land so as to encourage natural regeneration and to grow there a stand of oaks etc". At this point Miss Laptain completely retracted her recommendation for the preservation of the grassland.

In a letter of 7 February 1956 she claimed that the purpose of scheduling the site was "to have ten acres of land in which the course of the natural regeneration of oak could be followed". She went on to say that she had never heard that "the Trust wanted the area as grassland". This brought a sharply worded rejoinder from me quoting her own report and recommendation of little more than six months before and of my earlier letters and reports pointing out the presence of many butterfly species – some of them even then, like the chequered skipper nationally rare – dependent on grassland and woodland edge habitat. Her inconsistency was not entirely unexpected. She was one of a very small minority of NC officers who seemed to regard County Trusts as interfering voluntary bodies. Gilbert Sale was charming and helpful, but was not prepared to press the Forestry Commission for anything but minimal concessions. Accordingly I wrote again to Nicholson on 15 February 1956 asking that the Nature Conservancy should seek the agreement of the Commission to leave at least one third of the area unplanted and to use hardwoods on the remainder of the site. In urging this course of action I pointed out once again that it was the NC's delay in deleting the site from PNNR list that had inhibited the Trust from approaching the owner.

Sale meantime had had discussions with the Commission and arranged a site meeting with their Senior Officer to which I was invited. Whilst, apart from Sale, we had had little support from the NC, we were now more fortunate in our main contact with the Commission. Robert Payne, the Divisional Officer, was understanding and sympathetic – after retirement he became the Cambridgeshire Trust's Administrative Officer for several years. Conceding as much as he was able to do in the circumstances, he agreed to leave unplanted a strip of grassland of 1.8 acres at the top of the slope adjoining the patch of old woodland. It was to have a scalloped edge with a minimum width of thirty-five yards. We had to accept that the remainder would be ploughed and afforested, but Payne agreed to plant oak rather than beech, his original intention. The Trust then entered into an informal management agreement with the Commission for the small piece of grassland. It had been a sorry story, but I felt we had achieved all we could in the circumstances.

Unfortunately the troubles of Robert's Field were far from over. After a few years the oaks planted by the Commission failed in the thin limestone soil and were replaced by a close crop of Scots pine after the ground had been ploughed. Later there was yet another problem. Adjoining the grassland reserve at the top of the slope was a big hedge with a variety of trees and shrubs, and behind that some five acres of old oak woodland which had also been included in the PNNR proposals. We had called attention to the importance of this for butterflies in our negotiations for a grassland reserve. It provided shelter and a variety of food plants. In 1977 the Commission sought our views on an application to fell and replant the woodland with a mixture of oak and Norway spruce. It had been expected that after felling the estate would transfer it to the Commission for replanting, but in the event the owners decided to retain and plant it themselves. This was unfortunate since Payne would almost certainly have been sympathetic to the nature conservation interest. As it was, he could only advise me to write direct to the owner, Major the Honourable Mountjoy-Fane, to seek his co-operation in leaving a screen of old trees and shrubs between the grassland reserve and the area to be replanted. This I did with due tact, but in reply I received the most irascible and unhelpful letter that I ever had from a landowner. I reproduce it in full:

> Dear Smith
> Thank you for your letter of 20th. The Forestry Commission are my tenants and no doubt will do what they can to help but the land has to be used in a manner likely to produce something useful and not to breed butterflies. I guarantee nothing regarding the future of that piece of land. I am in the near future felling some oak nearby but this will be replanted with oak and hardwood and should do no harm to the biological value. I am sorry I cannot be of much help but if say ironstone is found on my land it has got to be taken whether I like it or not.
> Yours faithfully
> M M Fane.

The woodland area was felled but something of the old hedge survived and with the help of the Commission we won some concessions from the estate - through a more reasonable and businesslike agent – on the proportion of oak against spruce to be used, although the Trust's repeated offer to acquire the woodland was rejected. As a final indignity the Nature Conservancy Council decided in 1987 to de-notify Robert's Field as an SSSI, a site which thirty-five years before they had regarded as of national importance and whose loss was due in no small measure to their own vacillation and inaction.

Initially the Commission kept the grassland mown, but later it became neglected, and in 1985 the Trust concluded a more formal management agreement with the Commission. In spite of neglect the grassland had retained almost all its characteristic species although in much diminished quantity.

The destruction of the greater part of the wildlife interest of Robert's Field for the sake of a few rather wretched conifers was a conservation tragedy which I felt no less keenly as the years went by. So when a sympathetic Forestry Commission Conservator, charged at last with wider responsibilities for nature conservation, visited the Trust in 1988 I suggested to him that the Commission should transfer to the Trust their 999 year lease for the twelve acres of Robert's Field. To my surprise and pleasure he adopted the proposal and in 1991 we became virtual owners of the site with the bold intention to fell the pines and restore the limestone grassland. We knew it would not be easy, but expert advice from Terry Wells of the Institute of Terrestrial Ecology and others was encouraging and by 1998 the results of the first phase of the operation were impressive. Whether anyone will ever see again that marvellous galaxy of butterflies that I saw on that May morning forty years ago I cannot tell, but some of the beauty and interest has already been restored, as I recount in a later chapter.

Waddingham Common

While something has been salvaged from Robert's Field, Waddingham Common, another site of unique interest in Lincolnshire, has gone for ever. The Common was a twenty-two acre patch of fine gravelly alluvium with some peat lying in a hollow in the dip slope of the Lincolnshire limestone. A mile north of the village of Waddingham, isolated among the fields, it was approached along a green lane with a big hedge on the north side which contained, I remember, a lot of purging buckthorn sought out by brimstone butterflies. It was a delightful place, traversed by a little stony-bedded stream, its steep banks studded here and there with the pale rosettes of butterwort. Where it broadened out into a marshy patch, clumps of black bog rush stood stiffly over the little white flowers of brookweed and mats of bog pimpernel smothered in pale pink flowers wide open in summer sunshine. Elsewhere in damp patches there were bold spikes of fragrant orchid - the dense flowered form – and ferny-leaved saw-wort like a refined version of knapweed, whilst ling dominated the drier areas which were enlivened by occasional plants of petty whin. For me the star of Waddingham Common was the exquisite grass-of-Parnassus, the flower that had first attracted me on that school visit to the Derbyshire Dales in the 1930s. By 1950 the Common with its fascinating assemblage of calcicole and calcifuge plants was the last example in Lincolnshire of this unusual habitat.

The site had not surprisingly figured prominently in our 1951 Report to the Nature Conservancy and was included in the first schedule of Lincolnshire SSSIs published later that year. It was also high on our list of priorities for action since it was already in the 1950s suffering from uncontrolled use which had resulted in refuse tipping and fires. Proper management could have prevented this misuse, but although the Parish Council was thought to own the land, its legal status and any common rights attached to it seemed to be obscure and complicated. In the early 1960s the Trust was in contact with Lindsey County Council about the status of the Common, suggesting that a scheme of management might be drawn up under the proposed Common Lands legislation. The chief clerk in the Clerk's Department, Mr B C Duddles – with whom the Trust had many amicable dealings at Gibraltar Point and elsewhere – was asked to investigate. In addition, early in 1963, we sought a meeting with the Parish Council to discuss the Common, but that meeting was overtaken by events.

It came as a complete surprise to the Trust and indeed to the County and Parish Councils, when in May 1963 Mr J Owen Day, a large farmer from nearby Redbourne, claimed to have acquired the freehold ownership of the Common and intended to drain and plough it with the assistance of a £12 an acre ploughing grant and other incentives then available from the Ministry of Agriculture.

We immediately alerted the Nature Conservancy and Lindsey County Council and made contact with Mr Day. He confessed that he too had believed the land to belong to the Parish, but in seeking to purchase it had discovered that it belonged to another owner. Who that owner was and the nature of his title to the land he always refused to reveal. In spite of SSSI designation the Conservancy was powerless to prevent the destruction of the site, and the Ministry of Agriculture, whilst expressing the hope that the site could be spared – the Ministry's Regional Controller made an unsuccessful personal appeal to Mr Day – stated that they were legally obliged to confirm the ploughing grant if the applicant insisted.

By this time the case had received a good deal of publicity and had been raised in the County Council by Alderman Cottingham, a farmer from a nearby parish who declared himself appalled by Mr Day's intentions and proposed that the County Council take action to prevent it. At our request Day agreed to a site meeting with us, and Dick Cornwallis and I met him and his solicitor on the site. We further explained its biological interest and we offered to purchase it or lease it, or in some other way to compensate Day for any financial loss. If those options were unacceptable to him, we offered to manage the site in agreement with him so as to control rabbits and other pests and to safeguard the sporting interest of his nearby property with which he seemed to be much concerned. Dick, who was at that time also the Chairman of the County Branch of the NFU, made a strong personal appeal to Day, reminding him that land ownership carried responsibilities to the environment, and that the Common in any case represented only a tiny fraction of the many hundreds of acres which he already owned. Day, however, was adamant that he must get rid of what he described as 'an eyesore infested with vermin'. There was clearly a yawning chasm of perception between us. Nevertheless, although we considered the site to be already an almost minimal size for viability, we suggested in a final attempt to salvage something that if an area of not less than six or seven acres was left the wet heath plants might have a chance to survive if a reasonably high water-table could be maintained. In response Day offered to leave no more than one acre. Both we and the Nature Conservancy considered that to be totally inadequate and useless. He must have known that that was in fact a derisory concession. I still remember that depressing meeting on a chilly November afternoon. There was though a slightly comic element about it with Day and his solicitor retiring out of our earshot from time to time to discuss their tactics.

When it became clear that all efforts were in vain, we issued a press release on 3 December 1963, in which we recounted the situation as it had developed and drew attention to the national significance of the case in the following terms:

> *Here then is a small piece of land of unique interest in Lincolnshire which Parliament has caused to be scheduled as a Site of Special Scientific Interest, but which is now to be destroyed with the aid of a Government grant from public funds.*
>
> *The value to the nation of Scheduled Ancient Monuments is recognised by the legal protection afforded to them. Yet the Sites of Special Scientific Interest are just as valuable and equally irreplaceable. They are the living museums and the open - air laboratories of our landscape; they are an integral part of our national heritage, a local and national asset which will be increasingly valued and appreciated. They too should be accorded some real measure of protection which will ensure their survival for the benefit, interest and delight of our own and future generations.*

The matter was immediately taken up by the local press and received prominent notice in the Daily Telegraph of 23 December 1963. Our statement was also sent to Lincolnshire MPs, and the Member for the Gainsborough constituency Marcus Kimball (later Lord Kimball) put down a question to the Minister of Agriculture asking what steps he took to see that ploughing grants were not given for SSSIs. In reply the Minister recalled the attempts made to find a solution to the Waddingham Common issue and said he was 'extremely disappointed' that the intervention of the Ministry's Regional Controller had failed to secure an agreement. He had no option, however, but to admit the drainage and ploughing for grant. As a result of this incident Kimball presented a Private Members Bill for the better protection of SSSIs, and although it fell at second reading it was an important stimulus to finding an acceptable method of providing additional protection for SSSIs. At their January 1964 meeting Lindsey County Council resolved to seek ways of safeguarding Waddingham Common, but that was in effect a gesture of disapproval of its destruction which by that time was too far advanced to be halted.

That it was a significant factor in the campaign which eventually secured a better deal for SSSIs was, I suppose, some small compensation for the destruction of the Common, but the loss to Lincolnshire's wildlife heritage was grievous and irreparable. Nothing else like it existed anywhere else in the county, and of its rare plants one is now extinct and two others confined to single sites. I drove along the road from Waddingham to Redbourne recently. The only way I could recognise the site was from the hedge along the track which used to lead to it. Otherwise its obliteration was total. It is as though it had never been.

Kimball's Bill required farmers to give six months notice to the Nature Conservancy of potentially damaging operations on an SSSI, the Conservancy to use the breathing space to persuade the farmer to desist or modify his intentions. The government refused to allow the Bill to proceed, but it brought the issue to the fore and triggered debate within government – even at cabinet level – which led eventually to the strengthening of SSSI protection, beginning with the very modest provisions for management agreements in the Countryside Act of 1968.

By resolutely opposing the Waddingham Common destruction we had dared to challenge the agricultural juggernaut at the peak of its ascendancy. In doing so we had also challenged the mighty power of the Ministry of Agriculture. According to John Sheail's book *Nature Conservation in Britain* (1998) one of the Ministry's senior officials complained of the 'hectoring and intransigent line' that naturalists were perceived to have taken over Waddingham Common. We had nevertheless further exposed the agricultural subsidisation policy which was destroying irreplaceable SSSIs in all parts of the country and which was increasingly recognised as being indefensible and against the national interest.

Manton Common

Over large tracts of north-west Lincolnshire from the Isle of Axholme to Market Rasen boulder clays are overlaid with wind-blown sands derived from the Bunter Sandstone measures west of the Trent. To the east and south-east of Scunthorpe these sands cover the oolite ridge in places. Of the extensive wet and dry heathlands which they produced – graphically described by 17th and 18th century travellers as being 'like the sands of Arabia' – only fragments, like the Trust's Linwood Warren and Scotton Common reserves, now remain. The heaths in the vicinity of Scunthorpe were extensively destroyed by ironstone mining and industrial encroachment from the 1880s onwards; much of the rest disappeared in the 1920s, 30s and 40s under a blanket of conifers, and almost everywhere else the remnants have been eroded by intensive agricultural usage since the 1940s. One of the most extensive areas to survive until after the Second World War was in the parishes of Messingham, Manton and Twigmoor. A thick deposit of sand over the limestone ridge had created a sand-dune system which, in the late 1940s, after the destruction of the Lakenheath dunes in Breckland, was probably the finest inland example in England. Below the scarp to the west lay a great tract of wet heath extending into the parish of Messingham, part of it used as a practice bombing range by the RAF during the Second World War. The

WADDINGHAM COMMON TO BE PLOUGHED

Naturalist's offer to buy land

MEMBERS OF THE Lincolnshire Naturalists' Trust alleged this week that the 22-acre Waddingham Common, of unique interest in Lincolnshire, had been "claimed" by a wealthy Redbourne farmer who proposes to plough it up with the aid of a Government grant of £12 an acre.

On Wednesday night Mr J. Owen Day, of Southfield Farm, Redbourne, told the Lincolnshire Times, "I did not claim it. I bought it."

Grass of Parnassus

TED SMITH

The Common, about eight miles from Brigg, is described by the Trust as "a peat bog over limestone, the only example of this kind of habitat left in Lincolnshire."

It has, they say, a most interesting and varied community of plants, a remarkably high proportion being extremely rare or localised in Lincolnshire.

"Some, like the grass of Parnassus, the fragrant orchid and the sawort, are beautiful flowers by any standard. Some, like the butterwort, which traps insects, are of outstanding biological interest.

"Others, like the black bog rush, are rare because they need specialised soil conditions A stream rising from a spring in the limestone provides another feature of interest."

That is what the Lincolnshire Naturalists' Trust find attractive about Waddingham Common, which, they say, was one of the first "Sites of Special Scietific Interest" to be scheduled in 1951.

Tipping

They agree that the Common has suffered in recent years from uncontrolled use which had resulted in refuse tipping and in a number of fires.

"Proper management of the Common could have prevented this misuse but the legal status of the land its ownership and the common rights attaching to it, seemed to be obscure and complicated."

Following a Ministry of Agriculture pronouncement that there was a legal obligation to confirm the ploughing grant, the Trust had this to say: "Here then is a small piece of land of unique interest in Lincolnshire which Parliament has caused to be scheduled as a Site of Special Scientific Interest but which is now to be destroyed with the aid of a Government grant from public funds."

Purposes of the Trust's statement was to make the point that just as the value to the nation of "scheduled ancient monuments" was recognised, so the living museums and open-air laboratories should be accorded some real measure of protection to ensure their survival.

On Wednesday, Mr Day agreed that he, too, had been under the impression for years that this was common land and it was not until he had had solicitors at work for three years that he found who owned it.

"My first thought was to clear an eyesore, not to acquire more land, for the Common was vermin-infested. That was what realy bothered me, because I had farmland adjoining."

Mr Day said he had originally thought that the land belonged to the parishioners. "We set about seeing how we could buy land from parishioners but there proved to be another owner. We negotiated and bought it."

The Trust had hoped that those difficulties could be cleared up and a scheme of management agreed under the proposed Common Lands legislation.

Earlier this year the Trust had sought a meeting with Waddington Parish Council to discuss the Common, and that would have taken place had not subsequent events intervened.

According the Trust's statement issued this week, "It came as a surprise to learn in May of this year that Mr J. Owen Day, of Redbourne, had claimed the ownership of the Common, and had applied to the Ministry of Agriculture for a £12 an acre ploughing grant."

Compensation

Members of the Trust met Mr Day on the site and asked him to survey it, offering to buy or lease the land "or in some other way to compensate Mr Day for any financial loss.

They further offered to manage it in agreement with him so as to safeguard the sporting interests of the nearby property with which he was concerned.

The Trust acknowledged that Mr Day had offered one acre of the Common to maintain the biological interest, but that was considered by the Trust and the Nature Conservancy to be "totally inadequate."

LINCS. M.P. PLANS A BILL TO SAVE NATURE SITES FROM PLOUGH

A LINCOLNSHIRE M.P. is hoping to promote a Private Member's Bill in the next session of Parliament which would protect sites of scientific and other interest from being ploughed up.

The reason, says Mr. Marcus Kimball, M.P. for Gainsborough, is because the present machinery for protecting such sites is not strong enough.

Mr. Kimball made his decision after correspondence with the Ministry of Agriculture over recent ploughing on Waddingham Common, near Kirton Lindsey.

He received a reply from Mr. James Scott-Hopkins, Parliamentary Secretary to the Minister.

Arrangements

In his letter, the minister explained the general arrangements they had with the Nature Conservancy over agricultural operations affecting sites of special scientific interest.

Details of the sites involved are supplied to the Ministry by the conservancy, which is always consulted by the Ministry when proposals which might adversely affect the site are received.

The conservancy could then negotiate with the occupier concerned so as to safeguard the interest in the site.

But the Ministry could only operate this machinery when given advance notice of the agricultural operation in question.

Types of grant

A farmer wanting the Part I (£5 an acre) ploughing grant did not have to tell the Ministry until after the ploughing had taken place. Previous notification was necessary only for the more expensive or complex operations, such as that for the Part II (£12 an acre) grant, or for help under the new Grassland Renovation Scheme.

In either case, said Mr. Scott-Hopkins, the Ministry had to be satisfied that the condition of the land called for a more costly type of operation and that the programme of treatment was technically sound.

In the case of Waddingham Common this machinery was used fully. The occupier asked for a £12 an acre grant and a meeting was arranged on the site in an effort to reach some agreement acceptable to the occupier, the Conservancy and the Lincolnshire Naturalists' Trust.

No agreement

Agreement was not reached at that stage. Nor was it reached later when the Ministry's Regional Controller was called in.

The minister wrote: "We were extremely disappointed when this final approach also failed to lead to any settlement. But this was as far as we could go. In the circumstances, we had no option but to admit the ploughing for grant."

Mr. Scott-Hopkins said the problem could arise in areas not only of scientific interest, but also in national parks, nature reserves and sites of outstanding beauty.

The ministry could not, however, use present agricultural legislation either to protect these sites or disqualify them from grants to which an occupier was entitled under the conditions of Ministry schemes.

Made clear

Mr. Kimball told the Evening Telegraph that the minister's letter made it perfectly clear that in the case of Waddingham Common all possible negotiations were carried out before the ploughing grant was given.

The lesson to be learned was that the machinery for protecting sites of scientific interest "was not strong enough."

Since 1960, he said, 50 sites of great importance to nature conservancy had been damaged in this way, including Manton Warren, near Kirton Lindsey.

Consultations

In Mr. Kimball's view, the law would have to be amended. He intends to consult the conservancy, the Lincolnshire Naturalists' Trust, the Council for Nature, and other bodies interested in conservation.

He will then promote his Bill, to which he is confident Parliament will give sympathetic support, in view of the general growing public awareness about the need to conserve what is left of our natural heritage.

Grimsby Evening Telegraph
21 January 1964

whole area was one of great physiographical and biological interest and it was only narrowly rejected by the Wildlife Conservation Special Committee as one of their proposed Scientific Areas.

When members of the Nature Conservancy visited Lincolnshire in 1951 the then Director-General, Cyril Diver, and Professor Alfred Steers, looked at the area and called on Mr E H Davey of Greetwell Hall who owned most of Manton Warren. Davey gave them an undertaking that he would not reclaim any of the Warren without consulting the Nature Conservancy, yet within two years he had ploughed a large area of it north of the Greetwell-Messingham road with the encouragement of the Ministry of Agriculture's principal County Officer, but without any consultation with the Nature Conservancy. After cropping with rye for a couple of years this land was abandoned, reverting not to its former cover of sand sedge and heather but to rosebay willowherb, docks, nettles and thistles, a condition in which it remained for many years.

When Dick Cornwallis and I took Max Nicholson, the Director-General of the Nature Conservancy, on a brief tour of north Lincolnshire in April 1955, much of the heathland below the scarp was still intact and represented the largest area of wet heath of its kind in the county. Rare plants like bog asphodel, sundews and marsh gentian occurred in some abundance, and there were nesting snipe, redshank and curlew. Its subsequent total destruction was not a single catastrophic event like the elimination of Waddingham Common; it went on piecemeal for a number of years to final drainage and ploughing in 1974. Ironically it was Mr J Owen Day of the Waddingham incident who put an end to it. The land had been used for rough grazing by his uncle Mr R E Day who had been concerned particularly for the gentians and had refrained from reclaiming nearly 100 acres within the Manton South SSSI. When his nephew took over the land in February 1974, however, he immediately proposed a scheme to drain the remaining wet heath, including the SSSI, and applied to MAFF for a drainage grant.

After our experience with Mr Day at Waddingham Common, we left the negotiations largely to Nature Conservancy Council officers led by Michael Schofield, the Deputy Regional Officer for East Anglia, although we kept in close touch through our Conservation Officer Ray Collier. The negotiations were complex and frustrating, but followed a predictable pattern. In order to secure the drainage grant, Day offered to leave five acres (later extended to eight) out of an SSSI which by that time had already been reduced to about seventy-five acres. The area he offered in the south-east corner of the site did not include the best of the wet heath plant communities nor was it likely that adequate water levels could have been maintained in an isolated patch in the middle of a great area of arable. A scheme for that purpose proposed by Bob Myers, MAFF's ebullient Regional Drainage Engineer, would have been complicated (possibly necessitating pumping) and the cost of it would have fallen on the Trust. The Nature Conservancy Council's position, which we entirely endorsed, was that a minimum of twenty acres would be necessary to offer any chance of retaining wet heath conditions, and an optimum size would be that of the whole SSSI of seventy-five acres. Day refused to improve his offer beyond eight acres; the NCC refused to de-notify the SSSI, and in accordance with new inter-departmental regulations, agreed since the Waddingham affair, MAFF had to refuse him a drainage grant on the SSSI, although he went ahead without it and destroyed the lot.

By 1960 excavation of sand had begun in the north-west corner of the

Common and this proceeded until the late 70s leaving the complex of pits which now form the Trust's Messingham Sand Quarry reserve. There was more sand extraction to the north of the Messingham-Scawby road, but up the slope to the east some patches of heathland survived adjoining the Twigmoor Woods where until the 1950s the lakes were the breeding site of one of the largest black-headed gull colonies in Britain. This area, the Manton-Twigmoor SSSI, belongs to a very old Lincolnshire family, the Nelthorpes of nearby Scawby. The late Colonel Oliver Sutton Nelthorpe was the President of the Trust from 1951 to 1964. On the crest of the ridge parts of Manton Warren have remained reasonably intact although the once mobile sand-dunes have long since been stabilised.

Messingham Heath

To the west of Messingham village on either side of the road known as Carcar Lane there was another tract of wet and dry heath which was probably the finest of them all. Unfortunately it was not known to Dick Cornwallis and me when we prepared our 1951 report, and it was not until 1964 or 1965 that it was brought to the Trust's attention by local members Joe Duddington and Frank Brazier. By that time the Nature Conservancy had a warden naturalist, Martin Ball, stationed in Lincolnshire and living on the Saltfleetby-Theddlethorpe NNR. Martin and I inspected this site in July 1965 and said in our report: "We came away with the impression that the site is of great ecological value and top priority for conservation". On the south side of the Lane there was undulating mainly dry heath with sand-dunes rising to thirty feet and occasional blow-outs. Sand sedge, sheep's fescue, bell heather, ling, harebell, devil's-bit scabious and sheep's sorrel formed a turf close-cropped by rabbits. Lichens and bare sand patches provided an ideal habitat for the grayling butterfly in one of its very few Lincolnshire localities. These masters of disguise were on the wing in some numbers on the day of our visit, flying rapidly over the heath and then suddenly disappearing as they alighted.

The best of the wet heath lay on the north side of the Lane. Here every depression in the hummocky sand-dune surface had interesting bog communities growing usually through a cushion of bog moss. In some there was marsh cinquefoil, bog bean and marsh violet; in others cottongrass, marsh arrowgrass, bog pimpernel and hard fern. Bog asphodel and round-leaved sundew occurred locally, and in one or two hollows some of the finest specimens of marsh gentians I have ever seen. These boggy patches were interspersed with occasional birch and oak and there was a small birch wood at the western end. There were wheatears on the dry heath where they may well have nested, and Duddington had recorded the large heath butterfly there on what was then its most southerly station in eastern England.

The Trust urged the Nature Conservancy to schedule the site - about 140 acres of it - as an SSSI without delay. If that were done the Trust was prepared to approach the owners and tenants with a view to purchase or agreement which would safeguard its interest. The scheduling was done promptly, in October 1965, but early contact with the owner of the northern section, farmer Mr J Trought of Sandhowes Farm, was inauspicious. Whilst not unfriendly he made it plain straightway that he intended to reclaim and bring all the heathland into production over the next few years. The only concession he was able to offer was that the wettest area would be the last to go! Since reclamation would scarcely be economically feasible for him without government aid, the Nature Conservancy expressed the hope that MAFF would refrain from approving grant at least over the best parts of the site.

Within three months of the scheduling Trought applied for planning permission to extract sand over the whole of the site in his possession (a small area belonged elsewhere). In a letter of 1 March 1966 seeking the Nature Conservancy's views on the application, the Lindsey County Planning Officer, Robert Stirling, said that although it was an application to extract sand, "the real purpose of the operation is to restore the land to some agricultural use by the removal of accumulations of blown sand. That process", he went on, "has been carried out most successfully in other parts of the County, and from a purely planning point of view I have no objections to the proposal". The last remark of course caused great consternation, and I wrote to the Planning Officer on 11 March reiterating the Trust's strong support of the SSSI designation and expressing surprise at his statement to the Nature Conservancy that he would have no objection to the application from the "purely planning point of view". Did he not regard notification by a government agency of special scientific interest as a planning consideration? I further reminded him that at a meeting with Martin Ball and me the previous August his Deputy, Mr N Dickenson, told us that it was unlikely that the Planning Authority would grant permission for sand extraction at Messingham in the foreseeable future, especially if they allowed it (which they did) on the very considerable area of nearby Manton Common for which permission had at that time been sought. I asked that the Authority should not give extraction permission over any of the SSSI. In reply the Planning Officer assured me that the views of the Trust and the Nature Conservancy would be taken into account as a planning consideration in determining the application.

On 31 March 1966 the East Anglian Regional Officer of the Nature Conservancy, Dr Bruce Forman, his Deputy Michael Schofield, Martin Ball and I attended a site meeting at Messingham with Mr Williams of the Planning Department. We met Mr Trought who again explained his intention to excavate the whole of the area in the next twenty years. He would be prepared to leave the best piece of bog undisturbed provided he was granted planning permission for the remainder. However, if that were refused he would simply fill in the hollows and reclaim the lot for agriculture. It was the kind of rather crude blackmail with which we were already becoming familiar and against which we were totally powerless. In an attempt to save the small area we withdrew our objection to sand extraction on the rest of Trought's land, but since he was still unwilling to consider selling or leasing any land to the Trust or to enter into any kind of agreement the future looked bleak for the whole of the northern half of the SSSI which at the time of our visit was being grossly over-grazed and degraded by some 200 head of cattle. Nonetheless, we clearly identified the best patch of bog where marsh gentian and bog asphodel grew and over the next few years we kept a close watch on it.

When Dick Cornwallis and Mike Schofield visited Trought again in October 1967, the selected bog area was still intact, but now surrounded by sand extraction operations which were rapidly destroying the rest of the site. Indeed when Chris Walker, the NC's Assistant Regional Officer for Lincolnshire, visited the site in May 1972 he reported that the whole of the northern part of the SSSI was "virtually destroyed". Two years later when a further massive application was made to extract sand on other parts of the SSSI north of Carcar Lane it was not opposed by the Nature Conservancy. The applicants at that time stated their intention of creating lakes for fishing or water sports or both. Although the small boggy area was again excluded from the application, the NCC's Assistant Regional Officer, Derek Ungley (following local government re-organisation our South Humberside area was by that time in the NCC's north-east region) reported that: "the wildlife value of this strip may have deteriorated because of the drainage effects of nearby operations to the east of it. I am doubtful about its future for wildlife if quarrying takes place immediately to the north and west of it".

The continued degradation of the whole site was now inexorable and predictable. In 1977 Clugston Reclamation Ltd, a subsidiary of Clugstons of Scunthorpe, applied successfully to tip industrial waste on part of it. Driving along Carcar Lane, as I did about that time, the scene on the northern side was totally unrecognisable from what it had been when I first knew it little more than ten years earlier. Great heaps of sand, processing machinery, bulldozers, lorries, site offices, refuse tips: a chaotic wasteland. And yet miraculously the boggy area of little more than an acre with its marsh gentians and bog asphodels was still surviving in dwindling isolation, as county botanist Irene Weston reported to the Trust in August 1977. We now made renewed efforts to obtain some real security for this area first by talking to the General Manager of the Clugston Company, and when that yielded little, by writing to the Chairman of the parent company, Leonard Clugston, who was at that time a member of the Trust Council. Enquiry to him from the Trust's Conservator, Stuart Crooks, about the possibility of some management agreement, if not sale or lease to the Trust, received no reply. In 1983 Clugstons sold to British Industrial Sands Limited part of their Messingham property which included the little area which they still euphemistically called 'the nature reserve'. It was obviously inconvenient for BIS's planned extraction proposals and they included it in a planning application to which the NCC and the Trust both objected. BIS argued, correctly no doubt, that the area would deteriorate further because of operations around it and they proposed transplanting some of the wet heath flora to a 'restored' site nearby. When the Trust and the Nature Conservancy Council maintained their objections, BIS commissioned a study of the area – including the feasibility of transplanting and re-establishing some of the vegetation elsewhere – from Dr D M Parker of the Environmental Advisory Unit of the University of Liverpool. Dr Parker concluded that the site was in a "degenerating condition due to a drop in the water table caused by extraction of sand in adjacent quarries. This has resulted in drying out of the site ... and an increase in weed invasion into the natural vegetation". I wonder how much he was paid for that blinding revelation? Having the wishes of his clients in mind, no doubt, he concluded that transplantation of important vegetation was feasible. This 'expert' report was submitted by BIS to Humberside County Council in support of their planning application. The end had come at last for the pathetic little remnant of the northern part of the former SSSI. There was no point in continuing the struggle and both the Trust and NCC reluctantly accepted the inevitable and withdrew their opposition to the BIS application. It was a condition of the subsequent permission that they transplant some of the wet heath vegetation, and this was transferred to the Trust's Messingham Sand Quarry reserve (which was leased from BIS), where for a few years the marsh gentians struggled to survive.

It was another melancholy saga. Once again we stood no chance against massive commercial interests and we wasted nearly fifteen years in the attempt. The SSSI system was again shown to be completely toothless. With better planning of the use of mineral resources from the start and determination on the part of the Planning Authority, much if not all of the northern part of the SSSI could have been spared. Did the Planning Officer of Lindsey County Council in 1966 really believe that Mr Trought's intention in seeking permission for sand extraction was simply to restore the land to agricultural use? Was he being extraordinarily naive or was this just dressing up an extraction proposal in the guise of what he thought was a currently more acceptable agricultural purpose? One can hardly blame Mr Trought for threatening to destroy the site by perfectly legal means if he did not get his way on his sand extraction application. He no doubt did well out the whole business - even his farmhouse was eventually pulled down to extract the sand underneath it! And what of the powerful exploiters of the sand resource? Clugstons, while professing concern for conservation, were prepared to make no significant concessions. British Industrial Sands in their anxiety to be rid of the irritant of the little relict area, brought in Dr Parker to lend scientific respectability to their purpose. It was all a waste - waste of a splendid site and all its natural treasures, waste of our efforts in endless frustrating meetings, reports and representations, and perhaps a waste of my time in recording it.

The area of Messingham Heath SSSI to the south of Carcar Lane fared somewhat better than that to the north - at least some of it survived after a fashion. It belonged to a Dr H Jackson of Scunthorpe. His son was a builder and was believed to be interested in extracting sand, although no planning permission for this was ever sought. The land was tenanted by a farmer, Mr J Green of Carcar Farm. On the first contact between Mr Green and the Trust and the Nature Conservancy in 1965 he indicated his intention to bring some of the heath into agricultural production. He had in fact already begun drainage operations at the western end of the area which was to be scheduled. At a meeting with Martin Ball in October 1965 Mr Green explained his intention to drain, plough and use the land for pasture and arable farming. However, some thirty acres of dry sandy heath would be left untouched apart from a possible fertiliser application. It would be used for rough grazing. Like Mr Trought, Mr Green was unwilling to consider any Trust involvement by way of lease or purchase even if the owner was willing. In fact communications with Dr Jackson were always unanswered. In October 1967 Dick Cornwallis, then Chairman of the Trust, and Mike Schofield of NCC met Mr T Hardy of the Land Commissioner's office in Lincoln on the site, and discussed his plans for reclamation with Mr Green who was described by Schofield as 'pleasant and co-operative'. He repeated his intention to plough and re-seed part of the site but to graze the remainder with cattle. In July 1969, however, it was reported to the Trust that there was a herd of pigs enclosed on the latter area. Visits by Barrie Wilkinson, the Trust's Reserves Officer, on 25 July and John Blackwood of NCC on 6 August confirmed that some damage was being caused - up to 20% of the ground grubbed up according to Blackwood. Mr Green intended to extend the pig enclosures believing that disturbance of the soil encouraged fresh growth of herbage. He proposed, he said, to follow up with sheep or cattle. In spite of that assurance, however, Chris Walker of NC reported in May 1972 that "to the south of the road, most of the SSSI is occupied by pigs. Rooting has done considerable damage to the extreme eastern edge of

Remaining part of Messingham Heath SSSI.

*Grayling, confined to
a few of the north-west
Lincolnshire Heaths.*

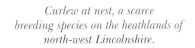

*Curlew at nest, a scarce
breeding species on the heathlands of
north-west Lincolnshire.*

143

Samphire beds – the first coloniser of the marsh covered by every tide.

BARRIE WILKINSON

Mature upper marsh with sea purslane on the creek banks.

GEOFF TRINDER

Saltmarshes

Freiston Shore with a reclamation bank building in the distance (left), 1980.

TED SMITH

144

the area and also along the southern boundary. The area nearer the road is less extensively damaged".

Walker and Wilkinson then recommended extending the southern part of the SSSI to include an area of undamaged wet heath at the western end, but in spite of further urging by the Trust this was not done until 1984 when the ruined northern part was finally deleted. Meantime Mr Green continued to use pigs alternating them with horses or ponies. In spite of its ill treatment the sandy heath survived and in 1978 and 1980 the Trust tried again to influence the treatment of the site by another visit to Mr Green by Stuart Crooks and Barrie Wilkinson, and by seeking a meeting with the elusive Dr Jackson who once again failed to respond. In 1991 a new character appeared on the scene, a Mr R W Price who informed NCC of his intention to seek planning permission for a golf course which would cover the whole of the revised SSSI. His proposal got short shrift from Helen Stace, NCC's Conservation Officer for south Humberside, in the following terms: "In the light of the high scientific interest of the site" she wrote "and the losses already sustained, I regret to inform you that I would be obliged to object to any planning application to extend the golf course on to the SSSI". The threat was averted and what remained of the original Messingham Heath SSSI survived into somewhat more secure times.

Saltmarshes

Saltmarshes are not the most immediately appealing wild places. They seem to have none of that variety of colourful flowers that make meadows and downland and even sand dunes so attractive. My impression of saltmarsh on that first late August visit to Gibraltar Point was of a uniform grey-green expanse of vegetation, simply the foreground to the more exciting mudflats beyond with their flocks of waders which were the main objective of my visit. In winter when the marshes can seem bleak and desolate places even the muted colours of summer drain away and leave bleached and withered stems and grasses. For the 18th century poet and parson George Crabbe they reflected the drab and miserable lives of the poor in the Suffolk coast villages:

> Here a grave flora scarcely deigns to bloom
> Nor wears a rosy bloom, nor sheds perfume:
> The few dull flowers that o'er the place are spread
> Partake the nature of their fenny bed.

I soon discovered that there is a lot more to saltmarshes than my first impression or Crabbe's dismal description conveyed. The plants adapted to periodic immersion by the tides have their own distinctive characters, like the sea purslane under whose sprawling grey leaves on the creek banks shore crabs scuttle for shelter – hence its local name of 'crabgrass'; or like the fine silvery leaves of sea wormwood with their clean aromatic smell; or plants like the creeping sea milkwort and the sea spurreys which stud the shorter turf with tiny pink flowers. Then in late July and early August the quiet colour of the saltmarsh is transformed into purple carpets of sea lavender and mauve patches of sea aster in bloom. And it is not only the colour, the flowers are alive with bees, hoverflies, butterflies and other insects.

There is another feature of saltmarsh which I came to value when I began to teach the rudiments of ecology to adult students: the living illustration of how vegetation changes in succession in response to a changing environment. In addition, compared with many other habitats, there are relatively few plant species that you need to identify to follow the succession. From the earliest colonists of the mudflats, the seablite and the glasswort (the Lincolnshire 'samphire'), you pass through various stages of the succession to the upper parts of the marsh reached only by the highest spring tides – that is of course if the saltmarsh has not been truncated prematurely by reclamation.

The birds of the saltmarsh have a special appeal. In spring there is the rapturous display of the redshank, its yodelling call uttered on bowed and quivering wings; the chorus of skylarks which was one of my first impressions of the marsh at Gibraltar Point; the 'parachute' song flight of the meadow pipit, and in contrast the inconsequential little song of the handsome reed bunting. In winter, finches, snow buntings and shorelarks forage for seed among the stems of glasswort and seablite; further out on the shore the brent geese 'talk' incessantly as they feed on the algae which coats the mud, whilst short-eared owls, the real spirits of the winter saltings, hunt in buoyant and effortless flight.

The saltmarshes support many other creatures, of course, some of them specially adapted to living in a habitat subject to periodic saltwater inundation. One such, the little scarce pug moth, a species largely confined to Lincolnshire and Norfolk, feeds on sea wormwood. We first found it at Gibraltar Point by lying flat on the ground to see the wriggling caterpillars silhouetted against the sky. Many spiders also live on the saltmarsh, and there is an abundant population of voles who retreat to higher ground in advance of tidal flooding. Overall, saltmarshes with their rich flora and fauna are an essential element in the whole intertidal ecosystem and a natural resource of the highest importance.

Out beyond the beds of glasswort and seablite the tidal mudflats teem with invertebrate life, most of it living below the surface: molluscs of many shapes and sizes, and marine worms tube-dwelling and free moving, all of them in vast numbers and all of them food for that great group of birds known as waders. From tall curlews to diminutive sanderlings all the waders have beaks of length and shape to pick or probe for their prey. These adaptations, their flock behaviour and their long distance migrations, which in many cases take them from arctic breeding grounds to winter in West Africa: all these contribute to making them one of the most attractive and fascinating group of birds. I have always been captivated by them from my early visits to Gibraltar Point. To ensure their future is a local, national and international responsibility.

Whilst there are extensive and developing saltmarshes on the north-east Lincolnshire coast from Saltfleetby to Tetney, those in The Wash are of special importance being the largest expanse of the habitat in Britain. That importance is now clearly recognised by a variety of international designations which give them the best possible security. When the Trust came into being in 1948 and for many years afterwards there was no such recognition or protection. The saltmarshes have been subject to reclamation at intervals since Roman times, but the frequency with which it took place had depended on favourable conditions for farming, and the extent had been determined by the cost to the developer and by the limitations of manual labour. Comparatively little had been done, for example, in the years of agricultural depression from the 1870s to the 1930s, but after the Second World War the pace accelerated dramatically, stimulated by Government policies and subsidies and by the availability of powerful earth-moving machinery.

In the past the long intervals between reclamations had allowed new saltmarsh to develop through its vegetation stages in front of a new bank. From the 1940s onwards not only were many of the particular reclamations on a large scale – one of the first at Wainfleet, Friskney and Wrangle in 1948 took in more than 400 hectares – they also took place at much more frequent intervals long before the redeveloping saltmarsh had reached maturity. By the 1970s old saltmarsh, the richest phase biologically, survived in the Wash in only two or three places, notably between the Witham and Welland outfalls. That was recognised as a serious loss to conservation, but the effects of the process on the whole ecosystem of the Wash was not fully appreciated until the 1970s.

In preparing the Trust's report and recommendations to the Nature Conservancy on Areas of Scientific Interest in Lincolnshire in 1950, saltmarshes posed a particular dilemma. There was no question of their scientific importance; the problem was their extent and the fact that reclamation was an accepted procedure which had never been seriously challenged. Faced with the same problem a few years before, the NRIC Sub-Committee, having named the whole coastline from Cleethorpes to the county boundary in the Wash as a Scheduled Area, recommended two particular sections for their saltmarsh habitat: Friskney Flats described as "typical 'salting' with littoral and saltmarsh associations", and Frampton/Kirton marshes where the "flora association varies from the above in many respects".

In 1950 there was no designation available to the Nature Conservancy for extensive areas like the Wash saltmarshes, and no particular site could be guaranteed to be safe from reclamation. Much of the Friskney Flats, for example, which the NRIC Sub-Committee had recommended, had already been eliminated by the 1948 reclamation. We decided nevertheless that one area of saltmarsh should be included in our recommendations to the Nature Conservancy in the hope that it could be kept "in its natural condition". It was indicative of our acceptance of the inevitability of further reclamation that one of the reasons we advanced for the preservation of at least one area was that "the results of observation and research in such an area might well be of value when applied to reclamation problems. It is obviously necessary, in this respect, that the conditions in which saltmarsh accretion takes place should be adequately investigated". The area we chose was Freiston Shore, a somewhat arbitrary selection perhaps (Frampton Marsh would have been a better choice) made on the grounds that it was an area well known to naturalists and was near to Pilgrim College in Boston which was used by the University of Nottingham as an Adult Education Centre and as a field centre headquarters for students of the University Department of Botany. For that reason it could be expected, we suggested, that considerable study of the area of saltmarsh would be made. More in hope than expectation perhaps we recommended "that the area be excluded from any further drainage scheme".

The Nature Conservancy accepted the recommendation and included Freiston Shore in the first SSSI schedule for the County of Holland in 1951. We subsequently pressed the Conservancy to join us in exploring the possibilities of protecting the area from reclamation suggesting that it would serve as a useful test case. As a starting point we arranged a meeting in October 1952 with

Gilbert Buchner, the influential Chief Engineer of the Witham Fourth Drainage Board which covered a large area of the Wash coast. He had been in charge of the 1948 reclamation of Wainfleet, Friskney and Wrangle. I attended for the Trust and Dr Verona Conway, one of its first senior scientists, represented the Nature Conservancy. Buchner listened sympathetically to our case, but we came away with little hope of achieving anything significant. In any case decisions on reclamation in any particular area lay with the frontagers and with the Crown Estates Commissioners who owned reclamation rights in much of the Wash and who were themselves undertaking large scale projects. Dr Conway's view after that meeting was that any further representations on the issue would be fruitless, a conclusion with which I reluctantly had to agree. Within the next few years reclamation of Freiston Shore by HM Prison Service from their North Sea Camp was started, being completed in 1981.

When the Holland SSSI schedule was revised in 1959 Freiston Shore was deleted "on the grounds that it is impractical to resist the agricultural reclamation which is taking place there". The Nature Conservancy's inability to offer any protection to the Wash saltmarshes at that stage was further reflected in the 1968 SSSI revision where they stated "The Wash is obviously an area of outstanding National and International importance, but it is impossible to define any particular area within it for the purposes of this Schedule".

The Trust was not entirely helpless in this situation. We had one notable success. We had long realised that the surest way to safeguard an area for nature conservation was to be in possession of it, preferably by owning freehold but by lease if that was not possible. So in 1976 we seized an opportunity to negotiate a twenty-one year lease from the then Anglian Water Authority of some 170 hectares of saltmarsh at Frampton, the area adjoining the River Witham outfall, known as the Scalp. This is some of the most mature saltmarsh in The Wash rich in plant life and of exceptional importance not only for migratory and wintering waders and wildfowl but for breeding birds also. It held a large black-headed gull colony – at that time the largest in Britain – common terns and an exceptionally high density of redshanks as well as oystercatchers, skylarks, meadow pipits and reed buntings.

The South Lincolnshire Wildfowlers' Club already had shooting rights over the area and we entered into a joint lease with them and a management agreement with the grazing tenant. We were satisfied that the wildfowling was responsibly managed and that continued grazing by cattle was a desirable form of management. Members of the Club formed a valuable nucleus of volunteer wardens for the reserve. A few years later in 1984 the Anglian Water Authority agreed to sell the freehold of the reserve to the Trust for a sum acceptable to the District Valuer. Wildfowling rights were let to the existing Club who continued to participate in the care and wardening of the reserve.

We were anxious to expand the reserve by the acquisition of adjoining land to a size which would justify the appointment of a full-time warden. We were aware that the RSPB was interested in acquiring land on the Lincolnshire side of the Wash, and we were disappointed that they failed to attend a meeting early in 1984 called by the NCC to discuss a tripartite strategy for acquisition. When a piece of adjoining marsh came up for sale soon afterwards we were prepared to make a bid, but refrained from doing so – perhaps mistakenly – because we understood that the RSPB, not being dependent on external funding, was willing to exceed the DV's valuation, something which we could not afford to do. In the event, however, the DV accepted their figure and they received a grant from the NCC. When another nearby piece came onto the market shortly afterwards we made an offer, but were outbid by the RSPB who claimed to be unaware that the other offer was from the Trust.

This rather sorry situation led to some slightly prickly correspondence between me and my old NCC friend Ian Prestt who had become Director of the RSPB. I urged that we make a new attempt to reach an understanding about acquisition in the Wash as a whole and about attitudes to the important issue of wildfowling which the RSPB were anxious to exclude from their properties. In the end we reached an amicable working arrangement about a common grazing policy on our respective marshes, and it was, of course, satisfying that one of the most important saltmarsh areas in The Wash had been safeguarded for conservation.

Meantime reclamation elsewhere continued apace through the 1950s, 60s and 70s taking in almost 3000 more hectares of saltmarsh, including the area opposite Gibraltar Point to which I referred in an earlier chapter. In the early 1960s a feasibility study was mounted to examine the proposal for the creation of a freshwater reservoir in the southern part of the Wash. The project was eventually abandoned, but it provided resources to carry out a great deal of basic research which shed new light on the history of the Wash, the process of accretion and the wildlife interest. That knowledge, together with a growing realisation that the intensive agricultural production of the previous thirty years was not sustainable, encouraged conservation bodies to mount a challenge to the reclamation process. The opportunity came in 1980 at a Public Inquiry into an application for planning permission to enclose 200 acres of saltmarsh at Gedney Drove End which the Secretary of State had decided to 'call in' to consider the national implications of the reclamation versus conservation issue. It was thus widely accepted that this would be a test case.

The applicants, supported by the Ministry of Agriculture, put forward the customary claim that there was a national need for more agricultural land and that in any case reclamation caused little long-term damage to wildlife. The objectors had formed a consortium of the Nature Conservancy Council, the Trust and the RSPB and were represented by a barrister, Mr David Mole. His first witness Mr John Bowers, an economist, showed that whilst reclamation would provide a valuable capital asset for the developer, the benefits to the nation were negligible. Most if not all the crops likely to be grown on the land were already in surplus in Europe. We neither needed the extra crops nor would they help Britain's balance of payments. The contention that little damage was being caused to wildlife by reclamation was attacked by Mr F J T Kestner, formerly of the Hydraulics Research Station, who explained that the amount of silt in the Wash is limited and that, contrary to popular belief, little new silt is derived from rivers or the sea. So although saltmarsh reformed rapidly outside new reclamation banks, the effect in the absence of adequate sediment replenishment is a progressive reduction in the area of intertidal mudflats on which so much of the wildlife depends including the internationally important migratory and wintering populations of wildfowl and waders. That view was reinforced by NCC scientists who showed that reclamation not only impoverishes the saltmarsh habitat by removing the older more interesting stages of its development, but that it was also removing intertidal areas permanently. The RSPB demonstrated the European importance of the Wash for birds including both wildfowl and waders, and species like redshank, skylark and reed bunting which nest on the saltmarsh. The Trust's Director Stuart Crooks explained the importance of the Wash for education, research and recreation in a Lincolnshire as well as a national and international context.

After about twelve months consideration the Secretary of State decided, in accordance with his Inspector's recommendation, that planning permission for the proposed reclamation should be refused. This decision coincided with the preparation of a consultation draft of Lincolnshire County Council's Coast Subject Plan which was inevitably much concerned with the reclamation issue. To provide an opportunity for an expression of views by all the parties concerned the County Council convened a discussion meeting in Spalding in May 1981. The Trust was strongly represented at the meeting by David Robinson, Stuart Crooks, Don Wright and myself. The views and arguments were to a large extent a repetition of those put forward at the Gedney Drove End Inquiry in the previous year. The draft Subject Plan subsequently proposed a total ban on reclamation on the north-east Lincolnshire coast – there had been no significant reclamation there since the middle of the 19th century – and a five-year moratorium on the Lincolnshire section of the Wash. This was endorsed by the Planning and Recreation Committee of the Council, but the powerful Policy Committee proposed to replace it by policies which would place no restrictions whatever on reclamation. This was announced in a County Council press release on 8 February 1982. The Trust responded with a press statement the following day expressing astonishment and concern at this attempt to overturn the Planning Committee's recommendation which was based on a careful assessment of all the evidence put forward at the Gedney Drove End Inquiry and the Spalding Consultation Meeting. The Trust then wrote to every County Councillor individually seeking their support for the Planning Committee's original recommendation. By an overwhelming majority the Council voted to retain the Planning Committee's proposal.

At the formal Local Inquiry into the Coast Subject Plan in June 1983 the Trust made a written submission, and evidence on behalf of the Gedney Drove End consortium of NCC, Trust and RSPB was given by Dr Patrick Doody of the NCC's Scientific Team and a leading specialist in coastal ecosystems. In spite of renewed objections from MAFF and others, the Inspector recommended no alteration to the Coast Subject Plan and the moratorium on reclamation came into effect. The Gedney Drove End decision, combined with the changing economic situation in the agricultural industry, had in fact effectively put an end to future reclamation in The Wash which now has an impressive array of international conservation designations and a separate management plan agreed by national and local authorities and by commercial, conservation and recreational users. That hard-won planning decision was also another indication that the writing was on the wall for the inflexible policies and die-hard attitudes which had dominated rural land use policies for the previous thirty years. The days of the Juggernaut were numbered!

A somewhat ironic footnote to all this is that Freiston Shore, which we had sought unsuccessfully to protect in the early 1950s, has now become the first substantial area in the Wash to be returned to intertidal saltmarsh and mudflats. It was acquired by the RSPB and re-flooded in 2002 after demolition of the sea bank in accordance with the Environment Agency's coastal realignment strategy.

This is obviously a cause for satisfaction, but in view of our earlier involvement in the site I cannot suppress the rather churlish feeling that it would have been fitting for the Trust to be able to undertake the project. In fact once again we had no knowledge of the negotiations which led to the RSPB's acquisition.

Woodlands

Most of my early exploration of the natural world was in woodlands within cycling distance of home. There were five or six of the ancient woods of the Middle Marsh which I frequently visited either with permission or in spite of 'keep out' notices and equally forbidding gamekeepers. Though I might have been to the same wood many times there was always a sense of eager anticipation of the sights and sounds and smells of the woodland. Spring and autumn were my favourite seasons for the woods. By July the colours were reduced to a dull greenery and the heavy foliage had become oppressive. I liked the winter where you could see the structure of the wood and the shape of the trees and the colour and texture of bark and twigs, but you were more conspicuous then and the feeling of seclusion was lost.

There were the familiar sights of the seasons: hazel catkins dangling in the February breeze; the ice white flowers of blackthorn against dark stems; the subdued colour contrasts of primrose and wood anemone in the recently cut coppices; the purple haze of the bluebell carpets; the autumn flushing of dogwood and field maple; the woodcock springing up at one's approach and weaving away through the trees. Sounds were just as evocative. Hearing impairment in old age makes me realise how important they were, the birdsongs and calls: the whispered cadence of the willow warbler, the brilliant virtuoso performance of the blackcap as if to an audience, and in contrast the quiet mellow song of the garden warbler singing as if to itself. The woods were full of scents too: the elusive fragrance of primroses, the musty sweetness of moschatel that most nostalgic of scents which I still seek out every spring.

Some particular encounters stand out in the memory like the first silver-washed fritillary described in my first chapter. Another I remember was my first lesser-spotted woodpecker. It was an early April morning in Mother Wood, a day of sunshine and squally wintry showers, the little bird moving about in the ash tops all black and white bars and much smaller than I had envisaged. I remember too where I found my first broad-leaved helleborine in Muckton Wood. When the Trust acquired the wood in 1983 I was able to take Barrie Wilkinson, the Trust's Reserves Manager, to the exact spot although I had not been there for thirty years or more. The plant was still there and flourishing! Another springtime recollection was cycling out after dark to Hoplands Wood where I had heard a nightingale during the day. I stood just inside the gate and listened to the bird in full song. In the soft stillness of the night it sounded magnificent. After a while a cyclist passed along the road; I half expected him to stop and listen. He passed on apparently oblivious to that thrilling voice!

Woodland memories like these keep flooding back, but I little realised then in the 1930s that the woods that I loved were already suffering a radical change of character. The rides were well kept, but the coppice-with-standards system on which they had been managed for many centuries was falling into disuse – had indeed already done so in many cases. The demand for small wood from the hazel and ash coppices for farm and estate uses – and earlier for mud-and-stud cottage building – had faded away. The coppices were becoming outgrown and the habitat diversity which their periodic cutting had produced was greatly impoverished. During and immediately after the Second World War in most of these ancient woods oak and ash standards were felled in response to timber shortage; old coppice stools decayed and bramble became rampant smothering the ground flora. Many owners, unwilling to undertake costly replanting, were only too willing to sell or lease to the Forestry Commission or enter into management agreements in return for subsidies. Some woodland was felled and cleared for agriculture although not nearly as much as in the years of Victorian high farming in the mid 19th century.

This process of change happened in all the main areas of ancient woodland in Lincolnshire: on the Middle Marsh boulder clays, on the Kesteven Uplands and in the Central Vale where the national ecological importance of the extensive oak-limewoods had yet to be recognised. Where it had not already been done, the Forestry Commission carried out extensive clear-felling and replanted with densely grown alien conifers or at best with conifer-hardwood mixtures. The research on woodland changes which I did for the Trust's *Nature In Lincolnshire* Report (1996) revealed that ancient semi-natural woodland as defined by the Nature Conservancy Council had declined from 6,500 ha in 1930 to only 2,700 ha in 1989.

The declines and extinctions among woodland flora and fauna listed in that Report are largely the consequence of the changes I have described, in particular the loss of structural diversity and of broad-leaved trees and shrubs which support vast populations of invertebrates. Plants like the saprophytic bird's nest orchid, common cow-wheat and the lovely wood vetch which I could find in a number of woods in the 1930s have all but disappeared from Lincolnshire. But perhaps the most spectacular losses were among woodland butterflies. In the space of less than twenty years from the late 1940s all four of the woodland fritillaries and the chequered skipper disappeared from Lincolnshire woods – as they did from the whole of eastern England. There can be little doubt – as most experts believe – that changes in the character and management of woodlands were a major cause, although, as I speculate elsewhere, butterflies may also have been affected by some form of aerial pollution caused perhaps by pesticides. Butterflies and birds too suffered also from the neglect of woodland rides and from the loss of marginal grassland. There are very few places now where woods are able to develop a 'skirt' into surrounding meadow or pasture. It is a habitat which the Trust is seeking to restore wherever opportunities arise.

The Lincolnshire NRIC sub-committee in their 1946 report had selected four ancient semi-natural woodlands as potential habitat reserves: Newball in the Central Vale; Legsby on the northern edge of it; Welton (embracing Welton High and Low and Willoughby Woods) on the Middle Marsh boulder clays, and Holywell and Newell on the county boundary in the south-west. They also recommended Forestry Commission woodlands at Twyford and Bourne where, in spite of much replanting, areas retaining some of the original character had survived. The latter, they suggested, might form national forest parks of the kind which the Commission were creating in other parts of the country. The information available to the sub-committee about woodland was largely limited to species – and that mainly of plants and insects – recorded at LNU field meetings and by individual naturalists. Newball, for example, was known to be one of the richest butterfly woods in the county, a stronghold of the chequered skipper among others.

In our 1951 Report for the Nature Conservancy, Dick Cornwallis and I sought to make our woodland recommendations on a somewhat broader habitat basis. We retained Welton as the largest block of ancient woodland in the Middle Marsh with its contrasting chalk and boulder clay soils and its variety of plant and animal communities. We added Muckton as a smaller and more compact example of Middle Marsh woods with a rich flora and a notable bird population including a flourishing heronry. We noted, however, that the cessation of coppicing there had already led to a prolific and smothering growth of bramble. Newball and several other Central Vale woods having been largely felled since 1946, we selected Stainton as "the most considerable and representative piece remaining". It was known to be an excellent butterfly wood, but we admitted a lack of information about its flora. Two other examples of old woodland were included: Troy Wood at Coningsby on the sand and gravel margin of the Fen; and Skellingthorpe on similar soils to the west of Lincoln. Most of the latter had already been felled and replanted, but parts of the old wood which survived were especially important for insects including the last marsh fritillary colony in Lincolnshire. We omitted Holywell and Newell because they were already designated as part of a potential national nature reserve.

In the light of the knowledge of Lincolnshire woodlands gained from survey and research in the last fifty years the recommendations in both the NRIC and the 1951 reports seem very inadequate. They were, however, based on the best information available, and certainly in 1951 our options were being rapidly restricted by the widespread clear-felling and replanting of woodlands. Four of those we recommended in 1951 – Welton (although restricted to the Willoughby section), Muckton, Stainton and Troy were accepted by the Nature Conservancy for the first (1951) SSSI schedules. Skellingthorpe (in part) was added at the first revision in 1959; Stainton and Muckton were deleted then, but the latter was reinstated at later revisions.

Designating woodlands, however, was a somewhat academic exercise. The Nature Conservancy had no real powers to prevent clear felling or deleterious changes of management, nor in 1951 did the Trust have the money to purchase any of the woods. We did nevertheless explore other possibilities of retaining some of them – or parts of them – in a semi-natural condition. In that we had some small successes. At Muckton, for example, already the subject of a Tree Preservation Order made in 1950 by Lindsey County Council, we reached an understanding in 1953 with the sympathetic owner, Mr P K Dennis, regarding the protection of the heronry; and when the wood was acquired in 1959 by the Forestry Commission we concluded an agreement with them for a plan to ensure that the heronry would not only remain undisturbed but that new trees would be planted into which the herons could move when the existing old oaks in which they nested had decayed. In the event the Commission interpreted the no-disturbance agreement so literally that when the Trust eventually purchased the wood in 1983 it had become virtually impenetrable! At Skellingthorpe the Commission agreed to leave unfelled a strip of woodland on either side of the main ride, although that failed eventually to retain the entomological interest. On the whole, however, we could do little to mitigate the destruction of semi-natural woodland that went on through the 1950s and 60s until it eventually came to an end. Before that happened, however, native broad-leaved trees which had been replanted in Forestry Commission woodlands were subjected to an extraordinary assault.

From its creation in 1919 planting conifers of largely non-native species had been the main objective of the Forestry Commission's silvicultural policy. This had applied moreover not only to new planting on moors and heaths – as in north-west Lincolnshire – but to many ancient woodlands which after clear-felling during and immediately after the Second World War were replanted with conifers or at best a conifer-hardwood mixture. As I have described elsewhere, the character of such woods and their plants and animals suffered a radical change. Even in some of the mixtures hardwood retention was called into question in the 1960s when the government decided that return of capital should be the Commission's aim rather than the original concept of building up a strategic reserve of timber. In the Eastern Conservancy of the Commission especially, one means of achieving the policy objective was to concentrate even more on growing conifers even to the extent of eliminating some of the oak already planted in pure or mixed stands. The cheapest way to do that was by aerial spraying of herbicides which would kill the oaks and other hardwoods but leave the conifers unscathed. Treatment began in the mid-1960s but it was some time before we became aware of the extent of what was proposed – no less than 8,000 acres of young oak to be killed in the East Midlands area. In 1968 the Nature Conservancy was notified of 456 acres to be treated in seven woods in the west of Lincolnshire, followed in 1969 by a further 720 acres in nine woods which included Mother, Greenfield and Tothill in the Middle Marsh.

As the scale of the destruction became more widely known, conservation and amenity organisations locally and nationally began to protest and public opinion found expression in letters to the press and to Members of Parliament. In September 1969, after discussion in the Trust's Scientific Policy Group, I raised the matter in the Lindsey County Council Countryside Committee and as a result Peter Thallon, Assistant Conservator of the Eastern Conservancy, attended the December meeting of the Committee to explain the Commission's policy. This was, he said, dictated by economic necessity complying with government directives. He did not say, however, why only the Eastern Conservancy had adopted the practice on such a large scale. Under hard questioning from the Committee he admitted that some damage might be caused to other woodland plants, but he played down any suggestion that animals or humans could be put at risk – the issue of chemical defoliants used in Vietnam was still fresh in people's minds. Neighbouring landowners and users were notified of spraying in advance, and to protect amenity a belt of broad-leaved trees was left around the edges of treated woods. Areas of high nature conservation importance notified by the Nature Conservancy were left untreated. After a somewhat half-hearted defence of the spraying policy Thallon announced that a brake had been put on the practice and that for the next three to five years there would be little killing of pure oak and other hardwoods. What he did not concede was that this suspension of the practice – in effect its discontinuance – was the result of public and political pressure.

I had also pursued the matter through the Conservation Liaison Committee of the SPNR on which the Forestry Commission had been represented by Peter

Garthwaite, a senior Commission officer, whose appointment as the Commission's first Wildlife Officer had been warmly welcomed by the nature conservation movement. In my SPNR capacity I had developed a friendly and productive working relationship with Peter who was vehemently opposed from the outset to the aerial spraying practice in the Eastern Conservancy. Although in December 1969 he had just resigned from his post in the Commission he continued to advise me on the spraying issue. In particular he sent me a copy of the instruction which George Stewart, the Commissioner for Forest and Estate Management, sent to all the Territorial Conservators on 9 December 1969, the day after Thallon had appeared at the Lindsey Countryside Committee. The instruction said that the justification for aerial spraying needed further examination, but until that had been done the destruction of broad-leaved crops by chemical or other means would cease. The 'further examination' was clearly a face-saver; it marked in fact the end of the practice. It was only in the Eastern Conservancy that the practice had been prolonged, and Garthwaite attributed that to the obduracy of the Conservator G W Backhouse.

We were still anxious to discover the full extent of the destruction of hardwood trees by this practice in Lincolnshire. At the Countryside Committee Thallon had spoken about 8,000 acres of young oak in the East Midlands Area and had said that 3/5ths of the pure oak had been treated and 4/5ths in mixed plantations. On Garthwaite's advice therefore I wrote to Peter Thallon – who was personally very helpful – in January 1970 asking for specific Lincolnshire figures. To my surprise I received a curt reply from Backhouse saying: "It is not the policy of the Commission to disclose the kind of information you request without knowing the purpose for which it is required". I had clearly touched a raw nerve! I saw no reason why the information should be secret; it was a matter of public interest and concern and the refusal to disclose it did no credit to the Commission. In welcoming the news that the practice had been halted in the Trust's newsletter of February 1970 we referred to the good work that the Commission had done in recent years for the conservation of the wildlife and amenity of its forests and for the provision of opportunities for their enjoyment, purposes for which it had an excellent record of collaboration with other bodies including the County Trusts. "We are reluctant therefore", we said, "to appear critical of an aspect of its policy, but the practice we have described has aroused such widespread concern that we cannot pass it over without comment. We hope that it will not be resumed". I sent a copy of the newsletter to J A (Tony) Spencer, Head of a new Conservation and Recreation Branch at the Commission, who had replaced Peter Garthwaite as the Commission's representative on the SPNR's Conservation Liaison Committee. I asked him at the same time if he could provide me with the statistics for Lincolnshire which Backhouse had refused to divulge. I received a frank and detailed response in which he said that, whilst their chief concern in such matters was to ensure a fair presentation of the situation, that had "always been the case in the published comments of yours that I have seen". The Commission's policy he went on to say was that in future all pure stands of young hardwoods should be grown on to secure a final crop, and wherever amenity and conservation interests were judged to be important all mixtures would be managed so as to keep open for as long as possible the option of producing a final crop of hardwoods. In Lincolnshire, he told me, 124 acres of immature oak stands had been replaced by conifers, and 660 acres of mixed stands converted to conifers, a total of 784 acres. Comparable figures for all other counties in East England were 1,503 and 1,113 acres respectively.

It had been a sorry episode, the sacrifice of long-term sustainable forest resources of timber and amenity and wildlife for short-term economic gain – and even that purpose was of questionable validity. On the bright side, however, the termination of the practice was indicative of changing attitudes and priorities in the Commission which would lead eventually to much greater concentration on native hardwoods in old woodland even to the extent of removing conifers in their favour. The wheel in full circle indeed!

Many of the Commission staff whom I had known were excellent naturalists and dedicated conservationists, disliking some of the intensive silvicultural management methods which they had to practise often to the detriment of wildlife and amenity. Several of them in retirement played an important role in the conservation movement, in the Wildlife Trusts in particular. Robert Payne the Eastern Conservancy Private Woodlands Officer became the Administrative Officer of the Cambridgeshire and Isle of Ely Trust; Morley Penistan, who succeeded Backhouse as Conservator in the Eastern Conservancy, became Chairman of the Gloucestershire Trust and an active member of the SPNR Council and Executive Committee until the time of his tragic and untimely death; my old friend Gerry Haggett, national authority on Lepidoptera, who was Head Forester in Lincolnshire and then in Thetford Forest, is still active in conservation; Hugh Tilney-Bassett, District Officer in Lincolnshire and then in the Chilterns, retired to Lincolnshire and chairs the Trust's Woodlands Team. There were many others.

It was in pursuance of a more cordial and productive relationship between the Trust, the Nature Conservancy and the Forestry Commission that a meeting of the three parties was held in December 1970 to discuss the conservation interests of Commission woodlands in Lincolnshire and the ways in which those might be safeguarded. As a result, the District Office of the Commission established master maps showing points of conservation interest notified by the Trust and the Conservancy so that damage to them could be avoided or at least mitigated during forestry management planning and operations. Exchange of information about the recreational use of Commission woodlands, including nature trails, was also agreed. Arising from the meeting a joint field exercise was held in Bardney Forest in June 1971 during which, incidentally, Little Scrubbs Meadow, which I refer to in the next chapter, was 'discovered'. Liaison meetings were held thereafter on a regular basis at least once a year; the Trust's advisory role on wildlife matters was acknowledged, and formal agreements concluded on six Commission sites including Little Scrubbs Meadow. The appointment of Morley Penistan as Regional Conservator later in 1971 gave further impetus to this new relationship with the Forestry Commission, one hopeful sign at least that the retreat of nature could be halted and perhaps reversed.

Woodland flowers drawn by Mary Smith

157

TED SMITH

The Wispington 'Prairie', 1977.

<u>Extent</u> of permanent grassland	in 1938	230,679 ha	
	in 1965	116,958 ha	
	in 1995	49,000 ha	(est)
<u>Extent</u> of meadow	in 1938	41,187 ha	
	in 1965	4856 ha	(est)
	in 1995	142 ha	(app)
	A loss since 1938 of 99.7%		
<u>Extent</u> of pasture unimproved	in 1938	189,576 ha	
or semi-improved grassland	in 1965	112,102 ha	
older than 5 years	in 1995	48,860 ha	(est)
	A loss since 1938 of 74%		

<u>Conservation Status</u>
SSSIs (18)   289 ha
  of which meadow   54 ha
  pasture   235 ha
Nature Reserves (including SSSIs)
      Meadow (14)   57 ha
      Pasture (12)   190 ha
      Protected Road Verges 17

Decline of permanent grasslands in Lincolnshire 1938-1995
(from 'Nature in Lincolnshire', 1996).

– 9 –

In the Path of the Juggernaut

A S IT had been in the first, Lincolnshire was in the forefront of the second Agricultural Revolution which was gathering momentum throughout the 1950s and 60s. The nation's survival in the Second World War had depended on increasing agricultural production. Grasslands had been ploughed, marshes drained, heathlands reclaimed; the production of bigger, more efficient machinery for all kinds of agricultural purposes had been accelerated. Nevertheless, as I described in an earlier chapter, it had been assumed that after the war farming would largely revert to its pre-war pattern albeit on a more efficient and prosperous basis. It was all too clear even by the early fifties that such assumptions had been utterly wrong. Post-war governments continued to encourage maximum home production of cheap food by a lavish subsidy system; agricultural methods and machinery continued to improve – and the number of farm workers to decrease in consequence. Bigger machines for ploughing and harvesting needed bigger fields, thus necessitating the large-scale removal of hedges. More intensive land drainage eliminated most of the remaining wetlands and turned pleasant streams into featureless drains. But perhaps the most significant feature of the new 'revolution' was the introduction of a vast array of new chemicals to promote plant growth and to control weeds and pests. These were to have far-reaching consequences for wildlife for the rest of the century.

Traditional patterns of cropping and cultivation were progressively abandoned and replaced by more intensive and predominantly arable regimes. Where grassland was retained it was usually in the form of short-term leys cropped for silage. Permanent grass began to disappear and the rate of decline accelerated throughout the sixties. Statistics that I researched for the publication *Nature in Lincolnshire* (1996) showed a fall of nearly 50% in the extent of permanent grassland in the county between 1938 and 1965, 230,700 hectares being reduced to 117 000. It was in areas where mixed crop and stock systems had been the traditional land use that landscape changes were most drastic: on claylands like the Lindsey Middle Marsh and the Central Vale and on the Spilsby Sandstone country around the southern edges of the chalk Wolds. Small hedged fields of plough and pasture were replaced by vast tracts of arable largely bereft of trees and hedges. The 18th century Agricultural Revolution had also brought radical changes to the old medieval landscapes of the Open Fields, and swept away fens and marshes and downlands, but what it created instead was a new landscape rich in scenic beauty and wildlife. The bleak, inhospitable arable prairies of the late 20th century had no such qualities.

As early as 1951 in only its third Annual Report the Trust had expressed its concern about the effects of drastic agricultural changes on landscapes and wildlife. Whilst recognising that many such changes were inevitable, the Trust, said the report, was not convinced that "the grubbing up of hedges and trees and the conversion of small streams into something resembling Fenland drains is in all cases either necessary or desirable". Too little consideration had been given to such problems as changes caused in the balance of predator/prey populations and to the neglected issue of long-term soil conservation. The Report went on to appeal to landowners and farmers not to destroy hedges and trees unless absolutely necessary and to replant wherever possible. It concluded: "We shall deserve as badly of posterity in this respect as the 18th century deserved well if we leave a countryside which is largely devoid of natural beauty".

That was 1951, and the agricultural juggernaut – 'the engine of destruction' as William Waldegrave called it when he was Minister at the Department of the Environment in 1984 – continued relentlessly for the next thirty years or more. In the path of it the Trust sought to salvage examples of special habitats such as heathland and marshland wherever it could, but as already described, many precious sites and their characteristic plants and animals were destroyed, some in spite of SSSI designation and of the Trust's strenuous efforts to save them. Nonetheless without the Trust's efforts in those years much more would have been irretrievably lost.

We recognised that it was important to seek practical solutions to land use problems and wherever possible to retain the goodwill and respect of the farming and land-owning community. Farmer and landowner representation on the Trust Council was strongly maintained through farmers like Dick Cornwallis who in the mid-60s was Chairman of both the Trust and the County Branch of the NFU. Notable among other supportive farmers was Jack Hargreaves of Goxhill, a considerable benefactor of the Trust on Humberside. We also developed useful working relationships with officers of statutory bodies concerned with various aspects of land and water management such as Bob Miers, the Senior Regional Drainage Engineer of the Ministry of Agriculture, and Geoffrey Phillippo, the Clerk of the Lincolnshire River Authority.

There were moves nationally in the late 1960s to promote better understanding between farming and conservation interests and to seek areas of compromise. These derived in part from 'The Countryside in 1970' series of conferences and from a ground-breaking conference in July 1969 at Silsoe in Bedfordshire between farmers, agricultural advisers and conservationists which I attended in my SPNR capacity. In the context of such national initiatives the Trust and the Nature Conservancy collaborated with the National Agricultural Advisory Service, the NFU, the Lindsey College of Agriculture and other bodies in organising local conferences and exercises. In 1970, European Conservation Year, those included a Lindsey 'Farming and Nature Conservation' conference at which I was one of the principal speakers; tree and nature conservation walks on farms at Willoughby in Lindsey and Wilsford in Kesteven; an exhibition in Lindsey on the selection, application and safe use of agricultural chemicals, and appreciation courses on conservation for NAAS staff. Further important exercises involving farmers and conservationists were held in 1971, based on a study of farms at Holywell in Kesteven and Low Toynton in Lindsey. In preparation for those exercises the Trust and the Nature Conservancy carried out intensive surveys of the wildlife interest of both the farms. Trust Area Groups were also active in contacting sympathetic farmers and arranging farm walks and Open Days. Later in the 1970s the Trust played a leading role in the establishment of the Lincolnshire Farming and Wildlife Advisory Group which organised further practical events and discussions, and encouraged farmers to seek advice about wildlife on their farms. For many years Honorary Officers of the Trust acted as vice-chairman or secretary of the Group.

Following Dick Cornwallis' death in 1969 the Trust's Executive Committee considered the possibility of purchasing a farm as a memorial to him. The purpose would be to demonstrate the compatibility of farming and wildlife, something which Dick had always believed to be possible. A paper prepared by the Honorary Secretary, David Robinson, early in 1970 outlined various options for the acquisition and management of such a farm, estimating that at least £50,000 would be needed for the project which would also require involvement by national conservation and farming organisations. It was an idea before its time, too ambitious for the Trust with its still slender resources which were in any case about to be committed to a major new appeal for nature reserve purchases. Acquisition of a farm was an idea that the Trust returned to from time to time, especially in recent years although by then the purpose was more to provide housing for the Trust's increasing stock of sheep and cattle rather than to provide a demonstration of compatibility between agriculture and conservation examples of which were becoming more widely available through Government sponsored agri-environment schemes.

Back in the 1970s the Trust, in association with the Nature Conservancy with whose local officers we developed a close rapport, devoted a great deal of time and resources to the kinds of exercises and consultations which I have mentioned. They may not have made much impression on the overall problem of wildlife on farmland, but they were worthwhile in fostering relationships between the nature conservation movement and some sectors of the farming community. The contacts thus established proved to be especially helpful when economic conditions began to impinge on farming prosperity and when conservation began to receive a greater political priority in the later years of the century. Moreover, as I now describe, the Trust was able to achieve some modest practical successes in saving examples of vanishing farmland habitats such as meadows; in influencing practices in the management of road verges and of rivers and streams; and in playing a part in national efforts to limit the damage to wildlife caused by the use of toxic chemicals.

Meadows

Meadows had been an essential feature of mixed husbandry farming. Managed without herbicides or artificial fertilisers they produced grasslands rich in variety of grasses and wild flowers, many of them familiar to country people for their herbal or medicinal virtues or simply for their legendary curiosity and beauty.

Cowslips and early purple orchids bring the first colour of the year to meadows followed closely by the tall-stemmed meadow buttercups. By June there are flowers in profusion and a medley of colour: ox-eye or dog daisies; handsome great burnet with reddish-purple flowerheads – burnet 'knobs' for winemaking; toothed-leaved betony; spotted orchids; saw-wort like a more elegant knapweed; dyers' greenweed, a dwarf broom, and of course meadowsweet in the damper places; and as hay-time approaches and the ripe seeds of the yellow or hay rattle rustle inside the pods, the colour of the meadow changes to a purplish mauve as the dense round pincushions of flowers of the devil's-bit scabious begin to open.

The wealth of flowers attracts countless insects, bees, grasshoppers and butterflies most conspicuously. Among the latter it is the 'browns' that are the most characteristic of meadows: the meadow brown and the smaller more colourful hedge brown or gatekeeper, the name I prefer; the attractively patterned wall, and the aptly named ringlet which prefers the shade of the hedgeside. The big hedges which surrounded old meadows had their characteristic birds whose songs contributed to what Matthew Arnold called "all the live murmur of a summer's day": the scribbly little song of the whitethroat, the contented 'purring' of the turtle dove, and the lazy 'little bit of bread and no cheese' ditty of the yellowhammer.

Viewed on a fine summer afternoon in the traditional country way – by leaning on the gate – when the breeze ripples through the grass there is beauty and tranquillity in old meadows reflecting a quieter and less hectic way of life which allowed man and nature to co-exist more harmoniously than is the case today.

Meadows were traditionally cut in mid to late July, the re-growth or 'eddish' as it was known in Lincolnshire, being often grazed by cattle or sheep for a few weeks in the autumn. Hay-making was one of the major events of the farming year; the fields of drying haycocks one of the most familiar sights and scents of the countryside in high summer. The essence of the scene was wonderfully distilled by Edward Thomas in his poem 'Adelstrop':

> *And willows, willowherb and grass,*
> *And meadowsweet and haycocks dry,*
> *No whit less still and lonely fair*
> *Than the high cloudlets in the sky.*

Herb-rich meadows had been such an abundant feature in areas of mixed husbandry that the need to preserve any of them had scarcely occurred to us until the 1960s. None appeared in the early SSSI schedules for Lincolnshire in the 1950s, a situation which applied throughout most of lowland England. Yet the statistics in *Nature in Lincolnshire* (1996) show that a massive decline of meadow grassland had already taken place by 1965, a drop from 41 000 hectares in 1938 to less than 5 000. It was often the decline of a particular species that highlighted the loss of its habitat, and in the case of meadows in Lincolnshire that species was the green-winged orchid. It was a relatively widespread plant of old meadows, associated with such familiar flowers as cowslip, meadow buttercup and great burnet. A sample survey of the orchid carried out by the Trust in 1965 revealed that in twenty-six meadows where it had previously been recorded it was then found in only five, and in a repeat survey in 1980 it survived in only one of the original twenty-six. Most of its meadows had been converted to arable and others to leys. Writing in the Trust's newsletter in November 1965 Martin

Ball, the Nature Conservancy's Warden Naturalist for Lincolnshire, called for the conservation of a few small meadows in various parts of the county as a matter of urgency. Nationally too, the rapid decline of old grasslands had highlighted their ecological significance which was acknowledged in the Nature Conservancy's massive survey of habitats and sites *A Nature Conservation Review* which started in 1965.

As we searched for old meadows it soon became apparent that their survival was depending increasingly on the older generation of small farmers unable or unwilling to convert all their holdings to intensive arable. Once they went out of business their land almost always passed into the hands of 'improvers'. We looked, therefore, for what were rapidly becoming old-fashioned farms, and we explored half-forgotten little fields down obscure green lanes.

The urgency of finding and preserving a selection of herb-rich meadows was highlighted by the destruction in the early 1970s of one of the best examples in the country. Meadows at the foot of the northern Wold scarp at Worlaby had been recognised by the Nature Conservancy almost immediately after their discovery as the outstanding example in the whole country of calcareous loam pasture, one of the fourteen groups into which neutral grasslands were classified in *A Nature Conservation Review* on the basis of environmental and floristic characteristics.

Within a year or so of their discovery the Trust learned that the Worlaby Meadows were for letting by tender. The owner lived in York, and David Robinson, who had succeeded me as Honorary Secretary in March 1969, went to see her there in an effort to persuade her to sell the freehold or give the Trust a lease without going to tender. His pleas unfortunately fell on deaf ears and the owner persisted in advertising for tenders for letting. The Trust made a bid but failed. With Nature Conservancy support we then sought to persuade the successful tenant to retain the fields as meadows and not to use fertilisers. In spite of some assurances, however, he went the whole hog the following year and drained and ploughed the fields. Ironically the drains clogged with silt and he lost part of the crop. Thus another piece of the country's natural heritage was destroyed to no-one's advantage.

Before the Worlaby disaster, however, we had achieved a notable success. In the winter of 1967/68 Barrie Wilkinson, then the Trust's Field Officer, gave a talk to the Women's Institute at Irby-in-the-Marsh, a village in the Lindsey Middle Marsh. In the course of it he showed a slide of green-winged orchids which prompted one of his audience to tell him about some old meadows in the neighbouring parish of Bratoft where orchids grew. Derek Wells, one of the Nature Conservancy's grassland specialists, identified the meadows in the following spring as of national importance and they were immediately designated as an SSSI. Enquiries revealed that the owner of three of the fields lived in Boston; he had probably bought them as an investment or as a result of some local attachment. Fortunately he was willing to sell and the Trust purchased his three fields, subsequently adding another three. Bratoft Ings – Ings is an old Scandinavian word meaning low-lying meadow or pasture – a tight mosaic of little fields and big hedges of hawthorn, willow and ash, is a remarkable relict of an older agricultural landscape. The fields are a mixture of meadow and pasture according to the way they have been managed and used. The meadows have a wealth of flowers of a kind which I have just described. Green-winged orchids are a particularly notable feature producing more than 2 000 flowering spikes

163

in most years. Derek Wells was so impressed by them that he conducted a five-year project of different kinds of management treatment in experimental plots. Thereafter with the assistance of Barrie Wilkinson he maintained an annual monitoring programme for thirty years.

The Trust was able to purchase the Bratoft Meadows largely from its own carefully managed finances. Much of the money it had been able to save for nature reserve acquisition had accrued from special fundraising by individual members. Outstanding among those was the redoubtable Winifred Heath for many years the District Nurse at Nettleham near Lincoln. 'Heathie', as she was affectionately known, worked tirelessly and selflessly to raise money for the Trust by selling almost anything she could lay her hands on. By 1969 she had contributed more than £1,300 towards our funds. She was particularly keen about meadows and, as recognition of her help and devotion, the Trust Council decided to attach her name in perpetuity to the Bratoft Meadows and commissioned a handsome plaque which was erected on the site in her honour. She was delighted. **Heath's Meadows** were the first of a series of meadows which the Trust managed to acquire over the next twenty years. Each one had its own characteristics.

The four fields which comprised the sixteen acres of **Moor Closes** at Ancaster were purchased in 1971 from a small farmer who grazed them – or rather under-grazed them with a few cows – together with his adjoining fields. They lie on the sands and gravels and alluvium in the floor of the great gap cut through the limestone ridge by glacial overflow waters from the Trent Valley. The low-lying parts beside the little Ancaster Beck have a rich marsh and wet meadow flora with such species as marsh arrowgrass, ragged robin, marsh valerian, devil's-bit scabious, and marsh and spotted orchids, the latter in some years numbering over 60,000. The higher drier parts have meadow saxifrage and the inland sub-species of thrift *Armeria maritima elongata* distinguished by its long slightly twisting stems. Once more widespread on the limestone in Lincolnshire and Leicestershire it is now confined in the whole of Britain to this and one or two other nearby sites. The Moor Closes Meadows make an idyllic scene: the wealth of flowers, the little stream with its old pollarded willows, the big thorn hedges laden with blossom in May time, and in the background across the adjoining fields the elegant spire of Ancaster church rising above the trees.

Little Scrubbs Meadow, a five acre ancient clearing in the middle of the Bardney Forest Limewoods, was discovered in 1970 as a result of a Trust-Forestry Commission exercise. Some of it had already been furrowed and planted, but the Commission agreed not to proceed and to transfer elsewhere some of the trees already planted and then to lease it to the Trust. For the early 1970s that was very enlightened action on the part of the Commission and an augury perhaps of future changes in their policy on conservation. Almost all the typical clay meadow plants occur here, and the woodland edge on all sides enhances its value for birds and for butterflies and other insects for which the Limewoods are famous. Scrub re-growth from the remaining plantings in the furrows has always been a problem, but mowing and more recently sheep grazing has kept it at bay.

In my own village of **Willoughby** one tiny meadow had survived the mass conversion to arable because it belonged to an absentee landowner, a hospital in Northampton which must have acquired it some time in the past as a result of a bequest. In its 1.3 acres there are nearly 150 kinds of flowering plants and grasses. These include all the characteristic species of Lincolnshire clayland meadows, and

Trust – Forestry Commission exercise in Bardney Forest with District Officer Hugh Tilney-Bassett (second right) when Little Scrubbs meadow was discovered in 1971 (below left) and as it looked twenty years later.

Farming and Wildlife exercises, organised by the Agricultural Development and Advisory Service, the Trust and the Nature Conservancy, 1971.

Manor Farm, Low Toynton

Lodge Farm, Holywell (Dr Rick Pilcher, Chairman of Trust Scientific Policy Committee, third from right).

Meadows

Derek Wells (Nature Conservancy, left)
and Barrie Wilkinson doing annual
monitoring of green-winged orchids (right)
at Heath's Meadows, Bratoft.

Nurse Winifred Heath
(Heathie)

Moor Closes in the Valley
of the Ancaster Beck.

Silverines Meadow near Goulceby
with meadow saxifrage.

Worlaby Meadows – lost.

Willoughby Meadow – saved.

perhaps because it lies on a belt of sands and gravels over boulder clay on the edge of wooded country, there is also tormentil, lady's mantle, bugle and the heath grass. In 1976 it came up for sale by auction and the Trust sought to purchase it. One neighbouring landowner generously agreed not to bid against the Trust, but there was nevertheless keen competition and we were forced to pay more than we had envisaged to secure it. Like all the other meadows though it has proved to be a wonderful investment. Twenty-five years later the Trust was able to purchase an adjoining five acre field which had been a grass ley for many years. This is being converted to meadow and pasture using seed from the original meadow. The whole forms a more viable and secure unit.

Silverines Meadows are also tucked away among big hedges in a stream valley. They lie not on clay but on the Spilsby Sandstone soils which surface along the southern and western edges of the Wolds. You look down on Silverines and the village of Goulceby from the downland of the Red Hill reserve on the chalk scarp to the east. Whilst they have many of the clay meadow species the Silverines fields also have an abundance of meadow saxifrage – I would like to think that they derive the picturesque first element of their name from its silvery-white flowers. The second element – 'ines' – is probably a variant of the familiar name 'ings' for damp meadows. In a marsh by a stream are kingcups, marsh orchids and ragged robins. Snipe used to nest there but sadly they have disappeared now as they have from most of their other sites on Trust reserves and elsewhere.

Old grassland on a woodland edge is now an exceedingly rare habitat in Lincolnshire, and the Trust has been fortunate to secure three excellent examples. **Porter's Lodge Meadows** lie on the calcareous boulder clay of the Kesteven limestone on the edge of the Tortoiseshell Wood reserve where there are splendid wild service trees. The meadows known as **Bottleneck** and **Jackson's** – another addition to the fascinating array of names of Trust reserves – occupy a similar position, being on the edge of the Lawn Wood reserve which overlooks the ancient village of Castle Bytham. The meadows were donated to the Trust as a memorial to David Harris.

Hatton Meadows adjoin the National Nature Reserve of Hatton Wood, one of the finest of the Lincolnshire limewoods in the Central Vale. They are damp meadows traversed by a small stream, and there is much meadowsweet, spotted orchid, ragged-robin, valerian and water avens, with giant bellflower along the woodland edge. The hedges which surround most of the meadows are magnificent. They contain both species of hawthorn, crab apple, field maple, blackthorn and purging buckthorn with ancient oak trees here and there. The rare and elusive brown hairstreak butterfly occurs here together with purple hairstreak and white admiral for which Hatton and other Bardney forest woods are a stronghold. The reserve is dedicated to Edward Mason, a devoted naturalist and benefactor of the Trust.

Two other groups of meadows lie in the Central Vale at **Sotby** and **Kingerby Beck**. The former lie on clayland nestling among big hedges in the valley of a little stream. The latter are on a patchwork of soils of glacial sands and Kimmeridge Clay, the flora consequently varying from one field to another. A colony of frog orchids, a great rarity now in Lincolnshire, was an exciting find there.

The rescue from the arable onslaught of this splendid collection of meadows is among the Trust's most important achievements. There is no doubt that without it most if not all of them would have been destroyed by conversion to arable or improved grassland. It is an achievement which has given me special satisfaction, partly, I have to admit, for nostalgic reasons because the meadow reserves are reminders of the countryside of my boyhood. More seriously, they preserve examples of agricultural management practices of great historical interest, although they are far from being just museum pieces. The species and communities of plants which they sustain and their relationship to soil types and environmental conditions are of immense ecological interest. They are 'reservoirs' of plants many of whose traditional herbal qualities may prove of new medicinal application. They are the seed source for new meadows now being created under Stewardship and other agri-environment schemes – the Trust harvests and sells seed for the purpose. In their landscape settings and with the profusion and variety of their wild flowers and insects they are places of delight and inspiration and that alone would more than justify their existence.

Roadside Verges and Hedgerows

I cannot think of any ecological system in Britain that so clearly has all the virtues inherent in the conservation of variety Charles Elton.

Road verges and hedgerows are one of England's great natural assets forming in many counties the largest remaining tract of semi-natural vegetation. They are of special importance in Lincolnshire where open downland was destroyed in the first agricultural revolution, and where the amount of old grassland has again declined drastically in the last fifty years as intensive arable cultivation has become the predominant land use. In this situation verges provide a vital refuge and reservoir for plants and animals many of which have become rare or localised as a result of habitat loss. Verges have other values too: they occur on all kinds of soils and they provide 'highways' along which plants and animals can spread and move.

Several of Lincolnshire's endangered plants are now dependent on road verges to maintain their status in the county. They include the beautiful perennial flax, man orchid, bastard toadflax and sand leek, the latter known from only one verge. Butterflies too find verges attractive and some are especially associated with them in their seasons: the orange tip, for example, with the May blossom and flowering cow parsley; the gatekeeper with the dusty roadsides of high summer. Some increasingly scarce species like the dingy and grizzled skippers occur - or used to do - on a few verges, and the only site for the lovely chalkhill blue in Lincolnshire was on the Ermine Street verges at Copper Hill near Ancaster – 'was' because alas it has been extinct there since the mid-1970s.

The richest verges in the county occur on the chalk and limestone hills where Enclosure Acts often provided for wide verges to be created for easier movement of cattle and sheep perhaps, or to compensate peasant farmers for loss of land by providing roadside grazing. Knapweed and scabious, marjoram and rockrose, pyramidal orchid, clustered bellflower and many others make a colourful summer display on some of the quiet, uncluttered byways of the Wolds and the limestone Heath.

On clay soils the flowers are those of the once abundant meadows: cowslip, meadow buttercup, spotted orchid, great burnet and the various umbellifers in their season. On acid soils on the north-west Coversands and on the Fen edge sands and gravels the verge flora contains many of the characteristic heathland species, although occasionally lime-loving plants occur where roads have been 'booned' with chalk or limestone.

Like all grassland, verges are the result of management. In the past they were often grazed, but the motor car put an end to that. Mowing for hay was the commonest form of management, but that practice too greatly diminished as arable farming became predominant after World War II. Already by the 1950s Highway Authorities and landowners were seeking alternative means of controlling the vegetation on verges in the interest of road safety and to prevent what some regarded as weeds from spreading onto adjoining land. Flail and rotary type mowers came into common use, but unlike haymaking they left the litter to make a mulch which if thick enough suppresses the herbs and encourages weed species. Many county highway surveyors were also attracted by the potential of the new agricultural herbicides for killing off taller, broad-leaved plants to leave a mainly grass sward which was easier to manage.

Conservation bodies became seriously alarmed at that prospect, and spraying experiment in some counties in the early 1950s created a public outcry when attractive roadside flowers became a horrid mass of deformed and dying vegetation. Drifting spray also damaged hedgerows and killed insects, birds and mammals. Pressure of public opinion and representations from the Nature Conservancy eventually resulted in agreement on the modified use of sprays defined in a circular to local authorities from the Ministry of Transport in August 1955. This recommended that spraying be restricted to trunk and class 1 roads and to certain dangerous corners on class 2 roads; that it should be limited to within ten feet of the road edge on wide verges; that special care should be taken on narrower roads to avoid spraying the hedge, and that in certain cases sections on class 1 roads should be left unsprayed where interesting plant species or communities occur.

The Trust was concerned with road verges from the outset. No less than six of the twenty-four sites in the Trust's 1951 Report on Areas of Scientific Interest in the County – on which the first SSSI schedules were based – consisted in whole or part of road verges. In seeking practical measures for the protection of those sites, therefore, we had early discussions with the County Surveyors for Lindsey and Kesteven, and in May 1951 I was able to report to the Trust Council a sympathetic response from both of them. It was then suggested in Council that a survey of other interesting road verges be made and brought to the notice of local authorities, especially in view of the new dangers posed by chemical spraying. Miss Joan Gibbons, the leading county botanist, was subsequently asked to put forward suggestions for that purpose.

The question of road verge spraying in Lincolnshire was first raised in the Trust Council in March 1955 when it was reported that Lindsey County Council was considering carrying out experiments. Correspondence with the County Surveyor was reassuring: experiments would be carried out but only in accordance with the national agreement referred to above. Verges of course were subject to all kinds of other disturbance: excavation for water and gas pipes for example, the dumping of road materials and soil from elsewhere to make up depressions. Since their maintenance depended increasingly on the Highway Authorities they had to be mown in the manner and at the time that suited the Authorities' programme. The County Surveyors of Lindsey and Kesteven, however, were prepared to be helpful, and the Trust had already begun to identify verges of outstanding botanical interest. What was needed at that stage was a practical scheme for the protection and management of a selection of them. Such an agreement was in fact precipitated by an extraordinary incident.

The incident on Tetford Hill

The weekend of the first Trusts' conference at Skegness in May 1960 was favoured with warm sunny weather, so much so that it was possible to hold the Saturday morning sessions on the lawn of the Trust's new field station at the Gibraltar Point nature reserve. The main Saturday afternoon excursion took delegates – who included some of the leading figures in the nature conservation movement – over the Wolds to the heathland reserve of Linwood Warren. On the return journey the bus in which most of them travelled called at the chalk downland fragment on the Red Hill, and then back on the Bluestone Heath road along the spine of the hills to Tetford Hill. The wide banks on the roadside there were well known for their variety of chalk plants which then included bee and pyramidal and the rare lizard orchid. The banks were scheduled along with the adjoining quarry and ashwood as an SSSI. Time would not allow a close inspection and tea awaited at the White Hart in Tetford, so it was arranged that the banks would be viewed from the bus as it drove slowly down the hill. As the banks came in sight, however, it was evident that something had happened to the vegetation which looked dead and blackened. It had in fact had been sprayed with herbicide! Tea turned into an indignation meeting. It was assumed that the spraying had been done by the County Council as the Highway Authority. That assumption was correct, and when Walter Lane, the Clerk of Lindsey County Council, came to address the conference on the Sunday morning on the role of local authorities in nature conservation, he encountered a barrage of protest. Lane, of course, knew nothing about the incident and was much embarrassed. He undertook to make urgent enquiries.

On the Monday morning indeed he telephoned me to say that he had asked the County Surveyor to carry out an investigation. It turned out that the local road man, who had been spraying pavements in Tetford village a few days earlier, had decided to clean out his tank on what he no doubt considered 'waste' ground on the hillside verge. The County Council expressed regret for the mistake and reaffirmed their policy of limited road verge spraying. Lane further proposed that the Trust should identify a selection of botanically rich verges in the county which the County Council would then mark appropriately and consult the Trust about their management and about any works likely to affect them adversely. The incident received much publicity in the local and national press, reflecting the widespread concern of the time about the treatment of roadside verges.

The conveyor of unwelcome and embarrassing news, especially when it receives much local and national publicity, is seldom popular, and Keith Tallack, the County Surveyor, whom I knew well, was decidedly cool towards me for several months afterwards. He mellowed, however, and became a staunch supporter of the Trust and member of the Council, acting for a few years after his retirement as our honorary land agent.

The Protected Road Verge Scheme

The Protected Road Verge Scheme adopted in 1960 by Lindsey and Kesteven

County Councils provided for consultation with the Trust and the Nature Conservancy on any developments such as road widening, pipelaying or tipping of material which might damage selected verges or change their character. Management prescriptions for mowing at the most appropriate times of year, for scrub control and other requirements would be formulated where necessary in consultation with adjoining landowners. The scheduled verges were to be marked by white posts lettered NR (for Nature Reserve) so that they could be readily identified by workmen. Partly no doubt because of the national publicity which it received, the Lincolnshire road verge scheme attracted a great deal of interest, and similar schemes were adopted in more than twenty other English counties in the following ten years.

We already had a short list of important verges derived from existing information and previous surveys, and our news bulletin of July 1962, welcoming the County Councils' initiative, reported that the first six verges – all on minor roads – had been notified to the County Surveyors and were in process of being marked. By 1968 the number had grown to 24, 14 in Lindsey and 10 in Kesteven. Thereafter increasing volunteer and staff resources and the strengthening of the Nature Conservancy's presence in the county enabled us to conduct survey and assessment of verges on a wider scale. The pioneering survey work on grasslands, including verges, carried out by John Blackwood of the Nature Conservancy with the assistance of Barrie Wilkinson, the Trust's Field Officer, in the late 1960s was especially valuable; and the employment of survey teams under the Government's Job Creation Project in the 1970s resulted in further enlargement of the scheduled list which stood at 31 sites in 1976 and more than 50 in 1993.

Roadside verges and their hedgerows are familiar to everyone who lives and travels in the countryside and their protection aroused great interest among the public and in the media. We accordingly devoted most of the Trust's March 1968 newsletter to articles on the subject. Nature Conservancy specialists, Dr Michael Way and Dr Max Hooper wrote about the general importance of road verges and hedgerows respectively; Dick Cornwallis and Dennis Townsend about birds, and Rick Pilcher about butterflies.

The scheduling process was slow but thorough. Consultation with the Trust about threats to scheduled sites was on the whole satisfactory, but this and other aspects of the scheme were somewhat dependent on the degree of importance which Divisional Surveyors applied to it. In several cases damage was avoided or mitigated. Being on a major north-south line of communication the Ermine Street verges, where there were no less than six scheduled sites, were particularly vulnerable. The important verges on Copper Hill at Ancaster were the subject of more than one round of consultation with water and electricity authorities; and further south at Blue Harbour we persuaded the water authority to take a pipeline across the road to avoid the scheduled verge which is one of the few sites in Lincolnshire for the blue flax. I remember a burly, bare-chested foreman being dumbfounded when I suggested the diversion. "What" he said, "cross the road for a b... flower!". We had a long talk and when I saw him again a few weeks later he had become an ardent conservationist anxious to be doing the right thing!

We found, inevitably, that the scheme had its limitations. It sometimes proved difficult to fit our ideal mowing times into highway maintenance contracts, and in any event, County Council mowing was usually restricted to a narrow swathe next to the carriageway, leaving the remainder of the verge in danger of scrubbing up.

That in fact is exactly what happened in a number of cases, the Tetford Hill site being one of them. Some adjoining landowners still mowed their own verges, but not always at the appropriate time. There were complaints reported to the Trust's Scientific Policy Committee in 1972, for example, about the mowing of verges at Calceby when the spotted orchids, a notable feature of the site, were in full flower. In April of the previous year the Committee had acknowledged that more management plans were required for individual verges.

Roadworks and pipe and cable laying were by no means the only potential cause of damage. Unauthorised rubbish dumping was a frequent occurrence; and where hedges had been removed there was always a danger of encroachment by ploughing from the adjacent field. That happened on at least two of the scheduled sites where the County Council had to erect concrete posts to demarcate the boundary. Rutting and compaction by heavy farm and other vehicles became an increasing problem especially on narrow lanes. We had instances too of people digging up primroses, orchids and other attractive wild flowers. What was needed was more regular inspection of verges and the reporting of any damage or mismanagement. To that end in 1975 we launched a Wayside Warden scheme appealing in newsletters in May 1976 and April 1977 for volunteers. The response was encouraging and we were able to report in September 1977 that wardens had been appointed for 18 of the then 31 protected verges. Within a few years almost every scheduled verge had its own voluntary warden and our management control was immensely improved. For all this time an impressive inventory of the biological interest of the verges was being built up with the use of special record cards. Even more information was obtained in the 1980s by the survey and monitoring work of Marson Peet, a former Honorary Treasurer of the Trust, who after retirement from business devoted himself to botanical recording.

In 1992 after more than thirty years experience Lincolnshire County Council and the Trust conducted a major review of the scheme with particular regard to the limitations and weaknesses which had been exposed. It was agreed that the solution lay in providing the Trust with resources to manage the scheduled verges either by letting mowing out on contract or by doing it with its own staff. In discharging its functions under this arrangement the Trust was to act in consultation with adjoining landowners wherever appropriate. It was expected that the money made available to the Trust by the County Council for the purpose would be supplemented by other resources, including, of course, volunteer input. The Trust was straightway able to appoint a part-time road verge officer to liaise with the Wayside Wardens and arrange for whatever management was deemed appropriate in each case. A road verge team was established to supervise and develop the work. The revised scheme – another first for Lincolnshire – was launched on 27 April 1993 at a ceremony held appropriately on Tetford Hill.

Rivers and Streams

Unquietly flows the Brook

The River Lymn is typical of Lincolnshire's small unobtrusive little streams. Rising at the base of the chalk scarp above Tetford it flows through the village where it once generated the first of its five mills. It then cuts the deep New England valley

A sprayed verge in 1973.

Protected verge on the High Dyke – the Roman Ermine Street in Kesteven – with one of the early marker posts.

PROTECTED ROADSIDE VERGE

This verge is specially managed for its wildlife interest

LINCOLNSHIRE COUNTY COUNCIL

The Lincolnshire Trust

Blue flax at Blue Harbour on the Ermine Street, one of only three sites where it grows in the county.

Alan Stennett of BBC Radio Lincolnshire inaugurates the revised Protected Roadside Verge scheme on Tetford Hill in April 1993 watched by Cllr Bill Rawson, Chairman of Lincolnshire County Council and Ted Smith (right).

Chalkhill blue butterfly

Wildlife on the Verge
Protected Roadside Verges

Your local grassy road verge could be a remnant of pasture that has been in use for hundreds of years.

The plants growing there could be uncommon or even endangered species, holding on in a last refuge on the edge of modern farming.

LINC⬤LNSHIRE
COUNTY COUNCIL

THE
wildlife
TRUSTS

Lincolnshire Wildlife Trust

Flowers of chalk and limestone drawn by Mary Smith

Kingfisher

River 'improvements'

on the River Lymn

at Northorpe Bridge

Top left looking upstream
July 1970
and
September 1970

Left looking downstream
March 1964
and
April 1971

through the sandstone where snowdrops carpet the slopes at the end of winter and kingcups brighten the floor beneath the alders in April. Past the village of Somersby the stream now swollen by tributaries soon enters a wider valley. The next mill at Stockwith retains its mill house, its mill race and wheel and you can enjoy tea and scones there now within sight and sound of rushing water. The valley narrows again through the sandstone ridge between Partney and Halton Holegate, but the river soon reaches the edge of the Fen and for the next six or seven miles to Wainfleet it has been canalised and is known as the Steeping River. Its old course though is still intact, a meandering reedy dyke where bur-reed, arrowhead and flowering rush, reed and sedge warblers and dragonflies have found refuge. It once met the sea at Wainfleet when the little town was a thriving port in the Middle Ages but now there is another two miles to the estuary at Gibraltar Point where it becomes Wainfleet Haven.

A modest little stream the Lymn, but it has a claim to fame that few others of its kind enjoy. It is the subject of a poem, part of which almost every school child used to know – though I doubt if many do now – because this is Tennyson's Brook, the original of his famous poem of that name. He played by it as a boy at Somersby and it became, like the Rectory garden, an important element in the landscape of his emotional experience in his early years at Somersby, years which inspired much of his finest lyrical poetry. In the popular poem *The Brook* it might be any little stream; but it is more clearly identified in the poem *A Farewell* – 'Flow down cold rivulet to the sea' – and more especially in *In Memoriam* where it appears in the poignant passages of regret at leaving Somersby.

> *Unloved, by many a sandy bar,*
> *The brook shall babble down the plain,*
> *At noon or when the lesser wain*
> *Is twisting round the polar star*
>
> *Uncared for, gird the windy grove,*
> *And flood the haunts of hern and crake;*
> *Or into silver arrows break*
> *The sailing moon on creek and cove.*

One fine morning in early spring in 1964 I stopped at Northorpe bridge where the road from Spilsby to Skendleby crosses the Lymn. The river at this point has cut a deep channel into the rich alluvial soil of the valley floor. The almost vertical banks provided ideal nest sites for kingfishers – I had stopped in the hope of seeing one – and there were little ledges at various water levels where grey wagtails and green sandpipers could search for food in winter. At each bend the river in spate had cliffed the outer bank and deposited a miniature sand bar, places where we often found otter spraints although even by that time they were becoming scarcer as the population went into steep decline. Above the bridge the yellow and dark red catkins of the alders were dangling in the breeze; below it the catkins of the bankside sallows were opening to reveal golden-tipped stamens in a sheath of silvery hairs. Old pasture on one bank, a potential flood plain, completed a scene of such pastoral tranquillity that I fetched my camera from the car and captured it on film. In view of later developments I was very pleased that I had.

Seven years later, in the winter of 1970-71, I had reason to take another photograph of the Lymn from the very same spot on Northorpe bridge. The 'improvers' were at work and the scene was one of bleak desolation. The channel had been widened and deepened, the banks had been graded to a smooth slope and the old willows cut down to stumps prior to removal. The dragline was still at work depositing the spoil over the pasture on the left bank. Whenever I have shown this 'before and after' picture, the stark contrast has always brought a gasp of horror from the audience. I have often looked at that scene again over the years. Upstream, where agreement with the landowner enabled the Trust to replant alders and willows, time has softened the impact of that drastic assault and the river has resumed something of its natural appearance. Downstream, however, although the banks have grassed over and the pasture on the left bank has – somewhat miraculously – survived, the channel still looks like a drainage engineer's blueprint of the 1960s.

The treatment of that stretch of the Lymn was typical of what happened to many similar small rivers in Lincolnshire in the 1960s and 70s. The intensive arable farming of the post-war years necessitated more intensive land drainage, and that in turn involved the 'improvement' of rivers and streams in order to convey water to the sea as speedily as possible and to allow valley pastures, meadows and marshes to be converted to arable. 'Improvement' usually took the form of regrading, widening and often straightening and embanking the channel, and that involved the felling of trees and shrubs on the banks, the elimination of shoals, cliffs and sand bars, and reed swamp and other marginal vegetation: in other words all the variety of riparian and aquatic conditions which the river had naturally created for itself. Many a pleasant stream became no better than a bleak canalised drain and many forms of wildlife suffered. Kingfisher nest sites and even its fishing perches disappeared; so did the erosion ledges and sand bars where waders and wagtails used to feed and otters brought their catches. Destruction of riverside trees and shrubs robbed many birds of nest sites and feeding places. Riverside pastures and marshes, home of cuckoo flower, ragged robin and marsh orchid, of snipe and lapwing quickly went under the plough and both those birds declined catastrophically. Lincolnshire's most extensive valley wetlands, the Welland washes at Crowland and Cowbit, were dried out after construction of the Coronation Channel, the Spalding flood relief channel.

Something of this kind had happened before in the first agricultural revolution. Listen to John Clare lamenting the effects on the landscapes of his native Helpston just over the Northamptonshire border from Lincolnshire:

> Ye injur'd fields, ye once were gay,
> When Nature's hand displayed
> Long waving rows of willows grey
> And clumps of hawthorn shade;
> But now, alas! your hawthorn bowers
> All desolate we see!
> The spoiler's axe their shade devours,
> And cuts down every tree.
> Not trees alone have owned their force,
> Whole woods beneath them bowed,
> They turned the winding rivulet's course,
> And all thy pastures plough'd.

There was a difference, of course, between Clare's world and ours – the difference between horse and tractor, between spade and drag line. With the spade you did no more drainage than was strictly necessary; now you provide against a flood that happens – or was calculated to happen in the 1960s – only once in a hundred years. The effects on landscapes, including rivers and streams, are correspondingly more drastic.

As early as 1951 in only its third annual report the Trust, whilst appreciating the need for flood prevention, expressed its concern about the effect on wildlife and amenity of what it considered to be unnecessarily drastic treatment of rivers and streams in the interest of land drainage. Responsibility for upland water courses or 'main' rivers had passed in 1948 to the newly created River Boards, one of which the Lincolnshire River Board covered most of the historic county, a small area in the south falling into the area of the Welland and Nene Board. Most lowland drains remained the responsibility of the Internal Drainage Boards which were dominated by farming interests.

In addition to management treatment of watercourses, we had long been concerned about the effect on flow levels of excessive extraction for domestic and industrial purposes and crop irrigation. In our Bulletin to members in January 1963, for example, we described the plight of the River Slea which in 1961 had gone dry leaving a few stagnant pools where it flows through Sleaford. At the same time Newsham Lake on the Brocklesby Estate dried up, the result apparently of heavy drawing of underground water supplies by the North-East Lincolnshire Water Board. Extraction was a problem to which we frequently drew attention in subsequent years.

The Water Resources Act of 1963 resulted in the conversion of River Boards into River Authorities. The Act also required the Authorities to 'have regard to' the conservation of wildlife and natural features in discharging their functions, a requirement further expanded in the Water Act of 1973. This provision was greatly strengthened in the Wildlife and Countryside Act of 1981 which gave both the new Water Authorities and the IDBs a duty to 'further' conservation.

The Trust began to develop contacts with the Lincolnshire River Board in the mid-1950s, a process facilitated by the interest of the Authority's Clerk Geoffrey Phillippo. A wiry figure with a grizzled beard and a gravelly voice with a strong Norfolk 'drawl', Phillippo was a forthright, formidable character who did not suffer fools gladly. I had known him slightly as a solicitor in Lindsey County Council in the late 1940s at the time of the Trust's formation. He had become the first Clerk of the Lincolnshire River Board and the successor Authority, and by the 1960s was an experienced and influential administrator. He was also a knowledgeable ornithologist, and in 1965 was elected to the Trust Council of which he remained a member for the next ten years. Taking the Authority's duty to further conservation seriously and following discussions with the Trust and Nature Conservancy officers, Phillippo convened a meeting in March 1970 to discuss in general terms the conservation of rivers and streams within the River Authority's area of responsibility. Phillippo and the Chief Engineer John Finn attended for the Authority, David Robinson and I for the Trust, and Mike Schofield and John Blackwood for the Conservancy.

Whilst recognising that the Authority was compelled to carry out operations not necessarily favourable for the conservation of wildlife and riparian habitats, it was accepted that with understanding and sympathy operations could be modified to take such factors into account. The Authority would give the Trust and the Conservancy as much notice as possible of proposed river schemes together with an indication of long-term intentions for the management of a river system as a whole. The Trust and the Conservancy would undertake surveys where works were proposed, identifying stretches of special interest and offering suggestions and advice on the treatment of banks, trees and other riparian features in order to minimise damaging effects. The agreement was formally endorsed by the three parties and came into operation straightway. In the following year the County Councils of Lindsey and Kesteven became associated with it.

The agreement came too late to secure modification of the Lymn scheme and another on the Waithe Beck in the north-east of the county, but – like the Tetford Hill incident in the case of road verges – those unpopular schemes were proof if any were needed of the timeliness of it. The Lymn scheme in particular drew considerable criticism in letters to the press and to the River Authority from local people. As a result I received a somewhat explosive telephone call from Phillippo about engineers and their lack of sensitivity! There was no doubt about his conviction that engineering methods needed to be re-examined, and engineers too were gradually persuaded that methods less damaging to the environment could be devised. On the Lymn it was only possible to arrange with a sympathetic landowner for some replanting of trees. On the Waithe Beck the Trust and the Conservancy conducted an emergency survey of the stretch which had been treated and the remainder which was due for treatment. Other than tree replacement, however, little could be achieved and the flood plain marshes, overlooked for a thousand years by the Saxon tower of Waithe church, were drained and ploughed and more pairs of snipe were dispossessed.

In spite of these initial setbacks the consultation scheme worked well and more than thirty projects were examined by the Trust and the Conservancy in the first two years, a third of them requiring site meetings with engineers and in a few cases with riparian owners. The Nature Conservancy's Assistant Regional Officer John Blackwood, Rick Pilcher Chairman of the Trust's Scientific Policy Committee, and the Trust's Field Officer Barrie Wilkinson undertook much of the early survey work and the preparation of proposals. These also became a major commitment for the Trust's first Conservation Officer who was appointed in 1971.

Agreement on maintenance of tree cover proved to be a less difficult problem than channel and bank treatment. Groups of trees and shrubs were retained on one bank or the other, and the Trust with volunteer labour carried out replanting in several instances. Gradually it was possible to secure retention of cliffs where there were kingfisher nest sites, and the Authority expressed willingness to leave cut-off meanders provided riparian owners would agree.

We never sought to exaggerate the practical value of this scheme, but it did produce worthwhiie results from the outset. And there was another value at least as important: the establishment of confidence and good relations between conservationists and engineers many of whom developed considerable interest in the wildlife management problems of their rivers. Eventually when Regional Water Authorities with wider terms of reference replaced River Authorities in 1973, their own fisheries officers and biologists assumed greater responsibilities in the field of nature conservation.

The Lincolnshire consultation scheme was the first of its kind in the country and established an important precedent for co-operation between a River Authority and nature conservation bodies. In that respect, incidentally, it was very much in the spirit of the 'Countryside in 1970' conferences which did so much to advance the cause and the understanding of conservation principles and practices. As a result of the Lincolnshire Trust's initiative and subsequent developments in the Trusts' movement as a whole, I was invited in my capacity as General Secretary of the SPNR to address the annual course for technical officers of River Authorities at Southampton in April 1972 on 'Conservation Aspects of River Management'. Later, in February 1974, I read a paper on 'The Impacts of Lowland River Management' at the British Trust for Ornithology's 'Birds and Freshwater' conference which provided the launching pad for the BTO's long-running Waterways Bird Survey. The paper was subsequently printed in *Bird Study* in 1975.

Toxic chemicals and wildlife

"I expect it's the stuff they're putting in the seed dressings that's done it", speculated the farmer as we talked about the score or so of wood pigeons and the several pheasants, house sparrows and chaffinches that were lying dead on his fields. It was 1961 and reports had been reaching the Trust for some time of heavy bird mortality in many parts of Lincolnshire apparently caused by the consumption of seed with toxic dressing. In one of our earliest annual reports in 1951 we reported on the potential dangers to wildlife of the new toxic chemicals which were being increasingly used in agriculture to control pests. An article in *The Times* in October 1951 had reported that on two fields in Gloucestershire 158 dead birds of several species had been counted, a figure which probably represented only a proportion of those killed. Toxic chemicals were suspected and we asked our own members to report any similar incidents to us so that we could pass the information on to the RSPB. Bird deaths continued to occur and 1961 was the worst year in Lincolnshire. The incident I reported at the beginning was a minor one compared with that on the Tumby estate in the spring of that year when 382 dead birds were picked up and several thousand others were estimated to have died, an incident described by the Parliamentary Secretary of the Ministry of Agriculture as a 'holocaust'. Casualties included wood pigeons, pheasants, partridges, chaffinches, greenfinches, blackbirds, skylarks, waterhens, magpies, carrion crows and rooks. Those were all seedeaters and analysis of corpses proved conclusively that poisoning was the cause of death. Even more disturbing were the deaths of predators in this and other Lincolnshire incidents – long-eared and tawny owls, kestrels and sparrowhawks – showing that poisons were being transmitted through food chains.

A decline in the population of sparrowhawks in Lincolnshire had been apparent from the early 1950s, and as reported in our newsletter in July 1960 kestrels had suffered a similar though less drastic decline. Various reasons had been put forward, trapping and shooting being the most popular explanations. Our newsletter appealed for information which might throw light on the problem. The answer in fact was to be found in the next newsletter in November 1960 which reported the suspicion – soon to be confirmed – that persistent toxic chemicals which were killing seed-eating birds were accumulating in lethal doses in their predators. The sparrowhawk had ceased to breed in Lincolnshire by 1962 and for the next twenty years it virtually disappeared from the county and from much of eastern England. In spite of fears for the kestrel its population remained reasonably stable at a somewhat lower level, probably because birds formed a much less important element of its food.

The heavy mortality among birds – which included many pheasants and partridges – and among foxes in 1960 and 1961 aroused great public concern which eventually forced a reluctant Ministry of Agriculture to negotiate a voluntary agreement by which seed dressings containing dieldrin, aldrin and heptachlor would not be used for spring sowings, and in autumn only where there was real danger of an attack of wheat bulb fly. Apparently as a result there was a marked reduction in birds deaths from poisoning in Lincolnshire in 1962. On the Tumby estate, for example, the scene of the 1961 'holocaust', 112 dead birds (excluding wood pigeons) were recorded, 59 of them being pheasants. The situation, however, was still very disturbing. Nest desertions had become common, hatchability of eggs remained well below normal, and analysis revealed that a very wide variety of birds, including raptors, owls, herons and even house martins, were being affected. Persistent chemicals had in fact infiltrated the whole ecosystem.

Through my membership of the England Committee of the Nature Conservancy I was aware of the difficult negotiations about the toxic chemical problem which had been taking place between government departments and agencies. The Ministry of Agriculture, entrenched and reactionary, and the chemical manufacturers had refused to accept that chemicals were the cause of bird deaths. When they had eventually to concede they sought to belittle the damage caused. Those negotiations are described in detail by John Sheail in his book *Nature Conservation in Britain: The Formative Years (1998)*. An absorbing personal account of relationships and the painstaking research into the whole complex problem of pesticides and wildlife conducted at the Monks Wood Experimental Station can be found in the autobiographical work *The Bird of Time* by Dr Norman Moore, then Head of the Toxic Chemicals and Wildlife Section at the Station.

It might be thought that there was little a local Trust could do about the pesticide problem. In fact we played an active role on several fronts, more important perhaps because Lincolnshire as a leading agricultural and predominantly arable county took the full impact of pesticide damage to wildlife. The number of poisoning incidents was more than twice that reported from any other county. First, we were able to collect information about bird and mammal mortality which we passed on regularly to the joint RSPB/BTO Committee which was set up to monitor the problem and whose reports had an important influence in the search for solutions. In the spring of 1961, for example, we sent the Committee information on more than forty incidents – including the one at Tumby – which had come to our notice through members and other sources. We were also able to arrange for many corpses, including those of predatory birds, to be sent for analysis, initially to the RSPB and later to the Nature Conservancy's Toxic Chemicals Section at Monks Wood.

Secondly, we sought to foster informed opinion about the extent and nature of the problem by reporting developments in our newsletters and by press releases which received both national and local publicity. *The Times*, for example, carried a lengthy report on 4 May 1962 about the effects of toxic chemicals and other threats to wildlife based on an interview which I gave to its Midlands correspondent.

Thirdly, we played our part in seeking political action to curb the use of the offending chemicals by writing to our MPs and by supporting representations by the RSPB and by the County Trusts' Committee of the SPNR which had just come into being. Not surprisingly the issue was high on the agenda at the Trusts' Norwich conference in 1962. The voluntary ban agreed in 1961 had eased but by no means solved the problem, and the voluntary conservation bodies continued to press for the complete prohibition of the organochlorine chemicals as recommended in fact by the Parliamentary Select Committee on Estimates. The case for prohibition was further strengthened by the widespread bird mortality caused by the severe winter of 1962/3 the effects of which were reported in our newsletter issued in May 1963. It became evident too that, although there were voluntary restraints on the use of pesticides in agriculture, the same chemicals were to be found in a number of garden insecticides which could be freely used. In the same bulletin we made an appeal to gardeners not to use insecticides containing those chemicals.

There was one other powerful influence on public opinion at that time, Rachel Carson's disturbing book *Silent Spring* which became a best-seller as soon as it was published in this country in February 1963. Her plea for recognition of the dangers of toxic chemicals and for more searching investigation of their effects closely reflected the views of the nature conservation movement and a growing sector of public opinion in this country. That, combined with the findings and courageous persistence of the Monks Wood scientists, led eventually to a thorough review of organochlorine pesticides by an Inter-departmental Advisory Committee whose recommendations for a ban on most uses of aldrin, dieldrin and heptachlor took effect in 1965. Their use and that of another persistent organochlorine DDT was further restricted in 1969.

There were other practical ways in which the Trust was able to make a small contribution to the investigation of the toxic chemicals problem. The persistent organochlorines were found to have contaminated marine and freshwater as well as terrestrial ecosystems, and one of the fish-eating predators studied by the Monks Wood team was the heron whose population had suffered a steady decline since 1959. Two long-established Lincolnshire heronries, at Troy Wood and Willoughby Wood, were chosen for intensive research. Both the owners, Sir David Hawley at Troy and Mr Jack Roughton at Willoughby, were members of the Trust – the former a member of Council for several years – and were readily co-operative. The research team was led by Ian Prestt whom I knew well from my Nature Conservancy involvement and who went on to become Deputy Director of the Conservancy and later Director of the RSPB. The work started in 1964 and for the next six years Prestt submitted progress reports for publication in the Trust's newsletter. Dead young and addled eggs and samples of fish were collected from below the nests and sent for analysis. They all showed varying degrees of contamination. At first a mirror on a long pole was used to look into the nests. Later in order to study behaviour at the nest a tower hide was erected in the Willoughby colony giving a view of thirteen pairs. One aspect of behaviour observed from the hide and caused by the effects of toxics was that some of the herons deliberately broke their own eggs which were also shown to have become thinner shelled than they were before 1945. The research made a significant contribution to our understanding of the effects of toxic chemicals, and incidentally of the breeding behaviour of the heron, the subject of a paper by members of the team in the journal *Ardea* in 1970.

In addition to liaising with the owners of the woods, the Trust was able to help by providing accommodation for the team at the Gibraltar Point Field Station, and by assisting through volunteers and its field officer in locating the main sources of fish and other food collected by the herons and fed to their young. The heronry is less than a mile away from home at Willoughby and the team often called on us for refreshment. On one occasion they had special need of it having been in the tower hide during a thunderstorm, an unnerving experience. The tower was no doubt safe enough, but it swayed in the wind and I doubt if it would have passed today's more stringent safety requirements! With some trepidation – I have no head for heights – I went up into the hide one fine April day. To see the herons and their reptilian-like young at close quarters in their green treetop world was a fascinating experience.

Postscript

The agricultural juggernaut ground on into the 1970s. The withdrawal of the persistent organochlorine pesticides – which took until 1983 to complete – came just in time to prevent even more contamination of the environment and save Britain's birds of prey in particular from further decline and allow them to make a gradual recovery. That, however, was not the end of the toxic chemical problem. Polychlorinated biphenyls (PCBs) used in the manufacture of paints, adhesives, cutting oils and many other substances also became widely dispersed in the environment and were implicated in the deaths of thousands of guillemots in the Irish Sea in 1969, and in the decline and virtual extinction of the otter from English rivers. We drew attention to the plight of the otter in an article in our newsletter in September 1969 when we appealed to members to report the occurrence of otters and to retrieve corpses for analysis at Monks Wood. Because of their growing scarcity we also supported the SPNR and other national bodies in a successful campaign to secure a ban on otter hunting. It was not until the 1990s that otters began to make a gradual return to Lincolnshire rivers.

Then there was the strange case of the disappearing butterflies, the subject of a major feature in our newsletter of spring 1968. During the late 50s and the 60s no less than twelve species of butterfly became extinct in Lincolnshire and another seven were reduced to remnant populations. Losses were especially heavy among woodland species: four fritillaries and the chequered skipper. The marsh fritillary disappeared from all its damp meadows; the marbled white and chalkhill blue from their limestone grassland sites in the south of the county; the Duke of Burgundy from Robert's Field, its only known locality at that time. Similar losses occurred over much of south-east England, and various reasons were put forward, destruction and deterioration of habitat being the most favoured. No doubt that was a major cause and we could quote specific examples like the destruction of the well-known marsh fritillary meadows and that of the Duke of Burgundy's limestone grassland at Robert's Field. There were, on the other hand, sites which seemed to have changed very little like some of the woodlands and the Trust's Kirkby Moor reserve where the magnificent dark green fritillary used to fly. The lost butterflies moreover came from a range of habitats and their extinctions happened over a comparatively short period of time of ten to fifteen years. These facts led me to believe that there were other contributory causes for these losses: the effects of toxic chemicals, acid rain or other forms of environmental pollution to which insects like butterflies might be particularly sensitive. Such a theory did not gain much credence from experts at the time,

High rise hide at Willoughby Wood heronry used by scientists from Monks Wood Experimental Station to study the effects of toxic chemicals on the eggs and young.

185

Sparrowhawk

but I have heard it more frequently propounded in recent years. Maybe current and proposed experiments to reintroduce some of the lost species will throw new light on the problem.

Agricultural practices other than the use of pesticides – some of which I have described earlier in this chapter – also had a drastic impact on wildlife. The widespread switch from spring to autumn sown grain, for example, which rendered crop land unsuitable for nesting lapwings and skylarks was a major factor in their decline. The absence of winter stubbles combined with the use of herbicides drastically reduced the supply of weed seed vital to species like corn bunting, linnet, yellowhammer, tree sparrow and grey partridge. The decline of these was already becoming apparent in the later 1980s and accelerated alarmingly towards the end of the century.

By the 1980s, however, there were signs of change in the agricultural situation. Over-production had resulted in grain and butter mountains, and set-aside was introduced to pay farmers for not cropping land. It had at last become apparent that the kind of government support for agriculture which had fuelled its intensity was neither justified nor sustainable. There was moreover a growing public demand for greater respect for the rural environment and its wildlife. These factors led to the introduction of agri-environment schemes like the Environmentally Sensitive Areas and Stewardship. Although no ESA was designated in Lincolnshire, in spite of strong representations from the Trust, opportunities for influencing land use and acquiring new nature reserves steadily increased. At the beginning of the new century the agricultural juggernaut finally ground to a halt! It left us a legacy of desolated landscapes, impoverished wildlife, and ironically – but predictably – an agricultural industry in crisis.

Gatekeeper

187

– 10 –

1958-1973 Growing Pains

THE FIFTEEN years between the Trust's 10th and 25th anniversaries was a period of growth and development. Membership grew from 540 to over 4,500; the volunteer officers and active members were reinforced by six members of staff; fourteen Area Groups were established based on major centres throughout the county; the number of nature reserves increased from eight to thirty; education and research work expanded beyond the most optimistic expectations of the 1950s. Most important of all perhaps the Trust became widely recognised as a body with an important practical contribution to make to the conservation of Lincolnshire's natural environment and wildlife. In this chapter I describe some of the means by which the Trust's structure and organisation was strengthened and adjusted to meet the needs of growth and expansion.

The Volunteer Force

Central Organisation and Area Groups

In 1958 the Trust was still almost entirely dependent on volunteers for its administration and nature reserve management, as it had been for the first ten years of its life. Expansion required yet more volunteer commitment and deployment. Centrally a hard-working Executive Committee had relieved the twenty-one member Council of much of the day-to-day policy implementation, and the Committee was gradually strengthened in the 1960s by the appointment of younger members such as David Robinson, Brian Tear and Dick Morgan who, as Chairman of the Grantham Area Group, played an important role in promoting the Trust's influence and activities in Kesteven. His early death in 1969 deprived the Trust of one of its most valued members. Dick Cornwallis maintained his invaluable role as Assistant General Secretary until he took over the Chairmanship in 1963. Marson Peet succeeded Tom Baker as Honorary Treasurer in 1958. For several years he had to deal personally with every financial transaction, and even later when office staff and facilities became available, he continued to handle a great deal of time-consuming financial business which grew steadily in volume and complexity. He served indefatigably for seventeen vital years of development, retiring in 1975 to be replaced by John Keily, a Chartered Accountant and a senior partner in a well-known Lincolnshire firm which also acted for the RSNC for several years. Robin Crane, who had established himself as a freelance film-maker in Lincolnshire, succeeded Dick as Deputy Honorary Secretary in 1966, although much of his time in that year was taken up by the making of the Trust's first film *Nature in Trust*, and he left the County in 1967 for Sussex where he played a leading role in the County Trust and later in the 1990s as Chairman of the Royal Society for Nature Conservation, the Trusts' national body.

During this period we were constantly seeking the best ways of using our volunteer resources to cope with the expansion of activity and commitment. In 1959 the Council adopted a plan to re-organise the Trust's administrative structure which provided, among other changes, for additional Honorary Officers to cover membership, publicity and education. There were further adjustments in 1963 when it was also agreed to change the name of the Trust to the more appropriate title of 'Trust for Nature Conservation'. In 1965 a Publicity Committee was established under the chairmanship of David Robinson. Among its early tasks were the selection of material for the newsletters and the planning of the first Handbook to the Trust's reserves which was published in 1966. In 1969 the Committee was converted into an Education and Public Relations Group, the title of 'Group' being preferred to 'Committee' to indicate that it was essentially a working body concerned with the implementation as well as the making of policy.

In parallel with the strengthening of the central organisation we sought to ensure that the increasing membership was organised to promote the Trust and its objectives throughout our far-flung county, the second largest historic county in England. We had experimented in the 1950s by creating Regional Committees. These had produced a number of notable volunteers, but, as described in an earlier chapter, had not fulfilled the broader purposes we had envisaged for them. The network of Regional Officers, which replaced the Committees, maintained a valuable link between regions and the centre, but most of the Regional Officers concentrated on reserve management and practical conservation tasks. A system was needed which would provide a service to members and enable them to participate in activities if they wished, and would promote the interests of the Trust and act as its eyes and ears in particular areas.

After extensive discussion in the Executive Committee and after taking soundings among members we decided to encourage the formation of groups to be known as Area Groups based on the larger centres where membership was mainly concentrated. The first of these was established at Spalding in December 1966 under the leadership of Arnold Smith, then the Trust's Honorary Auditor. Arnold was a great enthusiast and through his local professional connections was able to raise considerable sums of money. Unfortunately he took the view that the deployment of funds should be principally at the discretion of the local Group rather than the Trust's Executive Committee and Council. Whilst the latter were prepared wherever possible to satisfy local aspirations and proposals, their main responsibility was to the county as a whole and to conservation priorities which they determined on a county basis. Some of the Spalding Group's projects were certainly not in that category even for their own area. After strenuous but unavailing efforts to reach an accommodation with Arnold Smith and his Group, the Trust Council was left with no alternative but to disband the Spalding Group. Arnold subsequently set up a separate company - South Lincolnshire Nature Reserves Ltd - to hold a number of small properties which he had acquired or leased. In 1992 South Lincolnshire Nature Reserves was wound up and its assets transferred to the Trust which had meantime established a new South Holland Group.

That was not an auspicious start to our Area Group system, but in April 1967 a Group was established at Lincoln based on a constitution and procedures designed to contain it within the constitutional framework of the Trust and so avoid a recurrence of the Spalding problem. It was adopted as a model for all subsequent Area Groups. We owed that achievement to the legal and presentational skills of Richard Pepler, the Deputy Clerk of Lindsey County Council, whose membership of the Trust Council from 1966 and service as Deputy Chairman from 1974 to 1991 was to prove a great source of strength to the Trust. He became the first Chairman of the Lincoln Group with Brian and Anne Tear as Honorary Secretaries.

As a result of a meeting of Kesteven members in March 1967 Area Groups were next formed at Grantham and Sleaford and later at Bourne. Throughout the county the momentum was strongly maintained until by the mid-1970s seventeen Groups had been formed. It is a testimony to the durability of the concept that all but one of these Groups (a village group at Gosberton) are still in existence today. The fortunes of individual Groups have fluctuated as personalities and local circumstances have changed, but the full and varied programme of Area Group meetings which appears in each issue of *Lapwings* reveals a sustained wealth of activity.

In the late 1960s and early 70s the advent of Groups undoubtedly brought a new and exciting dimension to the Trust and brought it into closer contact with local communities and organisations. Members now had a real opportunity to participate in its affairs and promote its objectives. Most formation meetings were enthusiastically attended and Groups soon launched their own programmes of indoor and outdoor meetings, and mounted recruiting and fundraising events. Within the terms of the model constitution Groups were free to plan their own activities. Some adopted the full range of Trust work including surveys of potential nature reserves and the management of existing ones. Others concentrated on provision of meetings, events and publicity, leaving reserve management largely to volunteer wardens and work parties, a preference which gradually came to predominate as special Reserve Management Groups were established.

As part of the major reorganisation of the Trust's administrative and committee structure in 1969, the membership of the Council, as the governing body of the Trust, was expanded to allow greater opportunity for Area Group members to be appointed, bringing new strength to the Council. At the same time liaison between the centre and Area Groups was strengthened by the establishment of a standing conference of officers from both sides. One of its first actions was to formally approve the model constitution and financial arrangements for Area Groups. Later years have seen the liaison process further developed, and under revised Articles of Association each Group is now entitled to appoint a representative to the Council.

Managing the Nature Reserves

Most of our early nature reserves attracted support as soon as they were established, and we were fortunate in the competence and commitment of the voluntary reserve managers. Most of them were all-round naturalists who found great satisfaction in discovering more about their reserve, in putting management concepts into practice, and in the more mundane tasks of estate management and routine wardening. I have already referred by name to some of the early coast and heathland reserve managers; others who come to mind from the 1960s onwards include John Marshall and Alec Parker at the Decoy Wood, John Redshaw at Baston Fen and Surfleet Lows, Les Gostick and Geoff Atkin at Rauceby Warren, David Willey at Scotton Common, Bernard Featherstone at Langholme Wood, Brian Redman at Kirkby Moor, Ken Green at Crowle Waste, Peter Wilson and Brian Oxborrow at Linwood Warren, Angela Bates at Tortoiseshell Wood, Alf McGowan at Far Ings, Clifford Jukes at Tetney Blow Wells, John Walker at Sea Bank Clay Pits, Vivienne Booth at Donna Nook, Richard and Kay Heath at Moulton Marsh, Geoff Trinder at Epworth Turbary, John Moore at Muckton Wood, and Graham Johnson at Rigsby Wood. Some of those early managers moved on to other interests; others have continued to play a prominent part in the affairs of the Trust to the present day. Geoff Trinder's enthusiasm and sustained commitment brought much needed strength to our position in the Isle of Axholme generally. They were qualities which he later brought to its central administration together with his outstanding skill as a photographer.

In addition to the managers, almost all the reserves attracted a number of other helpers to assist with management tasks, and we encouraged the formation of reserve groups to support and assist the manager. In 1965 these groups were formally recognised and given terms of reference. They would be essentially working groups, responsible for the wardening and management of the reserve in accordance with an approved Management Plan. Each group was to submit to the Executive Committee – after 1969 to the Scientific Policy Group – an annual report on the management of the reserve. Their efforts were reinforced by school and college parties, Boy Scouts and Girl Guides recruited to help with special tasks. As already described, the national Conservation Corps also took part in major management tasks at Gibraltar Point in 1959, and at Linwood Warren and Scotton Common in 1961.

Earlier, in December 1960, the Executive Committee had decided to establish a mobile conservation corps to be recruited from three or four main areas. The corps was intended to supplement the work of volunteers on particular reserves and carry out special tasks. Whilst it functioned somewhat patchily, the mobile corps played a useful role in reserve management until 1977 when we established a new organisation the Viking Conservation Corps which, although sponsored and administered by the Trust, operated on a semi-independent basis. We acquired a van for it to transport tools, but transport of volunteers remained a limiting factor. The Viking Corps, initially under the leadership of Geoff Espin, gave valuable service to the Trust for the next fifteen years.

The appointment of the Scientific Policy Group in 1969 was an overdue recognition of the need for more detailed consideration of nature reserve acquisition and management and of the Trust's interests in the wider countryside, matters which up to that time had been dealt with by the Council and an overworked Executive Committee. Richard Pilcher was the obvious choice for Chairman of

Verdun Wray (left) with young naturalists at Gibraltar Point.

Marson Peet recording for the Rivers and Streams Survey, 1986.

Geoff Trinder, 1987.

The Bishop of Lincoln, the Rt Rev Simon Phipps, Ted Smith and Richard Pepler (right) set off on the sponsored Viking Walk, 1980.

Ray Collier the Trust's first Conservation Officer 1970-75.

Viking Conservation Corps clearing Claxby Spring, 1980.

Lindsey County Council Countryside Committee at Mausoleum Woods 1968.

Barrie Wilkinson interviewed by Radio Humberside at Mausoleum Woods.

Opening the Bardney Forest Nature Trails 1973.

Trust caravan at Grimsthorpe Park Nature Trail 1969.

the Group though after five years increasing deafness forced him to stand down and his place was taken by John Redshaw. John, who lived in the Spalding area, had been one of the earliest members of the Trust and had corresponded with me whilst still in his teens about Cowbit Wash and other places in South Lincolnshire, his reports often illustrated by meticulous plans and drawings. An excellent all-round naturalist, a man of quiet confidence and sound judgement, John has been one of the real stalwarts of the Trust for more than forty years. Among other early members of that Group were botanist Irene Weston, Don Wright and Keith Tallack, the former Lindsey County Surveyor, who in retirement gave valuable service to the Trust as Honorary Estates Adviser. Don, who was at that time Head of Biology, Science & Environmental Studies at Kesteven College of Education, had played a major role in promoting Trust Area Groups in Kesteven and was the first Secretary of the Grantham Group. He now brought his knowledge and experience as an ecologist to the affairs of the Trust in the Scientific Policy Group, in the management of Gibraltar Point and in the Farming and Wildlife Advisory Group of which the Trust had been a principal promoter.

The minutes of the first meeting of the Group in September 1969 illustrate the welter of business with which it had to deal. Among the items were reserve selection and acquisition policy, with seven sites for immediate consideration; the review of reserve management groups, and of progress with management plans; current surveys; policy on introductions including the recent SPNR policy statement on the subject which was approved; protection of seals and otters. Little wonder that the meeting did not break up until nearly 11 o'clock!

Promotion and Publicity
Membership of the Trust began to increase more rapidly after the mid-1960s. At the end of 1972 it stood at more than 3,400, the new intake in that year alone being over 1,000. This was the result of both Area Group recruiting activity and of new centrally organised promotional efforts and projects which included a major appeal for funds launched at a meeting addressed by Sir Peter Scott in September 1971.

The most exciting and successful of the promotional projects of the 1960s, however, was the making of a Trust film - two films in fact. The RSPB had been producing bird films for several years; we had shown several of them at area meetings. In 1965 the Berks, Bucks and Oxon Naturalists' Trust produced the first film about the work of a county Trust. By that time we had also begun to plan a film of our own, taking advantage of the technical skills and equipment in which Robin Crane had invested in establishing his film-making unit. To meet the cost of production we obtained sponsorship from business and industrial concerns, and hired and sold copies of the film to other organisations including the Lindsey Education Authority. Crane began filming in the summer of 1965 according to a programme prepared by the Trust's officers. He was able to feature most of the existing nature reserves with a variety of their plants and animals. The reserves were shown in their setting of characteristic Lincolnshire landscapes such as the Kesteven limestone hills, the Wolds and the Marsh. The unspoiled coastline of Gibraltar Point and Saltfleetby was contrasted with the holiday development areas around Skegness and Ingoldmells. Dick Cornwallis spoke to sequences which showed the impact of modern farming on wildlife. The great flock of pink-footed geese which then wintered on Croftmarsh; the high tide roosts of waders at Gibraltar Point, and a pair of Montagu's harriers which nested that year at Wainfleet were special highlights. Once the filming was completed I prepared a script, and the film was edited by a professional editor Douglas Fisher. I found it an exciting project in which to be involved.

The premiere of *Nature in Trust* was held in Lincoln on 4 April 1967 before an invited and widely representative audience of more than 250. The film made a great impact, and James Fisher, ornithologist and broadcaster, our principal guest, described it as of "Festival Hall standard". Five showings around the county in the following ten days attracted more than 1,400 people, and its popularity was sustained for several years. In connection with the film the magazine *Lincolnshire Life* published an attractively illustrated supplement about nature conservation in Lincolnshire and the work of the Trust. Robin Crane subsequently made a second film for the Trust *An Eye for the Country* in which wildlife and wild places are seen through the eyes of a young girl and a group of children. It was funded by British Gas and was shown for the first time in London. It was a good film, but it never achieved the popularity of *Nature in Trust* which even today retains much of its freshness and relevance.

Until 1964 we issued a duplicated newsletter to members at somewhat irregular intervals. The development of the Trust required something better, and in 1965 we produced the first of a twice-yearly newsletter in the form of a neat booklet illustrated by line drawings of plants and animals, many of them by my wife Mary. It contained current news of nature reserves and Area Group activities, and, as they developed, of publicity projects and membership, and of national affairs. It also carried the results of surveys and research. The first issue, for example, had an article on the Alder Carrs of the South Wolds, and on the Ponds, Pits and Quarries Survey which the Trust had just mounted. In subsequent issues there were articles on Lincolnshire rivers; on the impact of modern farming, including the effect of pesticides, on bird populations; on the status of the otter and the harvest mouse in Lincolnshire, and on the central Lincolnshire woodlands, the latter written by Dr George Peterken, the leading expert on ancient woodlands. One issue was devoted almost entirely to various aspects of road verges and their conservation, and we carried articles from officers of related organisations such as the Lincolnshire River Authority and the Forestry Commission.

When in April 1975 we switched to a more popular newspaper format for the newsletter, reports on surveys and research received rather less prominence. Change was desirable, however, partly because of the expanding membership and partly because of rising printing costs. The new format enabled us to carry advertising which made a significant contribution to the costs of production. It also enabled us to use photographs, an increasingly important feature. Whilst fully accepting the need for change I could not help regretting the demise of the little booklet, especially since early issues of the new style newsletter were printed on rather dingy paper. I had edited the booklet from the outset, latterly with David Robinson who now took over the editing, a task which he has continued to the present day. His experience and skills as writer, journalist and editor have made an invaluable contribution to the Trust's information service to its members.

Our promotion and publicity work was boosted in this period by increasing public concern about the conservation of the natural environment which seemed threatened by man-made dangers such as marine pollution and the effects on wildlife and on people of toxic chemicals used in agriculture and industry. These dangers were highlighted by publications like Rachel Carson's *Silent Spring*, Max Nicholson's *The Environmental Revolution*, and Fraser Darling's outstanding Reith lectures *Wilderness and Plenty*. By 1970 indeed the environment had become a major political issue and governments were under pressure to take action. 1970 was designated European Conservation Year, and the third of the series of influential 'Countryside in 1970' conferences was held under the presidency of the Duke of Edinburgh. 1970 was also fortuitously the Trust's 21st anniversary to celebrate which we published an attractive brochure and held a reception in Lincoln which was addressed by Christopher Cadbury, President of the RSNC, and Robert Boote, Chairman of the European Committee for the Conservation of Nature and Secretary of the 'Countryside in 1970' conferences. Mr Cadbury spoke of the debt which the whole County Trust movement owed to Lincolnshire "for leading us out of our parochial isolation into a strong united national movement with a much wider concept of the meaning of nature conservation". Mr Boote too described the Trust as a "true leader in this field". It was also a memorable occasion for me and my family since we were all presented with honorary life membership of the Trust.

Against this favourable national background, our Education and Public Relations Group, under Brian Tear's chairmanship, was active in mounting a number of special projects designed to inform people about the natural world and encourage greater participation in caring for it. We arranged for a national exhibition illustrating the work of all County Trusts to be staged in the City and County Museum in Lincoln and it was visited by more than 4,400 people. We also arranged Countryside Tours for the County Federations of Women's Institutes, 30 to 40 mile coach tours with commentary by experienced Trust members. These proved to be very popular, attracting more than 370 WI members. We also acquired, with the help of a Carnegie grant a motor caravan to serve as a travelling exhibition centre. But perhaps the most important development, for which the caravan was primarily acquired, was the launch in 1968 of the first nature trails sponsored by Shell as their contribution to European Conservation Year. None of the Trust's reserves was suitable or appropriate for a trail at that time, so we sought the co-operation of landowners for mounting trails in their parks and woodlands. The first two were on the Brocklesby estate in North Lincolnshire and at Well Vale near Alford where the trail became a regular feature for several years. In spite of a poor summer in 1968 the trails were a great success, more than 4,500 people walking the two of them. The following year 1969 one trail alone, at Willingham Forest, attracted some 6,500 people, and that figure was surpassed by the 8,000 visitors to the Normanby Park trail in August. Grimsthorpe Park, the home of our then Patron, Lord Ancaster, was the venue for the third trail of that year. It established a tradition of Trust trails at Grimsthorpe which continued for many years. In fact trails generally were assured of a regular place in Trust activities for several years ahead. Mounting a trail was a considerable task: for the initial planning; for writing the trail guide; for the physical job of laying it out with direction arrows, explanatory boards and plant and tree labels; and for the manning of the caravan each day. Preparing the trails on the ground became an annual task for Barrie Wilkinson, the Trust's Field Officer; and the new Area Groups played a vital part in providing volunteers for manning and publicity. Whilst they eventually ran their course there is no doubt that the trails proved their value as a method of interpreting nature and the countryside to the ordinary visitor. They encouraged landowners to allow controlled access to their estates, and they brought much favourable publicity for the Trust.

Education was one of the Trust's primary purposes from the outset and I have described how we sought to fulfil that purpose at Gibraltar Point in the 1950s. The appointment of Verdun Wray as Honorary Education Officer in 1959 was intended to help extend education to all areas of the Trust's activities. Verdun was a gifted teacher of Biology and Rural Studies with an ability to interest and inspire young people in the study of nature. It was a gift which he brought to the educational work of the Trust for the next twenty-five years. He began by liaising with schools using Gibraltar Point and other Trust reserves, and he soon began planning to establish a junior section of the Trust. This was not easy in such a large county with a scattered population, but progress was gradually made, especially when the Education and Public Relations Group was established in 1969 under Brian Tear's chairmanship. Brian, also an outstanding teacher with a gift for lively presentation, made the education and publicity work of the Trust his special interest, one which he has pursued with unflagging enthusiasm for more than thirty years. A primary schools Conservation Competition was sponsored by the Trust in European Conservation Year 1970, and was so popular that it was repeated in 1971. In the same year the Trust started a scheme to encourage schools to build and erect nestboxes. By 1972 Trust newsletters carried a Junior Members Section with news of local group activities. In 1974, when there were 350 junior members, the national organisation WATCH was established by the RSNC, the Trusts' parent body, and junior members began to receive the junior newsletter WATCHWORD.

Local Authority Relationships

There had been another outcome of the second 'Countryside in 1970' conference in 1965 which gave opportunities to the Trust to promote its aims. It was the recommendation from the conference group chaired by Walter Lane that County Councils should establish Countryside Committees which would encourage partnership between official and voluntary bodies in the care and conservation of the countryside. The Countryside Act of 1968 subsequently gave formal statutory acknowledgement to such Committees, but Lindsey County Council, closely followed by Kesteven, anticipated those powers and established Committees in 1966, in both cases including a third of the membership from bodies outside the County Council. For both Committees the Trust was invited to nominate a representative. Dick Morgan served on the Kesteven Committee and I served in Lindsey. The terms of reference for Lindsey – they were similar for Kesteven – were to consider and report on matters relating to the use and enjoyment of the countryside; to prepare a register of countryside 'treasures', and to maintain land held by the County Council for the enjoyment of the public. In the latter terms the Lindsey Committee took over the responsibilities for the Council's coastal estate. The Committee also sought to reconcile conflicting interests in the countryside, in particular those of recreation, nature conservation and farming.

At the same time in Lindsey the County Council was undertaking a countryside recreation survey assessing present and future demands on the countryside. The Trust was also represented on a Steering Committee for this survey, the report of which was issued in 1971. It showed what recreational facilities – country parks, picnic sites, footpaths and so on – and what opportunities for the study and enjoyment of nature were required and the areas where these might best be located. That survey was supplemented by a further study of recreational and conservation needs called the Project for the Improvement of the Environment (Lindsey 'Pie') which was financed by a grant from the Carnegie UK Trust. The Project Officer, John Leefe, liaised closely with the Trust.

There was certainly a great deal of activity in the Trust's field of interest in the later 1960s and it undoubtedly helped to promote our development and our public profile. As for the Countryside Committees, they flourished until local government reorganisation in 1974 when the new Lincolnshire County Council downgraded its Committee to a sub-committee of the Planning Committee. Though the Trust was allocated a place on Lincolnshire's sub-committee we regretted its loss of status which we believed – rightly as it transpired – would lead to its eventual demise. The new Humberside County Council did not create even a sub-committee.

Financing Development and Staffing

As the growth and development of the Trust gathered pace in the 1960s it became increasingly obvious that the momentum could not be sustained without a corresponding increase in administrative and financial resources which were already dangerously inadequate for the demands being made upon them. The implication was inescapable: some paid staff were needed to support the central administration. More of the time that I could spare from my University duties had to be devoted to the national association, and I was heavily involved both locally and nationally in many of the developments I have just described. Other Honorary Officers were likewise overburdened, and whilst new volunteers were constantly coming forward to assist the Trust, they were almost always people in full employment with limited time, and most of them in any case preferred to help in the field or with Area Groups rather than at headquarters. By 1967 the position had become critical and at a meeting of the Council in November that year the President Sir Weston Cracroft Amcotts and Richard Pepler were invited to examine the problem of increasing the Trust's income in order to provide a more adequate administration.

Since the Trust was closely associated and sharing costs with Lindsey County Council in the management of the Gibraltar Point reserve and in other ways, Sir Weston and Richard sought the cooperation of the County Clerk, Walter Lane. Walter had become Clerk in 1957 and had demonstrated straightway a concern for the countryside and for promoting understanding and enjoyment of nature. He had strongly supported the development of the Gibraltar Point reserve and its educational programme; encouraged the Council's efforts to protect other unspoilt stretches of the coast like Saltfleetby from development; promoted tree planting on a large scale by the County Council, and initiated with the Trust the first Road Verge Protection Scheme in England. In 1965 through his active role in the County Councils' Association he was closely involved in the proceedings of the 'Countryside in 1970' conferences and chaired the important Study Group which recommended more local authority involvement in conservation, including the establishment of Countryside Committees. It is not surprising that from the outset he and I found a great deal of interest in common. On a personal level we both had young children of similar ages, and we were both setting up new homes and developing new gardens.

Walter was always scrupulously careful, however, not to show favouritism or even support for the Trust unless it could be clearly and openly justified. So when he was approached about our financial problems he proposed that the Trust's finances and administration should be thoroughly investigated by the County Council's Organisation and Methods Officer, Mr T E H Dodds. We readily agreed to that and in November 1967 Mr Dodds presented a detailed report of his findings to the Trust Council. The Trust, he concluded, faced a serious crisis and new sources of help had to be found if the administration was to be strengthened in the ways he proposed. Pre-eminently it required a salaried administrative officer with adequate clerical support centralised in the new offices at The Manor House in Alford which the Trust had recently occupied. Management of the increasing number of nature reserves also needed greater resources.

The report was welcomed by the Trust Council who then agreed that application for financial assistance based on the report's recommendations be made to the three Lincolnshire County Councils. The application described the contribution which the Trust was making in a variety of ways to the protection of the natural heritage of the historic county, and the services and opportunities which it was providing for education and for public enjoyment of nature in the countryside. The Council also agreed that other new sources of financial aid be sought including an appeal to members for more covenanting, and publicity to attract legacies.

In Lindsey the application went to the Countryside Committee of which I was a member. When the Chairman reminded members to declare any interest more than half of them as members of the Trust left the room! The amounts requested from the Councils calculated on a population basis totalled £1,800 in 1968/69 rising to £2,650 by 1970/71. Lindsey and Kesteven met their quota for the first year but Holland fell short and the total amounted to £1,550. We decided nevertheless to go ahead with the appointment of an Administrative Officer in the salary range £1,200 to £1,400 pa. We were, I believe, the first County Trust to receive local authority grant-aid specifically for administrative purposes, and our advice on making an application was sought throughout the Trusts' movement.

The grants seem small by today's standards and they were in fact frozen for the next two years as a result of financial stringency imposed on local authorities. Nevertheless £1,550 represented about 20% of the Trust's total income for 1968. The comparable proportion in 2005 was less than 2%. The grants in fact saved the day and were a tremendous boost to morale. In 1970 the Trust re-applied to the three County Councils for financial assistance towards administrative, educational and conservation expenses. The Trust proposed the additional appointments of a Conservation Officer, a second Warden at Gibraltar Point for specific duties in connection with the field station as well as the nature reserve, and the full-time employment of the Field Officer whose services up to that time had been shared with the Nature Conservancy. The result of that application was an increase in County Council contributions from £1,550 to £2,600.

Paul Berkeley, a recently retired RAF Officer, took up the administrative appointment at the end of 1968. He served the Trust well for five years in a quietly efficient manner. He was a skilful negotiator and ambassador and played a particularly vital role in the establishment of the Area Group system. The increase in County Council grants in 1970 enabled us to proceed with the appointment of a Conservation Officer. He was to be responsible to the Honorary Secretary and work in association with the Administrative Officer and the Scientific Policy Group. The successful candidate was Ray Collier whom we had interviewed twelve years before for the Gibraltar Point Warden post. He had joined the Nature Conservancy and I had kept in touch with him when he was Warden of the Castor Hanglands Reserve in Northamptonshire. In 1970 he was in charge of the Inverpolly National Nature Reserve in Wester Ross. He came to the Trust on a five-year secondment, an arrangement which suited both sides. He typified in many ways the new kind of field officer which the conservation movement was producing. He was resourceful and energetic. He had a broad understanding of conservation management problems and he was skilled in the use of equipment being developed for management purposes. His contribution in those respects can be seen in the plans which he prepared for the Scientific Policy Group for new reserves like Snipe Dales, Moor Farm and Crowle Moors which were established during his time with the Trust. He encouraged and trained volunteers in reserve management groups, and developed recording systems including a photographic collection. He was also a popular speaker much in demand by Area Groups and outside bodies. He made contact with other Trust Conservation Officers and in 1973 he organised a three-day conference for them in Lincolnshire, the first time that professional and field staff of the Trusts had been brought together. At the end of 1975 he returned to the Nature Conservancy as Chief Warden in the East Midlands region and served in later years in senior posts in Scotland. His input to the Trust at a crucial time in its development was of great value.

Whilst increasing income from membership and grant-aid from the three Lincolnshire County Councils from 1968 had enabled us to appoint an Administrative and a Conservation Officer, funding the purchase of major new reserves depended on grants from outside bodies and special appeals to members and the wider public. So in 1971 when the opportunity arose to acquire Snipe Dales, Tortoiseshell Wood, Moor Closes and Moor Farm we boldly launched an appeal for £50,000 under the title 'Invest in Lincolnshire's Wildlife'. Sir Peter Scott gave it an excellent send-off at a reception in Lincoln in September and we attracted grants and loans from the World Wildlife Fund, the SPNR and four other Charitable Trusts.

The most encouraging feature of the appeal, however, was the response of our membership and the special fundraising efforts made by Area Groups and individuals who contributed some 30% to the eventual total. We also received generous support from firms and industries. When the appeal was wound up in October 1973 it had reached over £46,000. That was a considerable achievement, but some of the contributions were in five-year covenants and the Trust had to realise investments to meet the purchase costs of the properties. In addition the Trust agreed to sell the Snipe Dales property to Lindsey County Council for £10,000 on the understanding that the Council would lease it back to the Trust, an arrangement which ensured the future of that splendid reserve and the creation eventually of the adjoining Country Park. That contribution together with a supplementary appeal for Moor Farm enabled us to complete the purchase of all the four reserves.

It was nine years before we launched another major appeal for nature reserve purchase, and by that time grant-aid from national sources, in particular the

Countryside Commission and the Nature Conservancy Council, had become more freely available. In retrospect, however, the 1971 appeal was an outstanding achievement.

Change in Local Government

The radical re-organisation of local government in 1974 created serious problems for the Trust. We had enjoyed excellent relationships with the three County Councils and with some of the old Rural Districts, but the division of planning and other environmental responsibilities between County and the new District Councils required the establishment of a new set of relationships. The Government's original intention had been to create a new county embracing the whole of historic Lincolnshire, a proposal which the Trust warmly welcomed. At a late hour, however, the Government decided to create a new county of Humberside to include a large area of north Lincolnshire. We made our opposition to this known to the Government and to Lincolnshire MPs, and I was asked by Lindsey County Council to attend a meeting with a government Minister, Mr W Van Straubenzee to put the Trust's view as a voluntary body covering the historic county. The Minister listened but the Government had already made up its mind.

Lincolnshire and Humberside County Councils continued to grant-aid the Trust, the amounts being allocated on a population basis. We worked well with Lincolnshire County Council on existing projects like Gibraltar Point and Road Verges, and on new ones like Snipe Dales. We tried hard to establish a good relationship with Humberside, but in spite of adding 'South Humberside' to our title – thus making it the most cumbersome of any county Trust – and entertaining Council Chairmen and local councillors at Far Ings and at various events, we never got very close to the Council, who, I believe, wished to suppress the old Lincolnshire identity and create a new Humberside image. Lincolnshire and Humberside were also poles apart politically and that sometimes made our efforts to get on well with both bodies more difficult. We decided in 1991 to drop 'South Humberside' from the Trust's name, and it was something of a relief when Humberside county was abolished soon afterwards, although its legacy continued to create problems for us. Establishing relations with two new unitary authorities in North and North-East Lincolnshire was not easy, and neither produced any grant-aid. Moreover, the split in the old county was perpetuated on a regional basis and we had to deal with two Nature Conservancy Council regions based at Grantham and Wakefield, and eventually with two Regional Development Agencies, one of them covering the north of the county with the title of 'Yorkshire Forward'! Almost the only all-Lincolnshire bodies and institutions that remain today are the Diocese of Lincoln, the Society for Lincolnshire History and Archaeology, and the Trust! In all its fifty-seven years local government re-organisation has been the most troublesome and time-consuming development with which the Trust has had to contend.

Moving House

When Mary and I moved to our new home in Willoughby in 1956 we made an office for the Trust in a converted room in the outbuildings. By 1965 the expansion of the work of both the Trust and the national association (then SPNR) of which I was the Honorary Secretary necessitated new and larger office premises. They had to be within easy reach if I was to continue my voluntary role for both bodies. The Manor House at Alford is a fine brick and thatched building in the main street, a well-known local landmark. It dated according to older guide books from 1660, but recent investigations have shown that it was a timber-framed house of some fifty years earlier which was later encased in brick. It had been purchased by a local benefactor, Miss Dorothy Higgins, whose father and grandfather, agents to the Well Vale estate, had lived there. It had been unoccupied for several years and she was looking for some useful purpose for it, preferably in connection with the town and the county. Its future, however, was uncertain. It needed extensive renovation not least re-thatching of the roof. There was also an influential faction in the town, including some town councillors, that wished to see it demolished to make room for housing for elderly residents. I knew Miss Higgins well. She was an early member of the Trust, and she attended some of my university classes. I suggested to her that she might let the rooms on the upper floor to the Trust and the SPNR for a suitable rent. I also proposed to my University Department that one of the large ground floor rooms would make an excellent Adult Education Centre. That proposal also materialised in due course as a result of an arrangement between the University, the WEA and the Local Education Authority.

Meantime the office arrangements were agreed, and Wilf Dawson, the new SPNR Administrative Officer, and I with our secretary moved in in April 1965. The following Winter was severe, and outside the two rooms we occupied the house was empty and draughty. We survived nevertheless and gradually established Trust-SPNR administrations occupying eventually the whole of the first floor. Conditions were far from ideal, but we converted it gradually into an effective workplace for the SPNR for nine years and for the Trust for nearly twenty.

An incidental result of our occupation was to help to ensure the future of the Manor House. We demonstrated that it could be used to good purpose, and as a result local opinion swung in favour of preserving it. In 1967 the Alford Civic Trust was formed with the primary purpose of taking over the house and its extensive grounds. It has now (2006) been splendidly restored and renovated, but few of those who visit it today will be aware how close it came to destruction or decay forty years ago.

The Trust and the SPNR continued to share the Manor House offices until 1974 when the SPNR moved to Nettleham near Lincoln. The additional space then created enabled the Trust's growing staff to be more conveniently accommodated until it too had to seek more spacious quarters.

A Personal Footnote

The death of its Chairman Dick Cornwallis in June 1969 was a devastating loss to the Trust. For me it was the end of nearly twenty years of collaboration and friendship. No longer could I say – as I so often did – when a new situation or problem arose "I must talk to Dick about it". The Trust had to go on, and Richard Pepler, as a senior member of the Council, took the lead in proposing that I should succeed Dick as Chairman and that David Robinson should take my place as Honorary Secretary. The Council unanimously agreed to his proposal. I was initially somewhat reluctant to relinquish the secretaryship which I had held for twenty years, but the move seemed to be in the best interests of the Trust and it proved to be a sensible one for me. David took over the secretaryship with energy and determination. He had already shown great commitment to the Trust and he was at that time also the Honorary Secretary of the Lincolnshire

Naturalists' Union. He and I were already working together in adult education since his appointment in 1965 as Tutor Organiser for the Workers' Educational Association in East Lindsey. He was in fact to hold the secretaryship of the Trust for more than thirty-seven years.

For me relief from the detailed duties of the secretaryship was an important factor in enabling me to continue until 1974 as the University Resident Tutor in Lindsey, and to fulfil my voluntary commitments to the national association and to the Nature Conservancy/Nature Conservancy Council of whose England Committee I served as Chairman from 1971 to 1978. As Chairman of the Trust, moreover, I was able to stand back a little and concentrate on policy-making and on a general coordinating and overseeing role. The next thirty years as Chairman proved indeed to be just as rewarding as the previous twenty as Honorary Secretary had been.

TED SMITH

Alford Manor House, the Trust's headquarters 1965-1993.

Cover for the video version (1998) of the film 'Nature in Trust' which was premiered in 1967.

1970

INVEST
in
LINCOLNSHIRE'S
WILDLIFE

THE
LINCOLNSHIRE
TRUST for Nature Conservation

1971

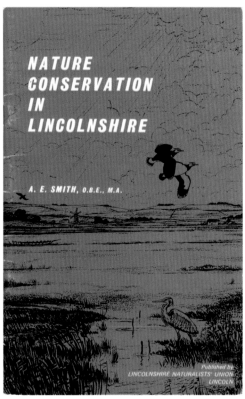

*Presidential Address to the
Lincolnshire Naturalists'
Union 1969.*

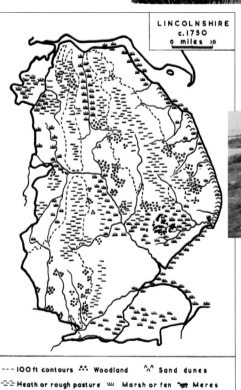

*Remains of Boreal forest trees on the
seashore at Huttoft 1920s.*

--- 100 ft contours ∴ Woodland ʌʌ Sand dunes
⌐-⌐ Heath or rough pasture ⱳ Marsh or fen ⱳ Meres

– 11 –

The Expanding Estate
1960-1975

I N THE 1950s we had concentrated on trying to secure the protection of those sites which appeared in the 1951 list. The story of our successes and failures has been recounted in earlier chapters. We were conscious from the outset, however, of the shortcomings of that list which was necessarily based on existing knowledge rather than on new survey. Having secured some of the important sites by the end of the decade we then turned our attention to the obvious gaps in habitat representation. We were receiving information about new sites all the time from members of the Trust and the Lincolnshire Naturalists' Union, and from officers of the Nature Conservancy who were responsible for producing and revising the SSSI schedules. Our knowledge of the distribution of plants in the county was transformed by the ambitious survey and mapping of the British flora conducted by the Botanical Society of the British Isles during the 1950s. Many Lincolnshire botanists participated. The ground-breaking Atlas published in 1962 provided a wealth of information for conservation planning and action. In 1967 we launched a systematic county-wide survey of ponds, pits and quarries, distributing a simple survey card to dozens of members. The survey yielded a wealth of information and we were able to investigate in more detail sites which seemed to be particularly interesting. A year or two later, as I described in an earlier chapter, we collaborated with the Nature Conservancy and the Lincolnshire River Authority in surveying rivers and streams. Knowledge about new sites and habitats in Lincolnshire was further augmented in the late 1960s by the National Woodland Survey conducted by the Nature Conservancy in which Trust members participated. Information was recorded about ownership, status and type of woodland, about its biological interest, habitats represented and notable species. More information about habitats emerged from the British Trust for Ornithology's five-year survey of the breeding distribution of all species of birds in the British Isles. The 120 observers who participated in Lincolnshire included many members of the Trust. The result of that survey was the publication in 1976 of *The Atlas of Breeding Birds in Britain and Ireland*.

There was another survey scheme which reinforced the search for sites of natural interest and gave them a kind of status. The 'Countryside in 1970' conference in 1965 recommended local authorities to compile registers of 'Countryside Treasures' defined as natural or man-made features of the countryside which were of public interest and heritage value. Lindsey and Kesteven County Councils adopted the scheme and distributed an explanatory leaflet inviting members of the public to nominate 'Treasures'. We made sure that all SSSIs and other sites of natural interest known to us were recorded and we offered help and advice in promoting the scheme generally. As far as non-SSSI sites were concerned this was in effect a forerunner of the Wildlife Sites Scheme of the 1990s. Unfortunately, like Countryside Committees and some other 'Countryside in 1970' initiatives, the active registration of Countryside Treasures did not survive local government re-organisation in 1974. The scheme fell into disuse and was largely forgotten.

All this extraordinary volume and variety of survey work was invaluable in helping us to formulate our reserve acquisition policy and to keep it updated. That was the subject of frequent consideration in the Executive Committee and after 1969 in the Scientific Policy Group. In 1972, for example, the Committee had a full discussion not only on acquisition policy, but also on management planning, practical work, recording, reintroduction and research and educational use of reserves. Another important contribution to this was the habitat survey work and analysis conducted by John Blackwood, the Nature Conservancy's Assistant Regional Officer in Lincolnshire. His article on Lincolnshire grasslands in our October 1968 newsletter contained new information about the extent and distribution of all types of permanent grasslands and their decline in the previous thirty years. His paper on 'Nature Reserve Acquisition in Lincolnshire' was presented to the Trust's new Scientific Policy Group in November 1970. All existing reserves were listed in the context of their natural regions, an approach of the kind which I had adopted in my Presidential Address to the LNU in March 1969. Entitled 'Nature Conservation in Lincolnshire' the Address was reproduced for sale as an illustrated booklet. Blackwood – who had been much assisted in his field work by the Trust's Field Officer Barrie Wilkinson – drew particular attention to the under-representation of certain habitats among the Trust's reserves, especially wetlands everywhere and grasslands on chalk, limestone and claylands. His paper stimulated further development of acquisition policies with particular emphasis on securing a representative sample of habitats characteristic of the various natural regions, especially those most threatened by land use changes. Whilst we had in the first twenty years concentrated on securing SSSIs, we now began to take a wider perspective and in the process, incidentally, acquired a number of sites which were quickly recognised by the Nature Conservancy as being of SSSI quality.

Management Planning

We recognised from the first that a plan was essential for the sound and consistent management of each reserve. Such a plan, although in a preliminary form, was an important element in the 1948 Agreement with the Lincolnshire County Council for the management of Gibraltar Point. The purpose and preparation of plans was a major topic of discussion at the course on Nature Conservation which I organised at Pilgrim College, Boston in 1956. Advice from Nature Conservancy officers was almost always helpful but they were in the same learning process about management as we were. There was one problem about plans with which the Nature Conservancy itself had to grapple: how much information about the reserve did you need before preparing a plan of action? Too little and you risked making mistakes; but wait too long, especially where successional change was rapid and perhaps aggravated by outside influences - as in the case of heathland and calcareous grassland - and you might find it more difficult to control or reverse a deteriorating situation.

At some of our early reserves, like Scotton and Linwood, the first plans were based on quite detailed vegetation surveys – Len and Betty Watkinson had produced a splendid vegetation map of Linwood, for example – and on identification of distinctive management compartments. A detailed plan for Linwood produced in 1960 was a model of its kind. Later versions of the plans have improved and refined prescriptions in the light of new knowledge, but the basic conclusions of those first plans - on scrub control, water management and so on – have remained valid. The real problem was that until recent years we did not have the resources to implement them successfully. Initially plans were prepared by central officers and reserve wardens and approved by the Executive Committee. After 1969 the responsibility passed to the Scientific Policy Group and the Conservation Officer. The Group made regular site visits to new and existing reserves to discuss the preparation and revision of plans.

New Nature Reserves
Coastlands
We had played a major role in the 1950s and early 60s in safeguarding Gibraltar Point and the Saltfleetby-Theddlethorpe Dunes at either end of Lincolnshire's sandhill coastline. In the central stretch between Skegness and Sandilands sandy beaches were backed by a narrow line of dunes, scrub-covered on the landward side. Much of the hinterland on either side of the Old Sea Bank road was old pasture until the 1950s. The coastal villages, whose economy was based largely on stock rearing, had been built or, in some cases, rebuilt a mile or two back from the sea which had been eating away at the bulge of the coast for several centuries. Five medieval churches had been lost in the process of which the devastating floods of 1953 were another episode.

When Gibraltar Point was inaccessible in wartime I had looked for migrants along this coast and watched the great flocks of lapwings and golden plovers for which it is an important winter range. Later this stretch of shore was the favourite place for family outings, and our children became enthusiastic and knowledgeable beachcombers. We collected shells, fossils, and worked flints. There was also a great variety of pebbles carried by ice from distant rock formations, and we still have specimen collections of them including semi-precious stones like agates, carnelians, types of quartz, and the rarely found amber. Low tides and storms revealed the clays beneath the sand and the stumps and boles of fallen trees, remains of Boreal forests killed by rising sea levels seven or eight thousand years ago. And in winter there were the sanderlings, diminutive waders in pearly-white plumage chasing the receding wave on twinkling black legs to pick up tiny morsels of food, and then scurrying back as the next wave broke. They were never more fascinating than on stormy days running fearlessly beside crashing waves. Beach nourishment in recent years has deprived the shore of much of this kind of interest, but at least the sanderling are still a great winter attraction.

By the 1930s holiday development was creeping along this coast wherever a pull-over gave access to the shore. The Lindsey Sandhills Act of 1932 had ensured that most of the sand-dunes themselves were protected, but behind them by the 1950s development was threatening to engulf the old dignified villages like Ingoldmells and Addlethorpe, and to cover more and more of the unspoilt stretches in a kind of ribbon development.

In 1948, whilst the Trust was in process of formation, I had discussions with the Planning Officer acting for the consortium of local Councils then responsible for planning control. I was impressed by his general approach to the coast where he was seeking to protect unspoilt areas and the character of the villages whilst providing for an expansion of holiday accommodation and facilities. After that discussion I wrote a letter to the *Lincolnshire Standard* strongly supporting the proposals. When Lindsey County Council assumed planning powers under the 1947 Town and Country Planning Act they adopted the same broad lines of policy which after all were implicit in their own Sandhills Act. Their first development plan in 1955 defined three stretches of coast – later expanded to five - where the conservation of the natural environment and the protection of sea defences would be paramount. The three conservation areas – as they later became known – covered the whole of the undeveloped coast between Ingoldmells and Sandilands. The Trust welcomed that policy and supported the Council in 1951 in refusing planning permission for large-scale holiday camps at Anderby, Sandilands and Huttoft Bank, the latter the site in the early 20th Century of a fanciful garden city by-the-sea project called Woldsea.

The Council's 1966 Coastal Conservation Policy Statement and Map – which defined two further Coastal Conservation Areas south of Skegness and north of Mablethorpe – reaffirmed the policy on conservation and defined the limited type of development considered appropriate in the Conservation Areas. Policies to regulate the use of access points and car parks to conserve the natural environment and sea defences were adopted in 1974. Meantime the area allocated for holiday development outside the Conservation Areas was substantially enlarged in 1973 and subsequently. The challenges to the Council's Coastal Conservation Area policy at Gibraltar Point in 1953 and at Theddlethorpe and Saltfleetby in the late 1950s and early 1960s had been decisively defeated. It was clearly re-stated in the county Structure Plan in 1981, in the more detailed Lincolnshire Coast Subject Plan in 1986, and in East Lindsey's Local Plan of 1985, although the latter made a subtle distinction between the Tetney to Mablethorpe and Skegness to Friskney Areas and those of the central stretch. The latter were deemed to be suitable for 'visitors engaged in more passive and outdoor-based or informal recreation and leisure pursuits', although built development and caravans would be strictly controlled to avoid spoiling the more natural landscape. In spite of that, much of the Ingoldmells to Chapel Area has been sacrificed over the years to holiday accommodation and entertainment facilities like the massive Fantasy Island leisure complex. There were breaches of policy in other Coastal Conservation Areas. The conversion of the derelict Bank House farm at Wolla Bank into a much larger restaurant and entertainment centre, for example, and the replacement of houses much larger than the originals and out of character with their surroundings between Skegness and Gibraltar Point. More positively, however, the District Council in its Local Plan expresses its intention of cooperating with the County Council and voluntary organisations 'in preparing and implementing a coastal management plan for the coastal conservation areas".

The Trust had been in contact with the County Council as early as 1948 about management as well as planning issues on the central stretch of coast. We held discussions from time to time with officers from the Planning and Land Agents departments about the management of the Council's own Sandhills properties. As a result there is more than one set of detailed proposals on the Trust's files for the enhancement and management of those properties, in particular the access points like those at Chapel Sixmarshes, Wolla Bank and Marsh Yard to Moggs Eye. Little came of such discussions partly due to frequent changes in County Council staff in the 1980s and 90s, partly to shortage of resources, and partly, it has to be said, to lack of interest in the Sandhills properties.

The Trust was fortunately able to secure its own property interest within this Area. After the destruction of much of the sandhills in the 1953 floods, clay was excavated from a series of pits, the **Sea Bank Clay Pits**, on the landward side of the Old Sea Bank road to be used for emergency repairs and to form banks behind the new concrete sea defences. It quickly became evident that the pits would become attractive to a wide variety of birds, especially when the marginal reedbeds had matured. The two southernmost pits could be viewed from the Old Sea Bank road, and on our family seaside visits we frequently stopped to look over them. Birdwatchers began to report interesting migrants and wintering species, and we discovered signs of otters small numbers of which frequented the Marsh drains before their population collapsed in the 1960s. At one of the pits where droppings were frequently found the otters had made a slide down a muddy bank into the water. One day in the mid-1960s I had a call from a man who was organising an otter hunt for a pack from another county – Buckinghamshire, I believe. He said he expected they would be able to draw the Sea Bank Pits as usual. I told him that I was not prepared to give any such permission, and when he questioned my authority I suggested that he contact my Chairman. I rang Dick Cornwallis straightway to warn him. His expletive of indignation is not repeatable here.

The developing flora and fauna, reedbed habitat particularly, and the proximity of the pits to the sea made them desirable candidates for protection and possible acquisition by the Trust. They were the property of the then Lincolnshire River Board whose Clerk, Geoffrey Phillippo, was a keen birdwatcher and became a member of the Trust Council in the 1960s. The Board's only interest in them was as a possible source for more clay where there was still some untouched ground. Through Phillippo's good offices we negotiated the sale of the two pits at Huttoft for £1 each, and the lease of the other three at a rent of £1 each per annum. The deal was completed in 1959. Subsequently we exchanged the smaller of the two Huttoft Pits – which had been excavated for clay to repair sea defences after a breach in 1947 – in exchange for a better access to the larger pit which can now be viewed from a memorial hide.

In 1965 we negotiated a lease from the County Council of a seven-acre site at **Wolla Bank** which had been scraped for clay in 1953 and which had developed vegetation of reed and scrub. It had attracted nesting reed, sedge and grasshopper warblers and reed buntings.

After a few years the reedbeds in the pits were alive with the chattering songs of reed and sedge warblers. Bearded tits began to appear in winter and for several years stayed to nest. The reedbeds also provided hirundine and starling roosts in autumn, and I sometimes took students on bird study courses at Gibraltar Point to see the spectacular numbers of swallows and martins. Over the years the pits have attracted a great variety of rare migrant and vagrant birds. My own 'firsts' seen there include little bittern, white-winged black tern, and great reed warbler – in full song. Among others that have occurred are red-necked and Slovenian grebes, purple heron, bittern and penduline tit. The Huttoft Pit has had breeding bittern, marsh harrier amd bearded tit in recent years, a remarkable record in only twelve and a half acres.

The bird interest and the aquatic and marginal fauna and flora quickly convinced the Nature Conservancy of the value of the pits, and they appeared in the revised SSSI schedule for Lindsey in 1960, the Wolla Bank Reedbed being added soon afterwards. The pits were the Trust's first wetland reserves. They also gave us a foothold status in the central stretch of coast. Enhancing that status by further freehold acquisitions would give us even greater influence on the protection and management of this Coastal Conservation Area.

By 1970 the Trust's commitment to the management of coastlands at Gibraltar Point and Saltfleetby-Theddlethorpe was quite as much as it could reasonably undertake or justify for the time being. The Scientific Policy Group, considering acquisition policy at its first meeting in September 1969, agreed that coastlands – with the exception of Wash saltmarsh – were adequately represented compared with other habitats and regions of the county. In any case we had not at that stage seriously investigated the potential of the coast north of the Saltfleetby-Theddlethorpe Dunes reserve. Donna Nook had been reactivated as the main RAF bombing range in 1976 and, although its attitude was soon to change, the Ministry of Defence had shown little interest in the nature conservation aspects of its estates. Our first Administrative Officer, Paul Berkeley, had been the Commanding Officer at RAF Donna Nook and he made enquiries from the Ministry about the possibility of establishing a sanctuary for little terns nesting on the outer ridges there. He established some useful contacts but nothing came of that particular proposal. The only site north of Saltfleet to appear on the SSSI schedules – and that not until 1968 – was the area of saltmarsh at Grainthorpe Haven. In 1955 Mr S H Mossop enquired about the creation of a sanctuary on part of the foreshore belonging to him. The Trust Executive Committee offered to support an approach to Lindsey County Council to investigate the possibility, but the suggestion was apparently not pursued.

On the Wash coast, following our early unsuccessful attempt to save Freiston Shore saltmarsh from reclamation, we had likewise made no further advances. In 1976, however, we were able to acquire the important area of saltmarsh known as the Scalp between the Witham and Welland outfalls. As I have described in an earlier chapter, we sought unsuccessfully to expand that holding. Our involvement at Frampton was possible because by 1976 we had a Conservation Officer and a Field Officer in post, and our volunteer force covering that part of the Wash coast had been considerably strengthened, especially by Brian Redman, another Trust stalwart and excellent all-round naturalist with intimate knowledge of the Wash saltmarshes.

Two years later the strengthening of our resources and a much more sympathetic attitude on the part of the MoD enabled us to secure a lease and management agreement covering nearly 3,000 acres of sand-dune, saltmarsh and intertidal area at Donna Nook, later to become a National Nature Reserve.

BARRIE WILKINSON

Caravans at Ingoldmells 1969

JOHN THOMPSON

Sea Bank Clay Pits at Huttoft, 1984

Huttoft Big Pit 1970s

*Hoplands Wood after coppicing hazel (below)
and regrowth of the coppice layer under
tall standard oak and ash (right).*

*Wild service trees on the edge
of Tortoiseshell Wood.*

*Below: Rigsby Wood now isolated in the arable Middle Marsh
is a great attraction on Bluebell Weekend, and bottom right a
demonstration of charcoal making on one of the open days.*

TED SMITH

DAVID ROBINSON

NEIL PAWSON

DAVE BROMWICH

BARRIE WILKINSON

214

Woodlands

The new Scientific Policy Group in 1969 selected woodlands and wetlands as priority habitats for nature reserve acquisition. At that time, twenty years after its formation, the Trust had only one ancient semi-natural woodland reserve, **Claxby Hoplands**. There were several possible reasons for this. One was the cost of purchasing woodland; another was availability or rather the lack of it. Much of the most ecologically interesting woodland was already in the hands of the Forestry Commission or within large estates. It was also a fact that we knew all too little about the general ecology of Lincolnshire woodlands at that time, the six woods in our 1951 List of potential nature reserves having been selected largely on the basis of known species interest. This is evident also from the early SSSI schedules for Lincolnshire in the 1950s which contain only four ancient woods and two so-called 'additional areas'. By the time of the 1968 schedule revision the number in Lindsey alone had increased to nine, seven of them in the oak-lime woods of the Central Vale which the research and survey work of Dr George Peterken and others had shown to be of national significance. The other two areas of ancient woodland in the county – on the Middle Marsh boulder clays east of the Wolds and on the clays of the Kesteven uplands – were still scantily represented in the pre-1966 schedules. There were only two, Willoughby and Muckton Woods, in the Middle Marsh and none in Kesteven. Even by the mid-1970s the situation was little improved. The Nature Conservancy's massive review of sites of nature conservation interest published in 1977 makes no mention of Middle Marsh woods and gives only an extremely tentative selection for the Kesteven Woods which, it states, had not been surveyed in detail.

Pursuing our policy of giving priority to the acquisition of SSSIs we made enquiries in 1960 about Willoughby Wood which we understood was on the market and was the subject of negotiations with the Forestry Commission. I was able to report to the Trust Council in June of that year that the agents had promised to consult the Trust before concluding any agreement about the wood. In the event they failed to honour that undertaking and I learned some time later that the wood had been sold to a local landowner and farmer, Mr J L Rougton, who subsequently concluded an informal understanding with the Trust about the protection of the long-established heronry. Willoughby Wood is still on the SSSI schedule (2005) but it has sadly deteriorated over the years. There are now few oak and ash standards, the coppice has become derelict, and the rides overgrown.

Most of the other Middle Marsh woods had been acquired by the Forestry Commission. Some had been clear-felled and replanted with conifers or a conifer-broadleaf mixture. Tothill, Greenfield, Mother, Haugham and Burwell all came into that category. There was one, however, which had retained many of its old oak and ash standards together with blocks of overstood hazel coppice. This was **Hoplands**, the wood where I had first heard nightingale song in the 1930s. I had visited the wood from time to time since then, and in 1948 Lenton Ottaway and I found a rich bird population and a flora which included herb Paris, broad-leaved helleborine and greater butterfly orchid.

Hoplands, like Rigsby three miles to the north, was on the Well Vale estate which at that time covered several thousand acres of farmland and woodland. Like many such families the Rawnsleys at Well had found it increasingly difficult to maintain the full extent of their estate. Major Richard Rawnsley had been one of the earliest members of the Trust in 1950, and his widow Mrs Susan Rawnsley had retained an interest in the Trust's activities. An invitation to Mary and me to see her garden and have tea gave me an opportunity to tell her more about the Trust. She said that she would like to help it in some way. As a result of that I wrote in May 1964 to the agent for the estate, Sir David Hawley, the Senior Partner of Chas. Martin & Co (who later became a member of the Trust Council) to enquire if Mrs Rawnsley would be willing to sell Hoplands to the Trust. Within a few weeks it was offered to us for £2,000 for its thirty-four acres, a generous offer which the Trust Council had little difficulty in accepting. The wood was subject to a dedication covenant with the Forestry Commission, but discussions with my friend Robert Payne, the Commission's private Woodlands Officer, confirmed that there would be no incompatibility between the dedication conditions and the Trust's plans for the wood. The payments under the scheme proved to be a welcome contribution to the cost of management, especially in the early years of restoration work. The decision to purchase was also significantly influenced by the availability of grant-aid from national sources: £500 from the World Wildlife Fund and £250 from the SPNR's Pilgrim Fund.

We also asked the Nature Conservancy to assess whether the wood merited SSSI status. On the basis of a detailed report by the Deputy Regional Officer, Brian Ducker, the wood was scheduled SSSI in 1966.

Managing our first ancient woodland was an exciting challenge for the Trust. A management group of local Area Group members was quickly established, and an area working party led by Peter Graves set about restoring hazel coppice and opening up glades and rides one of which had disappeared entirely and had to be traced from old maps. The first full management plan of 1972 prepared by Ray Collier served as a model for future woodland plans.

Hoplands today is an outstanding example of an ancient semi-natural oak-ash wood with large blocks of regularly coppiced hazel and many fine oaks of the 150 to 180 year age group. There is also a valuable younger range of 50 to 60 year trees. There are many fine ash standards also, but some of these suffer from heart rot and one or two fall every winter. Their gradual decay on the woodland floor provides another valuable kind of habitat. The old joiner in our village, who knew the quality of timber from particular woods, described Hoplands ash as 'carroty'. In addition to selling timber and firewood we have from time to time found a small market for hazel for making thatch spars and ledgers.

Hoplands also provides a splendid introduction to woodland ecology and is well used for the purpose. I acted as volunteer reserve manager for many years, and, whilst old age now prevents me from active participation in working parties, walking through the wood at all seasons of the year is still one of life's pleasures.

It was eight years before another ancient wood was added to our expanding estate. **Tortoiseshell Wood**, a fine example of Kesteven boulder clay woodland, came up for auction in spring 1971. The site comprised 28 acres, 23 of woodland and five of adjoining grassland. This was a priority habitat and the Trust Council agreed straightway that we should try to purchase it. The decision was reinforced by a report from Dr George Peterken who commented on the excellent structure of the wood and the large number of mature oaks and fine wild service trees, a comparatively rare species in Lincolnshire. Moreover, it differed significantly from other ancient protected woodland in the region. Sir David Hawley, by that time a member of the Trust Council, attended the auction on our behalf, but refused to bid beyond £8,750, the price realised. It was, he reported, in his opinion in excess of its value. Sir David, incidentally, was later to resign from the Council in disagreement over the price we paid for Moor Farm.

The Trust's Honorary Secretary, David Robinson, made contact with the purchaser, timber merchants Messrs Adcock of Bourne, who indicated a willingness to sell Tortoiseshell to the Trust for £10,500 on condition that we gave them the option of purchasing any timber that we might decide to sell. Sir David Hawley then agreed that the property represented reasonable value for the price and the purchase went ahead.

The wood lies on a north facing slope against a parish boundary marked by a fine bank. It has a typical structure and indicator species of old coppice-with-standards woodland, including abundant bluebell, primrose and wood anemone as well as yellow archangel, wood sanicle and rarer species like greater butterfly orchid. The wood lacked open rides and glades and these we had to create in the early phase of management. A notable feature of the fauna – in addition to nightingale, nuthatch, greater and lesser spotted woodpeckers and other birds – is a small herd of fallow deer. They created a serious management problem by browsing the young shoots of coppiced hazel. To retain the coppice layer we later reluctantly had to resort to erecting deer fences.

The access to the wood from the south is through two old meadows, Porters Lodge Meadows. The Trust's purchase of these in 1989 greatly enhanced the value of the wood. Wood edge grassland habitat has become all too rare in Lincolnshire in the last fifty years.

Three years later, in 1975, we secured the lease of another Kesteven wood, part of **Dole Wood**, a 6½ acre gem of coppice-with-standards woodland with a rich ground flora enjoyed by many visitors at the annual Bluebell Open Days.

The National Woodland Survey and information from members revealed several other Kesteven boulder clay woods which it would be desirable for the Trust to acquire. Apart from Lawn Wood near Castle Bytham, however, which was purchased in 1995, no feasible opportunities have since arisen. The Forestry Commission's change of policy in favour of maintaining and restoring native hardwoods – a policy which has also influenced private owners – has in some respects made woodland a less urgent priority for the Trust, although the acquisition of further examples of ancient woodland in all the main Lincolnshire areas of distribution remains an essential element of acquisition policy.

Most of the extensive woods in the Central Vale were already managed by the Forestry Commission, and although we made enquiries about several of the privately owned smaller ones, no suitable opportunity for acquisition arose in the 1960s and 70s. One of those woods, **Goslings Corner**, belonged to a farming friend of Dick Cornwallis, and we made a tentative approach in the 1960s about the possibility of purchase or management agreement. Goslings Corner is a twenty-five acre remnant of Langton Wood, most of which was destroyed between 1850 and 1870. It is a splendid example of the oak/lime woods of the area which are now nationally famous. Coppice of small-leaved lime, hazel and a variety of other shrubs form an understorey for oak standards. A variety of soils ranging from neutral to acid support a ground flora as rich and varied as in any of the neighbouring larger woods. Nothing came of our discussions at that time, but having 'discovered' Goslings Corner we kept it in our sights, and in 1987 a generous In Memoriam donation enabled us to persuade the owner to sell it.

We had also established an interest in the nearby Chambers Wood complex by the agreement in 1972 with the Forestry Commission to manage Little Scrubbs Meadow and by the acquisition in 1987 of Hatton Meadows on the edge of Hatton Wood. We had also mounted the first nature trails in the forest in the early 1970s. Our interest and input was recognised in 1990 when we were invited to be a party to the agreement between the Forestry Commission and the Nature Conservancy Council to designate the Chambers/Hatton Wood complex as a Forest Nature Reserve, later to become a National Nature Reserve.

Elsewhere, in the Middle Marsh, as described earlier, we had been active in securing the protection of part of **Muckton Wood** which we eventually succeeded in acquiring in 1983. Three years earlier we purchased **Rigsby Wood**, another property of the shrinking Well Vale Estate. This time the new owner could not afford to be generous; we had to pay the market price of £30,000. Nearly half of that was covered by national grant-aid, the bulk of it from the Countryside Commission whose interest stemmed from the fact that the wood was an important feature on the edge of the Lincolnshire Wolds Area of Outstanding Natural Beauty. Much of the rest of the purchase price we recovered from the sale of sycamore that had been planted in one of the compartments. Rigsby and the tiny remnant of the once more extensive Ailby Wood is an ancient woodland site with a splendid medieval boundary bank referred to in 12th century charters. Parts of it had been clear-felled in the previous thirty to forty years and replaced with a mixture of broadleaved trees and conifers. The ground flora was still exceptionally rich, however, even in those parts, and restoration of the traditional regime seemed perfectly feasible. Nevertheless the decision to purchase, which had to be taken at short notice, met with some criticism within the Trust. Few people visiting this wood today, however, after twenty years of restoration and re-coppicing, would be in any doubt that its acquisition was amply justified. Bluebell weekend at Rigsby has become a popular feature in the Trust's events programme.

The alder carrs of the south Wolds represent a distinctive type of woodland found in its most typical form in the valley of the River Lymn and its tributaries. Where the streams have cut down through the Spilsby sandstone into the Kimmeridge clay, waterlogged conditions in which the alders thrive give rise to a luxuriant swamp vegetation dominated by the primeval looking giant horsetail, hairy willowherb, meadowsweet and pond sedge, and in places by the mound forming tussock sedge. Marsh marigolds carpet the lower slopes in spring, and there are both golden-saxifrages, the opposite-leaved and the rarer alternate-leaved distinguished by its taller habit and larger, brighter flowers. Bluebells and red campion flourish on the upper slopes above the spring line where ash and in places the invasive sycamore are the principal trees.

Some of the best surviving alder carrs – many had been drained and ploughed in the 1940s and 50s – are in the valley of the Toynton Beck, a tributary of the Lymn. I had been introduced to one of them by the botanist Dr Francis Rose who carried out extensive surveys for the Nature Conservancy in its early years. This was Jenkins Carr which lies below the A16 road between Spilsby and East Keal. In 1964 through local contacts I got in touch with the owner who expressed willingness to consider an offer from the Trust. Sir David Hawley, our estate advisor at that time, was asked to value the property and negotiate for it. Negotiations unfortunately proved difficult and protracted and were eventually broken off by the owner. Subsequently, in spite of SSSI designation in 1966, much of the alder in the carr was felled and the valley floor extensively drained.

Against the background of an excellent article on the alder carrs of the south Wolds by Martin Ball, the Nature Conservancy's Warden Naturalist in Lincolnshire, published in the Trust's newsletter in 1967, we turned our attention upstream on the Toynton Beck to **Keal Carr**, a rich and little disturbed example which was also designated SSSI in 1968. Negotiations over this were complicated by at least three ownerships, but after several years we eventually succeeded in acquiring a major part of the Carr and a somewhat tenuous management agreement over the rest. Downstream below Jenkins Carr we were given a lease in 1994 by the County Council of **Lilley's Carr** as a memorial to Mark Newlands Lilley, the Assistant County Land Agent. It remains highly desirable to complete the protection of this little valley by acquiring and restoring Jenkins Carr.

Chalk Grasslands

I have described in an earlier chapter the Trust's campaign to salvage surviving examples of old meadows. The remnants of chalk and limestone grassland presented similar problems of conservation. Little had survived the 18th and 19th centuries enclosures and conversion to arable, and there had been further losses in the 1940s and 50s. We already knew most of the best sites from Lincolnshire Naturalists' Union records and field meetings, and our knowledge was further extended by the Trust's Ponds, Pits and Quarries survey, and by John Blackwood's grassland surveys in the late 1960s. Many sites were still threatened by conversion to agriculture, by afforestation and in the case of disused quarries by refuse tipping. It was the latter threat that led to the acquisition of the first of our chalk pit reserves at Candlesby Hill and at Claxby near Alford. Both were on Spilsby Rural District Council's list of potential landfill sites.

The **Candlesby Hill Quarry** is at the extreme south-eastern tip of the Wolds. From its top you see on a clear day the chalk cliffs of Hunstanton twenty miles away on the Norfolk shore of the Wash. This was the old Gunby Estate chalk pit and two of the 19th century lime kilns have survived. Chalk flowers have recolonised the floor of the quarry and the cliff face wherever they can find a crevice.

The quarry first came to our notice in 1961 as a result of a survey for our Ponds, Pits and Quarries project by local members of the Junior Section of the Naturalists' Union led by Andrew Sykes, an outstanding young naturalist whose early death in 1968 was a sad loss to Lincolnshire natural history. I made contact with John Trayner, the National Trust Area Agent, and discovered that the quarry was leased to a company for limited chalk extraction. He indicated at a site meeting in December 1961 that the National Trust would consider leasing the quarry to the Trust should the company not wish to renew. I then submitted detailed proposals to him on our management intentions, suggesting that in view of the cost of fencing which we should have to incur there should be a twenty-one year lease at a nominal rent. After discussion with his Chief Agent – with whom, incidentally I was discussing National Trust-Naturalists' Trusts relationships in my SPNR capacity – he offered to sell the freehold to the Trust for £150. This was possible because the quarry, unlike most National Trust properties, was held alienably. Some Trust Executive Committee members considered the price 'a bit steep' especially since we were asked in addition to meet the full costs of the conveyance. When we protested that our purpose was in line with the National Trust's own conservation policies, they relented and paid their share of costs! The quarry was conveyed to the Trust in 1964. In spite of that, Spilsby Rural District Council, without our permission, inspected the quarry in 1966 and announced their intention to acquire it as a refuse disposal site. When I reported this to the Trust Executive Committee they indignantly instructed me to tell the RDC that they found their action entirely unacceptable. I made it clear to RDC officers that they would meet ferocious opposition from the Trust if they took the matter any further. They did not!

If the negotiations for the Candlesby Hill quarry were relatively straightforward, those for the **Mill Hill Quarry** at Claxby, the next on our list, were exceptionally protracted and messy. This was a place familiar to me from boyhood, and in the first few years of our marriage Mary and I went every June to count the bee and pyramidal orchids. The quarryman expected us, and one year, when we were later than usual, he greeted us with a bunch of bee orchids which he had picked for us in case we missed them! We made sure that we went in good time the next year! Later our children got to know their chalk flowers there and searched for fossils in the cliff face. Both of them used the quarry for A-level projects: Alison for a study of nettles, and Helen for a survey of vegetation succession on the quarry floor.

Few places convey a more graphic impression of the interaction of man and nature. The Mill Hill, the site of a long-forgotten wooden post mill, was originally a Bronze Age burial mound. From its eminence you look eastwards over the Marsh to the distant sea; westwards you glimpse the two Neolithic long barrows half a mile away. You look down into the quarry at the mid 19th century lime kilns which the Trust has restored. Near the entrance to the quarry are the remains of a smithy used by a visiting blacksmith until comparatively recent times. The cliff face shows a classic exposure of the junction of the Middle and Lower chalk (the Upper chalk has gone) marked by a layer of marly material containing traces of volcanic dust.

The quarrying had ceased in the mid-1950s and the quarryman's bungalow was unoccupied. The quarry had been on Well Vale estate land, but by 1960 it had been sold with surrounding farmland to a remotely administered body Lady Renwick's Trustees who had obviously acquired the property as an investment. I got in touch with their solicitors, Messrs Pearson & Mackirdy of Helmsley in Yorkshire, to tell them of our interest in the site and to offer our help in its protection especially in view of the fact that it was already attracting refuse tipping, unauthorised shooting and vandalism of the bungalow. Negotiations with them started promisingly. In January 1961 I met one of the Trustees Sir Eustace Renwick and their solicitor Mr R W Pearson on the site. They seemed to respond sympathetically to my suggestion that they consider leasing the quarry including the bungalow to the Trust. They were concerned about fencing liabilities and I sought the advice of our solicitors on legal aspects and of the County Land Agent Tom Twigg on the practical problems of fencing. The Trust's Executive Committee agreed that we should offer to repair and restore fencing where necessary in return for a lease or agreement covering a reasonable number of years. Agreeing to put our proposition to the Trustees Mr Pearson added that it might also be suggested that the quarry be conveyed to the Trust "for a nominal consideration". Taking up that suggestion we made a further offer in respect of fencing liabilities and to cover the whole costs of a conveyance.

From that point, however, negotiations began to go awry. Repeated enquiries, in which our solicitors Andrew & Co were also involved, failed to elicit a positive response from the Trustees. In March Pearson failed to keep an appointment with me in Alford but wrote to say that Sir Eustace Renwick had authorised him to offer a 15-year lease to the Trust. In September he called to see me at Willoughby promising to send a draft lease "within three weeks" and handing me the key to the bungalow. The draft lease did not materialise in spite of urgent reminders from me in July and October 1962 telling him that we were already wardening the site, clearing refuse and repairing the bungalow. Four years then elapsed without any communication from Pearson until in September 1966 we were astonished to learn that the Trustees through their solicitors had offered to sell or lease the quarry to Spilsby Rural District Council for refuse disposal purposes. When our solicitors requested an urgent explanation Pearson said that his clients "subsequently decided that they would not grant a lease, but would permit the Trust to occupy the quarry rent free until such time as they might require it". Pearson claimed that this was what he told me on his visit in September 1962. That was blatantly untrue. We had been offered a 15-year lease in writing; we had accepted it and he had made no attempt to disclaim it when I sent reminders to him in 1962. Andrew & Co wrote to him stating that they had advised the Trust that a contract existed for a lease of 15 years from 1962 at a peppercorn rent. "As neither your clients nor Spilsby RDC," they wrote, "had the courtesy to inform the Trust of the proposal to use the chalk pit as a refuse dump, we have felt it necessary to protect our clients by registering the agreement for a lease in the Land Charges Register". They expressed the hope that the Trustees would still be prepared to confirm the Trust's occupation as agreed in 1962 by granting a formal lease as then promised. Otherwise they would advise the Trust to protect its rights by litigation if necessary,

The RDC's application to the County Council for planning permission met with widespread opposition from local people and organisations including the LNU, the CPRE Branch, the Rambler's Association and the Nature Conservancy, all of them joining the Trust in registering objections. There was another objection. Mrs Rawnsley of Well Vale had generously given to the Trust the little spinney adjoining the quarry along the roadside which she had retained from the sale of farmland to Lady Renwick's Trustees. Sir David Hawley of Chas Martin & Co, Mrs Rawnsley's agent, wrote to Pearson & Mackirdy expressing Mrs Rawnsley's concern at the refuse tip proposal. If that took place and the lease was not offered to the Trust it would make Mrs Rawnsley's generous gift quite pointless. He expressed Mrs Rawnsley's concern for the Trust "one of the most progressive and highly thought of in the whole country". In what amounted to a masterly reproof to the Renwick Trustees he said that the Rawnsley family had always supported public-spirited enterprises in the best landowning tradition.

The County Council rejected the RDC's application, and when the latter indicated that they would appeal, our solicitor Philip Race pointed out to Pearson & Mackirdy that at any public enquiry the officers of the Trust would regard it as their duty to give evidence fully setting out their position. The Trust, he went on, was already being asked for a statement by the local press. The Trust would refrain from making a public statement for a period of one week from the date of the letter to give opportunity for the Trustees to make known their considered views. After that time, however, the Trust would feel free to make any public statement that it considered necessary.

Facing the twin threats of legal action and public exposure the Trustees gave in and offered to sell the property to the Trust. Even then, however, they gave no sign of generosity or regret for their actions. Their Agent asked for £1,000, but David Hawley whom we asked to help us in the matter was finally able to agree a figure of £500. It had been a sorry business. Pearson & Mackirdy had treated the Trust in a casual and negligent manner amounting almost to contempt. Neither the Trustees nor at the last stage Spilsby RDC, who must have know of the Trust's occupation, came out of it with any credit. It was a relief to me that the matter was concluded, although in some ways I felt it a pity that it had not gone to a public planning inquiry. I should have enjoyed giving evidence at that!

Early in our occupation we attracted an enthusiastic band of volunteers both to carry out management tasks in the quarry and to prepare the bungalow and convert it into a small visitor centre which we intended to open at weekends in summer. Geological and other exhibits were collected and displayed on staging constructed for the purpose. Unfortunately the visitor centre project never really got off the ground. Winter damp made it impossible to keep exhibits there permanently and took its toll of the wooden building. It was used for several years by the local WATCH group, but eventually we reluctantly decided to demolish it. On the ground where it had stood for eighty years or more there appeared in the following spring a good number of corncockle plants, a rarity now in Lincolnshire.

Mill Hill Quarry continues to be one of the most attractive and most popular of the Trust's smaller reserves. Many come to see the chalk flowers, especially the thousands of pyramidal and spotted orchids and the magnificent stands of giant bellflower. Blackcap, whitethroat and spotted flycatcher are among the summer bird visitors, and goldfinches and linnets come for the abundant seed in autumn. The warm, south-facing slopes attract a variety of butterflies, bees and other insects, whilst pipistrelle bats roost in crevices in the chalk face. An original assessment of its value was confirmed in 1968 when it was notified by the Nature Conservancy as an SSSI.

On the scarp slope of the Wolds above the village of Goulceby quarrying in the past has exposed a conspicuous band of the red chalk, a well-known landmark appropriately named **Red Hill**, a scene painted in the early 19th century by the Lincoln landscape artist Peter DeWint. Above the old quarry is a rare remnant of chalk downland with all the characteristic flowers of the Wolds some now scarce and localised such as rockrose, thyme and basil thyme, yellow-wort, felwort and bee orchid. The Red Hill was in the 1946 and 1951 lists of potential nature reserves and it appeared in the first SSSI schedule for Lindsey also in 1951. It was therefore a prime candidate for acquisition or other protective action by the Trust and we began enquiries in 1956.

My first contact was Dr E C Cordeaux, the Chairman of the parish meeting – there was no Parish Council at that time. Dr Cordeaux was a member of the Trust and related to John Cordeaux, the late 19th century North Lincolnshire ornithologist and author of *The Birds of the Humber District*. I met him at meetings of the Lindsey Education Committee and we talked about the Red Hill and the possibility of creating a nature reserve. It was generally assumed that the land belonged to the parish having been allocated in the Enclosure Award to the Overseers of the Highways for extracting stone for the repair of public and private roads in the parishes of Asterby and Goulceby. In view of the damage being caused by motorbike scrambling and refuse tipping in the quarry there was some urgency for action, and I accordingly wrote to Dr Cordeaux in August 1956 asking if the parish would consider selling the site to the Trust to be managed as a nature reserve. In reply he promised his strong personal support but forecast that there might be resistance from some parishioners. His fears were well founded because at the parish meeting in 1957 the proposal to sell the land to the Trust was rejected by seven votes to five. Dr Cordeaux's disappointment was sharpened by the behaviour of the rector the Revd John Day who, having previously indicated his support, proposed at the meeting that there should be no further negotiations with the Trust.

We then decided to play the SSSI card, pointing out in further correspondence that the site was being damaged by misuse which the Trust was willing to help to control. In pursuance of this we convened a meeting in July 1958 of all the interested parties – the County and District Councils, the Nature Conservancy and the Parish. A strong Trust delegation met parishioners at a well attended meeting, explained our purposes and asked them to consider leasing the site to the Trust. The parish would be allowed to take chalk for road repairs but only from sites agreed with the Trust; public access would be permitted but people would be asked to respect the purposes of the reserve; an advisory committee with parish representatives would be established. This time the parish meeting agreed by a large majority to accept the proposal. However, a new difficulty then arose in that Mr H Blyth of the Manor Farm claimed that by manorial rights he was the legitimate owner of the site. He insisted that if the parish was to lease the land to the Trust they would have to prove their ownership. He then apparently threatened to plough the grassland and started to grub up some of the thorn trees. In response to this Dr Cordeaux sought the assistance of the County Council in affirming the claim of the parish to own the site.

Whilst this was happening we decided to talk directly to Mr Blyth, and Dick Cornwallis and I met him in May 1960. Contrary to report and expectation we found him entirely amiable and helpful, as I described in a report to Walter Lane the Clerk of the County Council. He said that he wished the Trust to manage the site, that he was willing to convey to the Trust whatever interest he might have in it, and to make a gift to the Trust of a further area of grassland on the adjoining scarp slope of which he was indisputably the owner.

Events now seemed to be moving in the right direction, but there was a further five year delay largely on the part of the County Council who eventually decided that the Council was the legitimate successor of the Overseers of the Highways and therefore the prior claimant to the land. Mr Blyth's offer was gratefully accepted, his land and interest being conveyed to the Trust; an agreement was concluded between the County Council and the Trust for the Trust to manage the whole eleven acre site which was subsequently declared a statutory nature reserve on 31 March 1971. Thus after fifteen years of tortuous negotiation, involving more than 140 pieces of correspondence and goodness knows how much of my time and that of other officers, Red Hill was secured. The remaining rubbish was cleared; the motorbike scrambling stopped, parking places defined; the red chalk exposure protected against erosion and a management regime of mowing and occasional grazing of the grassland was put in place. The successful outcome owed a great deal to Dr Cordeaux' support and persistence especially in the face of early opposition in the parish meeting. Sadly he died in 1963 before the reserve was formally established. When in 1998 the Trust acquired an adjoining fifty-five acres for restoration to chalk grassland the Red Hill, important in itself, also proved to be an excellent example of the 'reservoir' function of a nature reserve as a place from which surrounding areas can be recolonised by plants and animals.

Limestone Grasslands

Of the remnants of limestone grassland in Lincolnshire, apart from road verges, three were of particular interest to us: the Valley at Ancaster, Holywell Mound and Robert's Field the fate of which I have described in an earlier chapter. **Ancaster Valley** is the largest area of limestone grassland left in the county and it was an automatic choice for the 1946 and 1951 lists of potential nature reserves. It appeared in the first SSSI schedule in 1951. Narrow and steep sided, it descends gently from the plateau on the Heath into the floor of the Ancaster Gap close to Ancaster village. All the characteristic flowers of the Lincolnshire limestone are there including the beautiful pasqueflower in what is almost its most northerly site in Britain. On one side of the Valley there is a beechwood with a fringe of yew, box, wayfaring tree, barberry and wild clematis which further enhances the botanical interest. The property was owned by Mr H Johnson who lived at the farm at the head of the Valley. In April 1963 Brian Ducker, the Nature Conservancy's Assistant Regional Officer, Marson Peet and I visited Mr Johnson to discuss the management of the Valley. He was generally sympathetic but obviously unwilling to enter into any formal agreement. After further consideration, therefore, I wrote to him in July with a number of other suggestions designed to ensure the survival of the rich limestone grassland and its rare plants. Whilst emphasising the paramount importance of maintaining an adequate grazing regime I asked that Trust volunteers be allowed to remove some of the gorse and thorn scrub that was already spreading along both sides of the Valley. I also asked that we be allowed to have a wardening presence at weekends and to post a notice asking people using the public footpath through the Valley not to take wild flowers or leave litter. There was a very tentative oral agreement from Mr Johnson, but little was achieved until the appointment of Ray Collier as Conservation Officer in 1971. By that time with reduced grazing the scrub problem had worsened considerably and it required several work party visits to remove gorse from slopes in the upper part of the Valley. Before and after photographs show the results of that work. Some further progress was made after the formation of the Ancaster Reserves Management Group under Don Wright's leadership in 1973, but the grazing problem and continuing uncertainty about our status were severely limiting factors. The latter problem was exacerbated after Mr Johnson's death by a somewhat difficult relationship with his son who eventually terminated association with us and requested that we delete the Valley from our reserves handbook.

In 1978 we were alarmed to discover that two forestry-type enclosures had been erected in the Valley, one of them on one of the richest areas of limestone grassland. The intervention of the NCC at this point seems to have delayed any further action, but by 1981 birch and Scots' pine and a crop of kale had been planted following ploughing of part of the valley floor; a pond planted round with willows had also been excavated at the northern end near the entrance.

Then in 1982, just when further deterioration in the condition of the site seemed inevitable, the owner suddenly offered to sell it to us. A special appeal and grant-aid enabled us to complete the purchase and set about the major task of restoring the damaged grassland and providing by fencing and other means for appropriate grazing in future. We made a presentation to a well-attended meeting in Ancaster explaining the importance of the Valley and our management and access policies.

Securing the future of the Ancaster Valley, a site of high national as well as local importance, was another example of the complexities and difficulties of negotiation which could arise in such cases. It also illustrated the continuing ineffectiveness at that time of the SSSI system in safeguarding such places. Without the Trust's persistence the interest of this splendid site could well have been irreparably damaged or destroyed.

There are two gaps in the oolitic limestone ridge of western Lincolnshire, at Lincoln and Ancaster, both of them former courses of the River Trent and both of great strategic value in prehistoric and Roman times and still important lines of communication for road and rail. During the last Ice Age meltwaters flowing through the Ancaster Gap deposited great quantities of sand on the floor of the gap and spread it out over the dip slope to the east, giving rise to heaths and warrens. These have almost entirely disappeared, but something of their interest remains in the strip of land at South Rauceby between the A153 road and the railway. By the mid 1960s this had been largely excavated for sand, but patches of ancient turf had survived, and even on the disturbed ground the mixture of mildly calcifuge plants in the sandy surface layers and deeper rooted calcicoles was still apparent. In all over 320 plant species have been recorded in the twenty acres and they include some which are scarce or localised in Lincolnshire, and one, the smooth rupturewort, which is otherwise scarcely known outside the Norfolk and Suffolk Brecklands where similar soil conditions are found. Fluctuations in the water table are also of great interest. In most years towards the end of the winter the deeper excavations fill with water only to become completely dry again by mid-summer.

This fascinating piece of land was generously given to the Trust in 1968 by Messrs J W & J H Turnbull of Sleaford and became the **Rauceby Warren** reserve. With the formation of the Sleaford Area Group the following year volunteers were soon available to clear up rubbish and to control further unauthorised tipping. Members of the Group, Les Gostick and Geoff Atkin in particular, have since managed the reserve in exemplary fashion. We were fortunate too that in 1968 Roger Mitchell conducted one of the most intensive surveys of any of our small reserves, the results of which were summarised in an article in the Trust's newsletter in April 1969. Mitchell went on in much later years to become the head of English Nature's Species Recovery Programme.

There were two other sites on the Kesteven limestone which we sought to protect, both unsuccessfully. The Iron Age fort known as Honington Camp which occupies a strategic position above the Ancaster Gap was at that time one of four known sites in Lincolnshire for the pasqueflower. Several other scarce plants also grew in the ancient turf of the earthwork. The site had been badly treated: pigs had been kept on it and nettles and other weeds had proliferated on bare patches. Both its archaeological and botanical interests needed better care and protection. In 1968 we opened discussions with the owners of the land, Buckminster Estates, and David Robinson and Dick Morgan attended a site meeting with the Estates' Agent who was willing to offer the Trust a lease. The farm was about to change hands and the Agent indicated that if the Estate decided to sell the farm he would recommend that the Trust be offered the freehold of the site. The farm was sold; the new owner was told of the Trust's interest, but was apparently unwilling to take the matter further.

We had also made contact with the owners of the large disused Wilsford Heath Quarry on the plateau above the village. The quarry had been recolonised by a variety of calcicolous plants including the scarce and spectacular woolly thistle. There were also areas of scrub and mature woodland with an abundance of the evergreen spurge laurel in the shrub layer. Gregory Quarries of Mansfield, a family firm, were very supportive and willingly entered into a management agreement. When they decided to sell the quarry in 1977 the Trust made a bid for it but was unsuccessful. Discussions with the new owner about a continuing role for the Trust came to nothing and our association with the quarry came to an end.

North of Lincoln the limestone becomes a narrow ridge, the Lincoln Cliff, traversed by the Roman Ermine Street. On the edge of Broughton Far Wood near Brigg is an area of shallow, long disused limestone quarries known as **Clapgate Pits**. It was one of those small sites which miraculously preserved an unusual assemblage of limestone plants some of them rare in Lincolnshire. Most notable among them was the pasqueflower at what was probably then its most northerly site in Britain, and wall germander, a national Red Data Book species which is often a garden escape but considered at Clapgate to be of native origin. Pale St John's-wort and that delightfully named member of the bedstraw family squinancywort were among other Lincolnshire rarities. Like many such places the quarries were subject to refuse tipping and motorbike scrambling, and the open grassland was threatened by scrub invasion. In 1952 it was reported to the Trust Council that the owners, Westminster Estates, not knowing perhaps what to do with the place, had planted trees over it.

I consequently arranged to meet the local Agent for the Estates Mr T H Russell to make a plea to protect the rare flora. Miss Joan Gibbons, the county's leading botanist and member of the Trust Council, knew the site well and I invited her to accompany me. That proved to be a mistake. Her overwrought criticism of the Estate's action offended the Agent who was otherwise sympathetic. As a result I secured only a very minor concession to remove one tree from the vicinity of the pasqueflower plants. Over the years the site continued to deteriorate. The pasqueflowers were dug up by a vandal in 1969 and scrub enveloped all but a few patches of open ground. Then, as at Robert's Field, we were able to salvage the place by purchase of the freehold in 1996. The scrub was cleared by volunteers, and the site was fenced for occasional sheep grazing. Most of the limestone plants had just survived and have spread again, but some of the more vulnerable rarities like squinancywort and wall germander have disappeared. The moral of the Clapgate Pits affair, like that of Robert's Field, is never give up on a place as long as it retains something worth saving.

Other Grasslands
Erosion of the chalk along the southern and south-western edge of the Wolds has given rise to a broken landscape fretted by streams some of which have cut down through the soft Spilsby sandstone into the Kimmeridge clay. Alder carrs occupied the heads of many of the valleys; lower down it was mainly rough grazing. Many

of them were converted to arable in the agricultural intensification during and after the Second World War. John Blackwood's invaluable survey of grasslands in 1968/9 had aroused new interest in these lower cretaceous and Kimmeridge clay grasslands which the Trust's Scientific Policy Group at a meeting in September 1969 had acknowledged to be "seriously under-represented" in our Reserve Selection and Acquisition Policy.

One of the valleys which had survived was **Snipe Dales** in the parishes of Winceby and Lusby. The open valley had been more extensive - as I remember it in the 1930s – but in the 1960s the Forestry Commission planted some ninety-six acres of the lower part with conifers, mainly Corsican pine. The upper part, however, remained as rough grassland and scrub. There was evidence of more woodland there in the past, of oak and ash on the higher slopes, and willow and alder lower down, especially in the little lateral valleys whose names no doubt record former landowners or graziers - Isaac's Holt, Clarke's Water Holt, Tippings Holt. Wet flushes on the springline at the junction of the sandstone and the clay support kingcups, spotted orchids and tussock sedge, and later in summer a tall herb flora of giant horsetail, meadowsweet and hairy willowherb.

This was for Lincolnshire a wild, secluded valley almost invisible from any public road. The access at the head of the valley was through Winceby churchyard – the church had been demolished in 1964 – and Isaac's Holt with its flourishing rookery. Emerging from there the whole valley lies before you, the vista bounded in the far distance by the chalk Wold escarpment. It is a view that has delighted many thousands of people in the last thirty years.

Knowing that the Nature Conservancy intended to designate it an SSSI and that the property might be for sale, the Trust Executive Committee agreed in September 1971 to negotiate its purchase. The Administrative Officer reported to Council in June that the agents were willing to sell the 120 acres for £10,000 subject to boundary definitions. As reported in the previous chapter, the Trust having acquired the property agreed to sell it on to Lindsey County Council who then leased it back. An agreement between the County Council and the Trust set out the basic aims of management and those were approved by the County Council's Countryside Committee on a site visit in June 1972. The Council subsequently declared Snipe Dales to be a statutory Nature Reserve. Early management tasks carried out by volunteer work parties, supplemented by a week's task by the British Trust for Conservation Volunteers, were concentrated on establishing a pathway system including bridges, planting over 1500 trees and conducting experimental management of grassland which had not been grazed for many years. Close liaison was established with the Forestry Commission who sought the Trust's advice about the wildlife interest of their property and informally agreed to declare it a Forest Nature Reserve.

In 1984, however, the Forestry Commission announced their intention to sell their property. The Trust immediately explored the possibility of finding the funds to purchase it, but Lincolnshire County Council decided that they would do so in order to establish a Country Park. They proposed a management agreement with the Trust to cover both the Country Park and the Nature Reserve, an agreement which involved a full-time warden's post. It is an arrangement which on the whole has worked well in the interests of both the Council and the Trust for twenty years.

227

*Red Hill,
Goulceby 1960.*

*White chalk
Red chalk
Carstone.*

KEN ATTERBY

Giant bellflower.

BARRIE WILKINSON

Mill Hill Quarry, Claxby 1963.

DAVID ROBINSON

TED SMITH

*Snipe Dales Nature Reserve and Country Park. Inset: Trust President
Walter Lane plants a tree to inaugurate the Country Park in 1985.*

Ancaster Valley.

TED SMITH

GEOFF TRINDER

Pasque flower.

*Afforestation of heathland:
Ostler's Plantation,
Kirkby Moor, 1970.*

BILL DALES

Kirkby Moor reserve, early 1980s.

GEOFF TRINDER

Green woodpecker

TED SMITH

Kirkby Moor 1993.

Cotton grass in the Heath Field, Moor Farm.

JOHN HOWARD

BARRIE WILKINSON

Crowle Moors 1983.

Large heath butterfly

GEOFF TRINDER

TED SMITH

229

Heathland and Bog

Scotton Common and Linwood Warren, our early heathland acquisitions, were two of the best remaining examples of the once extensive Coversands heathland of north-west Lincolnshire. There is another area of heathland in the county about which in the 1950s we knew comparatively little. Sands and gravels deposited in delta conditions along the edge of the great Fenland lake in the last Ice Age gave rise to heathland soils and conditions, remnants of which survive in the vicinity of Woodhall Spa. The heaths were more extensive until the end of the 19th century. In his *Records of Woodhall Spa and Neighbourhood* (1899) the Rev'd James Conway Walter described the rich and varied wildlife as it was in the second half of the 19th century. Most of the plants he recorded can still be found, but some rarer species – especially those which flourish in boggy conditions – have gone, including marsh gentian, bog asphodel, grass of Parnassus, round-leaved and intermediate-leaved sundews, common butterwort and royal fern. The nightjar was a familiar heathland bird, and kite, buzzard and hen harrier all occurred until the mid-century. Walter recalls how as a boy he climbed the Tower-on-the-Moor, the remains of a 15th century hunting lodge, to take the eggs of a hen harrier, its last known nesting place in the area.

Much of the heathland in the parish of Kirkby-on-Bain – described in the Enclosure Award of 1776 as the 'Worst Moors' – had been left unenclosed as common pasture. During the 19th century, at times when cereal prices were high, and later when two World Wars required increased food production, parts of the moors were ploughed and cultivated with subsequent changes to the vegetation pattern. Commoners were allowed to enclose and manage allotments of land, and some of these became permanent features, as at Moor Farm and Jubilee Farm. Sir Joseph Banks' agent, John Parkinson, fulfilled an ambition by planting an oak wood on the moors which is still there, and in the 1940s the Forestry Commission planted an extensive wood of Scots and Corsican pine. I have a diary written by a naturalist Burtt Davy which describes a visit to Kirkby Moor in 1890 when the heathland was more extensive and more open. He describes how Tattershall Castle was clearly visible from it. To the west the heathland in the neighbouring parish of Roughton was likewise diminished and fragmented by the creation of a golf course and by the expansion of Woodhall Spa.

The only substantial area of open heathland that was left is the present **Kirkby Moor** nature reserve. That area survived because in the early years of the 20th century Woodhall Spa Water Company had acquired the area to make a reservoir to store water gathered naturally in the sands and gravels. The Trust had become aware of the importance of Kirkby Moor in the early 1960s, and when the Nature Conservancy announced their intention to schedule it as an SSSI we made contact with the owners, the East Lincolnshire Water Board whose engineer Ian Campbell was sympathetic to the Trust's interest. The Board had a problem in the form of heavy infestation of rabbits which they were being pressed to control. Because it was a gathering ground for water, gassing was not permitted and in the sandy soil would probably not have been very effective in any case. The Divisional Pests Officer of MAFF had recommended that to facilitate rabbit control the heathland be broken up and re-seeded and let for sheep grazing. The Board consulted the Nature Conservancy about that proposal, and the Conservancy then involved the Trust with the result that at a meeting with John Blackwood and me the Board's Deputy Engineer enquired if the Trust would be prepared to take a lease of the property and accept responsibility for rabbit control. I then had a site meeting with the Divisional Pests Officer from which it was clear that there was no alternative to fencing along three sides of the 140 or so acres – there was already a rabbit-proof fence erected by the Forestry Commission along the fourth side.

In a paper presented to the Trust Council in September 1968 I set out the costs of fencing, of bracken control and of means of reducing the rabbit population to manageable proportions. Up to 75% would be eligible for MAFF grant-aid and I put the total cost to the Trust over the first three years at £650 to £750. I raised a further possibility: that a lease might include the house on the site known as Foxhill Cottage, formerly occupied by an employee of the Board but then empty and no longer needed. That could enable the Trust to install a warden to give whole or part-time help in return for free accommodation. Our presence at Kirkby Moor might also enable us to extend our interests in the Woodhall area which was clearly still one of great natural interest. I proposed therefore that we seek a lease of not less than twenty-one years at a nominal rent (since we should be freeing the Board from the liability of rabbit control) and ask if the house could be included.

The Board agreed to our proposal. The lease was concluded subject to the continuing water supply function of the property. We accepted a responsibility for maintenance of the house and carried out repairs and renovation straightway. We determined, however, that the house should only be used in connection with the management of the reserve. We were fortunate to find a very suitable tenant who undertook part-time wardening of the reserve in lieu of rent. Peter Kalinowski was a biologist with the Lincolnshire River Board and he and his family enjoyed several years at Foxhill Cottage. Some of the subsequent tenants were not as satisfactory, so it is pleasing that the house is today (2005) occupied by the Trust's Assistant Director (Nature Reserves).

To demonstrate the value we placed on the new reserve we straightway asked John Redshaw to produce a management plan, a process in which he had shown great competence at Baston Fen and other reserves in the south of the county. He presented an outline to the Scientific Policy Group in May 1970. The first phase of management work involved bracken control on the heath and scrub clearance and mowing on the species-rich lakeside marsh. A visitors' path was established round the lake and the wet woodland on the west side of the access road. The successful management of Kirkby Moor over the years owes much to the knowledge and commitment of Brian Redman who has served from the outset as volunteer manager.

In 1976 we negotiated the purchase from the Lely Estates of the strip of heath and woodland between Kirkby Lane and Ostlers Plantation together with the oak wood on the other side of the Lane, some forty acres altogether.

When in 1979 Anglian Water abandoned water abstraction at Kirkby Moor we took advantage of the option in the lease to negotiate the purchase of the freehold. We offered £35,000; the Authorities Area Estate Surveyor estimated it to be worth £75,000. We increased our offer to £45,000 and that was accepted. Funding the purchase was one of the main objectives of the Trust's ambitious Appeal and Development Campaign launched in the spring of 1980. As part of the Campaign a special local appeal for Kirkby Moor brought a great response from members, and the *Lincolnshire Standard* newspaper gave strong support by launching its own 'Let's Save Kirkby Moor' appeal. At a packed public meeting in Woodhall Spa Peter (later Sir Peter) Tapsell MP and representatives of County, District and Parish Councils all spoke in support. With the additional aid of generous grants by the Countryside Commission and the World Wildlife Fund the acquisition was secured.

There is a northern moorland feel about our north-west Coversands heaths of Scotton and Linwood; Kirkby Moor in character and ecology belongs to the Brecklands of East Anglia which also lie on the edge of the Fenland. Remnant of a vanished landscape though it is, there is something of the spaciousness and solitude of the heathland about the place. I feel it whenever I cross the dusty track especially perhaps in spring when the woodlarks are singing that loveliest of bird songs, and on summer days of billowing white clouds in a blue sky and the heather showing purple. Jasper Petulengro's words to Lavengro come back into my mind: "There's night and day, brother, both sweet things; sun moon and stars, brother, all sweet things; there's likewise a wind on the heath. Life is very sweet, brother; who would wish to die". A magical place Kirkby Moor. It would be a great achievement to recreate more of it.

Kirkby Moor was not quite the first place that attracted the Trust's interest in the Woodhall Spa area. In the 1950s before it was completely built over, parts of Roughton Moor to the east of the Horncastle-Woodhall road were accessible from the road. One day, when I had been in Woodhall Spa organising an adult class, Mary and I explored what remained of the open moor. The ground sloped gently eastwards to a little stream – the parish boundary, incidentally between Roughton and Kirkby on Bain. Beyond that we discovered a wet pasture dominated in parts by various rush species – this we knew later was the aptly named **Rush Bottom Close**. In marshy areas we found fen bedstraw, marsh violet a favourite of ours with its modest pale lilac flowers veined with purple, devil's bit scabious and purple loosestrife. On the north side of the field there were patches of wet heath with bog mosses, bog pimpernel its green mat of leaves studded with bright pink flowers opening wide in the sunshine, lousewort, and most exciting of all round-leaved sundew. Visits the following year in spring revealed nesting snipe and lapwing. To the south of the field there were more extensive areas of wet heath and birch-oak woodland. I reported the 'find' to Trust colleagues and recommended further investigation. Other issues took priority, however, and it was not until 1970 that the new Scientific Policy Group visited the area together with staff from the Nature Conservancy. They were so impressed by Rush Bottom Close that they recommended the Trust try to acquire it, whilst the Nature Conservancy's Regional Officer recommended that together with the joining areas it be declared an SSSI. "There could be no doubt", he reported "that the area of marsh and wet and dry heath is of SSSI status both for the content of rare and unusual species and for the peculiar association of calcicoles and calcifuges".

The visit had been prompted by the knowledge that the farm to which Rush Bottom Close belonged was coming up for sale. A sympathetic owner, Mr J H Gillon, agreed to sell the Close together with the right-of-way from Wellsyke Lane. A price of £1,700 for the 16.8 acres was agreed and conveyance was completed by the end of that year 1970. We made an application to and received grants from the SPNR's Purchase Fund and the World Wildlife Fund. By this time the lease of Kirkby Moor had also been completed and a local management group was formed to cover both areas.

Further investigation of the area to the south of Rush Bottom Close revealed a fascinating mosaic of wet and dry heath and woodland which comprised **Moor Farm** with its small farmhouse and barn. Two of the largest fields were dry sandy heath with Breckland-type plants like cudweed, common centuary, crane's-bill and stork's-bill and rarer species such as creeping St John's wort and shepherd's cress. A low-lying field next to Rush Bottom Close was an acid bog with patches of cross-leaved heath and tussocky purple moor grass. The richest field floristically was the home field or, as we later called it, the heath field. There heath and common spotted orchids grew in abundance, and masses of flowering cottongrass created a striking spectacle. The rest of the 'farm' consisted of oak-birch-rowan woodland which had evidently grown up on rough pasture in the previous twenty or thirty years; the remains of boundary hedges and ditches can still be readily identified. When I went round with the old tenant who had been there for at least twenty-five years I remarked as we walked through the woodland that the farm must have changed a great deal during his time there. He replied that he hadn't really noticed! A real Rip Van Winkle.

The farm was not merely run down; it had almost ceased to function. Not surprisingly in fact we found that the owners Mr & Mrs Prime were willing to consider selling, and Paul Barclay, our Administrative Officer, conducted negotiations directly with them and through their solicitor. We offered £16,000 for vacant possession, but the owners did not wish to dispossess Mr Ranshaw their long-standing tenant. We therefore made a revised offer of £15,000 which was accepted. Since we needed possession of the property including the house, we agreed with Mr and Mrs Ranshaw that they would retire and live for a nominal rent in a house in Horncastle, Beck Cottage, which we acquired for the purpose. That enabled us to renovate the farmhouse for our newly appointed Conservation Officer, to convert the barn into a store for a tractor and other equipment, and to begin a programme of management for the reserve. Moor Farm has functioned ever since as a regional management base.

Kirkby Moor and Moor Farm together form one of the richest wildlife areas in Lincolnshire. The range of habitats includes wet and dry heath, old meadow, acid bog, marsh, open water and woodland. The variety of plants and animals is impressive: more than 250 species of plants, 275 of moths, twenty of butterflies, eleven of dragonflies and eighty of breeding birds. My own visits to both reserves leave many impressions, sights and sounds of the rich variety and fascination of their wildlife: the first flush of green on the birch trees; adders basking in the sunshine; a silvery slow worm sliding away from beneath a fallen log; brimstone butterflies around the alder buckthorn bushes; handsome little grizzled skippers flitting elusively along a sunny ride; the green woodpecker's yaffle ringing out over the heath; the nightingale's commanding song from the willow coppice, and a splendid male hobby – my best view ever – on a dead tree on the heath at Kirkby. Some sights and sounds are alas no longer there to be enjoyed: snipe no longer drum nor lapwings tumble over Rush Bottom Close, and the handsome dark green fritillary butterflies no longer search out the marsh valerian flowers. Nevertheless management has enhanced variety, and time may restore some of the losses which reflect widespread national declines of the species in question.

It seems extraordinary that what is now regarded as one of the most important National Nature Reserves in Britain was virtually unknown to the nature conservation movement, official and voluntary, only thirty-five years ago.

Crowle Waste (or **Crowle Moors** as we now prefer to call it) in the extreme north-west corner of Lincolnshire's Isle of Axholme, and Thorne Waste on the Yorkshire side of the county boundary, are the remnants of the great fens and peat bogs which once surrounded the head of the Humber estuary. Whilst the Trust had acquired the much smaller raised bog relics of Epworth and Haxey Turbaries in the Isle, we knew very little in the 1950s about Crowle Waste. It was a proposal by the Central Electricity Generating Board to investigate it as a site for dumping pulverised fly ash from the new Drax power station that first alerted us to its importance, although ironically we had just been discussing with the Nature Conservancy the desirability of making a survey of the site. In March 1969 the Lindsey County Planning Officer consulted us about the CEGB proposal. Whilst inviting our comments he pointed out, that although the two turbaries were SSSIs Crowle Waste was not.

Having researched natural history reports and records and made various enquiries I sent a holding response to the effect that the Waste was clearly of considerable ecological importance and that we had urged the Nature Conservancy to designate it as an SSSI. I had already alerted the Conservancy, and John Blackwood, the Assistant Regional Officer in Lincolnshire, told the Planning Officer that a survey of the area already planned would be brought forward. If as a result the scientific interest merited it, SSSI designation would be recommended.

In June 1969 a meeting took place between the CEGB, the Nature Conservancy and the Trust represented by David Robinson who was about to succeed me as Honorary Secretary. CEGB clarified their options for fly ash disposal and we agreed to produce a report on the scientific interest of Crowle Waste by mid-September. Meantime the Yorkshire Trust Council, in considering the threat to Thorne Waste, informed the Nature Conservancy's North Regional Officer that they did not intend to oppose the CEGB proposal should that particular site be chosen. The reason they gave was that "the Trust cannot oppose everything with which it is not in entire agreement"! Alarmed at the effect that this might have on our defence of Crowle Waste I wrote straightway to Colonel Newman, the Trust's Executive Officer, explaining our position and asking that his Trust should at least defer communicating their decision to the CEGB until we had had an opportunity to make further investigations and exchange views with them. Newman agreed to that and expressed their willingness to help in survey and collection of information of the scientific interest.

Survey visits to Thorne and Crowle arranged by the Nature Conservancy involved Rick Pilcher, the Chairman of the Trust's Scientific Policy Group. Local naturalists, mainly from the Yorkshire side, contributed information. They included Mr William Bunting, an expert on the Wastes and their rare plants and animals which made an impressive list. Whilst Bunting's intimate knowledge was undoubtedly of great value, his eccentric behaviour and confrontational approach were to prove something of an embarrassment to us in seeking permanent means of protecting Crowle Waste.

The report compiled by the NCC's North and East Anglian regions for Thorne and Crowle respectively confirmed beyond doubt the national importance of both, and the Regional Officers recommended SSSI designation for them. The Nature Conservancy, however, was still somewhat tardy in recognising just how important they were and in taking steps to ensure their long-term protection.

The CEGB eventually decided to tip their fly ash elsewhere, but the West Riding County Planning Officer in a letter to Dr Helga Frankland the NCC's North Regional Officer, in August 1969 pointed out that the WRCC's proposals for a regional airport at Thorne Waste would require the site to be reclaimed if not by fly ash then possibly by shale discarded by the National Coal Board. Thorne and Crowle Wastes it seemed were not to be allowed to escape even at the cost of building an airport on a bog! Identification of the national scientific interest and the opposition of the Lincolnshire and Yorkshire Trusts – the latter were strongly supportive once convinced – undoubtedly helped to counter the threats. Once they were behind us we set about trying to establish a reserve at Crowle.

Crowle Waste, an area of 400 acres, was granted for peat extraction to the tenants and inhabitants of Crowle as part of an agreement with Sir Cornelius Vermuiden in 1630 in connection with his drainage schemes. The peat deposits are thinner than on the Yorkshire side and this may account for the fact that there has been much more large-scale commercial extraction at Thorne than at Crowle. Most of Crowle Waste in recent times has been divided into 'ribbons' or strips, and in 1970 was in about twelve ownerships, including Fisons Horticultural Limited who owned some 292 acres in eight strips. Contact with Fisons, facilitated by the Nature Conservancy, established that they regarded the Crowle peat as basically surplus to their present requirements and were prepared to enter into an agreement with the Trust to establish a reserve. David Robinson took up the negotiations with great determination and saw them through to a successful conclusion in 1971 by means of a seven-year lease. The reserve thus established was the first by many years on any of the Wastes. During the next thirty years it was consolidated and expanded to more than 400 acres by the purchase of the freehold of Fisons' property and the acquisition of further strips from other owners. Establishing the reserve has given rise to problems of alleged common rights and ownerships of the often ill-defined boundaries of the strips, but the Trust can justifiably claim to have given the lead in securing the protection of what is now acknowledged to be the outstandingly important Humberhead Peatlands National Nature Reserve.

Wetlands

I described in an earlier chapter our unsuccessful attempts in the 1950s to establish nature reserves in the Humber Bank clay pits to the west of Barton. It was nearly twenty years later in 1973 when we gained our first foothold in the clay pits by the lease from Lindsey County Council of twenty acres of reedbed, open water and scrub adjoining the County Council's Outdoor Pursuits Pit to the east of Westfield Lakes, the reserve known as **Barton Reedbed**. It was a good start: bittern nested there, so did water rail, pochard and shoveler, and there was a high breeding density of sedge and reed warblers and reed buntings. The establishment of the reserve coincided with the formation of the Barton Area Group which participated in the survey of all the Humber Bank clay pits and provided an immediate management team for the new reserve.

Pressure for recreational use of the pits was increasing, and an application in 1972 to construct holiday chalets in connection with the Westfield Lakes Hotel prompted the Nature Conservancy to seek a meeting with the Planning Department and the Trust to discuss a policy for conservation and recreational development in the whole complex of clay pits from Far Ings Lane at Barton to

Immingham. As a result the conservation value of the pits was recognised in the County Council's Plan for the Barton Pits published in 1973. It was followed in 1978 by a subject plan for the pits produced by the County Council and Glanford Borough Council. Another stimulus to the planning process for the area was the likely effects of the construction of the Humber Bridge which began in 1972. That was going to involve in particular the excavation of vast quantities of spoil for which disposal sites would be needed. The Trust and the Nature Conservancy were fully consulted by the Planning Department, and extensive damage to the pits was avoided, although in 1977 a flooded pit between the bridge works and the reserve was unexpectedly used as a tip for chalk spoil. This was a result of a deal between the contractors and the owner of the pit and did not have planning permission. The spoil spilled over onto the reserve and we had to engage in legal action to have it removed and the damage repaired.

Expansion of our clay pits holding was henceforth a priority for the Trust. This was encouraged by a strong and influential Area Group which brought some outstanding people such as Martin Broadbridge and Sam van den Bos into the counsels and activities of the Trust. Although initially a little suspicious of the central administration, Sam in particular became one of the most stalwart and devoted workers for the Trust at county as well as local level. I specially valued his support. In 1982 we purchased Ness Lake and several other smaller lakes to the west of Westfield Lakes Hotel. This area, now known as the **Far Ings** reserve, contained some of the most extensive reedbeds in northern England, and also included the derelict farmhouse and attached farm buildings, a rare Lincolnshire longhouse. In view of their ruinous condition demolition seemed to be the only solution, but one day Sam took me into the house - a somewhat precarious venture - and described his visionary plan for the reconstruction of the building to serve as a Visitor Centre and Warden's residence. Tragically Sam did not live to see his inspiration become reality. He died in 1989. The Centre, splendidly restored, was opened in July 1991 in the presence of his widow Beryl and daughter Heather, both tireless workers for the Trust. On the same occasion Beryl unveiled the memorial stone recording the dedication of the Far Ings reserve to Sam. The reserve has continued to expand and, with the Visitor Centre, has proved to be one of the Trust's most successful and popular projects. Reserves have also been acquired in pits to the east of Barton. And the bitterns have returned!

Most of the major Fenland rivers were provided with washlands, areas adjoining the river which acted as flood reservoirs when the river overflowed. On the Welland, Crowland and Cowbit washes were drained after the construction of the Coronation Channel which took flood water round Spalding. The only washland then left in south Lincolnshire was **Baston Fen** on the River Glen, a narrow belt of ninety acres of rough marsh grazing and a flooded borrow pit along the foot of the riverbank. We knew comparatively little about its flora and fauna, but it was clearly of great interest with a variety of aquatic and marsh plants, some like greater spearwort, water violet, greater bladderwort and marsh orchid rare in Lincolnshire; and nesting snipe, redshank and lapwing. In winter when water levels were high and when it was occasionally flooded it held many wildfowl and was a favourite hunting ground of short-eared owls. Appropriate management, it was believed, could undoubtedly enhance the interest.

In 1967 the Spalding Area Group secretary, Arnold Smith, ascertained that the Deeping Fen, Spalding and Pinchbeck Internal Drainage Board were willing to sell the washland. As described in the last chapter, the Trust in 1967 was in process of parting company with Arnold Smith and his Spalding group, but he agreed that it was appropriate for the Trust with its greater management resources – rather than his South Lincolnshire Nature Reserves company – to acquire Baston Fen. The Trust therefore opened negotiations with the Drainage Board and a price of £4,500 was agreed for sixty-six acres together with herbage rights over a further twenty-four acres on the banks of the Glen and the Counter Drain. The sale was subject to continuing use of the land as a flood reservoir.

There was another interesting facet to Baston Fen. Since the drainage of Cowbit Wash it had been used as the main venue for skating in South Lincolnshire, and the National Championships had been held there. Skating, of course, only took place during hard ·frost when wildfowl and waders had moved to coastal saltmarshes or to other ice-free waters. Subject to proper control, therefore, the Trust offered facilities to the South Lincolnshire Skating Association and so helped to perpetuate a traditional Fenland sport. Milder winters in recent years, however, have effectively put an end to skating use.

Under John Redshaw's expert management over many years the reserve has flourished. Controlled winter flooding has been perpetuated and the Wash cut for hay or grazed by cattle. A parking area, waymarked route and hides have made it a popular visitor attraction. A severe national decline of both species has largely deprived it of its nesting lapwing and snipe, but it continues to attract many winter wildfowl, and investigation has revealed a rich invertebrate fauna including more than seventy species of non-marine molluscs. Together with Thurlby Fen Slipe reserve on the other side of the River Glen, Baston Fen, I hope, will form a nucleus of a much larger fenland habitat reserve which the Trust now aims to create.

The Trust acquired several other small wetland reserves during this period. Two of them were excellent examples of the natural artesian springs known as blow wells where water is forced up by pressure from the chalk through the overlying boulder clay. Such springs used to be much more numerous in the Lindsey Marshland but most have dried up as a result of depression of water tables through increased abstraction. One of these reserves is the **Barrow Blow Wells** on the edge of Barrow-on-Humber village. It was a generous gift from my old friend Jack Hargreaves to whom I have previously referred. He took me to see it before making the offer and was clearly very attached to the place. It had been noted for reed and sedge warblers and for cuckoos which parasitised them. The wood surrounding the wells may have been an old osier bed. The Barrow Beck on the northern boundary, once a clean and attractive chalk stream, had become badly polluted. An adjoining area of wet sedgy pasture of about an acre was also given to the Trust by Dr J R Bentley.

The other larger reserve was the **Tetney Blow Wells** for which the Trust secured a management agreement from the then North-East Lincolnshire Water Board. This was achieved through the good office of Cyril Cooper, the Board's Managing Engineer who was a long-term supporter of the Trust and served on its Council from 1967 to 1978. The thirty-six acres comprised not only the wells – which are still used for water supply – but a considerable area of grassland, damp woodland, marsh vegetation and reedbed which have developed on the site of the former watercress beds. It is a reserve full of interest.

In the south the Trust took a lease from Lindsey County Council in 1968 of a damp meadow known as **Surfleet Lows** beside the A16 road. Its eight acres have a rich flora with five species of buttercup including the uncommon hairy buttercup, and a number of brackish marsh species such as sea milkwort, distant sedge, glaucous rush and golden dock. It seems likely that in the Middle Ages it was saltmarsh within the tidal limits of the River Glen. The depression in the field is the site of an old creek. The grassland is summer grazed by cattle; winter floodwater attracts wildfowl like wigeon, and waders like snipe. It has been managed for many years, like Baston Fen, by the stalwart John Redshaw.

In 1971 the Trust negotiated a lease of disused gravel pits at Burton some 2½ miles north-west of Lincoln. Open water, reedbed and fringing woodland supported a rich variety of wildlife, notably water and waterside birds and wildfowl. The reserve proved to be particularly attractive to Lincoln members. Unfortunately over the years problems developed concerning tenure, relations with a fishing syndicate, and management and access arrangements. Those problems and the increasing cost of rental eventually (2003) forced the Trust to abandon the tenure.

BARRIE WILKINSON

Baston Fen 1986.

GEOFF TRINDER

Snipe

John Redshaw (left) building a bridge at Surfleet Lows, 1972.

RAY COLLIER

Ness Lake, Far Ings reserve 1984.

Sam van den Bos cutting reeds 1985.

*Unveiling of Sam's memorial stone by
Trust President Walter Lane with widow
Beryl and daughter Heather.*

*Derelict farmhouse and buildings in 1987 and after
restoration as the Far Ings Visitor Centre, opened
by Cllr Richard Bark, Mayor of Glanford in 1991.*

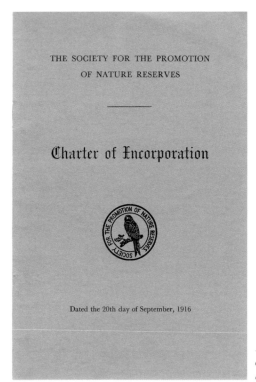

THE SOCIETY FOR THE PROMOTION
OF NATURE RESERVES

Charter of Incorporation

Dated the 20th day of September, 1916

*Cyril Diver, first
Director-General of
The Nature Conservancy.*

*Whiteslea Lodge on Hickling
Broad, venue of the 1957
discussions on national nature
conservation organisation.*

*L-R: Norman Riley,
Christopher Cadbury and
Ronald Hickling on
Hickling Broad when the
County Trusts' Committee
met at Whiteslea Lodge,
1974.*

Part III

Nationwide: The Trusts' Movement Develops

– 12 –

Wider Horizons

THERE was a national context, however tenuous, in the Trust's origins in the NRIC sub-committee for Lincolnshire. This, like all the other county sub-committees, was still nominally in existence in 1948 and my name as its Honorary Secretary appeared in the Handbook of the Society for the Promotion of Nature Reserves for that year. One of my first acts in November 1948 as its Honorary Secretary designate, therefore, was to notify the Honorary Secretary of the SPNR, Dr Herbert Smith, of the approaching formation of the Trust. The response of the Society's Executive Committee, which he promptly conveyed to me, was welcoming and sympathetic with a particular assurance of financial support for definite schemes. Shortly afterwards the Society established a formal link with the Trust by becoming a Life Member, as it had done already with Norfolk and Yorkshire.

The following year, 1949, I was invited to attend the Society's Official Luncheon in the Prince Consort Room at the Royal Albert Hall. The principal speaker was Lewis Silkin, the Minister of Town and Country Planning, who was at that time taking the National Parks and Access to the Countryside Bill through Parliament. I remember finding the speech disappointing but perhaps my expectations of politicians were youthfully naïve. The occasion was a grand if somewhat awesome experience for a newcomer from the country. I was indeed a stranger at the feast. I knew no one, but by good fortune found myself placed next to Phyllis Barclay-Smith, the redoubtable Secretary of the International Committee for Bird Preservation, who in the years that followed gave me much support and encouragement. Herbert Smith I met but briefly on that occasion. Already in his eighties he had directed the affairs of the Society for nearly thirty years. My impression was of an austere but courteous man. I had no further contacts of any significance with him before his death, still in office, in 1953. He was succeeded by joint Honorary Secretaries: Norman Riley, the Keeper of Entomology at the Natural History Museum – Herbert Smith had been the Secretary of the Museum

– and Phyllis Barclay-Smith whose acquaintance I had already made. Henceforth I was in frequent touch with the Society.

The Nature Conservancy came into existence in March 1949, little more than three months after the formation of the Lincolnshire Trust. The first Director-General, Cyril Diver, was also a member of the SPNR's Executive Committee and was thus aware of our Trust's formation and early activities. The same applied to another active member of the Council of the Nature Conservancy, Max Nicholson, the senior Civil Servant in the Office of the Lord President of the Council, and leading amateur ornithologist who knew also about the establishment of the Gibraltar Point Bird Observatory. I believe, but cannot be sure, that I was introduced to Max at the SPNR luncheon in June 1949. In any event I met him at a meeting of the Bird Observatories Committee of the British Trust for Ornithology at Bridlington in the spring of 1950.

The Nature Conservancy had been unenthusiastic about the powers given to Local Authorities in the 1949 Act to establish nature reserves, and it is clear from their first report for the period up to 30 September 1952 that they remained sceptical about the competence of Local Authorities to set up and manage reserves: "Though Section 21 empowers Local Authorities, in consultation with the Conservancy, to set up the Reserves, there are difficulties in the way of their doing so. The full cost must be met from rates or private subscriptions since there is no provision for Exchequer grants ... And it is far from easy to provide the skilled biological management which the maintenance of any reserve necessitates".

Nevertheless the Conservancy showed considerable interest in the initiative by Lindsey County Council and the Trust in establishing the reserve at Gibraltar Point. I was invited to speak about it at a meeting of the Conservancy in the spring of 1950, and, as reported in an earlier chapter, in August of that year Diver, Nicholson and the eminent Cambridge geographer, Professor Alfred Steers, visited the reserve. They went also to the Manton area in north Lincolnshire which had been considered for Conservation Area status by the Wildlife Conservation Special Committee. My own contacts with the members and staff of the Conservancy, and with Nicholson in particular, were further strengthened by the statutory declaration of Gibraltar Point in 1952 and the caravan site issue of the following year. By that time Nicholson had succeeded Diver as Director-General, and in 1954 was the speaker at the Trust's annual meeting, spending the following day visiting sites in north Lincolnshire with Dick Cornwallis and myself. In March 1956, in both my Trust and University capacities, I organised a weekend course in Lincolnshire on nature conservation and nature reserve management. Nicholson and the Conservancy's East Anglia Regional Officer, Dr Eric Duffey, were the principal speakers. The course, attended by thirty people – mainly Trust volunteers but including some from Leicestershire and Cambridgeshire – may well have been the first of its kind in this country.

It was during that weekend that Nicholson asked me if I would be interested in serving on the England Committee of the Conservancy. I felt diffident about the proposition, but he assured me that my practical experience – still a fairly rare commodity in the mid-1950s – would be of value to the Committee. My subsequent appointment to the England Committee – I attended my first meeting in autumn 1956 – proved to be the beginning of twenty-two years unbroken service on the Conservancy and its England Committee and successor body.

My contacts with national bodies and individuals, Nicholson in particular, stimulated my interest in national conservation issues. At the same time my Trust experience had already convinced me that local voluntary effort was essential for successful nature conservation and just as important as government action. In January 1954 the SPNR wrote to the secretaries of the regional NRIC sub-committees to enquire what had happened to them. In my response I explained how the Lincolnshire Trust had originated from the county NRIC sub-committee and I described the Trust's aims and achievements. I went on to express my conviction of the need for local voluntary action in conservation and my hope that the SPNR would encourage the formation of more county trusts. I concluded my response as follows: "My colleagues and I feel that some co-ordination is needed in the voluntary conservation movement in this country and that this will become more necessary as the movement expands. There is at present no national body performing just this function. Apart from anything else, we must obviously expect to have to fight on occasions to save important places from harmful development, as in the recent case at Gibraltar Point. A strong association of voluntary organisations might not only be of value in lending support when necessary in such cases but might also be of help to the Nature Conservancy. The SPNR would be just the body to perform a co-ordinating function of this kind. I make the suggestion very humbly for your consideration".

I was disappointed, therefore, when in June 1954 the SPNR formally wound up the whole NRIC organisation without attempting to encourage the formation of new Trusts even where some interest still existed. Even worse, it deliberately evaded any direct involvement in locally inspired opportunities for the promotion of nature reserves. Such opportunities, it requested, "should in future be brought first directly to the attention of the Nature Conservancy through its regional offices and not to this Society". After its brief resuscitation through the work of the NRIC the Society seemed about to revert once again to the empty shell of its inter-war years. To be fair to it, however, the response from what remained of the NRIC sub-committees had been very discouraging. The majority were moribund and there was, I must admit, little reason for keeping them in being as such. In his reply to me, moreover, Riley accepted that some co-ordination of local effort was desirable, and that the view expressed in some of the replies that everything could now be left to the Nature Conservancy was "a fatal attitude to adopt".

Riley had also invited me to give a talk about the work of the Lincolnshire Trust at the Society's annual Council meeting in June 1954. "It could", he said, "prove of great interest, and might tend to inspire others to set about creating similar Trusts". I did indeed take the opportunity in my talk – which was printed in the Society's Handbook for 1954 – to advocate the formation of more Trusts. Our Lincolnshire experience had already shown what could "be achieved by an independent organisation, devoted primarily to conservation, incorporated to hold property, with some financial resources and, most important perhaps, deriving its support from a much wider cross-section of the community than the average natural history society". In conclusion I summarised those features of the Trust and its work which seemed likely to be of interest to others considering the creation of a similar organisation. To any such I offered information and advice.

Promoting New Trusts

It so happened that opportunities to encourage the formation of new Trusts were about to arise. Early in 1954 the Lincolnshire Trust had acquired some thirty-seven acres of wet heathland on Scotton Common, a purchase generously assisted by the SPNR. There was little experience of nature reserve management of any kind in this country at the time, and advice was not readily available. We were recommended, however, to approach Dr Max Walters, a young Cambridge plant taxonomist and ecologist. He readily agreed to visit the reserve with us and gave us some very sound advice. Impressed by what he had seen and heard of the Trust's activities he invited me to Cambridge in the following year to talk to a small group of biologists and naturalists whom he believed might be interested in forming a Trust. As a result of that meeting the Cambridgeshire and Isle of Ely Trust came into being in November 1956, and I had the pleasure of speaking at the inaugural meeting.

Among the natural history and ornithological societies attracted to Gibraltar Point in the early 1950s none was more active and enthusiastic than the Leicester and Rutland Ornithological Society. Several of its members became regular visitors to the Bird Observatory. Foremost among them was the Honorary Secretary of the Society, Ronald Hickling, later to become one of Britain's leading ornithologists and President of the British Trust for Ornithology. Like Walters, he was impressed by what the Trust had achieved and convinced of the need for a similar organisation in his own county. He and other Leicestershire colleagues also attended Nicholson's inspirational lecture at the Lincolnshire Trust's 1954 annual meeting and the nature conservation course in Lincolnshire in March 1956. By that time, with strong support from local naturalists – the core of the NRIC sub-committee had remained active - and from the progressive and influential museum, preparations for a Trust in Leicestershire were well advanced, and I spoke at the formation meeting later in the year.

The formation of the Cambridgeshire and Leicestershire Trusts encouraged me to write to Lord Hurcomb, who had become President of the SPNR in 1951, to suggest that the Society should sponsor a series of regional conferences to promote the formation of more Trusts. The first, I proposed, should cover the eastern and south-eastern counties of England where the movement already had strength. The Lincolnshire Trust would be pleased to host the conference, but willing to assist with arrangements wherever it was held. I had no written response to that letter, although there is no doubt that Hurcomb was sympathetic to the proposition that the SPNR should play a more active role in promoting the conservation movement locally as well as nationally. Certainly he supported applications which the Lincolnshire Trust made to the SPNR between 1954 and 1956 for financial assistance for the purchase of properties at Linwood Warren and Scotton Common.

Over the next fifteen to twenty years Hurcomb played a major role in both the voluntary and statutory conservation movement. A retired senior Civil Servant of great eminence, he had been Chairman of the British Transport Commission and had played a major role in the organisation of wartime transport. He was cautious and deliberate in expressing opinions and making judgements, and somewhat withdrawn and distant in manner. In this he made a striking contrast to his close associate, the enthusiastic and voluble Max Nicholson. Whilst I never found our relationship easy, I believe Hurcomb had a genuine respect for my youthful enthusiasm and determination, and I owed a great deal to the support which he gave me in persuading the SPNR to 'adopt' the Trusts' movement.

Developing a Partnership

In 1957, however, there seemed little sign that the SPNR was ready to take on an 'umbrella' function for the Trusts, and I accordingly initiated discussions among the existing Trusts about the desirability of establishing some form of association to deal with matters of mutual interest and concern. I was already closely involved with the leaders of the Cambridgeshire and Leicestershire Trusts and I had been in contact over several years with my opposite number in Yorkshire, Clifford Smith, biology teacher and a national authority on spiders, who warmly welcomed the liaison. To establish and develop a Trust in the vast county of Yorkshire with its huge West Riding urban and industrial conurbations was a formidable task and for the first few years the Trust made little headway outside its York sphere of influence. Norfolk was a different proposition. Founded in the pre-history of the conservation movement, in 1925, it already held some of the finest nature reserves in Britain, a task which absorbed almost all its energies and resources. In consequence it had become inward-looking and had not only failed to use its own experience to promote similar action elsewhere, but had shown little interest in conservation developments outside Norfolk. So, for example, when I wrote to the Norfolk Trust to seek their support for our submission to the Gibraltar Point caravan site Inquiry in 1953 – Lincolnshire and Norfolk after all shared the Wash of which Gibraltar Point formed the north-west corner – I received a bleak reply from the Trust's Secretary, Miss Connie Gay, to the effect that they knew nothing of Jamaica (sic) Point and could offer no support. It came as no surprise, therefore, that the reaction to our proposals for inter-Trust discussions received a cool and equivocal response from Norfolk. It was only through Mr Aubrey (later Lord) Buxton that we had any contact with the Trust and it was on his invitation that we planned a meeting of Trusts to discuss the development of liaison at Whiteslea Lodge in the Hickling Broad reserve on 28/29 September 1957.

The Cambridge 'Declaration'

First, however, three of the Trusts – Lincolnshire, Cambridgeshire and Leicestershire – held a preparatory meeting in Cambridge on 29/30 June in that year. Yorkshire was unable to send a representative, and Norfolk declined. Dick Cornwallis and I represented Lincolnshire; Max Walters and Tony Vine (an old ornithological acquaintance of mine) Cambridgeshire and Isle of Ely; and Ronald Hickling and Trevor Walden Leicestershire. I acted as secretary to the meeting. The minutes recorded a wide-ranging discussion including the means of promoting new Trusts; the need of Trusts for outside support in defending nationally important sites; exchange of information on membership recruitment and fundraising and on educational methods; on services to members and on the establishment and management of nature reserves. We also discussed the need to make our views and concerns known at national level on government policy and parliamentary bills. We called on the Nature Conservancy to standardise its procedures in relation to all SSSIs – at that time there was considerable regional variation – and to afford some special recognition to those SSSIs which came under the effective management of Trusts but which were not statutorily declared by a local authority. We pressed too for a system of regular consultation with the Conservancy. The minutes concluded as follows:

Our main purpose was to satisfy ourselves that an association of Trusts is desirable. Our discussions convinced us that it is, and we agreed unanimously to recommend that it be established. We felt that each Trust, whilst losing nothing of its independence or local status, would benefit from association with the others and that the conservation movement generally would thereby be strengthened. We considered what form an association should take and we agreed that the Society for the Promotion of Nature Reserves should first be asked if it would undertake a co-ordinating function of this kind for which it seemed to us to be eminently suited. We envisage it performing for the voluntary conservation movement a function comparable in some respects to that of the CPRE.

We agreed that we would take the initiative in asking the Society's Executive Committee if it would be willing to send representatives to discuss the suggestion with the Trusts at a meeting to be held in Norfolk in September and, meantime, if it had the opportunity, to give the matter consideration. Another outcome of that meeting was an agreement to publish periodic joint newsletters to inform all our members about activities in the existing Trusts. The first of these, co-ordinated and edited by Lincolnshire, was circulated in January 1958; the second, for which Yorkshire was responsible, in June of that year. Four Trusts contributed.

A Proposal to SPNR

In pursuance of the Cambridge 'declaration', I wrote on 26 July to Norman Riley sending him a copy of the minutes of our meeting and inviting the SPNR to send representatives to the meeting in Norfolk in September to discuss the proposals with the Trusts. Riley's reply was encouraging. "I have no doubt whatever", he said, "that, were a proposal put up to our Executive to the effect that some kind of formal association should be built up between the Society and the Naturalists' Trusts, it would be heartily welcomed. Lord Hurcomb happened to come in this morning and he was delighted to hear of this meeting, and the proposals for future association". He then referred to consideration which the Society's Executive Committee had been giving to ways in which "the Society could play a more useful part in the nature conservation movement in this country than it is doing at present. So far we have not reached any decisions because of the difficulties of finance and staff involved, but I think I am not divulging any secrets if I tell you that a movement in the general direction of setting up a comparable organisation with the CPRE is much in our minds. This proposal of yours would fit in perfectly with such a scheme".

Up to that point we had been only vaguely aware of the discussions about a new national organisation which had been taking place in the SPNR Executive Committee. We surmised, however, that the prime movers in this were Hurcomb and, in particular, Nicholson. We therefore welcomed Hurcomb's intention to attend the Hickling meeting with Riley on behalf of the Society, and we readily extended an invitation to Nicholson to join us. The Yorkshire, Lincolnshire, Cambridgeshire and Leicestershire Trusts were all represented at the meeting, but Aubrey Buxton, who had made the local arrangements, withdrew before discussions began and the Norfolk Trust played no part in the proceedings.

The Trusts' representatives went to Hickling with a well defined, practical set of proposals based on the discussions at Cambridge in June. We envisaged a national organisation for nature conservation representative primarily of the autonomous County Trusts, the first task of which would be to promote the formation of a nationwide network of Trusts. It would be their machinery for co-operation and mutual self-help in many matters, including the defence of nature reserves and sites of interest; raising funds from national sources; facilitating the exchange of information and experience in such matters as the establishment and management of nature reserves for which it might establish its own panel of expert advisers. It would represent the interests of the Trusts at national level by liaising with other national organisations and government departments, and by making representations about Parliamentary Bills and government policy. It would give all possible support to the Nature Conservancy in its tasks of establishing and managing national nature reserves, and impressing on government, on local authorities, on industry and on the general public the need for the wise conservation of nature and natural resources. It would, of course, be able to offer criticisms if it disagreed with any of the Conservancy's actions or policies. Not least, the organisation would concern itself with publicity and education in the interests of nature conservation. A periodical bulletin designed to appeal to the amateur naturalist and the interested layman, giving information about the activities of the Conservancy and the Trusts and about problems of conservation in general, would be an important means of education and of enlisting support for conservation. Such a bulletin, it was hoped, might develop into a popular journal of conservation. The Trusts looked in the first instance to the SPNR to bring such an organisation into being. They already had links with the Society which was the only national organisation concerned with nature conservation as a whole. They hoped it would extend its scope and activities and re-shape itself to become the kind of organisation which they believed to be needed.

A Council for Nature: Solution or Diversion?

All this was embodied in a memorandum presented to the Hickling conference. Nicholson's ideas, however, as presented to the conference, were on a more ambitious scale. His concern was to muster the whole of the natural history and nature conservation movement in Britain through a national 'umbrella' body to support and promote conservation. Voluntary effort, he agreed, was essential but lack of combined action on legislation, on money raising and tax concessions and other issues, and the inadequacy of media coverage of nature conservation, left the movement weak and ineffective. The Nature Conservancy, he emphasised, could not "unaided and unsupported win all the necessary victories". He therefore proposed the creation of a body to be known as The Council for Nature, the main object of which should be (and I quote from a later memorandum of his) "to co-ordinate, and to assist by the provision of common services and otherwise, the efforts of independent associations, societies, clubs and individuals aiming in any way to promote the conservation of nature in the United Kingdom or overseas insofar as the United Kingdom can help to that end". He agreed that one of the principal objects of the Council should be "to encourage the movement for local naturalists' trusts where they already exist and by the formation of new ones in areas not yet covered". Full membership of the Council, he proposed, would be restricted to a limited number of national bodies adequately representative of the main subject interests concerned such as ornithology and botany, and functional interests such as field studies and nature reserves, and of the most important related interests such as amenity and sport. Local organisations would be represented only where they were particularly preoccupied with nature conservation and could not properly be represented through national bodies. This would apply especially to the local Naturalists' Trusts "which should always have high priority in the business of the Council". In his later memorandum he proposed twenty-four national bodies as founder members together with the six Naturalists' Trusts and the West Wales Field Society. The Council to be successful would have to develop "a mass influence through the media and would need its own first-class, semi-popular monthly illustrated journal or magazine with a paid editor". This would serve as a link between participating bodies and as a means of educating public opinion. A major money-raising effort would be required both to finance the operation of the Council and to assist its constituent bodies. A 'common fund for nature' would be established for this purpose.

Whilst this clearly had much in common with our own aspirations it went far beyond the relatively modest proposals which we had put forward. We were left, I think, somewhat bewildered and in danger of being blown off course. The position was neatly summed up by Norman Riley in a letter to me a few days later: "I hope you got home with a clearer idea of what we decided to do or recommend that others should do than I took away myself from our meeting at Hickling".

In the proposals which I subsequently drafted for the Trusts' representatives I attempted to reconcile our own plans with those of Nicholson – no easy task! There was no difficulty in agreeing some of the functions of the proposed body, in particular the promotion of publicity and education, parliamentary lobbying and a national journal, although we were insistent that the success of the whole organisation should not depend on that particular venture and that other activities should not suffer for the sake of it. We had emphasised throughout the discussions that a Council for Nature should somehow provide the machinery for co-operation among the Trusts in matters of mutual interest. This was after all our primary objective in going to Hickling.

The functions of the Council were one thing; its constitution, composition and procedures were a quite different problem. We had reached only vague and tentative conclusions about the latter, as Riley's letter indicated. In my draft, therefore, I proposed that the constituent bodies should be "the county Naturalists' Trusts and other local bodies devoted primarily to conservation, and those national organisations concerned with one aspect of conservation or another or with education or scientific studies likely to promote a better understanding and appreciation of the needs and problems of nature conservation in this country". The affairs of the Council would be managed largely by an Executive Committee of which, we proposed, the majority of members should be appointed by the Trusts and the others elected by the Council, the exact numbers to be decided when the exact number of national bodies became known. Among the special committees which would be needed was one to deal with nature reserves and practical conservation and this, we proposed, should consist largely of representatives of the Trusts.

Before I had had time to consult the Trusts' representatives about the draft, I received from Nicholson his detailed memorandum on the proposed Council for Nature to which I have already referred. In responding to it my first reaction was that it put too little emphasis on the work of co-ordinating and encouraging local effort in conservation to which we attached great value. I reminded him that the Trusts' representatives at Hickling had envisaged the organisation on two levels, as it were: first as a national association of many bodies to promote the interests of conservation generally; and, secondly, as a medium for closer co-operation among themselves and for the encouragement of more Trusts. Our main concern was to reconcile these two aspects so that each assumed a proper proportion. The concern that the co-ordinating and servicing function of the organisation would be overshadowed by the more spectacular publicity and educational work had emerged in the Hickling discussions and would not be entirely assuaged, I believed, by his memorandum. I made a number of detailed suggestions in an attempt to redress the balance and reassure the Trusts, whilst expressing the view that the whole problem of organisation needed more consideration.

Having secured the agreement of the Trusts' representatives to the draft I sent a memorandum to the SPNR on 2 November 1957 expressing the hope that the Society would agree to sponsor the proposed Council and seeking a further opportunity to discuss procedures. I had had no response from the Society by 30 November when to my surprise I received an invitation from Riley to attend a meeting in London on 5 December "to set up a committee to discuss plans for forming a Council for Nature". He did not say who else had been invited to the meeting, but in view of its apparent purpose I decided to attend in spite of desperately short notice. A further communication from Riley the day before the meeting stated that his Executive Committee supported the establishment of a body "representative of both the scientific and the widespread but diffuse public and popular interest in nature conservation evident throughout the Commonwealth". He gave a list of possible aims and objects of the proposed body (much on the lines of our memorandum) and the names of a working party appointed to give effect to the findings of his Executive's policy and to take fully into consideration proposals put forward by E M Nicholson. The composition of the working party was as follows: Professor W H Pearsall (Chairman), John Clegg (Hazelmere Museum), Dax Copp (Institute of Biology), Richard Fitter, Dr K P Oakley (Field Studies Council), Sir Herbert Griffin (CPRE), Nicholson, Riley and myself. I was immediately concerned to find that I was the only Trust representative appointed to this body and that no mention was made in Riley's notes for the guidance of the working party of our memorandum or indeed of our initiative at all.

It soon became clear at the first working party meeting that there were widely differing views on the nature and functions of the proposed body. There was, for example, a proposal that the Naturalists' Unions should be invited to join the Council. The admission of local natural history bodies was contrary to the recommendations made by ourselves and Nicholson who recommended that only the Trusts be admitted. It was eventually agreed that I should consult the Trusts about the admission of Unions. It was clear that some members of the working party, notably Oakley and to some extent Riley and the Chairman, wished to see natural history studies given as much or more prominence in the work of the Council as conservation. This indeed was a trend which was to develop and to threaten the whole of Nicholson's concept. I conveyed my unease to him in a letter written the day after the working party meeting. "I am most anxious", I wrote, "that my Trust colleagues should not get the impression that the matter has been taken abruptly out of their hands when they have given much time and thought to it ..... I have no qualms about urging special consideration for the Trusts. They will probably be able to contribute more to the Council than most other constituent bodies. They are prepared to give up the idea of their own association in favour of this wider organisation on the assumption that their interests will be adequately represented on it. I hope your suggestion of special recognition for the Trusts (including representation on the Executive) will be readily accepted by the Working Party ..... Any reluctance to agree to this would place me in a most embarrassing position".

On the same day I sent a report on the Working Party's discussions to my Trusts' colleagues. We had all come away from Hickling with some misgivings and these seemed to be confirmed by what I now had to tell them. Ronald Hickling's immediate reaction was that since what now appeared to be shaping was not the organisation we had resolved to form it would be better that we withdrew from the discussions and went ahead with our original purpose. I cautioned patience. I was unhappy about the working party, but I advised that we should only withdraw from it if it refused to approve the special recognition for the Trusts which Nicholson had proposed and which we had every right to expect. It had already become clear that the SPNR's funds were not going to be handed over to a new body (in the event the Society contributed a total of £2500 to the Council for Nature) but would still be available for Trusts to draw on for property purchase. We could still form our own association – and I believed we should – but we should also continue to support Nicholson's concept of a powerful national body representing nature conservation interests.

Max Walters was more phlegmatic than Hickling, believing that we should continue to uphold our own purposes in the Working Party's discussions. He was nevertheless also opposed to the admission of Unions and strongly of the opinion that the Executive Committee of the new body must consist of people who were vitally interested in conservation. We had to insist on adequate representation of Trusts. I had sent my report to our Norfolk Trust contact, Aubrey Buxton, who replied, apparently in a purely personal capacity, that being fully occupied at that time he was unable to express opinions on the points which I raised. He was content, he said, to leave the matters in my hands being in agreement with my attitude. I also sent my report to Professor Shotton, the Chairman of the newly formed West Midlands Trust, and to D G Sansbury, Chairman of the West Wales Field Society. Meantime Nicholson had reiterated to me his belief that only those Societies which "really have a major part in conservation and education as distinct from very general Natural History Societies" should be admitted as constituent bodies. Organisations like the Naturalists' Unions if linked at all, should be affiliated and not constituents.

The second meeting of the Working Party was in some respects more reassuring. Perhaps as a result of our pressure and our representations to Nicholson, the Working Party agreed to put into the objectives of the Council a specific reference to promoting and assisting Naturalists' Trusts, and to confine constituent membership among local bodies to the Trusts (at least initially). However, it was decided on a vote that only one, not two, of the five Executive places should be guaranteed to Trusts. I was not unduly upset by this as I believed we could secure adequate Trust representation through other nominations, a belief encouraged by Nicholson. However, when I received from Riley a draft of the constitution revised after the Working Party's discussion I found that the number of Executive members had been increased to seven. Although I protested to Riley that this was unauthorised and unacceptable to me, it was endorsed at the third meeting of the Working Party which I was unable to attend.

Back to the SPNR

I had proposed after the first meeting of the Working Party that the Trusts' representatives should meet again before the inaugural meeting of the new Council to clarify their position. Subsequent developments had made this even more necessary, and we met in Lincoln on 1 February 1958. Yorkshire was represented by Dr E W Taylor and C J Smith, Cambridgeshire by Dr S M Walters and A E Vine, Leicestershire by R A O Hickling, and Lincolnshire by R K Cornwallis, T J Winnall and myself. The West Midlands Trust sent their apologies and there was still no sign of any willingness on the part of Norfolk to be involved although I had kept them informed. We discussed the latest proposals for a Council for Nature to be put forward at the inaugural meeting on 19 February. We questioned in particular whether they would adequately fulfil the proposals in our Hickling memorandum, and whether the Trusts would have adequate representation on the Council. We saw the latter question not simply as a matter specifically for the Trusts, but also as an indication of the emphasis likely to be placed on conservation in the work of the Council. It was agreed that the proposed aims of the Council were too wide and too vaguely defined, and this fact, together with a reduction in the Trusts' position, was likely to result in insufficient attention being given to conservation problems. We agreed that, whilst supporting the proposed Council, we should try to ensure that it gave priority to conservation problems and that we should seek appropriate amendments to the draft constitution at the inaugural meeting for that purpose. We also agreed to propose that the number of Trusts' representatives on the Executive Committee should be at least two instead of at least one. At the same time, and more significantly for the future as it turned out, we also agreed that the collaboration already established among Trusts for purposes set out in the Hickling memorandum should be further developed. We unanimously agreed that the various Trust Councils should be asked to approve the immediate establishment of a joint Trusts' Committee, and that informal approaches should be made as soon as possible to members of the SPNR Executive known to be sympathetic to our aims with a view to securing representation for Trusts on the SPNR and making that body the medium for their collaboration. As an earnest of our intentions we agreed to produce the second bulletin for our members to which I have already referred.

After a very difficult few weeks I felt much happier after the Lincoln meeting. The way ahead for the Trusts had still to be negotiated but, as Clifford Smith wrote in a letter to me after the meeting: "we can now approach the London meeting with much more unity and confidence". We had held steadily to our purpose, and there was a feeling that we were firmly united in a common cause.

I conveyed our intentions to Riley as Secretary of the Working Party, and to Nicholson to whom I reiterated our concern at the emphasis being placed in the Council's priorities of general natural history activities rather than conservation, and at the reduction of the Trusts' representation on the Executive which we had resolved to try to reverse on 19 February. I then told him of our intention to approach the SPNR with a view to it becoming a central organisation for the Trusts, an idea which Nicholson himself had advocated to me in discussion. He had become impatient with the SPNR Executive for its failure to give a lead in strengthening the conservation movement. On the other hand, he undoubtedly respected the Trusts as bodies which achieved practical results. I assured him of our intention nevertheless to support the Council for Nature as a body to influence public opinion on a large scale and to represent the interests of the conservation movement as a whole at national level. Our principal aim, however, would be to extend and strengthen the Trusts' movement which would mean not only more reserves and protection work, but would create locally well-informed, influential bodies of opinion.

That then was the position on 19 February 1958, the day of the inaugural meeting of the Council for Nature held in the rooms of the Linnean Society at Burlington House. In a brief encounter with the Trusts' representatives before the meeting Nicholson reiterated his support for our approach to SPNR, but appealed to us not to rock the boat that evening by proposing constitutional amendments and disturbing the harmony which he apparently expected to prevail. In the event the meeting proved to be anything but harmonious, criticism of proposals coming not from the Trusts – as things turned out we decided not to intervene – but from the natural history interests which predominated at the meeting. Their main spokesman was the Earl of Cranbrook, a strong supporter of nature conservation in the House of Lords, but a man of strong, often idiosyncratic views and unpredictable utterances of which I had further experience when I served with him on the Nature Conservancy Council in the 1960s. He attacked in particular the proposal that the Council should consist of a limited number of major constituent bodies mainly concerned with nature conservation. He demanded that full membership should be open to any local or national natural history society. Nicholson strongly counter-attacked with a plea for a strong non-governmental voice in support of nature conservation. In the end the whole concept was sent back in confusion ("the biggest cock-up since Waterloo" was Dick Cornwallis's colourful comment) to the Working Party with instructions to carry out the widest possible consultation with all prospective member bodies. When the Council was re-launched in July, under the chairmanship of eminent zoologist Sir Landsborough Thomson, it was a very different body from that which Nicholson and indeed the Trusts had conceived.

The 19 February meeting nevertheless had one happy outcome. Nicholson had told me sometime before that I ought to make contact with Christopher Cadbury, who although resident in the West Midlands, was a long-time member and generous benefactor of the Norfolk Trust having lived for a number of years in Norwich as his family firm's representative in East Anglia. The full extent of Christopher's benefactions to the Norfolk Trust only became evident to me, incidentally, in later years. We met for the first time at that Council for Nature meeting and found ourselves in immediate agreement over a number of issues. In fact Christopher wrote to Riley the following day supporting a continuing role for the SPNR in co-ordinating the land-holding functions of the local Trusts.

I had supported the Council for Nature concept and had urged my colleagues to do so, but I had felt all along that it was too ambitious, that the movement was simply not ready for it, and that there were sounder if less spectacular 'bottom-up' ways of building the voluntary conservation movement especially through a network of County Trusts.

Any lingering doubts that we should defer our approach to SPNR were now dispelled, and, following hurried consultations, I wrote to Riley on 4 March informing him of the Trusts' intention to form a joint committee and requesting that the SPNR consider making provision for that committee to function within the Society. The expenses, I observed, would be modest and it would do its own administrative work, so imposing no additional burden on the Society's secretariat. It would, I added, "be desirable from every point of view that the committee should have close liaison with the Society's Executive Committee, possibly by the appointment of some of its members to the Executive and vice versa". If the Executive Committee was willing to consider the suggestion the Trusts would be ready to send representatives to discuss it with them. In reply Riley welcomed the Trusts' move to set up a joint committee and said he believed it desirable that the Trusts should have some direct representation on the Society's Executive Committee, although the composition of the Committee at that time, which was in conflict with the terms of the Charter, made it impossible to add any members to it. However, he suggested that, as this was very much in line with our own thinking, the Society might set up a special naturalists' trusts or nature reserves sub-committee. Our response discreetly kept up the pressure, and on 31 March Riley wrote again to say that his Executive had set up a small committee to consider how to take account of the needs of the Trusts. They would be pleased to receive a deputation from the Trusts for informal discussion and he invited me to make the necessary arrangements.

Meantime, there were signs of a new bout of activity at county level. I was already in touch with Dr Francis Rose and others who were moving to form a Trust in Kent. On 12 April Hickling, Walters and I spoke at a conference at London Zoo convened by the South-East Union of Scientific Societies with a view to promoting Naturalists' Trusts in south-east England. The time was obviously ripe for further stimulation of interest and lent urgency to the establishment of the SPNR committee for this purpose.

The meeting with the SPNR took place at the British Museum (Natural History) on 25 April 1958. The Society was represented by its Officers, by Cyril Diver and Professors Pearsall and Miles. Diver took the Chair, a fortunate choice for us since he was entirely sympathetic to our cause and had very clear views about the respective roles of the Society/Trusts and the Council for Nature. Five Trusts were represented – Lincolnshire, Cambridgeshire, Leicestershire, West Midlands and Kent (Yorkshire was unable to be present). Christopher Cadbury also attended in a personal capacity, but there was still no sign of any direct interest from Norfolk.

Diver opened the meeting by explaining the constitution of the Society and its advantages and limitations under the Royal Charter. Acknowledging the common interests of the Society and the Trusts, he then invited me to explain to the meeting what the Trusts had in mind. I referred first to the negotiations concerning the formation of the Council for Nature. Since it had become apparent that practical nature conservation would not be a primary objective of the Council, the Trusts had turned to the SPNR to assist their movement by creating a Naturalists' Trusts' Committee with a voice in the Society's affairs through representation on its Council. I then outlined the purposes of such a Committee which I had set out in a paper prepared for the meeting with the agreement of Trusts' colleagues. In general it would be consultative and advisory and would take no action affecting constituent bodies without their approval and consent. Its primary functions would be:

- To encourage by all appropriate means the formation of new Trusts.
- To enable Trusts to seek and exchange information, advice and assistance on all matters of common interest and concern. For this it would convene technical meetings and conferences in addition to its own regular meetings. It might sponsor research and courses in reserve management and practical conservation problems.
- To arrange for publication of bulletins about the activities of constituent bodies.
- To represent the interests of those constituent bodies through the Society in discussion with national organisations on matters of common concern.

The Society's representatives saw no constitutional difficulties in setting up a Committee and electing Trusts' representatives to the Council, but they foresaw practical problems because Officers of the SPNR were "all Honorary and very busy people", a fact incidentally that was to facilitate the Trusts' eventual 'take-over' of the Society. However, it was agreed that the five Trusts represented at the meeting together with Yorkshire should put forward names of candidates for election to the Society's Council which would be recommended to set up a Naturalists' Trust Committee on which other Trusts could also be represented as they were formed. Trusts' representatives would consider the criteria for recognition of new members. The main purposes and functions of such a Committee which I had outlined were approved. It was agreed in addition that it should meet at least once – perhaps twice – a year, and that conferences for general discussion of matters of common interest should be held in the areas of the various Trusts in rotation.

After the meeting we quickly took up the point about the lack of Society secretariat resources for the new Committee by offering to provide our own in return for modest secretarial expenses and travelling costs, not to Committee meetings, but to authorised representatives travelling in pursuance of the aims of the Committee.

The Regional Liaison Committee

The proposals of the 25 April meeting were approved by the Society's Council at its Annual Meeting on 7 July when representatives of seven trusts were appointed to the Council together with Christopher Cadbury, Max Walters and me as individual members. The Council decided that the Committee should be called the Regional Liaison Committee, a title which I did not favour and which was replaced within a year by the Naturalists' Trusts' Committee.

Because Riley was involved in the organisation of the Zoological Congress in Edinburgh in July, and then in attendance at an IUCN Conference in Athens in September, it was not possible to arrange the first meeting of the Committee until 12 November 1958, a frustrating delay. All this time I was continuing to act at the request of my colleagues as the spokesman and secretary of the Trusts' Joint Committee established at our Lincoln meeting in February. Diver, who had been appointed Chairman of the Regional Liaison Committee, sought my views on the Committee's terms of reference, and, at his request, I prepared some notes which formed the basis of the agenda for the meeting which was attended by representatives from seven Trusts, Max Walters for Cambridgeshire and the Isle of Ely unfortunately being unable to be present. In addition to the terms of reference of the Committee, the meeting was concerned with means of promoting new Trusts, of obtaining and exchanging information and advice, of representing the common interests of the Trusts and the Society, and of using and training volunteers. It was agreed that a Trusts' newsbulletin should be published as soon as practicable and that meantime Trusts' activities should be reported in the Society's Handbook. It was also agreed to be desirable that each Trust should allow access to its reserves to members of other Trusts on the same conditions as for its own members. The remainder of the meeting was taken up with discussion of relations with other bodies, notably the Nature Conservancy and the Council for Nature. It was acknowledged that each Trust would have to establish its own relationship with the Nature Conservancy, but there were many common aspects of those relations which could be discussed with the Conservancy through some form of liaison machinery. The functions of the Council for Nature in conservation presented a more thorny problem and one which for a time threatened to impede our progress in building up an organisation for the Trusts within the SPNR. Nonetheless we had achieved the main immediate objective of recognition by the SPNR, and so ensured that the Trusts' movement would develop in the counties and would benefit from the work of a national association.

The Society's involvement with the Trusts was generously acknowledged by the publication in its Handbook for 1959 of a description of the existing Trusts and their activities. In a preface Lord Hurcomb, the Society's President, welcomed the new liaison between the Society and the Trusts, looked forward to the formation of more Trusts and expressed the hope that all of them would be strongly supported by naturalists in their areas.

The problems of working out a relationship with the Council for Nature was a somewhat frustrating and, in the event, unnecessary diversion from the task we had set ourselves. Commenting on the dangers of cross-currents and overlapping, Diver in a letter to me of 30 December 1958 cited as one of the reasons for this that "many of the CN people are new to this game ..... and are unaware of the extent of the field already properly covered (now for nearly half a century) by the SPNR. A fairly close definition is, therefore, needed of what we intend to continue doing and what we are hoping the new body will take on".

Christopher Cadbury's personal initiatives – by despatch of letters and memoranda to a variety of people – to define the respective functions of the Council for Nature and SPNR did not prove entirely acceptable to other members of the Liaison Committee. He proposed to confine the Committee narrowly to land-holding and management questions; all other matters including education, public relations and general environmental problems – even those inseparable from reserve acquisition and management – would be the concern of the Council for Nature. To have to take one set of Trust problems to SPNR and another quite separately to the Council for Nature would have been quite unworkable. We had intended the Liaison Committee to be a forum for discussion of all problems of common concern to Trusts and most of us were content that the SPNR should represent our interests where appropriate at the Council for Nature.

The difficulty at that stage was that Christopher's conception of the functions of a Trust was based almost entirely on his Norfolk experience, and differed markedly from that of the new Trusts who had adopted a broader and more 'popular' role. Christopher's initial approach to the Trusts was cautious in other ways too. At our first meeting with SPNR representatives on 25 April he had expressed some misgivings about the long-term viability of some of the new Trusts and had suggested that SPNR might be the most suitable body to hold Trust reserves. He was still pursuing the same theme in a letter to Riley on 17 November 1959 in which he said: "Unfortunately, with changing conditions it would be a brave man who could feel certain that all the Nature Trusts being formed today will be in existence in fifty years time and adequately supported by voluntary subscriptions". In the following week he submitted a paper on the subject to the Society's Executive Committee. They agreed that the possibility of investing reserves in the Society should be drawn to the attention of Trusts, but they recognised at the same time that it was entirely a matter for the Trusts themselves to decide. Most of us in the Regional Liaison Committee were convinced that ownership of land was a powerful motivation for Trusts and we did not share Christopher's doubts about their viability. In the end it was agreed that Trusts should be recommended to include a provision in their Memorandum and Articles that in the event of any of them being wound up or dissolved their nature reserves should as far as possible revert to SPNR. That sensible compromise seemed to satisfy everyone. Christopher's misgivings soon disappeared and he threw himself wholeheartedly into the building of a strong Trusts' movement.

With several more counties moving towards the formation of a Trust and looking to the SPNR for advice, the production of a model Memorandum and Articles became a high priority for the Regional Liaison Committee. The Norfolk Memorandum and Articles of 1926, which had been used by Yorkshire and Lincolnshire in the 1940s, were in need of updating to reflect modern attitudes and requirements. Ronald Hickling offered to produce such a model adapted from the Leicestershire Trust's 1956 version, and this with minor amendments was the form adopted by most of the Trusts formed after 1959.

The Liaison Committee had recommended at its meeting on 20 October 1959 that I should become its Honorary Secretary provided that a reasonable allowance for clerical assistance was made. The recommendation was approved by the Society's Executive Committee in November, and £100 was allocated to me for the purpose for the calendar year 1960 to be drawn against vouchers submitted to the Treasurer. I had in fact been acting informally in that capacity for some time, but confirmation of the status and the financial provision were very welcome. I had throughout been strongly supported by original stalwarts like Ronald Hickling and Max Walters, and, as always, by Dick Cornwallis who was playing an increasingly influential role in the Liaison Committee.

It had also become clear by November 1959 that Diver's health would not allow him to continue as Chairman of the Liaison Committee nor for that matter of the Society's Executive Committee. I therefore suggested to Normal Riley in a letter of 18 November 1959 that the Executive should consider appointing Christopher as Chairman of the Liaison Committee to which he was already devoting much time and attention. Christopher was duly appointed in January 1960, and thus began the Cadbury-Smith working partnership which was to remain unbroken until my retirement as General Secretary at the end of 1978. We came from very different backgrounds and our approach to nature conservation was – at least initially – markedly different in some respects, but we never had any serious disagreements and we developed a close collaboration which was based on mutual understanding and respect and which was, I believe, very productive for the Trusts' movement.

The First County Trusts' Conference

The rapidly spreading interest in the formation of Trusts and in the problems and opportunities of nature reserve acquisition and management and of education prompted the Regional Liaison Committee to plan the first of the conferences which it had been agreed should be held in the areas of the various Trusts every other year. In addition to existing Trusts, invitations would be sent to people known to be planning to establish others, and to all the principal national bodies concerned with nature conservation. It was to be an opportunity to develop relationships as well as promoting the Trusts' movement.

In view of the need for secretariat input into the arrangements, it was agreed that an offer from the Lincolnshire Trust to host the conference should be accepted. Since field visits and management demonstrations were to be an important feature, the Trust proposed that the conference should be held in the spring of 1960 in Skegness where accommodation would be readily available at that time, and from where the Gibraltar Point and other reserves could be easily visited. May 13-15 proved to be the most popular weekend, and with sterling help from local Trust members – particularly Bob French the recently retired Skegness Postmaster – and the Urban District Council I began to make preparations wearing both my Trust and SPNR hats. Delegates were accommodated in hotels on the sea front, and indoor sessions were held in the Town Hall, in one of the hotels and at the Gibraltar Point Field Station where fine weather enabled us to hold the Saturday morning session out of doors on the lawn, the only distraction being the chorus of skylarks and the passage of whimbrels overhead!

The subjects for papers and discussion reflected some of the major current concerns in the nature conservation movement and were also designed to encourage the attendance of delegates interested in starting new Trusts. A civic welcome and a description of the Lincolnshire Trust reserves and other activities was followed by a session on Preservation of Coastline in which the Lincolnshire County Planning Officer, Robert Stirling, was principal speaker. Sessions on Saturday and Sunday were on Naturalists' Trusts and national organisations; acquisition and management of nature reserves and protection of sites of interest; the role of local authorities in nature conservation; public relations, education and information. Speakers were from national bodies and from Trusts, and the Chairmen of sessions were Lord Hurcomb, President of the SPNR; Max Nicholson, Director-General of the Nature Conservancy; Professor H W Miles, Chairman of the Executive Committee of the SPNR; and Christopher Cadbury, Chairman of the Regional Liaison Committee. In addition to Gibraltar Point, visits were made in continuing fine weather, to the Saltfleetby-Theddlethorpe Dunes and Linwood Warren reserves, to the Red Hill at Goulceby and to Tetford Hill. The latter visit was particularly memorable because Conference delegates found that this rich stretch of chalk grassland road verge had recently been sprayed with a weed killer. This was at a time of great concern about the effect of more extensive use of herbicides on road verges, and when the Clerk of Lindsey County Council, Walter Lane, came to address the conference on Trusts and Local Authorities on Sunday morning he ran into a storm of protest. The result was the first agreement between a Trust and a County Council for the protection of selected verges, a development which I have described in more detail elsewhere.

Many of the leading figures of the nature conservation movement attended the conference: for the SPNR Lord Hurcomb, Professor H W Miles (who had succeeded Diver as Chairman of the Executive Committee), Norman Riley, Tom Woodisse the Honorary Treasurer; for the Council for Nature Colonel Charles Floyd, Aubrey (now Lord) Buxton, Ted Lousley, Dax Copp the Secretary, and Brigadier Armstrong the Organiser of the Conservation Corps; for the Nature Conservancy Max Nicholson, Dr Eric Duffey, Dr Deryck Fraser, Bob Boote (later to become Director of the Nature Conservancy Council); for the RSPB Peter Conder then the Assistant Secretary (appointed Director in 1962). Lindsey County Council was strongly represented by Alderman Sumner representing the Chairman, and by the Clerk and three other senior officers; Skegness Urban District Council by the Chairman. The Lincolnshire Branch of CPRE was represented by its Honorary Secretary Flora Murray.

Seven of the eight Trusts already incorporated were represented as follows:

Norfolk – J C Cadbury, E A Ellis.
Yorkshire – Dr & Mrs E W Taylor, C Smith.
Leicestershire – R A O Hickling, H F Dixon.
Cambridgeshire & Isle of Ely – Dr A S Watt, W H Palmer.
West Midlands – Professor & Mrs F W Shotton
Kent – Dr F Rose, A Fletcher.
Lincolnshire – Colonel O S Nelthorpe, Dr R Hull, F T Baker,
A E & Mrs M Smith, R K Cornwallis, W M Peet, L & Mrs B Watkinson,
G H Seal, C L Ottaway, R French, F H Cliff, J S Chambers, K T Green.

Three Trusts in active process of formation were represented:

Berks, Bucks & Oxfordshire (BBONT) – R S R & Mrs M Fitter,
Mrs S Cowdy, G W Humphreys (who also had an interest in
Northamptonshire)
Hampshire & Isle of Wight – E Cohen
Essex – T H C & Mrs Bartop, Miss R G Foott, Miss G A Griffiths
West Wales (Field Society) – Dillwyn Miles

There were delegates also from the following counties where formation of a Trust was under discussion:

Derbyshire – T R H Appleby.
Suffolk – Lord Cranbrook, Sir Gervase Blois, D J D Shepherd
Wiltshire – Lady Radnor
Glamorgan – Dr & Mrs H J Hambury
Durham – Dr M E Bradshaw

The conference was covered for the national press and the BBC by journalist and writer John Hillaby who was no doubt the author of a lengthy report in *The Times* on 23 May. An article by Richard Fitter appeared in *The Observer* on 22 May. Local newspapers also carried generous reports.

The SPNR Handbook for 1960 carried a full account of the papers presented at the conference. It also published an article on *Progress in Nature Conservation* by Max Nicholson which incorporated much of what he had said in his brilliant summing up of the conference. The doubts and difficulties of the previous two years seemed to be resolved, and in the following terms he found many encouraging developments, including the 'new look' recently given to the SPNR:

Having launched the Council for Nature, the Society is now free to concentrate on its primary task of fostering voluntary effort in conservation in close partnership with the Nature Conservancy and with the increasing body of County Naturalists' Trusts, whose recent conference at Skegness in mid-May 1960 was a revelation both for what has already been done by the pioneer Trusts in Norfolk, Yorkshire and Lincolnshire and of the growing strength and enthusiasm of others which have recently been formed or are now in the process of formation. Through the Society's Regional Liaison Committee with Mr Christopher Cadbury (Norfolk Naturalists' Trust) as Chairman and Mr A E Smith (Lincolnshire Naturalists' Trust) as Honorary Secretary, the Society is now in the most intimate contact with the local Trusts and is able to help them with authoritative advice and in many other ways in addition to the financial grants which have long been available for such purposes. Thus, far from competing or overlapping, the Society and the Council for Nature are fulfilling complementary and mutually supporting roles.

Described in the Nature Conservancy's report for 1959/60 as "remarkable for its confident spirit and its practical and scientific approach to the formidable problems of conservation", the Skegness conference was an event of some importance in the history of the nature conservation movement in Britain. It was certainly a significant landmark in the development of the Trusts' movement. Within the next five years almost every part of Britain was covered by a County or Regional Trust. For me the conference was a satisfying climax to five years of seeking to create a national association for the Trusts. The challenge now was to make it work.

Delegates at the first County Trusts' Conference at Gibraltar Point, 1960.

Max Nicholson (centre) with Lindsey County Councillors (and Helen – seated – and Alison Smith) during the 1960 Conference.

Tom (Sir Thomas) Barlow (L), Helen Brotherton, Christopher Cadbury (2nd R) and others on Hickling Broad, 1974.

DAVID STREETER

With leaders of the Welsh Trusts at Gregynog in 1974. Bill Lacey is second from right.

Being interviewed by BBC presenter Bruce Campbell about the Trusts' movement for 'The Naturalist' programme, 1965.

Tony Tynan

Wilf Dawson, appointed Assistant Advisory Officer (later Assistant Secretary) SPNR, 1964.

– 13 –

The Trusts' Movement Expands 1960-1970

AT THE time of the Skegness Conference in May 1960 there were eight fully incorporated Trusts. By the end of 1963 there were thirty-six covering nearly all of England and Wales. It was a remarkable period of rapid growth and development, and I found it especially rewarding to be at the centre of it.

The Naturalists' Trusts' Committee of SPNR – the Regional Liaison Committee had been thus renamed in 1960 - set itself three initial aims: to promote more Trusts; to seek financial assistance for them from national sources; and to consolidate the status of the Committee and the Trusts it represented within SPNR and in relation to the Nature Conservancy and other statutory and voluntary bodies. It was an ambitious programme drawn up in the enthusiasm of the moment but with too little regard for the resources needed to carry it through. That was a problem that soon became apparent.

Nine Trusts were represented at the seventh meeting of the Committee in September 1960: Yorkshire, Lincolnshire, Leicestershire, Cambridgeshire, Kent, the West Midlands, Surrey, Essex and Hampshire. At that meeting it was reported that others were in various stages of formation in Suffolk, Sussex, Dorset, Glamorgan, Devon, Wiltshire and Derbyshire. The momentum continued to accelerate through 1961 and 1962, being given a further boost by the second Trusts' Conference held in Norwich in May 1962 which was attended by more than eighty delegates, and which firmly established a biennial sequence of such conferences. Papers covered a wide range of developments and problems in conservation including toxic chemicals, management of calcareous grassland and wet heath, and the research programme of the Nature Conservancy. Other topics covered the use of nature reserves for education and public enjoyment, relations with education authorities, and the work of the World Wildlife Fund. The Conference also, incidentally, marked a more outgoing attitude on the part of the Norfolk Trust and its fuller participation in the affairs of the national association.

In the great majority of cases the initiative for forming a Trust came from groups or even individuals in local natural history societies. In many cases too university teachers and museum staff were also strongly involved. So great was the enthusiasm that in one county two people sought to promote a Trust in ignorance of each other's intentions! The Skegness and Norwich Conferences were a great stimulus, and the early members of the Trusts' Committee helped to motivate others in their part of the country to explore the creation of a Trust. In any case most of the promoters made early contact with the SPNR to seek advice and assistance, and we were able to provide them with the model constitution to achieve the status of a charitable company to which I referred in the last chapter. Ronald Hickling also spoke about constitutional requirements at the Skegness Conference, and he reported to the Trusts' Committee in September 1960 that the model was being well used and proving of value. That was also true of the proceedings of the Skegness Conference. At the same meeting of the Committee a proposal that a guide for new Trusts on administrative matters should be compiled and published met with general approval. I undertook to see what could be done, but pointed out that it would be "a formidable undertaking".

In fact I was already involved in voluminous correspondence with promoters of Trusts and receiving invitations to meet them. Cadbury too was very active in communicating with some of the prospective Trusts, and Hickling was always ready with advice on constitutional matters. Nevertheless my own position soon became critical. In a letter to Norman Riley of 30 December 1960 I wrote: "I have been inundated with enquiries about new Trusts and correspondence with existing ones during the last few weeks. .... This business is snowballing and we shall have to look again at our means of coping with it". At that time my only clerical assistance was a few hours a week from a typist paid out of small allowances made by the SPNR (£100 a year), and the Lincolnshire Trust. Cadbury too was very conscious of the need for more administrative resources for the Trusts' Committee, and in March 1961 he enquired if I would become the full-time secretary of the Committee if means could be found to employ me. The suggestion was premature. Both Riley and Woodisse, the Hon. Treasurer, were obviously opposed to it, and from a personal point of view it would have been far too great a financial risk which, with a young family, I could simply not afford to take. Nor for that matter did I wish to give up my university adult teaching so soon.

I was anxious nonetheless to continue as the Honorary Secretary of the Trusts' Committee. We were doing, I believed, very important work at a critical time, and I found it very rewarding. There was a danger moreover that if I had to relinquish the post there would be renewed pressure to bring in the Council for Nature to fill it, and so jeopardise the independent position we had struggled to secure. I believed that I could continue to cope with the commitment in a voluntary capacity if I had a competent and full-time administrative assistant. It so happened that just such a person was available at that time in the person of John Ellis, a clerk in a local district planning office, who was keen to work in conservation even at a lower salary. Cadbury put a proposal to the Society's Executive Committee who agreed to contribute £500 a year for the appointment; the Lincolnshire Trust provided a further £150 and the University a smaller amount. It was a modest enough allocation, but – although he returned to the planning department after little more than three years – Ellis's appointment was crucial in enabling me to continue at that time as the Honorary Secretary of the Committee.

One major problem remained, however: the need to travel around the country to meet promoters of Trusts, to attend formation and inaugural meetings and to advise those Trusts already in existence about the possibilities of grant-aid and other means of development. Although there was some flexibility in my university programme, especially in the summer months, the time I could spend away was inevitably limited. I was very fortunate in the support I received from the Head of my university department, Professor Harold Wiltshire, who was always keen to encourage staff to contribute to social and cultural projects. He had quietly supported my request to SPNR for a full-time administrative assistant, and I talked with him again later in 1961 about my work in promoting the Trusts' movement. He then indicated a willingness to support an application for my secondment to the SPNR for a year, provided, of course, they could meet the costs. I discussed the possibility with Cadbury and other senior colleagues, and at their meeting in May 1962 the Executive Committee agreed to recommend to the Society's Council that a secondment be negotiated with the University of Nottingham for 11 months from the beginning of September of that year. Permission was sought from the Nuffield Trustees to use interest accruing on their loan fund (see later) to meet part of the cost, and an application describing the actual and potential contribution of the Trusts to research and education in the life and earth sciences was successfully made to the University in the name of the Officers of the Society with support from Max Nicholson and Professor H W Miles. The arrangement freed me almost entirely from teaching commitments for the period but left me responsible for organising the class programme for my area for the following academic year. So from the beginning of September I became the Co-ordinating Adviser to the County Naturalists' Trusts. That was a clumsy title but a fair definition of my function.

I had already attended a good many Trusts' meetings in the previous eighteen months, including discussions in Kent, Hertfordshire, Nottinghamshire and Northamptonshire, a formation meeting in Wiltshire, and inaugurals in Northumberland, Suffolk, and Dorset. At all these meetings I was hospitably entertained and made many new friends some of whom, like Tony Tynan in Northumberland and Helen Brotherton in Dorset, played a leading role in the Trusts' movement in the years ahead. Helen in particular became a family friend with whom I have always kept in close touch. I had worked closely with Christopher Cadbury on the visiting programme and he was a principal speaker at several formation and inaugural meetings including those in Glamorgan, Shropshire, Gloucestershire and Devon. My old friends and associates Ronald Hickling and Max Walters also took a share, the former attending the Lancashire inaugural, the latter that of the Berks, Bucks & Oxon Trust (BBONT) at Oxford. With their participation and that of some other members of the Trusts' Committee we were able to cover almost every formation and inaugural meeting throughout the country.

The autumn of 1962 was particularly hectic. I no longer have a record of my journeys, but the following extract from a letter to Christopher Cadbury on 10 October gives some indication of the volume of activity.

We got the Nottingham Trust formation committee on its feet at a well attended meeting last Thursday. After making one false start I think

*they will now go ahead ……… I shall continue to give them what help
I can during the formation stages. Today I go off to the Lake District to
speak at their inaugural meeting on Thursday, discuss their plans and
visit Merlewood to talk to Nature Conservancy regional and scientific
staff there. I shall be back home on Saturday evening. I have agreed to
speak at the Cheshire meeting in Manchester on 17 November. I look
forward to talking with you in London on the afternoon 23 October
and I shall be delighted to accept your invitation to stay with you when
I come to Hereford for their meeting on 29 November.*

During the next few months I attended meetings or made advisory visits to
many other counties including Surrey, Hampshire, Sussex, Somerset, Cornwall,
Gloucestershire, Essex, Bedfordshire and Huntingdonshire, Derbyshire and
Durham. With more time to devote to the work I was able in some cases to visit
sites in which the Trust had a special interest or was seeking funding to purchase,
many of them being Sites of Special Scientific Interest. The protection of SSSIs
was also of primary concern to the Nature Conservancy and my membership of
its England Committee proved to be mutually advantageous. Wherever possible
my journeys were made by train on a rail network which was to shrink drastically
in the next ten years. I derived great satisfaction from meeting dedicated people,
seeing wonderful places and knowing that in some small way I was contributing
to their conservation. The downside of my frequent absences from home – and
there were many London committee meetings in addition to visits to Trusts - was
leaving Mary to manage home and garden and two young children. I could have
not have done it without her loyalty and unwavering support.

Wales with large, thinly populated areas presented particular problems.
The West Wales Field Society, which covered the old counties of Pembroke,
Carmarthen, Cardigan and Merioneth, had been active in conservation since
the mid 1940s, but did not convert itself into an incorporated Trust until 1961.
Glamorgan under the enthusiastic leadership of Swansea surgeon Joe Hambury
who had been at the Skegness Conference, had started in 1961 but initially drew
the bulk of support from Swansea rather than Cardiff. I visited them in 1962,
spoke at an annual meeting and was given a detailed tour of the splendid Gower
peninsula including an inspection from the air! On the same visit I also spoke
to naturalists in Monmouth and Brecon who went on to form separate Trusts in
1964 after the failure of an ill-advised proposal to form a joint Trust for the two
counties. A meeting in Abergavenny to discuss that proposal which I attended
found little common ground and was chiefly memorable for an extraordinary
clash between the then Lord Raglan who was in the chair and Tudor Watkins the
MP for Brecon and Radnor.

A Trust covering the counties of North Wales was formally established in
October 1963 following a formation meeting which I attended earlier in the year.
The prime mover was Professor Bill Lacey of the University College of North
Wales, who became one of the leaders of conservation in Wales as a whole and a
valued member for many years of the SPNR Council and Executive Committee,
and a personal friend. He was also primarily responsible for bringing the Welsh
Trusts together in an Association which met regularly to discuss issues of particular
concern in Wales and to formulate common policies and action wherever
necessary. The move was welcomed by the SPNR and I attended meetings of

the Association whenever possible. I was always assured of a warm welcome, and my visits to the Association and to individual Trusts in Wales were some of the most memorable that I made. The Welsh Trusts also played a leading role in organising a successful three-day Conference 'Conservation in Wales' held at Aberystwyth in September 1969 as a contribution to European Conservation Year 1970 and to the 'Countryside in 1970' conferences. I spoke at that conference on the work of the County Trusts and the importance of the voluntary principle in conservation. 1970 also saw the publication of *Welsh Wildlife in Trust* edited by Bill Lacey. The North Wales Trust then hosted the biennial conference of County Trusts at Bangor in 1972.

By the end of 1962 some thirty Trusts had been formed covering parts of Wales and almost the whole of England where Somerset was a late comer in 1964 and Rutland had joined with Leicestershire in 1960. Most of the Trusts had got away to a good start and quickly consolidated their position, although for most of them growth was slow in the early years. A few unfortunately soon ran into difficulties. One of those was the three counties (Warwickshire, Worcestershire, Staffordshire) West Midlands Trust which was trying to cover too large and complex an area and lacked the kind of single county loyalty which others were able to exploit. After nearly four years it still had only about 120 members, and Dr Francis Rose, who was one of the founders of the Kent Trust, reported to me in June 1962 that he had addressed the West Midlands Trust's Annual General Meeting with an attendance of only fifteen. At about the same time a bulletin from the Bedfordshire and Huntingdonshire Trust indicated something of a membership and financial crisis after only two years in existence. The Sussex Trust reported that administrative problems were seriously hampering their progress. Surrey was in similar difficulties and I met their officers to discuss them. Suffolk were making heavy weather of the purchase of Redgrave and Lopham Fens and needed extra support. Hertfordshire was very slow to get off the ground, and Lancashire, where many large towns had tended to dilute county loyalties, had recurrent administrative crises. It was, of course, inevitable that the capacity and performance of the various Trusts would vary according to the degree of local support and the dedication of key people, but helping the weaker ones in particular to overcome their difficulties was henceforth one of the main concerns of the County Trusts' Committee and of demands on my services. It says much for the strength and validity of the concept on which local Trusts were based that eventually they all overcame their particular problems.

The formation of so many County Trusts in England and Wales in the early 1960s had not gone unnoticed in Scotland. I already had some contacts there in the 1950s, partly through my involvement in the Bird Observatory movement. As early as 1950 at a meeting of the Observatories' Committee of the BTO in Edinburgh I discussed the possibility of starting local Trusts in Scotland with George Waterston the publisher and owner of Fair Isle which he had recently purchased. He showed interest then and I was in touch with him again later in the 1950s about the possibility of a Trust for the Lothians. I also corresponded about that time with Elaine Bullard, well-known local conservationist and Secretary of the Orkney Field Club, who wanted to know about Trusts. More definite moves were being made in 1960 in Perthshire which was referred to in a meeting of the County Trusts' Committee in June 1962 as a likely candidate for a new Trust which we were encouraging.

Any further progress towards county-based Trusts in Scotland, however, was pre-empted early in 1964 by the formation in Edinburgh of the Scottish Wildlife Trust. The principal promoter and founder of the SWT was Sir Charles Connell whom I knew as a member of the Nature Conservancy Council. We had little prior information at SPNR about the foundation of the Trust, but in subsequent discussions with Christopher and me, Connell indicated that it wished to be fully associated with the County Trusts' Committee of SPNR, but as a national body covering the whole country it would expect to have special status. That was constitutionally achieved after some intensive negotiation by enabling the SWT to appoint a member of the Society's Executive Committee whose members were otherwise elected by the Council. When this provision was included in the revision of the Society's Charter in 1976 the Welsh Trusts (and later Ulster) were given a similar right of appointment. It was also agreed that the SWT would have two places on the Council.

The Scottish Trust faced a formidable problem of organising its support in a country with a relatively small population much of it scattered over vast areas. Fortunate in its first Executive Officer Bernard Gilchrist, it set about the task with determination forming branches and where that was not possible appointing representatives. It was recognised too that the Trust would need to establish its own relationships with Government departments and agencies which functioned on a country basis, but it nevertheless played its full part in the affairs of the County Trusts' Committee and SPNR.

In addition to my involvement with individual Trusts it was necessary in those early days to take every opportunity to make their aims and achievements more widely known on the national scene. To that end I gave addresses at several national conferences including that of the Botanical Society of the British Isles in 1963 on the Conservation of the British Flora when I spoke on 'Conservation in Practice'; and that of the British Association in Nottingham in 1966 when I gave a paper on 'Nature Conservation: Purpose and Practice'. Opportunities in radio and television were not as frequent as they are today, but I gave several broadcast talks and took part in discussions on 'The Naturalist' and other programmes.

Financial Assistance to Trusts

From its inception in 1959 the County Trusts' Committee recognised the need to seek funds to help Trusts to acquire and manage nature reserves, to launch educational projects and if possible to employ administrative staff. The latter, we recognised, would be the most difficult task. Then, as now, funding bodies preferred to support new developments and were reluctant to assist administration.

As in the case of Lincolnshire and Gibraltar Point, many Trusts had been formed with a focus on a particular site, and experience had shown that the early acquisition of a nature reserve or reserves was important to Trusts in demonstrating credibility and attracting support. The SPNR had made small grants for the purchase of reserves throughout the 1950s, and in 1961 agreed to establish from its own resources a loan fund of £5000 to assist acquisitions. At the same time Christopher Cadbury, who had some contacts with major funding bodies, secured £25,000 from the Nuffield Foundation for a similar purpose. The Nuffield Trustees had been particularly impressed by the educational value of many reserves already established. The Society's Executive Committee decided that loans should be made on the recommendation of the County Trusts'

Committee; that the maximum for any one property would be £2,500; that no loan should exceed 75% of the total cost of the property; that repayment would be made over a definite period, and that SPNR would be able to seek some security on the property if it was thought desirable. The purpose of the Fund was to assist Trusts to purchase reserves at short notice and then to give reasonable time to raise money for repayment of the loan by special local appeal or other means. The Fund was made available by Nuffield for five years, renewal being dependent on how effectively it had been used. In fact the Trustees were so satisfied with the use of the Fund that in 1964 they converted it into a gift to the Society which continued to use it as before.

Securing the Loan Fund was a major achievement. Not only did it enable many sites, including SSSIs, to be acquired; it also enhanced the status and influence of the SPNR and its County Trusts' Committee. The amounts loaned may seem small by today's values, but in the financial year 1963/64, for example, the 1,231 acres of reserves purchased with the help of the loans and grants cost an average of little more than £33 an acre. Notable reserves acquired by Trusts in the 1963-65 period with this financial aid included Hayley Wood (Cambridgeshire), the Wick Fingringhoe (Essex), Downe Bank, Yockletts Bank and Temple Ewell (Kent), Cors Goch and Ffestiniog Woodlands (North Wales), Roydon Common (Norfolk), Gower Cliffs (Glamorgan), Redgrave and Lopham Fens (Suffolk), and Borth Bog (West Wales).

In addition to the Nuffield loan and the £5,000 already committed by the Society for the same purpose, £3,000 was donated by the Pilgrim Trust in 1962 and allocated to small grants for nature reserve purchase. Two further £3,000 donations were made by the same Trust in 1963 and 1965.

The World Wildlife Fund established in 1961 proved to be another source of funding to the Trusts in the 1960s. Initially there was concern that the Fund's nationwide appeal for donations would adversely affect the appeals made locally. In order to clarify the position a meeting was held in August 1961 between representatives of WWF and the SPNR/Trusts chaired by Peter Scott. It was agreed that both parties would inform each other of any intention to launch special appeals; the WWF would invite the co-operation of local Trusts in any appeal it wished to make in the Trust's area, and joint appeals could be made where appropriate. Of the proceeds of WWF appeals one third would be available for in use in Britain and another third could be if agreed internationally. Applications from Trusts would be submitted through the SPNR, and grants would be available for land purchase and management, and for educational projects. Consideration would also be given to allotting a fixed percentage of 10% or 15% for administrative purposes, a particularly welcome proposal. A further outcome of the meeting was an invitation to SPNR to nominate a representative on the Allocations Committee of the WWF. Christopher Cadbury was subsequently appointed, and I also served on that committee at a later date.

Not all the above proposals were endorsed by the WWF and some were subject to differing interpretation. Concern continued to be expressed in the Trusts' Committee as the WWF appointed regional organisers and established local fundraising groups to conduct appeals often without the exchange of information and consultation which we had expected. Some of the organisers, who were simply money-raisers with little knowledge of the conservation movement, also saw Trusts as a convenient local peg on which to hang appeals, and proposed arrangements which would have left the Trusts financially dependent on the WWF. One such proposal in Northumberland so alarmed me that I wrote to Tony Tynan, then the Northumberland Trust's Honorary Secretary, warning that any unilateral arrangement with the WWF of the kind proposed would threaten the Trust's independence and the unity of the Trusts' national association. I received an immediate assurance that the Trust would not commit itself in that way. After the first two or three years in fact the WWF regional organisers developed other avenues for raising funds and largely lost interest in the Trusts. Meantime further meetings at national level helped to alleviate problems, but it was some time before the Trusts' Committee's concerns were entirely allayed.

WWF grant-aid nevertheless proved valuable to Trusts in those early years. The Fund did in fact contribute up to 15% of the cost of most nature reserve purchases including those already mentioned above. A variety of management and educational projects were also assisted, and in one case a grant was made towards the legal cost of representation at an important public inquiry. In the three financial years from 1962 to 1965 WWF contributed £3,300, £5,235 and £3,815 respectively for property acquisitions and other projects.

The Nature Conservancy was unable to make grants at that time for property purchase, but offered contracts for research, survey and monitoring, and for education and interpretation projects. Among the early grants of this kind made to Trusts were those for the first experimental nature trail in this country mounted by the Berkshire, Buckinghamshire and Oxfordshire Trust (BBONT), and the first information centre on a statutory reserve at Gibraltar Point in Lincolnshire.

By 1965 the County Trusts secretariat in SPNR was advising on and processing some twenty to twenty-five grant and loan applications a year. I found it one of the most interesting aspects of the work since it brought me into contact with practical conservation developments and problems, and the satisfaction of knowing that the assistance we were able to provide was of real benefit. It was, nevertheless, another major commitment and one that underlined the need for more administrative resources for the secretariat.

The value of the Nuffield, Pilgrim, and WWF funds in enabling the Society to assist Trusts in the acquisition of reserves was strikingly illustrated in summary figures for the three financial years 1961/62, 1962/63, 1963/64 published in the Society's Handbook for 1965. For an outlay of £27,374 from funds at the Society's disposal, property priced at £41,118 had been or was in process of being acquired by Trusts. The Handbook commented: "It is no exaggeration to say that had it been necessary for the Trust concerned to find unaided the means to acquire these reserves many would have been lost before adequate funds could have been raised".

The Trusts in SPNR

SPNR had agreed when the Trusts' Committee was established that all new Trusts should be invited to join as soon as they became incorporated. During the formation process observers would be invited. By 1962 twenty-one Trusts were represented on the Committee; a year later the number had risen to thirty-one. The vast majority of Trusts readily accepted and welcomed the SPNR's advisory, co-ordinating and supporting role, but there were one or two who seemed to regard it as a threat to their freedom of action especially in the channelling of grant-aid through the Society. Such suspicions were entirely misplaced. The

Society's sole objective was to secure funds for the use of Trusts, and it is highly unlikely at that time that Trusts individually would have been able to obtain grants on the scale of those provided by Nuffield and Pilgrim (and later Carnegie) or that those foundations would have been prepared to deal separately with more than thirty county bodies. Any misgivings on the part of Trusts were quickly dispelled by involvement in the work of the Committee, although in one case it took a few years to overcome an initial prejudice.

Several talented people among the early representatives on the Committee in the 1960s went on to play a leading role in its affairs and in the general work of the Society for the Trusts. It is perhaps invidious to mention names, but some that come to mind in that category include Ronald Hickling, Max Walters, Helen Brotherton, Dick Cornwallis, Richard Fitter, Bill Lacey, Edgar Milne-Redhead, Gren Lucas, Andrew Ruck, Dunstan Adams, Tom (Sir Thomas) Barlow, Francis Rose, David Streeter, Tony Tynan, Ian Mercer and Stan Jermyn.

Integration of the Trusts into the structure of the Society was further advanced by the decision of the Executive Committee to nominate Trusts' representatives on the County Trusts' Committee for election to the Society's Council. Under the 1912 charter the fifty members of the Council were appointed for life, and by the 1960s several long-standing members had ceased to take any active part in the Society's proceedings, having forgotten perhaps about their life appointment! A tactful approach to several of them produced willing resignations and their places were filled by nominees of Trusts who by 1963 numbered more than thirty, a majority of the Council.

The Trusts' element in SPNR was further strengthened in 1963 by the appointment of Christopher Cadbury as President of the Society in succession to Lord Hurcomb, and by my appointment as joint Honorary Secretary with Norman Riley following my year of secondment. There was further recognition of the close relationship in the decision to lease to appropriate Trusts the smaller properties owned by the Society. By 1963 in fact almost the whole of the Society's business was concerned in one way or another with the affairs and concerns of the Trusts. Symbolic also of the growing relationship was the production by the Society in 1963 of the first Trusts' Christmas cards, the small beginning of what was to become a common sales business.

A further test of the value which Trusts placed on the County Trusts' Committee came in 1964 when they were asked for the first time to make a contribution to the cost of developing the secretariat. As the SPNR was itself prepared to devote £2,500 per annum for an initial period of five years, the Committee agreed that the Trusts be asked to make a minimum contribution of £2 per hundred members, but that no contribution would be sought from a new Trust until it had completed one full financial year after the date of inauguration. This modest proposal was universally accepted, readily so by the great majority. Two years later the Trusts were confident enough in the work of the Committee to agree to an increase to £5 per hundred members. We always worked on the principle of asking the Trusts to contribute as little as absolutely necessary. The bulk of the funding needed for the secretariat we determined to seek from national sources. Nonetheless it was important to establish the principle that Trusts should contribute to maintain their own association.

The range and volume of business handled by the Committee grew rapidly. In addition to considering grant-aid applications and relations with other bodies, the Committee agreed on measures for the exchange of information among Trusts about access to nature reserves and about management problems. It established, for example, a working party on chalk grassland which produced a report in 1964. Another working party examined wild plant protection in collaboration with the BSBI and the Council for Nature. The effects of toxic chemicals in agriculture was another issue of general concern in the early 1960s, and the Committee encouraged Trusts to collect information and to lobby MPs for a compulsory ban on the chemicals which were having a devastating effect on birds and other wildlife. The Committee was equally active in matters of publicity and education, arranging for the exchange of annual reports and other literature among Trusts and for pooling experience on methods of interpretation like the nature trail and information centre. More mundane but nonetheless important matters such as the implications of the Charities Act 1960 and the problems of insurance were also considered and advice given to Trusts. Already by 1961 the volume and variety of business necessitated the appointment of a standing sub-committee to deal with some if it between meetings of the full Committee.

Administering the Society in the 1960s

After my eleven month secondment to SPNR I returned to full-time duties with the University of Nottingham in July 1963. I also resumed my honorary position with the Society, now as the joint Honorary Secretary, devoting what spare time I could afford to promoting the interests of the Trusts. It was not surprising perhaps that within a few months I once again found the pressures well-nigh intolerable. The needs of the new Trusts for advice and assistance – including visits – which I had helped to stimulate was growing all the time and we were now administering the distribution of considerable amounts of grant money as well as maintaining liaison with a widening range of other bodies. Norman Riley, the other Honorary Secretary, a delightful man to work with, had kept a room at the Natural History Museum for SPNR purposes. He conducted a good deal of correspondence with national bodies but could not deal with Trusts' affairs. More paid administrative assistance was the only answer to the problem, but the Society could still not afford to appoint a full-time senior executive officer or general secretary.

It was then suggested that I might seek partial secondment from my University post for an initial three-year period – it was later extended to four years – to act as Advisory Officer with the aid of an assistant and an office secretary. I accordingly prepared a detailed application setting out not only the basic educational purposes which such a post would fulfil, but also proposals for the maintenance and indeed expansion of adult education provision in my area of Lindsey. Harold Wiltshire, my Head of Department, was again sympathetic and the University, having obtained the approval of the Ministry of Education, agreed a scheme whereby I would devote 40% of my time as the Principal Advisory Officer to the Trusts, and an Assistant Officer and clerical staff would be provided at an office in Alford. I would continue to be responsible for the organisation of the University adult education programme in my area of Lindsey for which some additional organising help would be provided from the money payable by SPNR; I would fulfil a reduced teaching programme of my own; act as Director of Studies at the Gibraltar Point Field Station and continue to represent University Adult Education on the Lindsey Education Committee – which I continued to do until the Committee disappeared in local government reorganisation in 1974.

It was an enlightened decision by the University. For me it was going to be an exacting assignment, but I considered myself fortunate to be able to spend time on both the jobs in which I found great satisfaction. The Society was able to meet its share of cost of my employment, some £1,200 pa, through the generosity of an anonymous benefactor. There was little doubt in Trust circles about his identity!

The advertisement for the Assistant Advisory Officer produced a somewhat meagre field but there were two clear front-runners: Robin Crane who was the Honorary Assistant Secretary of the Lincolnshire Trust, and Wilf Dawson, a 31-year old forester who had just completed a spell of service with the Ministry of Natural Resources in Malawi. Since Crane was already working with me in the Lincolnshire Trust I left the selection to a panel appointed by the Society although they made it clear that their choice would have to be someone with whom I felt I could work satisfactorily. Dawson was the unanimous choice, but in order that I could be satisfied they asked him to spend a weekend with me in Lincolnshire. He clearly wanted the job and, although I would have preferred someone with more experience of nature conservation in this country, I was sufficiently impressed with his ability and commitment to accept the panel's decision. So we set up our office with a secretary in the Manor House at Alford in May 1965, accommodation that was shared with the Lincolnshire Trust until the SPNR moved to Nettleham in 1974. Crane was disappointed but accepted the decision with good grace and went on to play a prominent part later as Chairman of both the Sussex Trust and later the Royal Society for Nature Conservation (RSNC).

External relationships
The Council for Nature
In the negotiations to establish the Council for Nature in 1958 the Trusts then in being had agreed to support the Council, but for reasons which I explained in the last chapter had insisted on maintaining an independent association which they persuaded the SPNR to provide. There were unfortunately some who were closely involved with the Council for Nature who continued to agitate for Trusts' affairs to be dealt with by the Council. Even within the Society some of the older Honorary Officers – perhaps because understandably they shied away from extra work and responsibility – were opposed to the creation of a secretariat which became necessary for the development of the work of the Trusts' Committee. Woodisse, the Honorary Treasurer, made this quite plain to me; Riley's attitude was always somewhat equivocal, and Lord Hurcomb, although he had supported the Trusts' involvement with SPNR, would still have preferred them to go in with the Council for Nature. This became clear in November 1963 when at a 'Countryside in 1970' reception Hurcomb, the President of the Council for Nature, and Aubrey Buxton (now Lord Buxton), the Honorary Treasurer, asked me to consider becoming the Secretary of the Council. That unexpected invitation, flattering though it was, I promptly but politely turned down not only – as I wrote in a letter to Hurcomb – "for personal considerations", but because "I believe I can best serve the conservation movement in other capacities". It was comforting to know that in making that decision I had the full support of my closest colleagues in the Trusts' Committee. After that, apart from occasional sniping, relationships with the Council for Nature settled down.

Whilst strengthening the Trusts' association within SPNR, we continued nonetheless to support the Council which developed a valuable promotional and parliamentary lobbying role. The success of the 1963 National Nature Week which it organised led to the influential series of 'Countryside in 1970' conferences in 1963, 1965 and 1970 in which the SPNR/Trusts played a full part. The failure to implement Nicholson's original concept of the Council, however, continued to cause problems, and in 1967 its constitution was revised to strengthen the role within it of the SPNR/Trusts, the RSPB and several other national bodies, reverting more closely to the original form proposed for it. But even that failed to keep it alive for more than a few more years.

Shortly after Lord Hurcomb's approach, incidentally, I was asked by Professor Roy Clapham if I would consider becoming the Secretary of the Field Studies Council. Whilst that was in many ways a more attractive proposition than the secretaryship of the Council for Nature, I told Professor Clapham that I would not relinquish my university post for any reason other than to serve the Trusts' movement. At that time in fact my partial secondment for that purpose was already under discussion.

The Nature Conservancy

More important for the Trusts was their relationship with the Nature Conservancy. At the request of the Trusts' Committee I prepared a paper on the subject and this was discussed with the Director-General of the Conservancy Max Nicholson in December 1960 at a meeting attended for the Trusts by Cadbury, Walters, Rose and myself. The discussion concentrated on collaboration on safeguarding SSSIs and on the possibility of the Conservancy providing more financial assistance to Trusts for that purpose. Many Trusts had already provided information for the selection of SSSIs, and some of the older ones like Norfolk, Yorkshire and Lincolnshire were already managing a number of them as a result of purchase, lease or agreement. It was agreed that the Trusts should be encouraged to become involved in appropriate non-statutory type of work associated with SSSIs. That would enable Conservancy staff to devote more time to advising Trusts on nature reserve management and general conservation problems. Co-operation on survey and monitoring, and on collecting information about the effects of toxic chemicals were among other problems discussed. It was also recognised that to implement the proposals the Trusts would need adequate clerical assistance and funds to meet travelling and other legitimate expenses of volunteers. We had hoped that the Conservancy would be willing to meet some of those costs, but Nicholson proposed that the Trusts' Committee should apply to the WWF to finance such a scheme. The Committee welcomed the proposals in principle, but considered that, until the WWF's funding capacity and intentions became clearer, it would be premature to look to the Fund to provide the considerable cost which would be required.

Further meetings with the Conservancy were held during 1962 and a more definite liaison scheme was agreed in April 1963. It defined three phases. First, a joint review of SSSIs and consultation arrangements to cover other matters including the co-ordination of responses to Planning Authorities on development proposals. SSSIs would be placed in three categories: those demanding urgent attention because of threats or opportunities for practical protection; those in need of conservation management, and those which required only periodic report. Possibilities would be explored of collaboration on other conservation projects such as the selection of sites of interest outside the SSSI category, and the protection of road verges. The second and third phases would be concerned with the implementation of the arrangements. The Trusts would undertake periodic inspections of SSSIs subject where necessary to owner agreement, whilst Conservancy regional staff would advise Trusts if requested on reserve management plans and problems. Co-operation in the development of educational facilities for field studies would also be encouraged. The Trusts would discuss with the World Wildlife Fund a funding package to enable them to undertake the proposals, but the Conservancy would be prepared to pay an honorarium for surveys and other work carried out at their request. The liaison agreement concluded: "Close collaboration between Trusts and the Nature Conservancy is clearly of the highest importance. In developing this process it seems desirable to have a common code of practice and procedure which at the same time allows adequate flexibility for different circumstances. The above scheme is designed to provide this. It should help Trusts to formulate their conservation programmes. Formal acceptance of non-statutory responsibility for SSSIs, moreover, will enhance the status of Trusts and promote their development".

Admirable though it was, the scheme was somewhat utopian and premature. Most of the Trusts did not have the resources of money and manpower to implement it in full, and the WWF was still not ready to provide a funding package. There were also perhaps reservations about the involvement of Trusts on the part of some of the Conservancy regional staff. Nevertheless the scheme established the principles of collaboration and provided a framework for action on important issues of common concern such as SSSIs. It was followed up in 1964 by the establishment of a Joint Liaison Committee between the Trusts' Committee and the Conservancy which met regularly and covered a wide range of topics.

The Royal Society for the Protection of Birds
The other national organisation whose aims and activities were close to those of the Trusts was the RSPB. My acquaintance with the Secretary Philip Brown had kept me in contact with the Society throughout the 1950s, and by coincidence I had also made the acquaintance of Peter Conder, who had become the Assistant Secretary, during his spell as warden of the Skokholm Bird Observatory. Conder represented the RSPB at the Trusts' conference at Skegness in 1960 when we devoted a whole session to relations with other bodies. Describing the principal activities of the RSPB he suggested some possible areas of collaboration with the Trusts including law enforcement and the management of nature reserves of ornithological interest on which the RSPB would be willing to give advice. In September 1962 I visited the Society's new headquarters at Sandy and discussed with Philip Brown and his senior colleagues problems of mutual interest and concern. As a result of that visit I produced a paper for the County Trusts' Committee in November setting out proposals for collaboration, among them bird protection measures, the collection of information on the effects of toxic chemicals and the possibility of shared management of certain nature reserves – there was already such an arrangement for the Coombes Valley reserve in Staffordshire between the RSPB and the West Midlands Trust. Collaboration should also be encouraged in education where the RSPB were expanding their programme and services following the appointment of John Clegg as Education Officer. As further evidence of the close relationship between the two bodies at that time I was invited to write an article about the Trusts' movement for the

RSPB's magazine *Bird Notes* in which I was even allowed to appeal for support for the Trusts.

In order to facilitate co-operation on the above and other matters it was decided to invite the RSPB to send an observer to meetings of the County Trusts' Committee, and Peter Conder, who succeeded Philip Brown as Director at the end of 1962, fulfilled that role for several years. Attendance at the Committee and other contacts with the Trusts convinced him, I believe, of their importance and potential. He became a strong advocate of closer ties between the RSPB and the Trusts which led to his proposal at the Trusts' Bournemouth Conference in 1966 of a merger between the organisations. The outcome of that I deal with later in this chapter.

The Forestry Commission
Although in the 1960s the Forestry Commission had gradually begun to adopt more enlightened policies on nature conservation – as in the National Forest Parks created in upland areas - the focus of its policies and operations over most of the country were still on intensive timber production largely through the cultivation of conifers. In Lincolnshire, and no doubt elsewhere, heathland was still being afforested and ancient broad-leaved woods converted to conifers in the 1940s and 50s. On the other hand, many foresters were good field naturalists and within the narrow limits of their remit anxious to do whatever they could to conserve wildlife habitats. We had experienced both those aspects in dealings with the Commission in the early days of the Trust in Lincolnshire.

The establishment of the County Trusts' Committee now offered an opportunity to influence Commission policy at national level, to cater in particular for sites of special interest – remnants of heath and bog, for example, and woodland features of special ecological interest – which for one reason or another had survived in Commission forests. Many of these sites had been listed by the county sub-committees of the Nature Reserves Investigation Committee and some had appeared in the first SSSI schedules. The latter designation offered little real safeguard at that time, but the main threats were often from lack of vegetation management such as mowing or grazing.

At one of its earliest meetings in April 1961 the County Trusts' Committee agreed that we should seek discussions with the Forestry Commission with a view to securing a standard form of agreement between Trusts and the Commission to ensure the appropriate management of such sites. The first reaction of the England headquarters of the Commission was that such arrangements were best left to be made locally. However, when we persisted they agreed to discuss and I met the England Director, the formidable looking George Ryle (a naturalist who after retirement represented the Hampshire Trust for a time on the CTC) to work out the heads of an agreement. Since we were dealing with a government agency it took months to finalise a document, but it was eventually agreed and accepted with satisfaction by the CTC in June 1964. The agreement basically provided for a Trust to be granted a licence in return for an annual payment to manage a site according to a management plan agreed with the Commission. The licence was to run for fourteen years but could be determined by either party mid-way.

The facility provided by the agreement encouraged its wide use by the Trusts mainly for small sites like that at Roberts Field in Lincolnshire which I described in an earlier chapter, but there were also more ambitious examples of

Trust participation in site management as, for example, in Bedford Purlieus in Northamptonshire and in St Leonard's Forest in Sussex. Operating the agreement also helped to promote closer working relationships between the Trusts and local foresters which in most cases has persisted to the present day.

As the Commission gradually strengthened its nature conservation policies and practices it took over the management of many of the sites and the agreements with Trusts lapsed, although a few were still extant at the end of the twentieth century. It was generally acknowledged that the agreement had served a valuable purpose in rescuing sites from destruction and deterioration and sustaining their function as 'reservoirs' of biodiversity from which plants and animals could recolonise restored habitats around them. That happened at Roberts Field; it must have happened also at many other places.

The operation of agreements and collaboration with the Forestry Commission in general were greatly assisted by the appointment in 1964 of Peter Garthwaite as the Commission's first Wildlife Officer. Garthwaite was already an experienced senior officer of the Forestry Commission and was able to exercise considerable influence on policies and practices to the benefit of nature conservation. His wisdom and his breadth of vision were a great asset in the Society's Conservation Liaison Committee on which he represented the Forestry Commission until his retirement in 1969. I enjoyed a close and cordial working relationship with him. His successor as the Commission representative on the Liaison Committee, Tony Spencer, the Head of a new Conservation and Recreation Branch at the Commission, maintained a good relationship with us.

The National Trust

In the 1960s the National Trust already owned some of England's finest nature reserves – places such as Wicken Fen, Scolt Head and Blakeney Point – as well as great tracts of countryside rich in wildlife. Generally, however, nature conservation was not among their priorities: they had neither resources nor expertise for the specialised management requirements for habitats like chalk grassland, heathland and bog. As with Forestry Commission properties, the new County Trusts were aware of sites of interest on National Trust land and were prepared to assist in their management. The County Trusts' Committee therefore decided to seek discussions with the National Trust to offer assistance on the basis of management agreements or even leases.

Our consequent approach to the Trust's headquarters was warmly received. Christopher, Max Walters and I had an informal discussion with senior officers of the Trust, including the Legal Adviser, in July 1962. As a result we reported to the Society's Executive Committee in September that the Area Agents of the National Trust would be encouraged to liaise with the County Trusts in their areas to explore possibilities of involving Trusts in the management of appropriate sites. A further meeting with the Chief Agent of the National Trust in 1965 reaffirmed their readiness to consider suggestions from Naturalists' Trusts for management of National Trust property of special natural interest. As a result of these approaches the next ten or twelve years saw many examples of management agreements between the National Trust and County Trusts and of collaboration in raising funds to purchase new properties. So much so that the 1979 edition of the National Trust Guide reported "There can scarcely be one of the County Naturalists' Trusts which is not in league with the National Trust".

So, for example, the Charnwood Forest reserve at Ulverscroft is held by the Leicestershire and Rutland Trust partly by agreement with the National Trust. The nationally important woodland of Maentwrog in the Vale of Festiniog was acquired by a joint fundraising effort on the part of the North Wales Trust and the National Trust who then involved the Nature Conservancy in management. Some of the most important acquisition and management arrangements between the National Trust and County Trusts were made in pursuance of Enterprise Neptune, the National Trust's country-wide appeal for funds to acquire unspoiled stretches of coastline. We supplied information for Enterprise Neptune about coastal sites of special natural interest known to the County Trusts, and there was practical cooperation with the National Trust over several of them. The National Trust's acquisition of the important Whiteford Burrows reserve in Gower, for example, was made possible by a substantial loan from the Glamorgan Trust made available through the SPNR's Nuffield Loan Fund. Money had to be found as a matter of great urgency or the opportunity would have been lost. Perhaps the most outstanding example of joint fundraising by Enterprise Neptune was the public appeal for the acquisition and endowment of Brownsea Island in Poole Harbour in Dorset. Although only recently formed, the Dorset Trust, led by the indomitable Helen Brotherton, played a major role in raising £86,000 towards the sum required. The Dorset Trust then took a lease of half the island including the magnificent lagoon, and undertook the clearance of undergrowth and the restoration of the Villa as accommodation and laboratory, using volunteers for much of the work. It was largely in recognition of her work for Brownsea that Helen was appointed OBE which was later converted to CBE for services to the National Trust.

As with the Forestry Commission, collaboration on specific projects strengthened the general relationship between County Trusts and National Trust area staff several of whom, including Area Agents, served on Trust Councils and Committees. There were also instances, as in Hertfordshire for example, of County Trust officers being invited to serve on Area Committees of the National Trust. Relations with the Trust at national level were particularly close during Ivan Hills' period as Chief Agent in the late 1960s and 1970s. He attended Trusts' biennial conferences and was a main speaker at the conference at Oxford in 1970. By the 1980s, however, the National Trust was developing its own in-house capacity for habitat and wildlife management by employing ecologists in a special unit. It had less need for assistance from County Trusts and most of the smaller agreements over sites gradually lapsed although the major examples of collaboration like those mentioned above have survived.

There was another link between the National Trust and the SPNR itself. The latter was one of the bodies eligible under the National Trust's Charter to appoint a representative to its Council. I served in that capacity for eight years from 1980 to 1988. It was an interesting experience and I found the contacts very useful, but the Council seemed to be regarded more as a consultative rather than a policy-making body. More rewarding for me was a five-year stint from 1985 to 1990 on the Trust's Nature Conservation Panel whose business was much more directly concerned with policies and problems of management. Many such were similar to those confronting the Wildlife Trusts, and my membership of the Panel may have been helpful on occasions in promoting contacts and exchanging information and experience.

'The RSPBNR'? A Merger Too Far

I was aware that at the Bournemouth Conference in 1966 Peter Conder intended to propose a move towards a merger between the RSPB and the SPNR/Trusts, although there had been no substantive discussion about it before then. We had already established a Liaison Committee to consider matters of common concern such as legislation, relations with the Nature Conservancy and the effect of toxic chemicals on wildlife. The RSPB had been invited to send an observer to meetings of the County Trusts Committee, a role which Peter Conder himself fulfilled. At that time too (1962-7) I was a member of the RSPB Council as were two or three others who were actively involved in their County Trusts. The relationship between the RSPB and the SPNR/Trusts had indeed never been closer than it was in the early 1960s. There seemed to be a certain logic, therefore, in Peter Conder's proposal that we should take a step further and amalgamate. His proposal met with a positive response from Trusts' delegates at the Conference who recommended that the possibility should be investigated. There were nevertheless some cautionary voices, and in my own response I referred to some of the complex and vital issues which would need to be resolved not least the status of the individual County Trusts within a new body.

The two Societies had been further drawn together by their common concern about the Council for Nature, the constitution and functions of which had to be radically reconsidered following the debacle of its launch in 1958. Under the chairmanship of the eminent zoologist Sir Landsborough Thomson the Council in 1968 made amendments to its constitution designed to facilitate cooperation with the SPNR and the RSPB and other organisations, reverting in effect to the form of constitution originally proposed for the Council. The SPNR, representing the County Trusts, was allocated four of the twenty-three Council seats. The Council's functions were also redefined to be mainly Parliamentary work, press relations and publicity, national exhibitions and a newsletter for member bodies. Meantime as a temporary measure the RSPB had agreed to administer the Council in consultation with the SPNC.

These changes had barely come into force, however, when Sir Landsborough Thomson produced a plan for a tripartite merger between the Council for Nature, the RSPB and the SPNR. This he circulated as an Open Memorandum to all the bodies involved with the Council for Nature. It did not find favour as a basis for negotiation with the members of SPNR's Executive Committee who, at a weekend meeting held at Whiteslea Lodge on Hickling Broad, drafted an SPNR policy statement on the future of the voluntary nature conservation movement. The statement recognised the need in the long term for a new organisation with a proper balance between local and national interests. Meantime the re-constituted Council for Nature should be given the chance to work, and the relationship between the SPNR and the County Trusts should be further strengthened. The statement was strongly endorsed by the County Trusts' Committee at their meeting in June. Many of the Trusts' representatives spoke in a full debate emphasising the considerable progress which had already been made in coordinating the various parts of the conservation movement, and the need for the Society to continue its work of promoting the County Trusts whose importance in the conservation movement nationally was becoming evermore apparent. It was also suggested that mergers were not necessarily the best way to achieve progress.

Up to that point the SPNR/RSPB Liaison Committee had made little progress in discussions about a merger of the two bodies. They had to some extent been sidetracked by the Council for Nature problem on which they found much common ground, but, as many of us had anticipated, they had also encountered difficulties over some over the basic issues not least the status of the County Trusts in an amalgamated organisation. They agreed in November 1969 on recommendations made by Peter Conder and me to invite independent consultants to assist in drawing up a possible structure for a merged body, identifying the principles on which it should be based and proposing how it might be put into effect. A number of eminent people were approached of whom four agreed to assist: Dr Joe Eggeling, formerly Director in Scotland of the Nature Conservancy and Chairman of the RSPB's Scottish Committee; Walter Lane, Clerk of Lindsey County Council and member of the 'Countryside in 1970' Conferences Standing Committee; David Lowe, formerly secretary of the Carnegie UK Trust, and Ralph Verney, then Chairman of the Nature Conservancy's Committee for England. All four had considerable experience of various aspects of the voluntary conservation movement.

After an initial meeting with both sides of the Liaison Committee in February 1971, the consultants put a set of proposals to a further meeting in July under the title 'A New Look at the Voluntary Nature Conservation Movement'. In brief they recommended the creation of a single organisation based on the complementary strengths of the RSPB/SPNR-Trusts, retaining the autonomy of the Trusts, but as an integral part of the new body accepting obligations in respect of national policy. A membership would be basically of the whole organisation. The Council would be elected on a national and local basis, half appointed as representatives of each Trust, the other half by national ballot of all members except that for an initial three-year period the national half would be appointed by the outgoing RSPB Council. Properties would be acquired by the central body or a local Trust by agreement; existing ownerships would remain unchanged except for a transfer of RSPB and SPNR reserves to the new central body. There were other proposals regarding staffing and management of reserves, subscription structure and levels.

The Liaison Committee agreed that the basic principles should be put to their respective bodies and I circulated copies to all Trusts for consideration. The outcome of the County Trusts' Committee meeting in February 1972 was that twenty-six Trusts supported the consultants' principles in their entirety; eight supported them with reservations, mainly concerning their effect on their autonomy; three had major reservations but agreed that negotiations should continue; one rejected the principles outright and one other felt unable to express an opinion without balloting all its members.

I reported to the Committee that the RSPB had decided that they could not accept the consultants' principles, but instead had adopted a much less definitive interpretation of principles to be put forward as a basis of further discussion. They made no mention of parity of representation and were less specific than the consultants had been on the autonomy of Trusts. In discussion the members of the Trusts' Committee were unanimously agreed that parity of representation in the governing body and retention of local autonomy by Trusts were essential principles.

After a further meeting with the consultants in April 1972 I reported to the County Trusts' Committee that although the RSPB representatives on the Liaison

Committee had agreed to put the consultants' proposals to their Council, there was little enthusiasm for the idea of an amalgamation on their side. In particular it was apparent that they were unhappy about the principle of parity and asked for further information on the membership income and assets of the SPNR and Trusts. We agreed to provide this on condition that similar information was made available about the RSPB and that an independent assessor should be engaged to collate and examine the information. The RSPB agreed to provide information, but I told the Committee that if valid comparisons were to be drawn the voluntary input to the Trusts would have to be quantified as the consultants themselves had already indicated.

The collection of information had no sooner started than I received from Peter Conder a new set of proposals, drawn up by the RSPB's Administrator Cecil Winnington-Ingram on behalf of the RSPB members of the Liaison Committee, which were apparently intended to replace those of the consultants. I sent the proposals straightway to my Executive Committee, but I pointed out to Peter that I would be working on the assumption that we were still pursuing the consultants' proposals by collecting information about assets and resources which the RSPB had requested. Was the RSPB now rejecting the consultants' proposals? Winnington-Ingram's proposals involved retention of autonomy by both the Trusts and the RSPB, but the latter would add 'conservation of nature' to its title and objects. There would then be a new body elected by the Trusts and the reconstituted RSPB with a kind of coordinating and servicing role. When the Society's Executive Committee and later the Council discussed the proposals they did not consider that they offered a practicable or acceptable basis for negotiation, and in any case they held strongly to the opinion that a conclusion on the consultants' scheme ought to be reached before alternatives were discussed. The consultants' plan was formally rejected by the RSPB in March 1973, having been accepted by almost all the Trusts and SPNR twelve months earlier.

That was not quite the end of the merger marathon. In October 1973 a group of RSPB employees circulated on their own initiative to all Trusts and a number of other bodies a proposal involving the dissolution of the County Trusts and their replacement by local and regional committees of a national organisation in control of finance. The SPNR Council immediately agreed that if Trusts had any comments on the proposal they should be reported to the Council to be discussed by them before any public comment or any reply to the authors be made by Trusts individually. It was an unfortunate and ill-judged intervention which Trusts' deemed it best to ignore.

After nearly eight years both sides were suffering from negotiating fatigue and it was something of a relief in the end when we drew a line under it. Negotiations failed, I believe, basically because the RSPB perceived itself to be the stronger body and was therefore reluctant to accept the principle of parity on the governing body. The consultants, however, had found no significant disparity in resources between the two parties when the vast amount of voluntary help available to the Trusts' was taken into account, and for them the principle of parity was fundamental and one which they were not prepared to forego or to modify.

We cannot know whether the voluntary nature conservation movement would have been stronger overall had the merger gone ahead. As it was the RSPB and the Trusts have flourished in their respective roles attracting public support on a scale unimaginable in the 1960s. And even if the Trusts' national association the Royal Society for Nature Conservation (RSNC; now the Royal Society of Wildlife Trusts) seemed sometimes to have lost its way in recent years, the dire predictions of Landsborough Thomson and others in 1969 that without mergers the movement would suffer "in its practical effectiveness and in its public image" have proved to be completely unfounded.

Throughout the merger negotiations the Liaison Committee had continued to discuss other matters of current concern to the two bodies such as the Council for Nature problem, National Trust properties, barrage schemes, oil pollution, and representation on Sports Councils. Now that those negotiations had ended Peter Conder and I set up a series of meetings to explore future cooperation between our two bodies on specific subjects. One result was our joint approach to the Regional Water Authorities and the production of a manual on river management which I have described elsewhere. We also established a common position in 1972 on the future of the Nature Conservancy.

The negotiations had absorbed a great deal of time and energy, but they had given us a better perception of the strengths and weaknesses of the Trusts and of the role of the Society in providing their national association. Pending the outcome of negotiations on the consultants' proposals the Society had deferred plans for developing its services to the Trusts. The time had now come for it to move ahead.

Property	Trust	Year purchased	Acreage	Price £	Nuffield Fund Loan £	Pilgrim Fund Grant £	World Wildlife Grant £
Hayley Wood	Cambs. & Ely	1962	122	5,000	2,500	250	1,250
Fingringhoe	Essex	1961	100	4,000	2,250	250	1,000
Downe Bank	Kent	1962	11½	930	450	250	233
Buckfastleigh	Devonshire	1961	11	1,775	1,775	250	—
Cors Goch	North Wales	1962	28	950	950	250	250
Gower Cliffs	Glamorgan	1963	159	3,500	2,677	250	898
Redgrave and Lopham Middle Fens	Suffolk	1964	186	1,343	1,050	250	350
Welton Chalk Pit	Lincolnshire	1963	4	150	—	50	—
Cranberry Rough	Norfolk	1963	20	400	—	100	100
Roydon Common	Norfolk	1963	135	1,975	1,200	250	405
Yockletts Bank	Kent	1963	60	3,300	2,475	250	—
Temple Ewell Down	Kent	1964	100	5,000	500	250	2,300
Cors Goch	North Wales	1964	86	2,350	1,750	250	600
Cardigan Island	West Wales	1963	40	475	300	25	450
Maentwrog Woods .	North Wales	1965	180	10,000	2,500	500	1,500
Borth Bog	West Wales	1964	95	880	660	250	250
Hawthorn Dene	Durham	1965	65	725	295	250	180
Buckingham Canal	Northants	1965	24	200	150	65	70
Hoplands Wood	Lincolnshire	1964	35	2,000	1,500	400	500
Ouse Washes	Cambs & Ely	1965	15	635	450	150	175
Hempton Plain	Berks., Bucks., & Oxon.	1965	61	3,800	2,500	500	1100
Llanmadoc Woods	Glamorgan	1965	8	400	300	100	100
Holme (with house)	Norfolk	1965	5½	5,200	2,500	500	1,300
Lopham Great and Little Fens	Suffolk	1965	128	800	345	250	200
Whiteford Burrows	Glamorgan	1965	700	30,500	10,000	—	—
Hurley Chalk Pit	Berks., Bucks., & Oxon.	1964	3	250	—	75	100
26 Properties	*Total*		**2,382**	**86,538**	**39,077**	**5,962**	**13,311**

The total area of land now managed by County Trusts is over 16,000 acres, of which 6,500 are freehold; and the Trusts have grown from eight in number with 3,000 members in 1960 to 36 with 18,000 members in 1965.—J.C.C.

Grants and loans to Trusts through SPNR 1961-1965

Selection of the earliest SPNR Christmas cards for sale by Trusts (from 1963)

No. 13   Autumn 1976

Conservation REVIEW

PUBLISHED BY THE SOCIETY FOR THE PROMOTION OF NATURE CONSERVATION

IN THIS ISSUE

Wetland features on
Dragonflies Otters
Endangered Flora
and Geological Conservation

new charter
new name
new look

The granting of a new Royal Charter with the change of the Society's name to the Society for the Promotion of Nature Conservation was announced publicly for the first time to assembled representatives of the trusts and allied organisations at their 9th biennial conference in Newcastle in July. David Attenborough used the occasion to launch a new look for the Society and outline the challenges and opportunities that face it and the Trusts over the next few years.

For the first time the Society has a Charter which fully recognizes not only the Trusts' involvement in the Society as their national association but also the Society's involvement with something more than nature reserves—with the promotion of nature conservation in its broadest sense and the education of "the public in the understanding and appreciation of nature, the awareness of its value and the need for its conservation". It is significant that associating itself with and supporting the Trusts is the first of a number of powers vested in the Society to achieve these broad objectives.

The 40 Nature Conservation Trusts become Corporate Members and each appoints a member on the SPNC's Council with the remainder of the 60 places filled by individuals from the ordinary membership. All of our readers, as members of Trusts become Associate Members of the SPNC.

With the new name and Charter comes a new look for the Society; the new badger symbol will become a familiar sign of SPNC activity and already features above in our new look colour production of *Conservation Review*. While the *Review* is more attractive and easier to read, regular features remain with major conservation topics discussed in the centre pages—this issue looks at the endangered wetland wildlife—nationwide conservation news, SPNC news, publications and news from Trusts.

60 years ago we received our first Charter. We are re-organising and looking ahead to 2036!

New Royal Charter for the SPNC 1976.

Headquarters of the SPNC at Nettleham 1974.

– 14 –

Re-structuring the SPNR

BY 1971 all the Trusts had nominees serving on the Council of the Society and it was decided to wind up the County Trusts' Committee after more than ten years of productive activity, and transfer its functions to the Council. The Executive Committee had for some years been acting in the interests of both the Council and the Trusts' Committee. The process of converting the Society into the association of the Trusts was thus completed in practice, and in 1976 was enshrined in a new Royal Charter under which the Trusts became Corporate Members of the Society each with a place on the Council in its own right. The new Charter also gave the Society a specific power to encourage and support the Trusts. In recognition of its broader aims and objectives and those of its Associated Trusts the name of the Society was changed to the Society for the Promotion of Nature Conservation (and from 1981 the RSNC).

In an article entitled 'County Conservationists' Philip Lowe, writer on environmental issues of the Bartlett School of Architecture and Planning, described this transformation of the Society as "the culmination of a long process of growth and adaptation since its founding in 1912, from obscurity and an ineffectual past into one of today's most important conservation bodies". "The Society", he continued, "lacking direction, with an archaic constitution, small membership and having difficulty in adapting to modern times, would have declined even further and eventually died a natural death. However, just as an old building whose original use has finished and whose structure is incompatible with modern demands can nevertheless be renovated and its internal structure altered for new uses, so the SPNR provided old 'premises' for the newly developing county Trust movement".

The new Council of the Society met twice a year. With a representative from each of the Trusts together with the Officers it was a large body. Attendance was good, an average of about thirty-five. There were some lively debates on controversial issues, but the atmosphere at meetings was almost always good-natured and constructive. It reflected the remarkable degree of cohesion which the Trusts' movement had achieved by that time. The Council was criticised in later years, especially by those who wished to get rid of it, as being ineffective. It was alleged that Trusts tended to appoint representatives who could most easily attend weekday meetings in London and who were not always Honorary Officers or members with real influence, and who sometimes failed to communicate Council business effectively to their Trust. These criticisms undoubtedly had some validity, but did not in my experience seriously detract from the value of the Council as a body where every Trust had a voice and a vote and where policy decisions affecting the whole movement were made by common consent. No Trust came under pressure to take part in cooperative projects, like the sale business; the only obligation was the payment of the levy to the Society and that was always discussed and agreed in Council.

The Executive Committee of twelve members including Honorary Officers met usually four times a year conducting a great volume and variety of business some of it fed in by the specialist groups on administration and publicity and on conservation. To further relieve the pressure there was a Finance and General Purposes Committee which met as required, and later in the 1970s a Nature Reserves Committee to deal largely with the Society's own reserves or those in which it was closely involved. Christopher Cadbury presided over the Council and chaired the Executive Committee, a dual responsibility which became increasingly onerous for him. One of my earliest associates in promoting the movement Max Walters was the Vice-Chairman, but to my regret owing to other commitments he found it necessary to resign in 1971. But for his untimely death in 1969 Dick Cornwallis would almost certainly have succeeded Max and would probably have become Chairman of the Executive Committee in due course. As it was Christopher continued in both positions until 1977 when Walter Lane, who had become increasingly involved in nature conservation, was appointed Chairman of the Executive, a position which he held for the remainder of my time as General Secretary. David Robinson, the Lincolnshire Trust's Honorary Secretary, who succeeded Dick as the Trust's representative on the SPNR Council, went on to play a prominent role in the affairs of the Society over the next twenty-five years, including membership of the Executive Committee and the Editorial Board of *Natural World*, and the chairmanship of the Education & Promotions Committee.

When Tom Woodisse retired as Honorary Treasurer of the Society in 1966 Norman Riley relinquished the joint secretaryship and bravely volunteered to be Honorary Treasurer, a considerable responsibility which he discharged with his usual competence and good humour. His retirement from the post in 1972 virtually severed the long-standing connection between the Natural History Museum and the Society. I was very pleased then when Ronald Hickling, another of my old pioneering friends, volunteered to become the Honorary Treasurer, a post which he held for a further five critical years. For the remainder of my time as General Secretary Andrew Ruck was the Honorary Treasurer. The Executive Committee played a crucial and effective role throughout the 1970s in the work of the Society in promoting the development of the Trusts. We were indeed fortunate both in the Honorary Officers and in the membership of the Committee including experienced Trusts' leaders like those mentioned in the last chapter.

After my four years of partial secondment I returned in October 1968 to full-time employment with the University, reverting to being once again the Honorary Secretary of the Society. At the office established in Alford I was able to exercise a supervisory role and to attend Council and Executive meetings. Most of the day-to-day work, however, now fell to Wilf Dawson, but he soon had the help of an assistant administrative officer, a post which the Executive Committee had agreed to create at the end of my secondment. It was a post occupied over the next few years by a number of people including Dick Hallett, a retired naval commander, and Freddie Thomas who after a distinguished war-time service in the RAF had been the first secretary of the Devon Trust and who later in the 1970s conducted a special appeal for the Lincolnshire Trust.

A secretariat of two full-time officers, half the time of a secretary-typist and myself in a voluntary capacity was clearly inadequate to deal with the increasing amount of business being generated by the County Trusts' Committee and by Trusts individually. Contributions from Trusts, which in 1969 totalled around £1,400, were far short of the cost of the secretariat which in the same year amounted to £4,800. The remainder of the cost was met from the modest profit on sales, the interest on the Nuffield Fund balances and general donations. Any further expansion of the secretariat had to depend on increasing income from those and other sources. In fact a considerable increase in Trusts' membership almost doubled their contribution in 1970; and in 1971, as a result of further growth in membership and an increase in the capitation levy, their contributions amounted to £5,372, rising to £6,500 in the following year. This together with further generous donations by Christopher enabled a further appointment to be made for administrative and sales purposes, and a full-time office secretary and part-time typing assistant to be employed.

The accommodation at Alford Manor House had never been regarded as more than a temporary base for the Society. After three or four years it was indeed proving inadequate and unsatisfactory and there were particular problems in housing the growing sales business. I had made it clear to the Executive Committee on more than one occasion that I was quite prepared to relinquish the honorary secretaryship if the best solution to the accommodation problem was to move the office away from Lincolnshire. Since they reaffirmed their request that I should continue to exercise overall responsibility in an honorary capacity, however, it was obviously necessary for me to have reasonable access to the office. Dawson therefore prepared a paper for the Executive Committee analysing the future accommodation requirements of the Society in relation to the expansion of its existing administrative and sales services. He recommended that office accommodation be sought in Lincoln or nearby, giving better accessibility to London and other parts of the country and offering better opportunities for recruiting office staff. When the Executive Committee considered this paper in November 1971 they were advised that there were two other possibilities which might meet the Society's requirements. One was Charnwood Lodge near Loughborough which had recently been bequeathed to the Leicestershire and Rutland Trust; the other Christopher Cadbury's house Beaconwood near Rednal in Worcestershire, which he indicated might be bequeathed to the Society at some time in the future. It was decided that both these possibilities should be investigated and a small working group visited both places. They reported to the Executive Committee that Beaconwood was a possibility but not for seven to twelve years ahead when Christopher might no longer wish to live there. Charnwood Lodge would involve a considerable capital cost and running costs in excess of £2,000 a year utilising even the minimum amount of accommodation available there. Although both places might be suitable as permanent headquarters in the long term, neither offered a short or even medium term solution to the problem.

It was therefore agreed that the most satisfactory immediate answer would be to purchase a suitable property in the Lincoln area out of capital resources which could be considered as a medium-term investment.

We were fortunate in finding a suitable property within a few months in the shape of the Old Church Institute at Nettleham, a large village on the outskirts of Lincoln. The building with a timber-framed frontage stood prominently overlooking the village green. It could be readily converted to provide several offices and a reception area. The large meeting hall could be used as a sales store and packing room. A visit by the Finance and General Purposes Committee confirmed its suitability and in November 1973 it was bought at auction for £10,000. After conversion for office use and furnishing it was ready for occupation by the summer of 1974. Five years later we purchased for £17,500 the adjoining house and garden to provide extra accommodation for staff, so relieving what had by that time become an overcrowded main building.

In 1975 with the new accommodation available the small secretariat was reinforced by the appointment of Tim Sands as a joint assistant secretary. Tim was already well known in the nature conservation movement having been first the Information Officer and since 1972 the Secretary of the Council for Nature. An important aspect of his work for the Council was liaison with the All-Party Parliamentary Conservation Committee, and we made arrangements to make his services available through the Council to maintain his contacts with that Committee. His experience in publicity and media relationships was also to prove of great value to the Society. His wife Lesley who had worked as secretarial assistant for the Council for Nature also joined the staff at Nettleham. Tim went on to play a uniquely important role in nature conservation for the next thirty years. Thanks to the growth of Trusts' membership – it passed 100,000 in the middle of 1975 – their contributions to the Society together with other sources of income enabled us to maintain a secretariat better equipped to deal with the expanding workload.

The move to Nettleham caused me to consider my own position. Although it had been suggested to me on more than one occasion that I should become the paid secretary of the Society, I knew that whatever my own feelings might be the Society did not have the financial resources to employ me at the same level of salary that I was earning as a University Senior Lecturer. In 1974, however, an opportunity arose to overcome that problem. The Carnegie UK Trust had just completed its five-year programme of financial assistance for the County Trusts carried out in association with the Society. The Trustees had already been impressed with the results of their aid and their satisfaction was well expressed in their Annual Report for 1973: "The Trustees believe that the SPNR and the County Trusts have a great potential in the field of practical conservation, in involving the public as a whole in the problems of managing resources and an increasing appreciation and understanding of the natural environment". The success of the Carnegie programme for staff appointments for Trusts – extended beyond 1972 in respect of educational and interpretation projects – owed much to the personal interest of the Secretary of the Trust Michael Holton and his predecessor before 1970 David Lowe. Michael not only gave great attention to each application, but had also stimulated new thinking about administrative and educational problems and about the purposes and functions which the Trusts fulfil. So impressed was he with their work and purposes that after he left the Carnegie Trust to return to the Civil Service at the end of 1975 he became for several years the Honorary Secretary of the Society. I had developed a close working relationship with him, and he suggested in 1974 that if the Carnegie Trust was prepared to fund the post I should consider using my experience by devoting the five years to my retirement to full-time work for the Society strengthening the service which it was giving to the Trusts. The suggestion was warmly welcomed by the Council and Executive Committee who assured me of their full support.

I now had to make a decision. Financial security, the lack of which had previously been a deterrent would be assured with Carnegie grant-aid at university Senior Lecturer salary level, although pension provision would be more complex – and as it turned out less favourable – than if I stayed with the University. The previous five years had been hard going. Reconciling a full university adult education programme with my voluntary responsibilities for the Society and the Lincolnshire Trust was exacting in terms of time and concentration. They were also critical years for my chairmanship of the England Committee of the Conservancy with the transition from Nature Conservancy to Nature Conservancy Council in 1973. All those commitments had often involved sacrifice of leisure time and the curtailment of holidays, and Mary had had to take more than a fair share of the management of home and garden at a time when our daughters were taking exams and making decisions which would determine their future careers. A full-time job with the Society would be demanding, but it would release me from the pressure of trying to reconcile two major obligations. It would also give me the opportunity, as Michael Holton had said, to spend a further period of service in promoting the cause which I had espoused thirty years earlier.

With Michael's advice the Society submitted an application to the Carnegie Trust and I had discussions with Lady Albermarle, the Chairman of the Trustees. They subsequently made a grant of £25,000 to the Society spread over five years for my employment, and the Executive Committee straightway confirmed my appointment as the Society's first General Secretary (and David Robinson followed me in the university post).

Committee Structure and Implications
In parallel with the constitutional changes and the strengthening of the secretariat we also undertook a review of the Society's committee structure and functions. In order to deal more efficiently with the increasing load of business we had set up two advisory groups in 1965, one on conservation and the other on administration and publicity. Both groups enabled us to draw on the expertise and experience of many more people from the Trusts in addition to Council members, and by 1970 both were playing a vital role in the Society's advisory and support services to Trusts.

Education, Promotion and Public Relations
The Administration and Publicity Group was reconstituted in 1968 as the Education and Public Relations Committee under the chairmanship for several years of Sir Thomas Barlow. That dealt with an increasingly wide range of topics including national advertising, the production of educational material such as wall charts; the development of a sales business; the promotion of nature trails; the production of a magazine for Trusts, and the organisation of the biennial conferences. Some of these deserve special mention.

A Magazine for Trusts

Through the biennial conferences and through bulletins from our headquarters and visits by staff we had sought to disseminate information of common interest among the Trusts. There was a growing demand, however, for a newsletter or magazine for circulation not just to Trusts' officers and activists but to all members. Discussions with a national publishing company to take over an existing countryside magazine came to nothing, and after discussion during 1969 in the Education and Public Relations Committee and in the Council, the Executive Committee put forward a proposal for an eight-page magazine to be produced by SPNR three times a year (in the event we could only fund a twice-yearly issue) for circulation by Trusts to all their members. The magazine would carry information about conservation issues, developments and practices of common interest and concern, and news and articles of particular local interest, and would when appropriate express the agreed views of the Trusts' movement on national problems. Like the biennial conferences it would help to foster a sense of unity and cohesion in the movement without in any way infringing the Trusts' local autonomy and initiative. It would complement Trusts' own newsletters and by covering national and background information and events enable them to publish more local news. To pay for this publication and for an expanding sales service which was also proposed contributions by the Trust to the Society would have to be increased from one shilling to two shillings per member. The increase was accepted by all the Trusts and the first issue of *Conservation Review* appeared in autumn 1970.

In an editorial note in that first issue we explained that the *Review* was intended to convey news about national developments in nature conservation, about the activities of the various Trusts and about the work of the Society in supporting and assisting them. We expressed the hope that it would encourage members to redouble their efforts to build up their own Trust while giving them a sense of belonging to a wider movement.

In that first issue in autumn 1970 there were articles celebrating the Trusts' achievement in recruiting 50,000 members and the acquisition of more than 500 nature reserves. There was a list of awards made to Trusts under the 'Countryside in 1970' Countryside Awards Scheme, and an account of the biennial conference at Oxford in a particularly significant year for conservation. Six Trust appeals were featured. The Comment column expressed the hope that the new Conservative government would maintain and strengthen the measures already taken or proposed by the previous Labour administration. "The voluntary movement", it said, "will soon want to see action: on anti-pollution measures and on positive conservation through, for example, strengthening the Nature Conservancy and the Countryside Commission". That pattern of content was followed in subsequent issues, the emphasis always being on the Trusts' achievements and aspirations and the means of promoting them. New reserve acquisitions and major events, for example, were regularly reported and nature trails publicised.

Conservation Review was a modest, attractively produced publication which I still find it a pleasure to read. Producing it in-house and collecting material for it helped to ensure that headquarters staff were always in touch with current developments in the Trusts. For me that was a very important bonus. I regard *Conservation Review* as one of the highlights of my years as head of the Society's staff. It provided a unique overview of the progress of the Trusts' movement until it was replaced by the more ambitious magazine *Natural World* in 1981.

CONSERVATION
REVIEW

Autumn 1970

For Members of the County Trusts for Nature Conservation

About this review . . .

THIS review has been produced by the Society for the Promotion of Nature Reserves, the National Association of the County Conservation and Naturalists' Trusts. It is being distributed by the Trusts to all their members who are also associate members of the Society. It brings you news about national developments in nature conservation, about the activities of the various Trusts, and about the work of the Society in supporting and assisting them.

The strength of the Trusts' movement lies in its involvement of people in caring for the natural environment and its wildlife, and in its appeal to local loyalties and concerns. The independence of the Trusts and their freedom of initiative are vital, but they have recognised that they need to help and support each other and that cohesion and a sense of unity are necessary if they are to realise their potential influence as a national movement. SPNR has tried to provide a medium of association and support to strengthen the Trusts individually and collectively without interfering with their autonomy. It is hoped that this review will contribute to that end by encouraging members to redouble their efforts to build up their own Trust whilst giving them a sense of belonging to a wider movement.

Five Hundred Reserves

1970

. . . and the total still grows!

THE announcement in June of 11 new nature reserves in Northumberland by agreement between the Forestry Commission and the Northumberland and Durham Naturalists' Trust brought the total number of reserves established by County Trusts to over 500. Representing over 70% of all nature reserves in Britain, this is an impressive achievement by any standards; that it has been attained almost entirely through local voluntary effort largely within the last eight years is remarkable.

It is particularly gratifying that the total of 500 reserves has been reached during European Conservation Year but this cannot mean any slackening of effort. Nature reserves of all kinds occupy less than 0.3% of the land surface of England and Wales. There is obviously a limit to the amount of land which can be set aside as reserves, but the present tiny proportion comes nowhere near the aim of protecting a representative sample of all natural and semi-natural habitats nationally or locally.

The Nature Conservancy is currently engaged in a comprehensive review of areas of scientific interest and of its programme for selecting and establishing nature reserves. Provisional results indicate nearly 600 sites which are of national or international importance. This compares with an existing total of 127 declared and 42 proposed national reserves. In addition there are many more sites of regional or local importance.

The County Trusts agreed at the recent Oxford conference to formulate with the Conservancy a joint strategy for the acquisition of nationally important sites. Trusts will of course also be interested in acquiring sites of local importance for educational and public use.

Clearly the demand on overstretched financial resources will increase. Since 1962 the Trusts have spent over £200,000 on the purchase of some 5,000 acres of reserves. 80% of this sum was raised from local sources with the help of short-term loans of over £80,000 from the SPNR. The balance was received in grants from the SPNR and the World Wildlife Fund. Some purchases for which Trusts are currently appealing are described elsewhere in this review.

Continued on page 2, column 2.

"As President of the County Trusts Association it gives me particular pleasure to introduce 'Conservation Review' to every County Trust member in the country, and I hope you will enjoy reading it. The achievements and activities described are certainly impressive and are almost entirely due to the skill and vigour of voluntary effort and initiative. Members not only give us our basic financial support, but it is through them that our activities and influence are expanded both locally and as a national movement. Several County Trusts report record increases in membership during 1970, three have recently passed the 3,000 mark bringing the total for Britain to around 50,000. This is encouraging, but there is still a vast potential to be tapped. I therefore urge every Trust to redouble its efforts to convert into practical support the great interest which ECY and other events have created in the natural environment and the problems of its conservation.

I hope this review will give interest and encouragement to existing members and will help all Trusts to recruit new ones."

Christopher Cadbury

Mr. Cadbury welcomes Prince Philip to the Conservation tent at the East of England Show, Peterborough.

Published by the Society for the Promotion of Nature Reserves (S.P.N.R.), The Manor House, Alford, Lincs.

First number of Conservation Review, 1970

Shell/County Trust Nature Trails 1972

Taking the family for a drive? Why not make your
more interesting by walking one of the 19 nature
Shell and ACT—the Association of County (Nat
Conservation) Trusts—have arranged for your e
this summer.
    This leaflet tells you where the trails are
there. The trail leaflets themselves will be av
Service Stations in the area and at the start of
leaflets are free of charge but in some cases
small fee for car-parking.

A Nature Reserves Handbook

SPNC
Gifts catalogue 1978/79

Society for the Promotion of Nature Conservation
The Green, Nettleham, Lincoln LN2 2NR
Telephone: Lincoln (0522) 752326

*A guide to a selection of
Nature Reserves of the
Nature Conservation Trusts
and The Royal Society for
Nature Conservation 1982.*

A Trusts' Reserves Handbook

There was another publication produced by the Society with which I was especially involved. In the late 1960s suggestions were made in the County Trusts' Committee for the production of a guide to a selection of Trusts' nature reserves throughout the country. I was asked to look into the possibility. The idea was attractive for several reasons. The number and variety of Trusts' reserves was growing rapidly – 500 by 1970 – and access facilities for members and in some cases for the general public were increasingly provided. To enable more people to see their reserves would encourage more interest in the work of the Trusts and more support for it. There was another very important reason for such a guide: it would symbolise the cohesion and sense of unity which the Trusts had developed through the Society without in any way infringing their essential local autonomy. As I wrote in the introduction to the Handbook when it was eventually published: "We hope it will enable members in all Trusts to derive greater interest and enjoyment from their membership by visiting reserves outside their own locality and in so doing strengthen the feeling that they belong to a nationwide Trusts' movement".

'Eventually' published! In fact it took twelve or more years to get there! This was partly, I acknowledge, because the Handbook, although important, was not among the most urgent matters with which our small secretariat had to deal. It would have been completed earlier though if all the Trusts had produced the required information more readily. The minutes of the Council in the 1970s record frequent appeals by me for responses. The main difficulty was that, although the great majority were entirely in favour of the project, there were a few who harboured doubts and reservations largely through the fear – completely unfounded in the event - that their reserves and their volunteer wardens would be inundated by visitors and suffer as a result. In an attempt to overcome these doubts I drew up a set of criteria for reserves to be included in the Handbook which it was agreed would be available only to members of Trusts. In general the reserves would be those most likely to be of interest to visitors from other counties, especially where waymarked paths, trails and other facilities were available. Reserves held by agreement with private owners would not normally be included, nor would others considered by the Trusts to be too small, too fragile or too vulnerable to disturbance. In addition, we drew up a general set of conditions for visiting reserves to ensure that use and enjoyment did nothing to damage their vegetation or disturb the wildlife. Those conditions for visiting were set out in the introduction to the Handbook. There was one benefit from the long delay in completion, namely that we had an increasingly wide choice of reserves: there were over 1,200 of them by the end of the 1970s.

The 363 reserves described were grouped in regions – in the main those adopted by the NCC – for each of which I wrote an introduction describing the principal geological and ecological characteristics as the setting for the individual reserves. Each of these was briefly described with advice on how to get there and any special conditions of access. There was a location map for each region drawn by John Redshaw, a fair number of photographs and a few of my wife's line drawings of plants. It was offered for sale through the Trusts from 1982 onwards at the modest price of £3.50. In spite of its long gestation period, editing it was a satisfying experience, and I believe it made a valuable contribution to the progress of the Trusts' movement.

Conferences

The biennial conferences came to have a particularly significant role in the development of the Trusts' movement. Beginning at Skegness and Gibraltar Point in 1960, then in Norwich in 1962, York in 1964, Bournemouth in 1966, Canterbury in 1968, Oxford in 1970, Bangor in 1972, Brighton in 1974 and Newcastle in 1976, they all provided the opportunity for delegates from Trusts and many associated bodies to hear papers from specialists and practitioners on the latest ideas and developments in all aspects of nature conservation and environmental education. In that respect they assumed a wider national significance than simply internal Trusts' occasions. Speakers at the Oxford conference in 1970, European Conservation Year, included Max Nicholson; John Cripps, Chairman of the Countryside Commission; Ivan Hills, Chief Agent of the National Trust; Martin Holdgate, Head of the Government's new Central Scientific Unit on Pollution; Bob Boote and Peter Scott. Equally valuable were the opportunities at conferences to meet members from other Trusts, to exchange impressions and experiences and generally to bring to the association something of a 'family' atmosphere. Many friendships were made and cemented at the conferences. Field visits during the weekend enabled delegates to see at first hand some aspects of the work and achievements of the host Trust. They were all distinctively memorable occasions, landmarks in the progress of the Trusts' movement in the 1960s and 1970s.

There were other conferences arranged by the secretariat. Administration and finance were the subjects at Monks Wood in 1971 and at Losehill Hall in 1973. Among the topics discussed were Trusts' committee and group structures, subscription levels, fundraising, local authority relationships and aid. Interpretation techniques were studied at Leicester in 1975 when representatives of thirty-two Trusts attended; and the educational use of nature reserves at Gibraltar Point in 1972. The biennial conference at Bromsgrove in 1978 was devoted to Nature Reserves, the first conference in the UK on the subject for more than thirty years.

The first conference of Conservation Officers – many Trusts had such appointments by the early 1970s – was arranged in Lincolnshire in 1973 and led by Ray Collier, the local Trust's Conservation Officer. It was the first time that Trusts' professional and field staff had been brought together to exchange ideas and experiences. Regular liaison arrangements between Conservation Officers were agreed and the first of a series of periodical bulletins was issued. Among its contents were management plans, event recording, site investigation and use of tools and machinery. Another conference for Conservation Officers was held in Devon in 1975.

In addition to internal conferences, the Society played a considerable part in European Conservation Year 1970, and in 'The Countryside in 1970' conferences on whose standing, organising and public relations committees we were represented. I presented a paper to the first of those conferences in 1963 on the 'County Naturalists' Trusts', and I served throughout on Study Group 8 which, under Walter Lane's chairmanship, considered the protection of sites and objects of scientific, historic and cultural importance. We also mounted a special exhibition for ECY entitled 'What's in it for him?' illustrating the work of the County Trusts. Designed and produced by Tony Tynan and his staff at the Hancock Museum, Newcastle-upon-Tyne, it was first staged at the Forestry Commission's Jubilee Exhibition in Edinburgh in 1969 and then at the Trusts' biennial conference at Oxford in 1970. It was subsequently shown at many places in England and Wales including the Natural History Museum in London. In association with the 1970 conferences we also administered the Countryside Awards scheme, a task which we shared with CPRE and the County Councils' Association.

Nature Trails
The annual programme of Trusts' nature trails figures prominently in the minutes of the Education and Publicity Committee in the late 1960s and early 1970s. In 1967 one or two Trusts began to experiment with nature trails, basically a route on which the natural features and wildlife are described in a leaflet. It was a technique already well developed in the USA. In the following year 1968 we concluded a promotional deal with Shell which enabled the Society to channel grants of £250 each to several Trusts for setting up trails. Their number then grew steadily each year until by 1972, the last year of Shell's involvement, twenty trails were mounted in various counties in England and Wales from Northumberland to Devon and from Pembroke to Essex. The trails devised and prepared by the Trusts were almost always manned by volunteers. A brochure produced by the Society briefly describing all the trails for the year was widely available at Shell service stations and elsewhere. Trail leaflets were available on site and at Shell garages in the vicinity. AA signs guided people to the trails over a wide area.

Some trails were on Trust reserves, but the majority were on private estates, on land belonging to public authorities or on public footpaths or other rights of way. I have described in an earlier chapter how one such trail was organised in Lincolnshire, the success which it achieved in attracting public interest and support, and the benefits accruing from cooperation with other landowners. The same, I am sure, applied everywhere else. Shell ended their sponsorship after 1972, but the nature trail - sometimes in modified form - became a regular feature of many Trusts' educational and interpretative programmes.

A Sales Business
The Education and Public Relations Committee was also responsible initially for the development of a sales business. This had started in a very small way with the production – largely at Christopher Cadbury's instigation – of a set of three Christmas cards in 1963. They were followed by greetings cards, notelets, calendars and an increasing number of other small items mainly of stationery type. At a later stage a Trusts' tie with the badger motif was also produced. For illustrations we commissioned designs from some of the best wildlife artists of the time: Mary Grierson, Eileen Soper, Robert Gillmor, Eric Ennion, Dennis Harle, Norman Cusa, to mention but a few. I have kept a sample of almost all the Christmas cards, calendars and wall charts up to about 1978. They are still a pleasure to look at.

By 1972 there was a net surplus in trading of some £7,000 to the Society and £15,000 to the Trusts. We had created a Sales Officer post to arrange production of items selected by the Committee and to organise distribution to the Trusts. But the system of supplier-Society-Trust-customer was cumbersome and inhibiting of further development. It was proposed therefore to convert the business into a centralised mail order service to Trusts' members in addition to direct over-the-counter sales by Trusts. It was convincingly demonstrated that this would reduce distributing costs and relieve Trust volunteers and staff from time-consuming mail order processing. It would also reduce the amount of capital tied up by the Trusts in stocks of sales goods and enable them to concentrate on expanding sales at meetings and other outlets.

Some Trusts were initially unconvinced by the proposal fearing perhaps some loss of control over the business. At the Conference for Trusts' officers at Losehill Hall in May 1973, however, Stan Jermyn, the secretary of the Essex Trust, in a brilliant piece of advocacy convinced the doubters and carried a proposal for the development of a competitive, centralised mail order service. After further examination by a working party the proposal was adopted by the Council and put into effect for the 1975/76 season. The large meeting room at the Society's new premises at Nettleham was converted into a sales store and packing warehouse, a full-time professional Sales Officer, Anne Rule, was appointed and staff recruited locally. The response to the sales catalogues distributed by the Trusts was very encouraging, and by the third year of operation 1977/78 the turnover exceeded £200,000. In addition to the profit on sales, more than £5,000 in donations was received with orders, most of it attributable to the Trusts. In my last year as General Secretary the gross turnover had exceeded £250,000, £6,500 was received in donations, and the operation resulted in some 1100 new members being recruited for the Trusts.

Successful though it was, however, there were still some doubts about the long-term viability of the centralised sales business. It required considerable resource input from the Society including the time and attention of some of its senior officers and staff and of the Council. There were indeed complaints on more than one occasion about the time spent on considering the design of stationery or the suitability of some new item, all at the expense of basic Council business. More seriously there was doubt whether, in spite of its rapid growth, it would ever reach a point where long-term commercial viability was assured, especially since competition from other charity sources was rapidly increasing. Nevertheless the business had justified the confidence placed in it and was making a significant contribution to the income of Trusts and to their general well-being. Moreover by developing over-the-counter sales outlets the Trusts were also gaining the experience and confidence they needed to set up their own sales business which eventually many of them did.

Conservation Policy Practice and Achievement

The other Group, set up in 1966, was charged with advising on a wide range of conservation issues and practices. Within two years the scope and importance of the Group's deliberations persuaded the Society to convert it into a full committee and to invite other bodies to be represented. So was created the Conservation Liaison Committee which over the next fifteen years was the leading national body in promoting discussion and cooperation among many voluntary and statutory bodies, a role assumed after 1980 by Wildlife and Countryside Link. A list of those bodies and some of the issues they discussed and in some cases acted upon will give substance to my contention. Most of the following were regularly represented at Committee meetings; a few attended on special occasions: The Royal Society for the Protection of Birds, Botanical Society of the British Isles, Fauna Preservation Society, Nature Conservancy and its Biological Records Centre, Ministry of Agriculture, Forestry Commission, Farming and Wildlife Advisory Group and

Council for British Archaeology. As many as thirty representatives of the SPNR and the associated bodies were involved at any one time and they included many of the leading figures in their particular fields.

The Committee's terms of reference are worth quoting: first, to advise the Society and the Trusts and other voluntary bodies on all aspects of conservation research and management and arrange for publication of information; secondly, to provide a forum for discussion and exchange of ideas and experience in conservation management and to co-ordinate policies on conservation matters; thirdly, to act as a liaison body in practical conservation and research between the Nature Conservancy and the bodies represented on the Committee, and generally to promote and encourage awareness and understanding of conservation principles and their application. The matters the Committee dealt with are too numerous to detail here, but as an example in one year in 1973 their deliberations and recommendations for action where appropriate included Dutch elm disease, forestry policy, grey squirrel control, badger culling, road verge management by local authorities, straw and stubble burning, the use of Asulam in bracken control, the publication of endangered species lists, the use of herbicides on aquatic vegetation, a register of ornithological habitats, codes of conduct for wildlife conservation, and comprehensive wildlife legislation.

Servicing the Committee and follow-up action occupied much of the time of SPNR staff. I found it a particularly stimulating Committee at the leading edge of conservation planning and activity and I gave high priority to attendance. I regard it as one of the major achievements of the Society during my time with it. Its success, however, was due in no small measure to the highly competent chairmanship of my friend David Streeter, lecturer in biological sciences at the University of Sussex. David seemed to have his finger on the pulse of almost every conservation issue of the time and was highly sensitive to the political background of many of them.

The Conservation Liaison Committee promoted and influenced many policies and developments in nature conservation in the interests of the Trusts and of the conservation movement as a whole. The following achievements are especially significant.

A Biological Sites Recording Scheme
One of the first and most important projects which it undertook was the preparation of a Biological Sites Recording Scheme, designed primarily for the use of Trusts, to assist in preparing conservation policies and plans for the management of nature reserves and other sites of wildlife interest. It was devised primarily by David Streeter and Dr Franklyn Perring, the Head of the Nature Conservancy's Biological Records Centre, with advice and assistance from a number of specialists and field workers. A conference for Trusts' representatives was held at Monks Wood in June 1967 to explain the scheme which was based on the now familiar habitat and species recording cards system. It was published by the Society in 1969 as Technical Publication No 1 and distributed to Trusts for immediate use. Stocks of cards were held at the Society's headquarters and at Monks Wood. The recording system was a major contribution to nature conservation planning and management in the UK, but I suspect that most naturalists who use it today are unaware of its origins.

Technical Publication No 2, prepared by the Conservation Liaison Committee and published by the Society in 1970, was concerned with another important issue in conservation management: the introduction of plants and animals into nature reserves. Some alien species introduced into the countryside whether by design or accident have had far-reaching impacts on native wildlife, and nature reserves which often sustain specialised habitats and species are particularly vulnerable. There are, of course, quite justifiable reasons for wanting to reintroduce to nature reserves species which once occurred but which had died out because of habitat change or disturbance. The policy therefore, whilst urging that introductions to reserves be kept to a minimum, set out certain principles to be observed in considering them and recommended procedures to be followed in such cases including careful monitoring and recording of the consequences. The policy adopted by the Trusts was followed by the RSPB and other voluntary bodies and almost identically by the Nature Conservancy.

Further SPNR publications emanating from the Conservation Liaison Committee included a leaflet *Scrub Clearance – a conservation code*, and 'focussed' pamphlets on bats, badgers and marine life.

Wildlife legislation
Among the Committee's early deliberations was the problem of wildlife legislation. The principle of protecting wildlife by law had been accepted in the case of birds since the 1860s, and the Protection of Birds Act of 1954 had replaced in a single Act a succession of piecemeal Acts and the chaotic system of county schedules of protected species. By 1970 there were also Acts which provided some protection for deer and seals, and there was a demand for similar legislation in respect of badger, otter and bats. The SPNR itself was involved through the Conservation Liaison Committee in drafting a Wild Plant Protection Bill, a revised version of a bill unsuccessfully introduced into the House of Commons a few years previously. With the prospect of a further confusing proliferation of separate bills for single species or groups, the Committee set up a working party in 1970 to consider the desirability and feasibility of a comprehensive Wildlife Act. The working party, having obtained the approval of the full Committee for the general principles on which a bill should be based, began the considerable task of drafting its contents. By March 1973 it had completed the drafting of the schedules listing various degrees of protection for species, and by November of the same year the draft bill were ready to go out to wider consultation with all interested bodies.

In order to promote the case for a comprehensive measure I described the Committee's proposals to the All-Party Conservation Committee at both Houses of Parliament at Westminster on 22 November 1972. This was arranged through the parliamentary contacts of the Council for Nature of which Tim Sands had become the Secretary and of which I was then one of the joint Honorary Secretaries. I was pleased with the thoughtful reception which the proposals received from Members of both Houses of Parliament who asked that they should be printed and circulated to all Members of the All-Party Committee. An excerpt from the report of the meeting signed by Lord Craigton the Chairman, Arthur Blenkinsop MP Vice-Chairman, and John Farr MP Secretary, attached to the text of my talk concluded: "It was considered that such comprehensive legislation was desirable and should be adopted. It was agreed that Ted Smith's proposals would form a suitable starting point".

One of the MPs present at the All-Party Committee meeting was Peter Hardy one of the principal advocates of nature conservation in the Commons. Two years later he introduced as a private members' bill the Conservation of Wild Creatures and Wild Plants Bill in the drafting of which the Society played a prominent part. The Bill afforded protection to six animal species and twenty-one plants. It recognised too for the first time in parliamentary legislation the need to protect even common wild plants from unnecessary uprooting. The fully comprehensive legislation which the Society advocated was still some way off, but Peter Hardy's Act was a step towards it and elicited from the Government a request to the Nature Conservancy to conduct a wide review of wildlife legislation. The pioneering work of the Conservation Liaison Committee in this and other ways was crucially important. It has not, I believe, received the recognition which it deserved.

Concern with the protection of species in no way diminished our advocacy of the basic need to conserve habitats, especially on SSSIs and other sites of natural interest. We constantly urged the need for stronger legal protection for SSSIs which were still being destroyed and damaged in all parts of the country, and sought the support of other land owning and land-managing bodies.

Rivers and Streams

One of our special concerns was the treatment of rivers and streams and the effects of land drainage, problems with which I had become all too familiar in Lincolnshire. In collaboration with the RSPB we established relationships with the Regional Water Authorities which were set up under the Water Act 1973. We also began work on an ambitious Rivers and Wildlife Handbook. Liaison with Water Authorities resulted in meetings, most of them on a regular basis, between Trusts and Authorities in the North-West, Severn-Trent, Southern, Wessex, Yorkshire and Northumberland. Most of these resulted in the kind of consultative arrangement that I described for Lincolnshire in an earlier chapter. We found some encouragement in the re-stated requirement in the Water Act 1973 for Water Authorities 'to have regard' to the needs of conservation, and even more so when in 1981 The Wildlife and Countryside Act gave the Authorities and Internal Drainage Boards the duty to 'further' conservation. At the British Trust for Ornithology's annual conference in 1974, which marked the launch of that Trust's long-running waterways bird survey, I gave a talk on 'The Impact of Lowland River Management' describing the effects of intensive land drainage and river management on birds and other wildlife, and suggesting ways in which damage could be mitigated. My paper was published in *Bird Study* in December 1975. I had spoken on the same theme under the title 'Conservation Aspects of River Management' at the annual course for technical officers of River Authorities at Southampton in April 1972. The RSPB-RSNC *Rivers and Wildlife Handbook* was eventually launched in 1984 at a ceremony in London attended by William Waldegrave, Parliamentary Under-Secretary for the Environment. I spoke on behalf of the RSNC on that occasion.

Nature Conservation and Agriculture

There were many other land use and environmental problems which occupied the attention of the Society's Council and Conservation Liaison Committee during the 1970s, all of them affecting the work and welfare of the Trusts in one way or another. It was a time in particular when intensity of cultivation and production in agriculture was being seriously questioned. Two almost complementary Statements were of particular significance in this respect, one entitled 'Nature Conservation and Agriculture' by the Nature Conservancy Council; the other 'New Agricultural Landscapes: Issues, Objectives and Action' from the Countryside Commission. Both were concerned with the radical landscape changes and the consequent decline in wildlife that had resulted from agricultural intensification in the previous thirty-five years. Both made proposals to solve some of the problems. The NCC's document issued in 1976 called for a national land use policy in which, whilst agriculture would remain the primary land use over most of the country, nature conservation would be recognised as an important national objective, and in defined areas would be accorded priority. The NCC also emphasised the importance of nature reserves and SSSIs whose owners they urged should be asked to give formal notice before changing the agricultural or forestry management of such a site.

The Countryside Committee's document, a follow-up to their earlier 'New Agricultural Landscapes' study, called for a major effort to conserve lowland countryside, to stop unnecessary destruction of features of landscape value, and make advice more freely available to landowners and users, and achieve higher standards of planning control. Both policy statements were closely studied by the SPNC Council and committees, and the spring 1977 number of *Conservation Review* was largely devoted to them and to a supporting article by Dr Norman Moore, Chief Advisory Officer to NCC. Our editorial comment in *Conservation Review* which reflected attitudes in the Society's Council, welcomed both documents but was critical of certain aspects of them. NCC's failure, for example, to consider the concept of conservation zones, areas of countryside which retain more variety of wildlife habitat and are often the setting for nature reserves; their failure also to give more attention to the possibility of improving practices in modern farming technology. All agreed, however, on the need to sustain the debate about land use and conservation.

While seeking change in agricultural policies and practices, the Trusts recognised the need to develop cooperation with the farming community wherever possible. The National Conference of Farming and Conservation Interests which I attended at Silsoe in 1969 resulted in the formation of the Farming and Wildlife Advisory Group which aimed to promote similar local groups and mount exercises involving farmers and conservationists. As evidence of the importance which the Society attached to this initiative we agreed to fund the appointment of a full-time FWAG Advisory Officer jointly with the RSPB. Likewise in most counties the Trusts were among the principal promoters of local FWAGs.

The Future of the Nature Conservancy

The status and strength of the Nature Conservancy was of particular importance to the Trusts most of whom had established close working relationships with the Conservancy's regional staff and were benefiting in various ways from work carried out at its experimental stations. Monks Wood, with its breadth of research on habitats and species and pollution and its facilities and accommodation for training and for conferences, was especially appreciated by the Trusts. It was a matter of great concern, therefore, when the Government announced its intention in 1972 of splitting the Conservancy by creating a Nature Conservancy Council to discharge the conservation functions, whilst leaving the research element in the Natural Environment Research Council within which the Conservancy had

Speakers at the Trusts' biennial conference, Oxford 1970:

top: Bob Boote, Deputy Director, The Nature Conservancy (later Director General, Nature Conservancy Council)

centre: Peter Scott

bottom: TV and radio personality Johnny Morris

Tim Sands
Joint Assistant Secretary
SPNC 1975

Freddie Thomas
Administrative Officer
SPNC 1977

David Streeter
Chairman SPNC Conservation
Liaison Committee

The impacts of Lowland River Management

Reprinted from 'Bird Study'
Vol. 22, No. 4   December 1975

1975

POLICY ON
INTRODUCTIONS TO
NATURE RESERVES

S.P.N.R.
CONSERVATION LIAISON
COMMITTEE

TECHNICAL PUBLICATION No. 2

1970

Wildlife and the Law - the case for a comprehensive approach

The text of a talk given to the All-Party Conservation
Committee of both Houses of Parliament by
A. E. Smith, O.B.E., M.A.

1972

Monks Wood Experimental Station 1972.

operated since that Council's establishment in 1965. The relationship between the two bodies had been a troubled one. Many in the Nature Conservancy considered that it had suffered financially and that its broad conservation purposes were being inhibited by NERC. NERC officials on the other hand complained that for a research body the Conservancy had sought too high a public profile, as for instance in the leading role that it took in the 'Countryside in 1970' conferences and in European Conservation Year 1970.

At their meeting in February 1972 the County Trusts' Committee strongly supported the view that the Conservancy's research and executive function should not be separated, and invited individual Trusts to make representations to that effect to their local Members of Parliament. An article in the spring number of *Conservation Review* that year recounted how the problems had arisen, emphasised the importance of the Conservancy's executive and managerial role in conservation which was different from that of any other part of NERC and had suffered from inadequate resources. Since 1968, the article observed, NERC had been able to find less than £100,000 for the purchase of new nature reserves by the Nature Conservancy, whilst County Trusts alone in the same period had voluntarily raised over £200,000 for the purpose. The article called for the restoration to the Conservancy of an independent status with access and responsibility to a single Government Minister. "Given the degree of public and scientific support which it enjoys", the article concluded, "the Conservancy should be perfectly capable of standing on its own feet". By the time the Council of the Society met in September (having replaced the County Trusts' Committee) the Nature Conservancy Council Bill had been published and was virtually certain to be enacted. I commented that, regrettable though the 'split' would be, there was one important gain in the Bill which could be of particular benefit to Trusts, namely the power for the NCC to make grants to official and voluntary bodies and private landowners for land acquisition and management purposes. Grant-aid from the Nature Conservancy had previously been confined to research and survey projects. We now had to bring to an end, I suggested, the difficulties and uncertainties which had beset the Conservancy and make every effort to ensure the success of the new system and to press the Government to provide adequate resources to the NCC to fulfil its functions satisfactorily.

Under the Nature Conservancy Council Act 1973 the new NCC regained a large measure of independence, but it was at the expense of losing its major research function. That was now discharged by a new body the Institute of Terrestrial Ecology from which the NCC was expected to obtain and pay for research. It was, however, allowed to conduct some research of its own, that which was necessary for conservation requirements at local and regional level.

When I first read the Bill I was astonished to find that although there was provision for statutory Committees for Scotland and Wales there was none for England. I straightway made contact with Lord Craigton and several other members of the All-Party Conservation Committee to seek an amendment in the House of Lords to give England the same provision as Scotland and Wales. I found encouraging support, and when an amendment was proposed, the Government, whose case was feeble and illogical, readily conceded and England got its statutory Committee.

Rutland Water filling up, 1975.

Redgrave and Lopham Fens, Suffolk.

Coppicing in Bradfield Woods, Suffolk.

302

– 15 –

Nature Reserves: The Changing Role of the SPNR

O NE OF the main sources of satisfaction in my years with the Society was the expansion of the number and variety of nature reserves established by the Trusts. When the County Trusts' Committee was formed in 1960 the first few Trusts had about fifty reserves covering some 4,000 acres; by 1970 there were 500; by 1974 the number had grown to 800 and the acreage to 60,000. Before I retired as General Secretary in 1978 the number had passed 1,000 and the acreage was approaching 90,000. The reserves represented an exciting variety of landscapes and habitats: woodlands of all kinds including valley oak woods; coppice-with-standards woodlands on lowland claylands; alder carrs by streams, pine and birch on mountains and heaths; moors and heathlands and downs; ancient meadows; wetlands; saltmarshes, sand-dunes, estuaries and cliffs; limestone pavements, and mountain country in the Pennines, Wales and Scotland. Many of the reserves were already SSSIs; some have subsequently been accorded National Nature Reserve status.

At SPNR headquarters we were able to keep in constant touch with the nature reserve acquisition process through processing grant applications, through site visits and personal contacts, through Trusts' newsletters, and *Conservation Review* where new acquisitions were regularly reported.

Every Trust had its own reserves acquisition policy which was revised from time to time to reflect changing priorities, new threats, enhanced knowledge and availability of resources for acquisition and management. As a means of conservation the nature reserve had stood the test of time, but by the 1970s other measures had become increasingly necessary and important for conservation purposes: providing advice to planners and land users, influencing the treatment of the environment and its wildlife on a wider scale, and using education to create a better understanding of the natural world and the need to protect it. Nonetheless the purposes of nature reserves, so perceptively defined in the 1947 report of the Wildlife Conservation Special Committee (Cmd. 7122), remained entirely valid. Indeed the 'reservoir' function had assumed even more importance as intensive land use had put greater pressures on landscapes and wildlife habitats.

The demand for the use of nature reserves for research and education had also exceeded the expectation of 1947.

More than twenty-five years on from Cmd. 7122, however, it seemed opportune to re-examine the policies by which Trusts selected and established reserves. The decision to do so was further prompted by the expected publication of *A Nature Conservation Review*, the NCC's massive review of more than 700 biological sites of national importance. There was now an opportunity to work out a comprehensive strategy for nature reserves which took account of regional and local as well as national programmes of acquisition, and to identify the part which the Trusts and other voluntary bodies and landowners could play in such a strategy. I described the need for this in an article in the autumn 1975 issue of *Conservation Review*, and after discussion in the Society's Council and committees we put forward a case to the NCC who offered a contract to the Society for a two-year study. We appointed a young biologist, Dr Cameron Easton as Project Officer to collect and analyse data. He was directly responsible to me as the General Editor and nominated officer for the contract, and the project was supervised by a small Steering Group consisting of David Streeter and Ian Mercer from the Society and Dr Brian O'Connor Deputy Director of the NCC.

The Study appraised existing reserve selection criteria, both scientific and functional, used by the Trusts; assessed the effectiveness of various forms of reserve tenure; reviewed the progress in formulating and implementing reserves programmes; assessed the financial and other resources available for acquisition and management, and analysed existing reserves held by Trusts in terms of habitat coverage and in relation to SSSIs and to the site gradings in *A Nature Conservation Review*. Information was collected by discussion with officers of Trusts some of whom were visited for the purpose, with NCC officers and other voluntary bodies; by questionnaires, literature searches, and some field survey mainly concerned with management problems and resources. We presented preliminary conclusions from the Study in three papers at the Trusts' Conference on Nature Reserves at Bromsgrove in Worcestershire in April 1978. Cameron Easton left shortly afterwards and I completed the drafting of the conclusions and recommendations and the general editing of the two volumes under the title *A Nature Reserves Study*.

The Study presented a detailed picture of the nature reserves holdings, policies and management practices of the Trusts in the mid-1970s. Among its principal conclusions and recommendations were that the Trusts with SPNR support should seek more resources for site conservation, training of volunteers and strengthening of staff, including a Conservation or Reserves Officer and wardens to supplement the work of volunteers; prepare more management plans and carry out more regular monitoring of reserves; seek an expansion of NCC grant-aid to assist in purchase and management of reserves and encourage Local Authorities to become involved in acquisition of sites and in providing Trusts with resources to manage them.

The Study was a major undertaking and occupied much of my time in my last months as General Secretary of the Society and beyond. Whilst much of the statistical information is now only of historical interest, the Study made an important contribution to the progress of nature reserve expansion and improved management into the 1980s. It set the Trusts' work into a wider national context and it influenced the NCC's policies in making grant-aid available to the Trusts.

In processing grant-aid applications from Trusts for property purchase we became familiar with many of the new reserves being acquired in the 1960s and 1970s. This was not only through descriptions in applications, but also in some cases by visiting the site to offer advice and assistance, especially where acquisition negotiations were difficult and complicated. Way back in the 1950s before the County Trusts' Committee was set up I had been involved in my Lincolnshire Trust capacity in an attempt to secure protection and appropriate management for the Hills and Holes at Barnack which was only two or three miles beyond Lincolnshire's southern boundary. This long abandoned quarry in the oolitic limestone had supplied the stone for many of the medieval cathedrals, churches and monasteries throughout East Anglia. It was worked out by the end of the Middle Ages and had developed a superb limestone flora including man, bee and fragrant orchids and pasqueflower in profusion. Grazing which had been practised had ceased by the 1950s, coarse grasses were becoming dominant and the site was being invaded by turkey oaks from a nearby plantation. It was urgently in need of care and management. Since there was still no Trust in Northamptonshire I tried to arouse some interest among local naturalists including John Chandler, a leading Northamptonshire botanist with whom I had considerable correspondence. I also arranged a meeting with the Agent for the Burghley Estates, John Langton, who after retirement returned to live in his native village of Langton near Spilsby in Lincolnshire. Although little came of that meeting immediately, it paved the way for later negotiations with the Estate which led to a lease of part of the site to the Northamptonshire Trust and eventually to National Nature Reserve status for the whole of it.

Another exciting project with which I had some direct involvement was Rutland Water. The vast reservoir project was originally planned by the former Welland and Nene River Board, and having viewed the proposed site I accompanied officers of the Leicestershire and Rutland Trust to a meeting with officers and members of the Board where we were able to set in motion negotiations which led eventually to the creation of the nature reserve and to the Trust's status as its manager. I also had a hand in the appointment of the first warden of the reserve for which we secured grant-aid for the Trust.

There were several instances where the Society was asked to acquire a site because the Trust concerned did not have the resources for it. One such was Cors Goch in Anglesey, an area of fen and limestone scarp of national importance which was purchased by the Society in 1962 and handed on to the North Wales Trust which was then in process of formation. I have already mentioned the cases of Whiteford Burrows and the Ffestiniog Woods. In other instances where the Trust was in difficulty in meeting the costs of purchase in spite of the usual level of grant-aid we were able to find extra money for them. Redgrave and Lopham Fens in Suffolk was a good example. These Fens in the headwaters of the Waveney were the finest of the East Anglian valley fens, and I renewed my acquaintance with them more than thirty years later when my daughter Helen went to live at the edge of them and became a leading authority on the great raft spider one of their outstanding features.

We also provided the Nature Conservancy with funding to enable them to meet purchase costs in excess of the official valuation in the case of Wye and Crundale Downs in Kent on condition that they established a Joint Advisory Committee with the Trust. A similar arrangement was in negotiation in 1969 for

Martin Down that lovely stretch of downland on the Dorset-Hampshire border for which we had already sought the interest of Hampshire County Council and the Commoners on behalf of the Hampshire and Dorset Trusts. Unfortunately the Nature Conservancy was unsuccessful in acquiring it at that stage. Whilst being willing to assist the purchase of important sites we were very reluctant to get involved in management. That condition applied to two sites which we were asked by Trusts to acquire in 1973, one within the Cotswold Water Park in Gloucestershire, the other Long Meadow in Wiltshire.

We also became involved in 1971 in efforts to save the nationally important area of limestone pavement at Gait Barrows in Silverdale in North Lancashire. The pavement was being destroyed by the extraction of the weathered limestone for sale as rockery material. Whilst the business did not have planning permission, the owner of the site was able to continue extraction by exploiting the weaknesses of the planning system. He was reputedly willing to sell the site, but only at a price well in excess of the District Valuer's valuation. The Nature Conservancy therefore invited the SPNR and the Lancashire Trust to discuss the possibility of putting together a funding package to enable the Trust to acquire the site or to find the difference between the asking price and the DV's valuation to enable the NC to do so. When the former seemed to be the more feasible option we made considerable progress in the search for the ten to twelve thousand pounds that would be required to purchase the vital central area of the site. A new approach was made to the owner, but he was unwilling to consider selling to the Trust. After another five years of frustrating negotiation the NCC at last succeeded in purchasing the site, an outcome I refer to in my later chapter 'The Conservancy Years'.

The most important case in which the Society had a direct involvement was the purchase of Monks Park and Felsham Hall Woods at Bradfield in Suffolk. These were two of the finest ancient coppice-with-standards woods in East Anglia, particularly valuable because they had a recorded history of at least 700 years of coppice management which had been sustained in recent times by the use of coppice produce for manufacturing rakes, scythe handles and other wooden tools by a local rural industry Welnetham Woodwork. A large part of Monks Park Wood – which had once belonged to the Abbey of Bury St Edmunds – had been clear-felled for agriculture in 1966, but a temporary Tree Preservation Order, later confirmed after a Public Inquiry, had prevented further destruction. In 1969 the remaining areas were offered for sale together with the Welnetham factory as a result of a liquidation. It was important to ensure their future before any further attempts were made to fell them or radically change their management.

Several local people who were prepared to support the purchase of the woods by a conservation body and to operate the factory approached various organisations for help including the Suffolk Trust and the Society. The Trust indicated that it was in no position to take on management responsibilities, so the requests were considered by the Society's Executive Committee in June 1969. They had received a report on the scientific and historical interest of the woods from Drs. Rackham and Dymond of Cambridge University, and they invited the Nature Conservancy's Deputy Regional Officer Colin Ranson to the meeting to advise. He reported that the Conservancy intended to schedule the woods as an SSSI. In view of the Suffolk Trust's inability to act, the Committee decided to make funds available for the purchase and to support the local group in launching a public appeal for funds. The secretary of the group Mrs Litchfield attended the meeting and was congratulated by the Chairman on her efforts to win support for the purchase of the woods. He assured her that the Society would continue to supply raw material to the rake factory which she and her husband intended to buy, and would ensure that that policy would continue if management responsibility passed to another body in the future. The 103 acres of Felsham Hall Wood were purchased in 1970 followed by the remaining 58 acres of Monk's Park Wood in 1971 and 1978. An Advisory Committee chaired by Tom Barlow, a member of the Society's Executive Committee, was established. A woodman and a warden were employed and the coppicing regime was sustained. The ownership and management of the woods was passed eventually to a much strengthened Suffolk Trust, but without the Society's actions at a critical time one of the finest woodland National Nature Reserves in the country might well have been destroyed.

Those developments occurred at a time when I was returning to full-time work with the University after my four years of partial secondment, and whilst I visited Bradfield Woods and met the local group, much of the negotiation and arrangements for management were very competently handled by Wilf Dawson with support from Tom Barlow, Colin Ranson, Max Walters and others.

When the County Trusts' Committee was formed in 1959 the Society still held a mixed bag of nine nature reserves in various parts of the country. Most of them had come into its possession before and immediately after the Second World War as gifts from individuals and local naturalists' organisations. They were looked after by local groups or individuals; some were maintained in reasonable condition, others had deteriorated through lack of management like the little fritillary meadow at Mickfield in Suffolk. By far the most important of them was Woodwalton Fen in Cambridgeshire, one of the most notable of the fenland relicts, which owed its survival to the generosity of Charles Rothschild who acquired it for the Society in the early years of the last century. Like some of the others it posed formidable management problems. Lowering of the surrounding water table by more intensive land drainage and consequent drying out of the Fen had allowed invasion of scrub and woodland which by 1950 was dominating much of the reserve. In 1954 therefore the Society had taken the sensible step of transferring the Fen to the Nature Conservancy on a long lease, retaining its own interest through a Joint Advisory Committee on which the Society and the NCC each appointed four representatives together with a Chairman agreed by both parties. It was a Committee which I had the pleasure to chair for twenty years following my retirement from the Nature Conservancy Council in 1978.

Once Trusts' representatives had a working majority on the Society's Council the decision was taken to lease most of the other reserves to appropriate Trusts, and by 1968 this had been done in all but a few cases. Here too the Society retained its interest when appropriate by appointing a representative on the reserve management committee and by receiving annual reports.

With Trusts covering the whole country it was not anticipated that the Society would henceforth need to acquire reserves itself or be directly involved in management except where a Trust for some reason was unable to act. Such a situation in fact arose in 1969 in the case of Bradfield Woods as I have just described. Many Trust appeals for property purchase had benefited from Christopher Cadbury's generosity and he had earlier enabled the Norfolk Trust to acquire some of its most important reserves. Christopher, however, had his own ambitions for establishing reserves which in the first instance at least he wished to realise through the Society. There were two places dear to his heart from childhood and family holidays. One of them was the delightful Welcombe and Marsland Valleys which fall down to the sea on the north Devon-Cornwall border. Beginning in 1959 with the purchase of the lower Welcombe Valley, Christopher by painstaking negotiation personally conducted, often at weekends, with owners of numerous plots, eventually put together a reserve of some 520 acres in the two valleys which he transferred to the Society. In 1972 he also gave the Society the house at the bottom of the Marsland Valley for occupation by a warden. The annual rental income from property already purchased would meet some of the cost and Christopher offered to guarantee the balance initially for three years. A warden was duly appointed and the reserves were managed by the Society for the next twenty years. A committee with representatives of the Society and the Devon and Cornwall Trusts was appointed to oversee the management.

For me visits to Welcombe and Marsland, usually combined with visits to west country Trusts and occasionally with family holidays, were a real bonus. The banks of primroses – I have never seen them in such profusion – the fritillary butterflies and the dippers and grey wagtails and buzzards, and the rock pools on the shore were a delight long remembered by our children. Thanks be to Christopher! It is fitting that in this reserve that he loved a memorial stone plaque – unveiled by Sir David Attenborough in 1997 – commemorates Christopher's outstanding contribution to the conservation of Britain's wildlife.

Another place with which Christopher had family connections was Benmore Coigach in Wester Ross, and there he succeeded in 1975/6 in acquiring a 13,500 acre estate of mountain, moorland and birchwood, a spectacular wilderness overlooking the Summer Isles at the mouth of Loch Broom. At about the same time he took the initiative in aquiring the Rahoy Estate on the peninsula of Morvern in Argyle, an area especially notable for its arctic-alpine flora. The World Wildlife Fund and private owners also contributed to the costs of the purchases. The Scottish Wildlife Trust – which was initially more enthusiastic about Rahoy than about Benmore Coigach – was brought into joint management of the Rahoy Hills Reserve as it became known, to the purchase of which it had also contributed. John and Faith Raven, who played an important role in local management, added part of their adjoining Ardtornish Estate to the reserve.

The Society's Council and Executive Committee had gratefully accepted these Devon and Scottish reserves for which Christopher had provided initial endowment. There was some concern about the additional responsibilities for the small secretariat, but whilst there was some extra work involved in employing wardens, managing the reserves caused little distraction especially since Christopher himself was always actively involved. And eventually of course it was all to the benefit of the Devon and Scottish Trusts.

Similar concern had been expressed two years earlier when Christopher purchased the Seychelles island of Aride for the Society. Managing a remote island thousands of miles away did indeed seem a daunting proposition, but again Christopher himself made most of the arrangements for management and the involvement of the secretariat was fairly minimal. On a wildlife cruise visit to the Seychelles Christopher had been captivated by the wealth and beauty of the island's wildlife. Its flora was outstanding and it was second only to Aldebra in that part of the Indian Ocean for the variety of its breeding seabirds. The political situation in the Seychelles at that time was volatile and a foreign body acquiring land had to tread with particular care. Christopher wisely negotiated an agreement with the Seychelles National Parks and Nature Conservancy Commission for Aride to be declared a Special Nature Reserve, and he was appointed a member of the Commission. He brought together a small management group of people living or working in the Seychelles all with special knowledge of the islands. One of these was Tony Beamish who produced a film of the island's wildlife. The management group and a series of dedicated wardens appointed by the Society managed to sort out the problems that inevitably arose from time to time. Christopher was always anxious that I should visit Aride, but Mary and I were anxious at that time to take holidays in Europe and the opportunity to go to the Seychelles did not arise. The acquisition and establishment of the Aride reserve was one of Christopher's most remarkable achievements. It was an important contribution to international nature conservation and it enhanced the reputation of the Society. It deserves to be more fully described, but it had little relevance to the main work of the Society in assisting and advising the local Trusts in the UK.

The same is true of New Island and two smaller ones in the Falklands that Christopher acquired for the Society in association with the Fauna Preservation Society, although in that case management was the responsibility of the FPS and the SPNR did little more than hold the freehold.

Back in the UK, acquisition of the wetland site of Upton Warren and the rich grassland of Eades Meadow with its rare meadow saffron in his home county of Worcestershire was funded largely by Christopher. Both were acquired for the SPNR to be managed by the county Trust on a long lease. The same applied to Martham Broad in that case to be leased to the Norfolk Trust. Freehold ownership of all these properties was eventually transferred to the Trusts in question.

Funding the Nature Reserves

For nature reserve purchases the Trusts continued to make full use of the Society's Nuffield and Pilgrim Funds and of the World Wildlife Fund's grant-aid. In 1970 alone, for example, Trusts established more than ninety new reserves totalling some 4,700 acres. For those purchases six Trusts took Nuffield Fund loans amounting to nearly £11,000; twelve received £4,650 in grants from the Pilgrim Fund and from another fund established by Christopher Cadbury; and sixteen had WWF grants amounting to £10,450. There could scarcely have been more convincing evidence of the value of all these Funds. They were clearly fulfilling the purpose for which they were established.

What Trusts now needed, however, increasingly urgently, was financial assistance for the employment of staff for administration and nature reserve management. Without it not only would further development be inhibited, but volunteer input would become increasingly frustrated by the sheer volume and complexity of the work.

The Carnegie UK Trust

When the Carnegie UK Trust announced in 1968 that countryside projects would be eligible for grants during its next quinquennium we made an immediate approach to them to put the case for financial assistance for Trusts for staff appointments. The Trustees were impressed by our application and agreed to make available a fund of £30,000 for five years from 1969 to 1973 to enable the Trusts to appoint administrative or conservation officers or nature reserve wardens; and to provide educational facilities in nature reserves and elsewhere in the countryside for public use and benefit. Grants for staff were to be spread over three years on a reducing scale to a total maximum of £12,000. Applications would be made through the SPNR who would make an assessment of them and advise on their preparation, but payment would be made directly to the applicant Trusts. These and other conditions were embodied in a joint policy statement signed in December 1968 by David Lowe, the Secretary of the Carnegie UK Trust, and by me for the Society.

That the Carnegie fund was a very important and timely break-through into funding was immediately apparent by the response from the Trusts. In the first year fourteen Trusts received grants amounting to over £15,000, and by the end of the third year the fund was almost exhausted. Impressed with the use being made of it, the Trustees agreed to extend it and gave the Society discretion to use some of the money to assist smaller Trusts, in some cases on the basis of agreed cooperative schemes. At the end of the five years the Carnegie Trust had granted a total of £38,000 to more than thirty Trusts to assist the appointment of eighteen Administrative Officers, ten Conservation Officers and six field officers and wardens. Although the Trustees were not able to extend the fund for a further period, they did assist two or three more appointments by smaller Trusts, and they continued to make aid available for educational and interpretative projects such as visitor centres, mobile units and nature trails. As I have already described, the Carnegie Trust made another significant contribution to the SPNC by providing a substantial part of the funding required to enable the Society to appoint me as its first General Secretary in 1974.

I was very fortunate in the two Carnegie Trust Secretaries with whom I had to deal in the ten years in which the Trust provided financial assistance to the Society and the County Trusts. David Lowe with whom I negotiated the original Fund in 1968 was unfailingly helpful and encouraging, a wise counsellor and a good personal friend. I always enjoyed my twice-yearly meetings with him in London, and once during a family holiday in Scotland visited him at the Carnegie Trust's headquarters in Dunfermline and at his home there. He acted as one of the consultants for the SPNR-RSPB merger negotiations in 1972. His successor at Carnegie Michael Holton also became a personal friend, and as already described was equally supportive.

The Society was able to supplement and replenish the original Pilgrim and Nuffield Funds to assist land acquisition by loans and grants, first by a generous donation from Christopher Cadbury, and after 1973 by the Paul Ayres Memorial Fund of £105,000 derived from a gift and a legacy from Mr H J Newlin. At the end of my period as General Secretary in 1978 the Society also received a loan of £250,000 for ten years from an anonymous donor for the purpose of assisting the purchase of land or property for nature conservation purposes.

The Countryside Commission

Another important source of funding became available after the creation of the Countryside Commission by the Countryside Act of 1968. The Commission, provided with necessary powers, offered grants for the purchase of land especially of landscape and amenity value, and for the provision of facilities for public enjoyment and understanding of the countryside. We concluded an agreement with the Commission in 1972 defining the conditions and procedures for grant applications from Trusts. As in the case of the Carnegie Trust, the Commission asked that such applications be channelled through the Society. Over the next few years most of the Trusts received grants from the Commission ranging from small projects to substantial land acquisitions and new visitor centres. Among them – to cite just a few examples – were the purchase of Castle Woods in West Wales, Windmill Hill in Worcestershire, Swanage Quarries in Dorset, Strensall Common in Yorkshire and visitor centres at Gibraltar Point Lincolnshire, Fyne Court Somerset, Haverfordwest in West Wales and a purpose built mobile centre for Dorset.

As with Carnegie and the WWF, channelling Countryside Commission applications through the Society proved to be of real benefit to the Trusts. We had gained useful experience in framing applications to the particular grant-aiding bodies and we were able to advise Trusts accordingly. Every application and its outcome was reported to the Society's Council. As with the other grant-aiding bodies we had established good working relations with the staff at the Countryside Commission and they respected our endorsement of applications, very few of which failed. Understanding between the Society and the Commission was also helped by collaboration in other fields such as the regional conferences held to discuss the Commission's 'New Agricultural Landscapes' report. It was further evidence of the value that the Commission placed on the work of the Trusts that they invited the Society to put forward names for possible appointment to National Park Planning Boards and Committees to represent the interests of nature conservation.

Local Authorities

Since the great majority of Trusts are county-based bodies it was natural that they should look to their County Councils for support and assistance. In some counties there was a close association from the outset between the Trust and the County Council, especially where the Council was actively involved in countryside management or where the Trust attracted the interest of influential councillors or officers. The recommendation of the 1966 'Countryside in 1970' conference that County Councils should establish Countryside Committees with a proportion of co-opted members from a range of relevant bodies offered a new point of contact with the Councils for those Trusts who secured membership. Unfortunately the recommendation was not as widely adopted as had been hoped, and in several cases where a committee was created it was in an advisory rather than a statutory role and so had no direct control of funds.

Walter Lane, the Clerk of Lindsey County Council, who had spoken on County Council-Trusts relationships at the Skegness conference in 1960 and who chaired the 'Countryside in 1970' conference group on the role of local authorities, provided helpful guidance notes on the subject in the 1966 SPNR Handbook. He spoke again at the Trusts' Bangor conference in 1972, and arranged for an article on County Trusts to appear in the County Council's Gazette. The article published in October 1972 described the grant-aid already being given to Trusts by County Councils, and emphasised in particular the value of grants for the employment of staff which resulted in more and more effective voluntary input. To enable the Society to offer advice and guidance in the matter, Trusts agreed to provide information about local authority assistance of all kinds which they were receiving. Out of twenty-six Trusts in that category eleven received contributions from their Councils for administrative support, five of those in amounts ranging from £1,000 to £3,500 a year, and the others in amounts from £20 to £370. Other grants from County Councils were for a variety of purposes such as property purchase – Yorkshire, for instance, received £6,000 for the purchase of Wheldrake Ings, and Essex £2,500 for Colne Point – and educational projects. Whilst I have no reliable information after 1972 I believe that the grant situation improved somewhat after local government reorganisation in 1974. Most of those Trusts with existing grants seemed to have retained them, some down to the present day.

The far-reaching changes in local government organisation which followed The Local Government Act of 1973 created problems for Trusts, in particular the need to be in contact with more than three times the previous number of planning authorities created by the transfer of most planning control powers from counties to the new district councils. The implications of this were considered by the Society's Council at meetings in 1972 and 1973 when serious concern was expressed about the weakening of the county planning authorities and the possible dispersal of their staff. A number of Trusts – Yorkshire, Lincolnshire and Somerset, for example – were drastically affected by the dismemberment of their historic counties. It was agreed that if asked to do so the Society should offer guidance and assistance in such cases.

Another result of reorganisation was the disappearance of the statutory Countryside Committees which were either disbanded or replaced by advisory groups. It was suggested that Trusts should seek financial support from the new district authorities, and the Society was asked to offer guidance in making such applications. In the Trusts' movement as a whole in the 1970s the amount of assistance provided by local authorities of all kinds was somewhat disappointing. Much more had to be done to convince them of the real and potential value of the environmental and educational work of the Trusts. That process was assisted in the 1980s by changing attitudes and policies towards the environment.

The Nature Conservancy Council

The Nature Conservancy's powers to make grants was confined to research, survey and monitoring projects. Whilst they interpreted that provision as liberally as possible and assisted a number of Trusts, the scope was necessarily limited. When the Nature Conservancy Council secured much wider grant-aiding powers, therefore, there were expectations of more financial help for Trusts, and the Society held discussions with the NCC to explore ways in which aid could most effectively be deployed. After those discussions in 1977 the NCC issued an important declaration of intent, reaffirming their support for a strong voluntary nature conservation movement to mobilise "the enthusiasm, knowledge and skills of many sections of the community for conserving the natural environment of which wildlife is a major component. Voluntary bodies offered opportunity for participation in practical conservation, and also provided a channel for the expression of public opinion on environmental issues". The statement went on to emphasise the crucial importance of the independence of the voluntary bodies, and the need to develop their capacity "to tackle important tasks for the NCC and bring identifiable benefit to their own organisations". The NCC would provide funds to enable the Trusts to carry out specific functions without being related to particular staff posts. The statement listed several areas of Trusts' activity which the NCC was especially concerned to encourage: site safeguard, education and interpretation, survey and monitoring, and the participation of volunteer members and others in all those activities.

Under the programme agreed with the Society each Trust was to receive £5,000 for each of three years: seventeen Trusts in 1978/79, a similar number starting in 1979/80 and the remaining few to begin in the following year. The order of reception was determined by the availability of a full application and by the readiness of the Trust to make immediate use of the grant. It was a fair and transparent process which was fully reported to and accepted by the Society's Council. The first seventeen Trusts duly received their grants, but then suddenly the NCC was forced to suspend funding because of a drastic reduction in their financial allocation by the Government which had run into serious financial difficulties. The Trusts expecting their grants in 1979/80 and thereafter were severely disappointed; those who already had theirs were embarrassed; all of them felt a sense of injustice and, led by the Society, made strong representations to Ministers and to their Members of Parliament throughout the country. The representations were renewed to the new Government after the General Election of April 1979, but it was some time before NCC was able to resume the level of aid to Trusts envisaged in their 1978 declaration. The disappointment was compounded when the Countryside Commission was also forced to suspend its grant-aid programme, the scope of which had only recently been expanded to include land purchase and management.

For me it was a somewhat sour note on which to end my span as General Secretary. Although this was completely outside my control I nevertheless felt a sense of responsibility for the disappointed expectations of the Trusts who had been waiting to enter the scheme. The great majority of them were understanding, but there were one or two who after the event expressed resentment at not being included in the first batch.

Time to Go

I had fully intended to complete my five-year assignment as General Secretary, but by the fourth year 1978 I was tiring. My blood pressure problem had flared up from time to time and my doctor friend advised avoiding stress as far as possible. Commuting the thirty odd miles to Nettleham each day was no problem for most of the year, but in winter the journey over the Wolds could sometimes be difficult. More seriously, after the closure of the Grimsby to Peterborough main line through Willoughby in 1969 my four or five visits a month to London involved a round journey of 100 miles to Grantham and back for a train, nearly six hours travelling at the best of times.

There were other reasons for my concerns in 1978. I was aware that there was some criticism that I was not sufficiently ambitious in promoting the Society itself and seeking to expand its staff. My successor as General Secretary called it – somewhat unflatteringly – 'the sleeping giant' of the conservation movement. It may be that my long experience of managing on a shoestring had made me over-cautious, but my concept of the Society's purpose had always been to promote and serve the interests of the Trusts and not to seek a separate role for itself. The bigger it became the more likely it was – as I saw it – to follow its own agenda, to seek its own justification and drift away from the Trusts. Of course it had to be recognised convincingly on the national scene as the representative body of the Trusts, and in that I believe it had succeeded not in terms of national media coverage perhaps, but by earning the respect of government and other statutory and voluntary bodies for sound and practical policies and judgements. There was plenty of scope for building on that, but the foundation I believe was solid.

There was another aspect of Society expansion that troubled me then: the greater levy demands which we would almost inevitably have to make on the Trusts, and that at a time when most of them were building their strength and needed all the resources they could muster to employ staff, to acquire and manage nature reserves, and to develop their educational and promotional work.

In spite of those doubts I recognised that some expansion and restructuring of staff was becoming increasingly necessary if we were to continue to provide adequate services to the Trusts. In a memorandum to senior Honorary Officers in May 1977 I recommended a review of the staff size and structure which the Society was likely to need and could afford in the years ahead. Such review should include the post of General Secretary and the responsibilities to go with it. Some redefinition and readjustment of roles of senior staff were made at that time, but it was thought appropriate that any major changes should await a new General Secretary, another reason why I thought it better that my departure should be brought forward by twelve months.

I was quite contented to go at the end of 1978. I had, I believed, largely achieved what I set out to do more than twenty years before: to help promote the formation of a country-wide network of Wildlife Trusts, and at the same time to give new life and new purpose to the near moribund SPNR to act as the Trust's national association to support and assist them. Continuing the carefully planned development of the Society was clearly necessary to fulfil that purpose, and I thought it timely that someone else should take charge of that next phase.

I retired as General Secretary being succeeded by Dr Franklyn Perring at the end of 1978, but at the request of the Executive Committee I continued to work part-time for the Society for another three years as a Special Adviser concerned with special projects, mainly with the completion of the Nature Reserve Study and the Handbook to Trust reserves which was finally published in 1982.

Thereafter I served until 1995 on the Society's Executive Committee, and on the Council until 1998, in the latter case as an Honorary Vice-President.

Fyne Court on the Quantocks, the Somerset Trust's Visitor Centre, one of several Trusts' centres which received a grant from the Carnegie UK Trust.

TED SMITH

Marsland Valley, Cornwall.

Benmore Coigach, Wester Ross.

Loch of Lowes, a Scottish Wildlife Trust reserve noted for its nesting ospreys,
aided by purchase grant from The Pilgrim Trust.

Nature Conservancy Council 1974.

Audrey Lees, Walter Lane (left) and Ted Smith, three successive chairmen of the NC/NCC Committee for England 1970s and 1980s, at Gibraltar Point 1987.

Unveiling a plaque to record the opening of a new office at Slepe Farm near Wareham, Dorset with Professor Fred Holliday, Chairman NCC, 1977.

Lord Howick of Glendale, Chairman Nature Conservancy, in the garden at Pyewipes during visit to Lincolnshire 1969.

Part IV

The Conservancy Years

– 16 –

M Y RETIREMENT from the general secretaryship of the SPNR at the
end of 1978 coincided with the end of my twenty-two years of service
as a member of The Nature Conservancy and its successor body The
Nature Conservancy Council, and as Chairman of the England Committee of
both bodies for nine of those years. When I first joined the England Committee
in 1956 the members were predominantly scientists, mainly professors, eminent
in their particular fields. Somewhat awed at first, I found nevertheless, as Max
Nicholson had forecast, that my practical experience in conservation enabled me
to make a distinctive contribution to discussion and to indicate the policy and
position of the voluntary sector, the Trusts in particular, on a range of problems
common to both organisations. My experience of the work of the Conservancy
was immeasurably widened by my appointment in 1966 as Chairman of a Visiting
Group to the English Regions through which I was able to learn at first hand
from regional staff of their particular achievements and problems. It was an
exacting but enjoyable task and an excellent preparation for the chairmanship
of the England Committee to which post I was appointed in 1971 succeeding
the eminent geographer Sir Dudley Stamp. With both Stamp and his equally
eminent contemporary Alfred Steers I enjoyed a very friendly relationship, and
I was able to give some assistance to the former in the preparation of his New
Naturalist volume *Nature Conservation in Britain*.

When I transferred to the Council of the Nature Conservancy in 1968 I
soon became aware of the differing opinions on the status and functions of the
Conservancy. Although originally created by Royal Charter reporting to the Lord
President of the Council, the Conservancy in 1964 had become a component
part of the new Natural Environment Research Council. This led to increasing
tensions over the Conservancy's role in land management and in promoting
nature conservation on the one hand – it had, for example, played a leading
role in the 'Countryside in 1970' conferences – and its research functions on the
other. Powerful figures in the Conservancy such as Professor Sir Harry Godwin
and Sir Ralph Verney advocated separation from NERC, a view supported by the
majority of the Council, but not by the Chairman Lord Howick. Amid growing

controversy the Council of NERC appointed a committee chaired by C E Lucas to recommend a solution to the problem. I was appointed to the three-man delegation led by Harry Godwin to put the Conservancy's case for independence with its research function intact. My particular brief was to explain the importance of the Nature Conservancy's role in securing public understanding and support for nature conservation and in advising and encouraging the voluntary movement. In spite of our plea the Lucas Committee recommended that the Conservancy should remain in NERC. The Government's eventual solution, however, was to split the organisation placing the nature reserves and advisory functions in a new Nature Conservancy Council as an independent body funded by the recently created Department of the Environment, and leaving the research function with NERC in a new Institute of Terrestrial Ecology. That policy was explained to the Council of the Nature Conservancy at a meeting in July 1972 by Peter Walker, the Secretary of State for the Environment. He was accompanied on that occasion by the Permanent Secretary of the Department, Sir David Serpell.

The above is a grossly oversimplified account of a complex dispute which involved Government departments and Ministers to the highest level including the Prime Minister herself. It was also a matter of intense interest and concern to the voluntary nature conservation movement as I have indicated in an earlier chapter. It has been admirably described in detail by John Sheail in his book *Nature Conservation in Britain: The Formative Years*.

I had actively supported the majority view in the Council in my evidence to the Lucas Committee and in another capacity through the voluntary movement. I then found myself thrust unexpectedly into a more prominent role. Lord Howick had died suddenly following an accident early in 1972. The Preparatory Committee of the new Nature Conservancy Council was due to meet in April to consider the draft NCC Bill then before Parliament, in particular the extent to which the Council should be able to conduct research itself in addition to commissioning it from other bodies notably the new Institute of Terrestrial Ecology. The Committee also considered the amendment to the Bill to give the Committee for England the same status as that for Scotland and Wales, an issue to which I referred in an earlier chapter. As the longest-serving of the three country committee chairmen I was appointed to chair the meeting of the Preparatory Committee, and I continued thereafter as acting Chairman until a new one was appointed. I received no formal recognition in that role, but I enjoyed much support and encouragement from senior staff and members of the Preparatory Committee, notably from Sir John Cripps, the Chairman of the Countryside Commission.

There were many other problems at that time, not least that Duncan Poore, who had succeeded Max Nicholson as Director of the Nature Conservancy in 1966, had resigned, and his deputy Bob Boote was left holding the fort. I had worked closely with Bob, a keen supporter of the voluntary movement, over several years – he had attended the Trusts' first 1960 conference. He was an obvious and eventually successful contender for the post of Director of the new body. As soon as it was announced that the new Chairman was to be Sir David Serpell, who was about to retire from the Department of the Environment, I sought a meeting with him. Serpell was courteous if somewhat reserved and understandably cautious. He was after all one of the most distinguished civil servants, the principal architect of the new Department of the Environment. I was completely unknown to him. But that first meeting 'broke the ice' and we went on to develop a mutual understanding and a close working relationship over the four years of his chairmanship. He made numerous visits to the English regions with the Council and some with me to meet staff and to see achievements and discuss problems. We have maintained a friendship by regular correspondence ever since.

The new Council, which included David Attenborough, had a well balanced membership. It met monthly in the first year to consider policies and practices, and issued a Statement of Policies in November 1974. It also delegated much responsibility to the Chairmen of the statutory Advisory Committees for England, Scotland and Wales whilst also seeking their advice on a wide range of issues. I could not have wished for a more talented, more assiduous or more supportive Committee than that for England to which I was appointed Chairman. Under the new regime each of the three countries had to appoint a Director. Under the Nature Conservancy the principal officer for England had been the Conservation Officer, a post occupied for several years by Dr Bruce Forman with whom I had worked on a close and friendly basis. Bruce was disappointed that he failed to secure the new directorship, but he went on loyally to serve as Deputy to the new Director Dr Michael Gane who came with considerable managerial experience but little knowledge of nature conservation in Britain. Towards the end of 1975 England headquarters moved from temporary accommodation in London to new offices at Banbury in Oxfordshire where the Committee usually met thereafter. It was a long drive for me, but a pleasant change from London where NCC Council meetings and RSNC business still took me two or three times a month.

We adopted a thematic approach in the new England Committee selecting some special aspect of nature conservation for discussion at many of our meetings. As with its predecessor, however, the Committee always had a full agenda of case work: of SSSI scheduling and protection; National Nature Reserve plans; county structure and local plans, and a great variety of national issues. The impact of the Channel Tunnel project on the natural environment; ball clay extraction on the Arne peninsula in Dorset; oil and gas exploration problems, and reservoir proposals which included Rutland Water and Kielder, are just a few examples of such issues. We visited a number of areas to see problems at first hand, in particular the pollution problems of the Norfolk Broads; conservation of the Essex coast in relation to the Maplin Sands airport proposal; wetland management on the Somerset Levels and the Ouse Washes, and the preservation of the finest limestone pavement in England at Gait Barrows in north Lancashire which was being destroyed by excavation for rockery stone. The latter was a particularly vexed problem which planning law had been unable to control over more than a decade. In the end the owner agreed to sell the site to the NCC, and I had the pleasure in May 1977 of introducing Sir David Serpell, shortly after his retirement as Chairman of the NCC, to unveil a plaque on the site to celebrate its declaration as a Silver Jubilee National Nature Reserve. The establishment and declaration of such new NNRs in England was an especially rewarding aspect of the work of the Committee. Other NNRs established during my chairmanship included Orfordness; Barnack Hills and Holes with which I had earlier been associated through the Trusts' movement; Wyre Forest, and the Lizard Heaths and Coast. These declarations and the other business of the Committee were extensively reported in the NCC's Annual Reports.

I had always found the NC/NCC work of absorbing interest, and I had never encountered any serious conflict of interests or loyalty between it and my work for the Trusts through the RSNC. Collaboration between the Government agency and the voluntary nature conservation movement was at that time very close and their work was in many ways complementary. I had devoted much time and attention to my England Committee chairmanship. To ensure that it did not prejudice my responsibilities to the RSNC required a strenuous programme of work and meetings, fulfilled often at the expense of leisure time and holidays. Having decided to retire from the general secretaryship of the RSNC somewhat earlier than I had originally intended, I had hoped for a further two-year extension from 1978 of my NCC appointment, and I was disappointed initially not to receive it. However, having served for a longer period on the NC/NCC than almost anyone before or since, I recognised that my replacement had become inevitable. What really disappointed me, however, was the clumsy and unnecessarily secretive way in which the termination of my appointment and the appointment of my successor was handled. It also aroused considerable concern and indignation among members of the England Committee. But all that was a long time ago and I look back now with pleasure and satisfaction on my Conservancy years.

Partly as a result of my Conservancy service I inherited two interesting assignments: the chairmanships of the Advisory Committees for the Breckland and for Woodwalton Fen. The former had a dual function: to provide advice to the Nature Conservancy Council, the Norfolk and Suffolk Trusts and the RSPB on the management of the Breckland National Nature Reserves, and to advise generally on matters affecting conservation throughout the area. The four constituent bodies co-opted up to ten other committee members with special knowledge of the area based on research and experience. One of the twice-yearly meetings usually included a site visit. Reconciling nature conservation with other land uses in Breckland of forestry, agriculture and increasingly also recreation presented many challenging problems, and the Committee provided a unique opportunity for the conservation bodies to consider them and advise on appropriate action.

The Committee played a major role in the preparation of a conservation strategy for Breckland which set out eight key areas for action designed to reverse the decline in the region's special wildlife and restore its unique character. The strategy was launched at a conference in March 1993 attended by landowners and land users, local authorities, the Forestry Commission, and ecologists with special knowledge of Breckland. This was a high point of my fifteen years as Chairman of the Committee from which I retired in 1995.

The Woodwalton Fen Advisory Committee was established as a condition of the SPNR's lease of the reserve to the Nature Conservancy in 1954. It consisted of four representatives of each of the two organisations, a co-opted representative of the Middle Level Commissioners, and a Chairman agreed by both parties. I succeeded Professor Alfred Steers in that office in 1978 and served for twenty-one years. The Committee met in spring and autumn in the wooden bungalow in the reserve, a period piece built by Charles Rothschild who gave the Fen to the SPNR in 1919. Most nature conservation committee work was inevitably concerned increasingly with the political aspects of land use and development, so it was a refreshing change to be able to concentrate as we did at Woodwalton on the management of habitats and species – the future of the reintroduced Dutch race of the large copper butterfly was a matter of particular concern – at a time when the process of reclaiming open fen habitats from invasive scrub and woodland was a primary objective.

Mary usually accompanied me to Woodwalton meetings and spent the time exploring the Fen. We enjoyed our journey through the Fens on the 'abbey route' through Spalding, Crowland and Thorney. It was a pleasure also to continue my association with former Conservancy friends and colleagues like Eric Duffey, Norman Moore and Terry and Derek Wells – all names embedded in the early history of the Nature Conservancy and the Institute of Terrestrial Ecology – and to continue to meet the remarkable Dr Miriam Rothschild with her unique and long-standing association with the Fen and the SPNR. When I retired from the Committee in 1999 I was succeeded as Chairman by Lincolnshire Trust stalwart and Fenland specialist John Redshaw.

Ruined limestone pavement, Gait Barrows, 1977.

Introducing Sir David Serpell to unveil plaque built into a cairn to celebrate NNR declaration of Gait Barrows, 1977.

Breckland landscape

Woodwalton Fen

100th meeting of Trust Council, December 1987.

Standing (L-R): John Adams, Geoffrey Grantham, John Keily, Sam van den Bos, Tom Twigg, Angela Bates, Brian Redman, Derek Golicher, Barrie Wilkinson (Field Officer), Bill Markham, Christine Underwood.

Sitting (L-R): Geoff Trinder, Don Wright, Philip Race, Richard Pepler (Deputy Chairman), Ken Wilson, Tom Baker, Jane Ostler (NCC), Walter Lane (President), Vi Wilkin, Ted Smith (Chairman), Midge Gilleard (Administrative Officer), Stuart Crooks (Conservator), Irene Weston, David Robinson (Hon Secretary), Pam Lyon, Bob Prentice (Hon Treasurer).

Absent: Donovan Fry, Andrew Hodson, Richard Holland, Bruce Leggott, John Redshaw, Brian Tear.

Board of Trustees, July 2006.

(L-R): Clare Harrison, Stuart Crooks (Director), Don Wright (Chairman), Ted Smith (President), Bob Prentice (Hon Treasurer), Peter Thorpe (Asst Director, Finance), Cheryl Aggett (Director's PA), Brian Tear (Deputy Chairman), Dave Bromwich (Asst Director, Reserves), Tom Twigg, John Redshaw, Geoff Trinder, David Sheppard, David Robinson (Hon Secretary).

Absent: Angela Bates, Caroline Steel (Asst Director, Conservation).

Part V

The Lincolnshire Trust up to Now in Outline

– 17 –

THE TRUST'S Silver Jubilee year of 1974 was celebrated throughout the county by a great variety of events in which the recently formed Area Groups played a full part. The highlight was the opening of the new Gibraltar Point Visitor Centre by Sir David Attenborough, and his lecture on 'Conservation Worldwide' to an enthusiastic audience at Riseholme College. It was at the end of that first twenty-five years that I intended to end this account of the Trust, but I find on re-reading that that would leave too many loose ends, so in a final chapter I will outline some of the major trends and developments since then in the hope that some future chronicler will describe and evaluate them in greater detail.

Constitution and Administration
Governance

The principal task which faced the Trust in its second half-century was to ensure that its human and financial resources were at all times adequate and appropriately deployed to fulfil its ever-growing commitments and aspirations. A major revision of the constitution in its Memorandum and Articles undertaken in 1976 was designed to assist that purpose. The role of the Area Groups – eventually seventeen of them – in promoting the strength and activity of the Trust was recognised by enabling them to appoint six representatives to the Council through the medium of appropriate combinations of Groups. This brought new experience to the Council, but the procedure was cumbersome, and at the next major review of the Articles in 1999 each Group was given the right to appoint a member to Council. The 1976 revision had also given the Council greater flexibility to order the Trust's affairs, in particular powers to delegate its functions to committees and groups of members which no longer had to consist entirely of Council members. The general effect of the changes was to enable the organisation of the Trust to be broadened and strengthened by providing more opportunities for members to participate in the running of its affairs.

These changes, coupled with the reappraisal of the status and functions of

323

the central committees, served the Trust well for the next twenty years, but by the 1990s the growing complexity of administering the organisation and the increasing legal responsibilities of the Trustees and Company Directors for charity law, for health and safety, for conditions of staff employment and so on, demanded more radical changes.

It had become patently obvious that the twenty-five members of the Council could not effectively fulfil all the responsibilities by that time expected of them as Trustees. Nor did the Executive Committee, although smaller, have the status and authority necessary to fulfil the required role. It was consequently decided in 1999 that the responsibilities of the Trustees and Company Directors should be devolved to a Board of twelve members to replace the existing Executive Committee. The Council was to comprise the members of the Board, nine members elected at Annual General Meetings, and one member appointed by each of the seventeen Area Groups. The Council would appoint the members of the Board and would continue to formulate policy and guide the future development of the Trust. These changes were embodied in a new Memorandum and Articles which also redefined the aims of the Trust in line with modern legislation and best practice. The success of the new system undoubtedly contributed to the significant progress of the Trust in the early years of the new century.

In making these constitutional changes it was also decided after thorough debate at all levels to change the name of the Trust from the Lincolnshire Trust for Nature Conservation to the Lincolnshire Wildlife Trust, so bringing it into line with the overwhelming majority of the other County Trusts. We made it abundantly clear, however, that the change of name implied no loss of autonomy as a symbol of which we retained our own Lapwings logo. I accepted the inevitability of the change and I recognised that the term 'wildlife' had achieved universal recognition, but I still regret the loss of the word 'nature' from the title. It somehow expressed a wider concept of conservation which embraces the whole of the natural world and man's place in it.

Constitutional change was accompanied by a radical reorganisation of management. With the growing complexity of the Trust's operations the two main Committees dealing one with conservation, the other with promotion and education, had spawned several sub-committees and the whole structure had become cumbersome and overloaded. It was decided therefore to replace all committees by a variety of teams covering all the main aspects of the Trust's work including human resources, education, membership and publicity, publications, biodiversity, nature reserve development and the main habitats with which we are concerned in the reserves and elsewhere. Committees dealing with three of the major reserves – Gibraltar Point, Far Ings and Whisby – were also converted to teams. Teams consist of members and appropriate staff on an equal footing. They report and make recommendations direct to the Board, but they have some delegated authority within established policy. A Board member has special responsibility for a team or a group of teams. With a few adjustments the system has worked well. It has involved more members with experience and expertise in policy-making and management processes, and it has further cemented the already close working relationship between members and staff.

Personnel
Local government reorganisation in 1974, which involved the demise of Lindsey

County Council, brought one incidental bonus for the Trust and for the cause of conservation country-wide. Walter Lane, after seventeen years as Clerk of the Council, decided to take early retirement and immediately accepted nomination as the President of the Trust to succeed Sir Weston Cracroft Amcotts who wished to retire. Walter brought to the affairs of the Trust sound judgement and a wealth of experience in local government and in nature conservation and environmental matters locally and nationally. He served as President for twenty-five years and continued thereafter as a valued member of the Board. The Trust owes a great debt to him for his discerning support and guidance over more than forty-five years. I have made references in earlier chapters to the important role which Walter played in promoting the Trusts' movement nationally. He served also on the National Trust Council, on the Forestry Commission's Committee for England, and most notably on the Nature Conservancy Council of which he chaired the England Committee for nine years. For services to the NCC he was appointed CBE in 1985. His sudden death in February 2006 was a serious loss to the Trust. For me it was the end of a long friendship and collaboration in the cause of conservation.

After thirty eventful and rewarding years as Chairman I decided that the 50th anniversary year 1998 would be my last in that office. Walter then graciously relinquished the Presidency to allow me to be elected. My obvious successor as Chairman was Don Wright who in various capacities had served the Trust with great dedication for more than thirty years. His experience and knowledge and sheer hard work had been of inestimable value. The same applied to Brian Tear, that other popular pioneer and promoter of education, who became the Deputy Chairman.

David Robinson was willing to continue as the Honorary Secretary, becoming now (2006) after thirty-seven years in the post almost certainly the longest serving senior officer in the same post of any of the Wildlife Trusts. He has also continued his invaluable role as the editor of *Lapwings*. I have referred elsewhere to David's services to the RSNC as a long-serving member of the Executive Committee and of the Editorial Board of *Natural World* and as Chairman of the Education and Promotions Committee. He also served for several years as the Honorary Secretary of the Watch Trust for Environmental Education. In 1997 he was appointed OBE for services to 'journalism and to the community in Lincolnshire'. In both those respects his service to the Trust must rank highly.

The post of Honorary Treasurer requires special knowledge and experience of financial management. We were very fortunate that John Keily's retirement as Honorary Treasurer after nine years of sound financial management coincided with the retirement of Bob Prentice as the Chief Executive – and previously Treasurer – of Lincolnshire County Council. He was already in great demand by voluntary bodies, and we were fortunate that he readily accepted our invitation to become the Trust's Honorary Treasurer. It was satisfying too that the Trust's reputation as a leading environmental body was an important factor in his decision. His confident guidance and perceptive planning during a period of rapid growth have been a vital element in the Trust's progress.

The post of Honorary Land Agent was specially created by the Trust Council to give formal recognition to the role of Tom Twigg who volunteered to assist the Trust following his retirement as County Land Agent for Lincolnshire and previously for Lindsey County Council in which capacities he had been closely associated with the Trust's work at Gibraltar Point and elsewhere. His professional advice and supervision have been invaluable in the maintenance and expansion of the Trust's estate. The creation of the post of Honorary Architect gave similar recognition to the equally valuable contribution made by Neil Taylor who has given freely of his time and expertise.

It is interesting to compare the present (2006) Board of Trustees with the members of the original Council in 1948. In addition to the Honorary Officers and Tom Twigg, and Walter Lane (until February 2006), the Board consists of Angela Bates, retired Managing Director of an animal foodstuffs company and authority on organic farming methods; Clare Harrison, farmer, housewife and botanist; Geoff Trinder, lecturer and former art teacher, expert photographer and the Trust's anchor man in north-west Lincolnshire; John Redshaw, retired Senior Engineer with Anglian Water, authority on the natural history of the Fens; and David Sheppard, a senior scientist in English Nature (now Natural England). Most of the Board members are also active in Area Groups and in various teams, some of them as Chairmen and Convenors. Their experience indeed extends over the whole range of the Trust's policies and activities.

Membership and Area Groups

The mid-1970s were somewhat difficult years for the Trust financially, reflecting perhaps the depression in the national economy. The 4,500 membership of 1974 grew painfully slowly, and the elusive 5,000 target was not reached until 1983. Thereafter, however, as the Trust's reserves and activities expanded and the Area Groups flourished, membership gathered momentum passing 7,000 in 1987 and reaching 8,000 in the 40th anniversary year 1988, a total which included 1,000 Watch members. Our next target was 10,000 for the Golden Jubilee year 1998, and by a special recruiting campaign and efforts to reduce fallout that target was achieved. Then in the next four years in an astonishing surge in recruitment the total doubled to 20,000, and by the beginning of 2004 it stood at more than 23,000, and although the rate of increase then slowed down the 25,000 target was reached in 2005. That achievement was due very largely to new methods of recruitment using agencies and paid recruiters for the purpose: door-to-door, and face-to-face in supermarkets, garden centres and the like.

The rapid increase in membership achieved by those means has had several consequences, most obviously the boost to the Trust's income. It also has potentially far-reaching implications for the character of the Trust and its membership, 60% of whom are now members recruited by the new methods. The vast majority of those probably regard themselves as contributing to a good cause rather than joining an organisation in the traditional sense. They may be less likely therefore to have the same loyalty to the organisation or to participate in its activities as members who have been recruited by the more traditional means of personal contact, through Area Groups and through attendance at Trust events and reserve open days. The voluntary character of the Trust is very much dependent on a core of activists at all levels. Without that it could become an organisation run largely by professionals, the members' role becoming akin to that of football club supporters. That must not be allowed to happen, but to avoid it will require more attention to recruiting methods and processes, to promoting the Trust's aims and purposes, and to the means of involving members through rejuvenated Area Groups and other means. In the meantime full advantage can be taken of the higher income and the influence which goes with a large membership.

In that context Area Groups clearly have a continuing role of vital importance in the Trust. Over the last thirty years they have fluctuated individually in strength and activity, but all have maintained a full programme of indoor and outdoor events, manned sales points and reserve open days, and supported many centrally organised events. Most of them participate in the sales business by selling goods at meetings, and in two or three cases organising Christmas shops. In the 1980s and 90s they also raised several thousands of pounds a year for the Trust's general purposes and made special efforts for Appeals. Their fundraising has diminished in recent years, however, perhaps because of an unfortunate perception that the Trust is much wealthier and has no need of relatively small contributions. That probably applies also to individual members who on their own initiative held coffee mornings and such like which raised small but very welcome funds.

For many years the distribution of *Lapwings* and *Natural World* has been organised through the Area Groups whose members deliver most of them by hand, so saving the Trust up to £10,000 a year. It also often provides an opportunity for deliverers to make the acquaintance of members, a welcome personal touch. Although recently the discrepancy in the timing of issue of the two magazines has necessitated the distribution of *Natural World* by post, *Lapwings* continues to be delivered mainly by the Groups.

Contact between the Groups and the Trust centrally has been maintained by regular visits to Group meetings and committees by Honorary Officers and staff. That liaison has been strengthened in recent years by Group representation on the Trust Council as already described. In 2004 the Forum for Area Groups which used to be a regular feature of the calendar was successfully revived. The need to reach out to members and give them a sense of belonging has never been more urgent and Area Groups are one of the main channels for achieving it. They also have a potential role in representing nature conservation interests in planning and other environmental issues in their own areas. Some of them already fulfil that role for which community strategies now offer new opportunities. Area Groups have attracted many dedicated volunteers and there are outstanding examples of service to the Trust especially among Chairmen and other Group officers.

Wildlife Watch

I described in Chapter 10 the Trust's early organisation for young people which became part of the national Watch Club in 1974. As with many youth organisations, membership numbers have fluctuated over the years. The 500 or so of 1980 had risen to nearly 1200 by 1990. Numbers then fell away but rose again with the new recruiting campaign to a record total of 4,600 by mid-2004. This substantial increase, which is in line with that of adult members, was largely due to the popularity of family membership.

Providing opportunities to explore the natural world has always been the main purpose of the provisions we make for children. It has been pursued through local Watch Groups and through participation in national surveys and projects. Its success has been due in no small measure to dedicated Group leaders whose work has been coordinated for the last twelve years by Clifford Jukes, an example of outstanding voluntary service for which he was awarded Honorary Life Membership. The Trust's capacity to organise WATCH activities from the centre, including the production of a Lincolnshire newsletter to go with the national magazine Watchword, had already been considerably enhanced by the appointment in 1986 of Mary Edwards (now Porter) as our first Promotions Officer.

In addition to the Watch programme, children's events and activities have long been a feature of work at Gibraltar Point, Far Ings and Whisby. This work received special impetus from the three-year Education and Community Action Programme 2002-05, funded largely by the Heritage Lottery Fund, which enabled us to expand our provision both for institutional and informal education.

Staffing

From 1970 to 1975 there were two headquarter's officers: the Administrative Officer Paul Berkeley and his successor Nigel Ellis-Gray, and Conservation Officer Ray Collier. Overall direction and coordination of management was the responsibility of the Honorary Officers, in particular at that time of David Robinson the Honorary Secretary. It was not a satisfactory solution for the long term, and it was agreed that our aim should be to appoint a principal Executive Officer. At that time unfortunately we could not afford both that and the two existing posts, so when Collier returned to the NCC in 1975 we decided to make the principal appointment to cover also the Conservation Officer role until we could afford to reinstate that as a separate post.

Many of the other Trusts had a Conservation Officer by that time and in my SPNR capacity I had met most of them on my visits to Trusts and at conferences. One of them, Stuart Crooks, the Cheshire Trust Officer, had made a particularly favourable impression on me for his understanding of the purposes and practices of his job, for his initiatives and for his maturity and dedication to the cause. He had worked as a designer in industry, and had been a founder member of the Herts and Middlesex Trust and an active volunteer before deciding to seek a career in conservation. He applied for the Lincolnshire post as soon as it was advertised, and was duly appointed and settled here with his wife and young family in August 1976. We gave him originally the title of 'Conservator' because it seemed to encapsulate the essence of the post, but we eventually adopted the more popular 'Director' title. For nearly thirty years Stuart has administered the Trust's affairs and managed an increasing complement of staff with skill and confidence. When he started he was supported by only two headquarters staff, the Administrative Officer and a Field Officer, together with two clerical assistants. The only outposted field staff were the two wardens at Gibraltar Point. Today the staff number more than forty. Stuart has also developed the Trust's working relationship with a wide range of official and voluntary bodies, raising the Trust's profile in the process. His appointment was a landmark in the progress of the Trust. Apart from its intrinsic value, it enabled the Honorary Officers to concentrate on policy-making and planning, promotion and public relations. As one of the most experienced and respected Trust Directors he has also played an important part in recent years in the reform of the governance of the national body (now the Royal Society of Wildlife Trusts) and of its financial management – another Lincolnshire contribution to the Trusts' movement.

Further expansion of the staff was made possible in the 1980s by the Trust's improving financial position, and by special arrangements with local authorities for the management of particular sites, notably Gibraltar Point, Snipe Dales and the Whisby Nature Park. The first new post to be created following Stuart's

Trust Chairman Don Wright (R) making presentation to Eric Simms, Volunteer Manager, South Witham road verge reserve.

Bob Prentice Hon. Treasurer.

Deputy Chairman Brian Tear in the Trust's Lincoln Wildlife Gift Shop.

Tom Twigg (L) and Hon Secretary David Robinson at Far Ings.

Stuart Crooks, Trust Director.

L-R: Brian Redman (Volunteer Reserve Manager, Kirkby Moor) Caroline Steel (Asst Director Conservation) and Geoff Trinder (Convenor, Heathland Team).

Peter Thorpe, Asst Director, Finance.

L-R: Angela Bates (Trustee), Dave Bromwich (Asst Director, Conservation) and Peter Graves (Snipe Dales Warden).

Retirement presentation to Barrie Wilkinson, 2002.

Kevin Wilson,
Gibraltar Point
Manager.

Lionel Grooby, North Lincolnshire Regional Warden
(right) and Roly Barber, Volunteer Reserve Manager,
Scotton Common.

Mary Porter with Countryside
Minister Eliott Morley at
Banovallum House, 1998.

Dave Vandome,
Volunteer Reserve
Manager, Deeping
Lakes.

HRH The Duke of Edinburgh plants
a tree at the opening of Whisby Natural
World and Education Centre (2001)
with Nature Park Manager Phil Porter.

Official opening of Banovallum House, the Trust's headquarters
(above) by Lord Cranbrook, Chairman of English Nature, 1993.

appointment was that of a Mid-Lincolnshire Warden. That was funded in part by a 'capacity' grant from the Nature Conservancy Council, a three-year programme of financial aid to the County Trusts to which I referred in an earlier chapter. The first occupant of the post, Peter Roworth – now on the staff of English Nature like several other former Trust employees – took up residence in the old farmhouse at Moor Farm from where he covered the expanding Kirkby reserves and others in the central areas of the county.

The field staff build-up continued with a new warden post at Snipe Dales created by the agreement with Lincolnshire County Council for the Trust to manage the Country Park as well as the Nature Reserve, the County Council bearing part of the cost. It is a post now occupied by Peter Graves who was for many years one of the Trust's most devoted voluntary workers at Snipe Dales and then as leader of the Alford area working party. The acquisition of the Far Ings reserve and subsequent restoration of the farmhouse as a visitor centre and warden's residence led to the appointment as warden in 1988 of Mark Tarttelin, succeeded after four years by Lionel Grooby who had spent a successful spell at Snipe Dales. The post was initially sponsored by CEGB through the Worldwide Fund for Nature. In the same year, 1988, a partnership agreement with Lincolnshire County Council and North Kesteven District Council to develop the Whisby Nature Park included the appointment of a full-time Project Officer, the cost being shared by the Trust and the Local Authorities.

Meantime at headquarters in 1988 more grant-aid from the NCC made it possible to reinstate the post of Conservation Officer to deal with wider countryside and planning issues and scientific recording; and to upgrade Barrie Wilkinson's Field Officer post to Reserves Manager. For Barrie it was well-deserved recognition of the key role he had already played in his twenty years of service to the Trust. He tackled the new job with his usual determination until retirement in 2002 when he was succeeded by David Bromwich for whom this was the fourth post in the Trust over a twenty year period. That – and the Conservation Manager post now occupied by Caroline Steel – have more recently been designated Assistant Director posts.

As further evidence of the growing strength and confidence of the Trust in the late 1980s, the post of Promotions Officer was created to provide support and advice to the Trust's Area Groups and other volunteers, to publicise the work of the Trust, and promote its aims generally. Through talks to a great variety of audiences and frequent broadcasts on local radio the occupant of that post Mary Porter soon became one of the most familiar faces and voices of the Trust. Less prominent externally but equally vital was the creation of a full-time Accounts Officer post to replace a part-time book-keeper.

The day-to-day administration of the Trust's finances became increasingly demanding as membership, landholdings, grant-aid schemes and staff all increased. In 1995 Peter Thorpe, a Chartered Accountant, was appointed Finance Manager and a new Membership and Finance Department was created under his management. The post – subsequently designated Assistant Director (Finance) – has been a vital element in the growth and development of the Trust in the last ten years.

A New Home for the Trust in Banovallum House 1993
The removal of the SPNR staff to their new headquarters at Nettleham in 1974

had allowed the Trust to occupy the whole of the first floor of the Manor House at Alford. The office accommodation and facilities there were never ideal but they continued to serve the Trust's purpose for a further period. By the late 1980s however, staff had increased to the extent that the accommodation had become inadequate and working conditions inefficient. In 1990 the Trust presented proposals to the landlords, the Alford Civic Trust, for the redevelopment of the Manor House to provide more space both for our operations and for their Folk Museum. Plans for the enhancement of the garden and grounds as a visitor attraction were also included. When the Civic Trust declined to consider these proposals we concluded that a new headquarters was necessary. It would have to be in a reasonably central location for the county and provide adequate office space and facilities including meeting rooms, car parking space and if possible attractive grounds for visitors.

Having considered and inspected several properties we decided to purchase Banovallum House in Manor House Street in Horncastle. It had been on the market for some time and the asking price had been progressively reduced to attract buyers. The house is a handsome 18th century building which had been extended in the 19th century. It had adequate space which could be adapted to meet our needs; it is close to the centre of the town but stands in three acres of grounds with walled garden, a meadow, an area formerly used as a garden centre and some 300 yards of river frontage – with frequent sighting of kingfisher! For good measure it had associations with the great naturalist Sir Joseph Banks having once been part of his Revesby estate. It was indeed as near to the ideal as we could have hoped to find.

The purchase of Banovallum House was a bold move for the Trust at a particularly difficult time of national economic recession when we were otherwise having to keep a tight rein on expenditure. It was necessary to borrow to meet the cost, but we had a firm expectation of selling a small but valuable strip of land at Rauceby Warren which was needed for access to a new housing development. Moreover, financial prospects generally were beginning to look somewhat brighter and indeed improved markedly from 1994. As a result we were able to pay off the mortgage within a few years.

Except for the second floor, the renovation and adaptation of the building – supervised by Honorary Architect Neil Taylor – was completed in time for a Grand Opening in May 1993 performed by Lord Cranbrook, Chairman of English Nature, in the presence of a large number of members and guests from many associated organisations. There followed two weeks of celebratory events including a sale of antiques, books, prints and stamps; an art and craft exhibition and sale, and illustrated talks, most of them held in a large marquee on the meadow. A sponsored walk on parts of the Viking Way attracted many participants and raised a substantial sum for the Trust. It was all a strange contrast to the almost unnoticed arrival of the Trust at the Manor House in Alford twenty-seven years earlier.

Renovation of the second floor of Banovallum House followed in 1996 with the aid of HLF and European funding. It provided more office space and a library and archive room designed to enable volunteer members and others to use the Trust's records and to assist in a variety of ways, including the vetting of planning proposals.

The establishment of the Trust at Banovallum House was another important landmark in its history and development. It has provided a splendidly appropriate and dignified headquarters enhancing the Trust's reputation and prestige. It was a major achievement especially for Stuart Crooks who led the planning and negotiation with skill and foresight.

Biodiversity, Land Use and Planning

Knowledge and information about habitats and their wildlife is essential for planning and implementing practical measures of conservation: nature reserves, species protection, advisory services and promotion of education and understanding. For the earliest selection of nature reserves we had had to rely largely on existing information from the Naturalists' Union's records, but by the 1960s, as I described in the Chapter 11, other sources of information also became available from local survey work undertaken by the Trust and English Nature, and from national surveys. In the 1970s and 80s the Trust's surveys of ponds, pits and quarries and of rivers and streams – the latter in association with the then Lincolnshire River Authority – greatly enlarged our knowledge of those habitats and sites. The Government's Job Creation and Community Enterprise Programmes in the 1970s enabled us to employ teams of ecologists to carry out surveys of a variety of habitats, and these provided even more information about the county's heathlands and grasslands, woodlands and wetlands and their wildlife. The LNU's publication of *The Flora of Lincolnshire* and of *The Butterflies and Larger Moths of Lincolnshire* were other important contributions to the county's natural history.

All this work provided the Trust with invaluable information on which to base its nature reserves and general conservation policies and practices. It also confirmed what we had long suspected that the more specialised habitats in particular were being progressively decimated and impoverished and that individual species of plants and animals were being lost at an unprecedented rate. It was clearly important, therefore, to identify those species most at risk and to examine ways of ensuring their survival. So at the request of the Trust's Conservation Committee I convened in 1985 a working party of specialists for that purpose. The result of our research and investigation was the publication in 1988 of a Red Data Report *Endangered Species in Lincolnshire and South Humberside*. The Report described the principal habitats in the county, the causes of decline and extinction of species, and the conservation measures already taken together with recommendations for further action. Species of vascular plants, mammals, birds, reptiles and amphibia, fishes, non-marine molluscs, insects and other invertebrates were listed with a brief description of present status and particular threats. Our research had revealed that over the previous fifty years no less than forty species of plants and twelve of butterflies – almost a third of the latter which occurred before the 1940s – had disappeared and there had been losses among other animals. In addition many other plant and animal species had been reduced to scarce, fragmented populations which were in danger of suffering the same fate. The Report with a foreword by Sir David Attenborough was attractively illustrated with line drawings and photographs. As the first of its kind for any county in the UK it attracted wide publicity in the conservation movement.

The Trust's Conservation Committee acted swiftly by appointing an Endangered Species Team to carry out the recommendations in the Report and initiate further action. The Team began by establishing a monitoring system for

NATURE IN LINCOLNSHIRE

TOWARDS A BIODIVERSITY STRATEGY

The Lincolnshire Trust
for nature conservation

1996

ACTION FOR WILDLIFE IN LINCOLNSHIRE

Industry on the Humber

Coast at Gibraltar Point

THE LINCOLNSHIRE

BIODIVERSITY ACTION PLAN

A leaf beetle

Lapwing

2000

endangered species applicable primarily to Trust reserves, but wherever possible for the county as a whole. With necessary modifications the system is still in use at the present day. Its implementation was greatly facilitated by the introduction of a computer system for storing and retrieving data, a development which was to prove invaluable for the Trust's success in managing reserves, in influencing planning issues, and in offering advice to planners and land users. In 1995 it became possible to appoint a Conservation Assistant for data work. Until then much was achieved – as in so many other fields – by voluntary help.

The Endangered Species Team also prepared recovery programmes for the most threatened species. The successful reintroduction of the natterjack toad to Gibraltar Point, and the reinforcement of the small pasqueflower population of the Ancaster Valley are examples of some of the methods employed. Elsewhere special attention to habitat requirements in reserves benefited other species.

Five years on we embarked as envisaged on a revision of the Red Data Report. By that time, however, biodiversity – a new word for an old concept – had entered the conservation vocabulary, and as a result of the Earth Summit in Rio in 1992 the Government had published a national Biodiversity Action Plan and called for similar action at local level throughout the country. On our own initiative we then developed what was intended as a simple revision of our earlier Report into a more comprehensive study concerned as much with habitats as with species, and with means of protection and recovery for both. In effect it became a kind of local BAP – it was sub-titled 'Towards a Biodiversity Strategy' – serving as an information and policy document for the Trust and as a contribution to further planning and action for the conservation of Lincolnshire's biodiversity.

As its editor I was determined that we should provide the statistical data to demonstrate convincingly both the decline in species and the changes in habitats which had occurred over the previous fifty years. Collating and analysing information for this purpose from a wide variety of sources proved to be one of the most time-consuming tasks I have ever undertaken, but I believe that it gave the report weight and authenticity, and provided invaluable material for the county's Biodiversity Plan which followed four years later. We were able to show – to give just three random examples – that meadow grassland had declined by over 99% since 1938; that bog asphodel had disappeared from all but two of its seven pre-1938 sites, and that the snipe was rapidly heading for extinction as a breeding species in the county.

I was assisted in preparing the report by a team of specialist contributors and by members of the Trust's headquarters and field staff. Without their input it would have been an impossible task. Since plants formed by far the largest species list I must make special mention of the contribution to this and other investigations of Rene Weston, the County Botanical Recorder.

Entitled *Nature in Lincolnshire* the report was launched in Lincoln in August 1996 before a widely representative audience. It was a timely complement to Lincolnshire County Council's recent report on the state of the environment. Shortly afterwards a Steering Group involving some forty other statutory and voluntary bodies began work on the county BAP assisted by a full-time coordinating officer based with the Trust. Whilst I remained for a time a member of the Steering Group I was very pleased when my colleague Don Wright was prepared to bring to the chairmanship of the Group his energy and wealth of experience. Completion and publication of the BAP in May 2000 owed much to his skill and dedication.

Following the publication of *Nature in Lincolnshire* I prepared a set of detailed recommendations and targets under the title 'Habitat Targets for the Trust' to supplement the general recommendations set out in the main document. It is interesting now to look back at those proposals – some of them subsequently embodied in the Lincolnshire BAP – and see how many of them have been implemented. One of them, applicable to all habitats, was the expansion of existing nature reserves and the preparation of maps showing what would be desirable in various cases. It is satisfying that much has been and is still being achieved in that direction.

Research for *Nature in Lincolnshire* had revealed a great deal about the county's wildlife resources. It was not, however, the only means used by the Trust to secure such information. In 1996, for example, we supervised a project to identify basic habitat features in the Lincolnshire Wolds AONB using colour aerial photos. More ambitiously, largely through Stuart Crooks' initiative, we played a leading role in the audit of the features, habitats, and land use and ownerships of the Lindsey coast from Tetney to Gibraltar Point. The report *Towards a Strategic Approach on the Lincolnshire Coast* contained detailed recommendations accompanied by maps showing the survey results and photographic records of car parks and access points. It provided invaluable baseline information for planning, management and improvement of the coastal zone.

From the outset, as earlier chapters recount, the Trust had been closely involved in planning issues. Structure and local plans produced by county and district councils from the 1960s onwards all dealt with environmental issues and all demanded examination and comment by the Trust. Our submissions undoubtedly had some influence on the content of plans especially in promoting the importance of natural resource use and environmental policies. On a regular basis individual planning applications likewise needed to be examined for any implications for nature conservation. The magnitude of this task can be gauged by the fact that in one year 1993/4 some 10,000 planning applications were examined and approximately 250 required comments by the Trust. The appointment of a Conservation Officer in 1988 greatly strengthened our capacity to be involved in the wider issues of local planning and land use, but initial examination of planning applications continued to be made by volunteers some of whom had had experience in the planning field.

Planning issues in a changing planning system have continued to occupy much of the attention of the Trust's Conservation Department now headed by Assistant Director Caroline Steel assisted by a Conservation Officer. The introduction of the Regions into the planning system has resulted in far-reaching changes. Local Plans are being replaced by Local Development Frameworks which have to conform with the Regional Spatial Strategy and National Planning Policy Statements. Allocation of land for housing and other development will be prescribed through this system. The picture is even more complex for the Trust since we have to relate to two Regions – East Midlands, and Yorkshire and Humberside as well as Lincolnshire County Council, the two unitary authorities and seven District Councils.

There are other kinds of planning of concern to the Trust, not least the Environment Agency's Shoreline Management Plans which determine, among other actions, coastal areas for realignment. The Trust currently has a close interest and some involvement in three such schemes: at Alkborough at the confluence of the Humber and the Trent, at Chowder Ness and at Donna Nook, both the latter adjoining our reserves.

There are also new issues to be considered, most recently the location and density of onshore wind farms. This can be a particularly difficult problem. The Trust supports sustainable methods of energy production which help to combat global warming, but the siting of turbines or too many of them in a particular area can be seriously damaging to wildlife.

The Conservation Department is concerned with biodiversity in other ways, in particular through the Trust's role in the implementation and revision (in 2005) of the County Biodiversity Action Plan. Collection, processing and dissemination of information is essential for biodiversity conservation planning and action, and the Trust has played a major role in the creation of the County Environmental Records Centre, a major achievement for Lincolnshire.

Nature Reserves Acquisition and Management
Selection Criteria

By 1988, its 40th birthday, the Trust had acquired more than 90 nature reserves covering some 3000 hectares. Up to that time acquisition had concentrated largely on sites identified in the 1950s and other outstanding examples revealed through subsequent investigation. Those scheduled as SSSIs had received the highest priority with the result that by 1991 the Trust had acquired as freehold or was managing by lease or agreement 48 of the 99 SSSIs (excluding purely geological SSSIs) in the county covering 2,240 hectares, some 80% of its total reserve hectarage, the rest being 578 hectares of 43 non-SSSIs. Similarly nearly 80% of the total cost of managing the Trust's reserves (£235,600 in 1991) was attributable to the SSSIs, and that took no account of the very considerable volunteer input in management at all levels which totalled 10,600 man/hours in the year in question.

I researched those figures to submit to Derek Langslow, the Chief Executive of the NCC, in support of the case which his Council was making to the Government for a scheme of payment to voluntary conservation organisations towards the cost of managing SSSIs. Under a Wildlife Enhancement Scheme the NCC was already compensating private landowners for SSSI management costs – more than £26,000 a year in one Lincolnshire case listed in the NCC's report for 1988/9. A new scheme for voluntary bodies known as the Reserves Enhancement Scheme came into operation in 1992. However, in spite of the detailed analysis of our position which I had provided and the fact that we knew our SSSI management commitment to be greater than most of the other early applicants, we were not granted entry into the scheme until the third tranche in 1994, a delay which led to some interesting correspondence between Langslow and myself. Once we were in receipt of payment, however, it made a very significant difference to our ability to manage the SSSI reserves, especially by such measures as introducing grazing regimes, restoring habitats and providing appropriate machinery for various purposes.

Whilst SSSIs remained a high priority for acquisition throughout the 1980s, periodic reviews of our acquisition policy were looking increasingly at other options. We were already managing a large proportion of the county's SSSIs, and in any case opportunities for acquiring others were occurring less frequently,

LINCOLNSHIRE AND
SOUTH HUMBERSIDE

TRUST FOR NATURE
CONSERVATION LTD

WILDLIFE *for* TOMORROW

WE NEED YOUR HELP TO MAINTAIN & ENHANCE THIS SPLENDID COASTAL RESERVE

AND THE FACILITIES WHICH IT OFFERS FOR ENJOYMENT & STUDY

GIBRALTAR POINT

A NATURE RESERVE FOR ALL SEASONS

At least £30,000 is required
for habitat conservation and
creation, and £10,000 for improvements
to visitor services
and to the Field Station.

The Gibraltar Point National Nature Reserve, which is managed by the Trust on lease from Lincolnshire County and East Lindsey District Councils, is renowned for the scenic beauty and wealth of wildlife of its spacious seashores, sand-dunes and saltmarshes.

Some of the habitats in the reserve have been improved by cattle and sheep grazing and scrub control, and others, notably the Mere, have been created.

Further diversification of habitat is now planned by restoration of the old dyke system and the ponds on the freshwater grazing marsh and by the creation of a large brackish lagoon to attract migrant and breeding waders.

Shelduck

Spotted Redshank

Gadwall

Dunlins

Crispin Fisher '85

Teal

Redshank

Curlew Sandpiper

Little Stint

Artist's impression of the planned Brackish Lagoon.

1985

especially since owners were being encouraged by the Wildlife Enhancement Scheme to manage them themselves. Experience had shown moreover that to wait until the top priority sites became available risked losing opportunities to acquire others lower down the list perhaps but capable of improvement by management. The acquisition of Rigsby Wood in 1980 and more recently of Legbourne Wood are good examples of the latter.

We had always had a supplementary selection of potential reserves even with the 1946 and 1952 lists. More intensive investigation of the county's wildlife, which I have just described, was constantly revealing new sites – as happened, for example, in the case of old meadows. One eventual outcome of that process of discovery was a formal recognition of what became known as Sites of Nature Conservation Interest, now simply Wildlife Sites.

With the widening of options for reserve acquisition there is increasing recognition of the desirability of expanding existing reserves many of which are small and vulnerable remnants isolated in an intensively farmed countryside. In most cases this can only be achieved by restoring or re-creating appropriate habitats on adjoining land, a technique which is making rapid headway as a result of research and experimentation in the conservation movement. The restoration of limestone grassland at Roberts Field – the story of which I recounted in an earlier chapter – was one of our first such ventures. That success is being repeated at the Red Hill, Far Ings and Croft Marsh at Gibraltar Point.

The stronger protection now afforded to SSSIs was long overdue, but with the role of English Nature in relation to them changing from advisory to supervisory we have unfortunately lost something of the understanding relationship which existed between the Trust and EN staff such as John Blackwood and, in more recent years, John Shackles who after retirement has continued to assist the Trust as a volunteer on Teams and in other ways.

The pattern of nature reserve development was changing but we continued to acquire and safeguard SSSIs wherever possible. The acquisition of the Ancaster Valley in 1982, one of the jewels of the first list of potential reserves, and of the Humber Bank Claypits to the east of Barton were particularly important achievements. The recent purchase of Deeping Lakes shows that we still have a commitment to safeguard SSSIs, but the much stronger legal protection now afforded to them and the requirement to manage them to English Nature's sometimes narrow and rigid prescriptions has diminished both the need and the incentive for acquisition by the Trust, a process which in many cases had previously been the only way of securing their protection.

Management Issues

More reserves and habitat restoration projects demanded greater management resources by way of staff and volunteers, tools and machinery. The NCC's Reserves Enhancement Scheme was a powerful incentive for us to take on additional commitments, and it was followed in 1998 by the Heritage Lottery Fund's Nature Reserves Capital Works Project which enabled us to undertake major management tasks on fifty-nine of our nature reserves and to appoint extra staff for the purpose including a Project Officer and a South Lincolnshire Warden, a post we had long wanted to create. The grant over five years amounted to £921,000, some three quarters of the total costs involved. The balance came from Landfill Tax credits, from our own resources and from a vast amount of volunteer input much of which was allowable as matching funding against grants.

Grazing by sheep and more especially by cattle had long been an essential management practice for our grassland reserves, although we experienced increasing difficulty in finding graziers as livestock farming continued to decline. In the early 1990s we also began to consider using grazing to control scrub on heathlands encouraged by the prospect of being able to carry out more extensive fencing through the Nature Conservancy's Reserves Enhancement Scheme. The first experiment at Linwood Warren where the heath was dominated by the tussock forming wavy hair grass was a great success. We had been impressed by the effect of grazing by Hebridean sheep on Skipworth Common in Yorkshire. Hebrideans, a rare breed, are small and very hardy. They browse as well as graze and are therefore particularly effective in devouring regrowth of birch. So in 1993 we decided to establish our own flock of Hebrideans, meeting much of the initial cost by Trust member sponsorship - £30 paid for a breeding ewe. The flock was based at Far Ings under the management of South Humberside Warden Lionel Grooby and Assistant Warden Karen Gray who became a skilled and devoted shepherdess. After a successful initiation at Epworth Turbary the sheep were gradually spread out to other heathland reserves and to grasslands and sand-dunes at Gibraltar Point and Saltfleetby.

Whilst sheep do a very effective job, there are circumstances in which heavier cattle are more appropriate – in damper areas, for example, or for controlling coarser vegetation. Aftermath grazing by cattle on meadows was a traditional practice which the Trust has sought to maintain where necessary. In recent years we have also used cattle on wet heath reserves like Epworth Turbary and Scotton Common, using Dexter cattle of our own to supplement sheep grazing. In 2003 we purchased our own small herd of Lincoln Red cattle – now quite a rare breed – based initially at Snipe Dales and later at Gibraltar Point. Meeting the need for grazing on our reserves by expanding our own stock of animals and by seeking arrangements with other graziers is now an important issue.

Grazing is already practised on nearly fifty of the Trust's reserves and has become an indispensable means of management. We have learned, however, that it needs to be applied with discrimination taking account of the needs and conditions of each reserve and the likely effect not only on vegetation but of animals such as snakes and reptiles and birds like nightjar and tree pipit. Overgrazing can be just as damaging as neglect.

Funding for Acquisition and Management
For matching funding for purchases and initial management projects we mounted a series of appeals which built on the experience of the 1971 'Invest in Lincolnshire's Wildlife'. So an appeal in 1980 enabled us to purchase the freehold of Kirkby Moor and Rigsby Wood. Another, the Coast and Country Campaign in 1985, assisted the purchase of several new properties including parts of Crowle Waste, Sow Dale, Goslings Corner Wood and the creation of a new Visitor Centre out of the ruined farm buildings at Far Ings. That Campaign, which also aimed to increase membership, ran for several years and was boosted in 1987 by a visit from Sir David Attenborough who addressed a gathering of representatives of industry, business and local government. There was an appeal in 1996 for coast projects, including the purchase of further land at Gibraltar Point, and another in 2001 to secure the freehold of Moulton Marsh and the purchase of additional

land adjoining the National Nature Reserve at Saltfleetby. More recently in 2004 we made an appeal for the purchase of Legbourne Wood. All these appeals have been vital in raising the money needed to complete acquisitions and projects. They have also had the effect of publicising the Trust and rallying the Area Groups and individual members to assist. The increasing strength of the Trust's finances as a result of growth in membership and increasing numbers of legacies was another important factor in enabling us to take advantage of grant-aid opportunities for land purchase and management.

Another crucially important factor influencing reserve acquisition from the 1970s onwards was the availability of more grant-aid from national sources for purchase and management. As I have previously described, grants had been made during the 1950s and 60s by Charitable Trusts and by the SPNR and the WWF, but as land prices increased these were sometimes inadequate to enable purchases to proceed. Then in the 1970s financial aid on a larger scale towards land purchase became available from a variety of other sources: from the Countryside Commission and the NCC; then from the National Heritage Memorial Fund, and after 1994 from the Heritage Lottery Fund; and more recently from Landfill and Aggregate Tax sources. This variety of assistance enabled us not only to expand our acquisition programme but to be somewhat bolder in site selection, taking more account, for example, of additional criteria like landscape qualities and potential for education and public enjoyment of nature. Larger and more expensive purchases could also be contemplated.

The Nature Conservancy Council's Reserves Enhancement Scheme enabled the Trust to improve the management of its SSSI reserves, and in some cases – like Scotton Common – to retrieve habitat conditions which had deteriorated through lack of management resources. In 1991, a year before the RES came into operation, another government initiative was launched, designed to mitigate and repair some of the damage inflicted on landscapes and wildlife by thirty years of intensive agriculture. The Countryside Stewardship Scheme offered financial support for a ten-year period for projects to maintain, improve or restore landscape features and wildlife habitats on farm land. This scheme provided another source of management funding for the Trust and within the first four years we were able to enter fifteen of our reserves which were either managed by grazing like Sow Dale and Frampton Marsh, or where habitats were being re-created as at the Red Hill and Jackson's Marsh at Gibraltar Point. By 1994 annual payments from Stewardship amounted to almost £16,500. With further entries, expanding properties and more regeneration of projects the income had reached more than £31,000 by 2005. In addition to Stewardship the Trust's productive grazing land now receives subsidy under the Single Payment Scheme which in 2005/6 amounted to nearly £33,000.

A new agri-environment scheme Environmental Stewardship launched in 2005 offers financial support for good land management and conservation. The Trust is taking advantage of this at both Entry and Higher Level. The latter, which attracts more resources, is designed for management of more specialised habitats like heathland and wetland and is therefore especially applicable to many of our reserves. Existing Countryside Stewardship agreements are transferred to the Higher Level Scheme at the end of their ten years.

Environmental Stewardship schemes should produce great benefits for wildlife and landscapes throughout the countryside. For the Trust the income from these various schemes including Woodland Grants will be of major significance for the management of existing reserves, and by providing an assured income for at least ten years ahead will be a critical factor in reaching decisions on further land purchase. The conditions of the Schemes, especially the HLS, are complex, specific and detailed and are regularly monitored. They require the kind of clear-sighted planning and meticulous administration which David Bromwich, the Trust's Assistant Director (Reserves) has devoted to them.

Habitat Representation

The expansion of our reserves over the last twenty-five years has continued to be based primarily on habitat representation. I give a brief update of major developments.

Coastlands

Gibraltar Point. I described in Chapter IV the establishment and securing of the Gibraltar Point nature reserve, the development of management and of facilities for education and public interest and enjoyment. Much of the routine management of the reserve over the last thirty years has been concerned with means of reconciling those uses with the conservation of its internationally important wildlife and natural features. Rare and endangered plants and animals like the little tern had to be specially safeguarded, and invasive species like rosebay willowherb and the pernicious Australian swamp stonecrop *Crassula helmsii* had to be controlled. The natterjack toad, which had occurred at Gibraltar Point until the early years of the 20th Century, was successfully reintroduced by a meticulous and painstaking process and by appropriate habitat management.

During this period the reserve was also considerably expanded and ambitious habitat creation projects undertaken. The first of these was a saline lagoon excavated in 1991 at the northern end of the old saltmarsh adjoining Bulldog Bank. The water level from springtide flooding was controlled by a sluice. Islands provided nest sites for waders and hopefully for terns, whilst hides at the east and west ends gave excellent views for bird watching. The construction of the Fenland Lagoon as it is named was generously funded by Fenland Laundries whose Managing Director Donovan Fry has been a lifelong supporter of the Trust and was for several years a member of its Council. The lagoon attracts a variety of passage waders and is used from time to time as a high tide roost by waders especially by redshanks. Oystercatchers and little ringed plovers have nested on its islands, but as a nesting site for reasons not fully understood it has never quite lived up to early expectations.

The reserve was expanded in 1998 when we were at last able to acquire the forty acres of wet grassland and scrub at the northern end of the freshwater marsh, an area which the County Council had tried unsuccessfully to purchase at an earlier stage. Most of it is now incorporated in the freshwater marsh grazing paddock. An exciting new development came in 1995 when we purchased the twenty-acre arable field adjoining Sykes Farm, meeting the greater part of the cost by funds derived from a legacy left to the Trust by Mr George Jackson of Hogsthorpe in whose memory the area is named Jackson's Marsh. Our intention was to create an area of grassland and wetland with shallow pools and marginal reedbeds. After survey and hydrological investigations a plan of the new layout was prepared and excavation of pools, sowing of the meadow grassland and construction of a large hide were completed by 2001. The spoil was used to construct a 'dune' system along the southern edge so that the hide is approached through a sheltered hollow hidden from the marsh.

There was one detail of that restoration which gave Mary and me particular pleasure. When we surveyed the flora of the reserve and its immediate surroundings in the early 1950s we discovered several plants of marsh mallow in a damp hollow – the site of an old creek – along the southern edge of what is now Jackson's Marsh. A few years later they were in danger of being destroyed by the dumping and burning of potato haulm, so as a precaution we moved some of them to the edge of one of the ponds along the Mill Pond Road in the reserve where they have flourished and spread over the years. Mary raused plants from seed and these were planted among the reeds on the original site. This year 2005 I could see the flower heads protruding above the reeds. A plant of brackish marshes, marsh mallow is rare in Lincolnshire and this site is at the extreme northern edge of its range on the eastern side of England. Its pale pink flowers and sensuously soft velvety leaves make it one of the most attractive of our coastal plants.

To the north of this area a private landowner had also excavated a lagoon known as Tennyson Sands (the Tennyson connection with Gibraltar Point persists) from which the spoil had likewise been distributed as a dune along the eastern edge screening the lagoon from the public road. This new dune, quickly clothed with vegetation helped by the sowing of appropriately chosen seed mixtures, has provided an excellent habitat for butterflies and other insects. In 2000 we were offered the freehold of the Tennyson Sands lagoon along with two adjacent fields on Croftmarsh, a total of 60 acres. The price was high but with some generous grant-aid and access to the Stewardship scheme we were able to complete the purchase. The extension of the lagoon and reedbed and the conversion of the rest of the former arable land to pasture is now completed. Cattle and our own Hebridean sheep are already grazing grassland areas here and on Jackson's Marsh, re-establishing a traditional Outmarsh regime. Two hides give excellent views over the whole area, and a new footpath and cycle track created in conjunction with the County Council traverses the whole length of the new property parallel to the public road. This project of wetland and pasture re-creation, carried out under the experienced supervision of our Gibraltar Point Site Manager Kevin Wilson, involved many people, staff and volunteers and our skilled contractor Maurice Coupland. It is a splendid extension to the habitat mosaic of the old reserve and has already brought a great variety of migrants and breeding avocets, common terns, oystercatchers, and little ringed plovers, and, equally pleasing, the return of nesting lapwings after an absence from the reserve of ten years or more.

There was one other notable piece of restoration of a different kind at Gibraltar Point. When we bought the farmyard of Sykes Farm in 1977 the only building left was the cart shed and barn above, and that was a roofless ruin. All that had survived were the three remaining bay arches and the lower part of the walls, and there was just enough left of the northern gable to see where the owl 'window' had been. For years we nursed an ambition to restore this once handsome building, but without any immediate use we could not justify the costs. By the late 1990s, however, office accommodation at the study centre had become seriously inadequate for the administrative use of both the centre and the nature reserve. So we returned to the idea of restoring the Sykes Farm building close to which we had already sited a workshop and tool store. On the basis of a costed plan prepared by the Trust's honorary architect Neil Taylor we succeeded in attracting funding from the European Rural Development Fund, from Landfill Tax credits and from Lincolnshire County Council. Reconstruction carried out during 2000 by local specialist builders has given us a superbly restored building – it should have had an architectural award – incorporating the nature reserve office and an assistant warden's accommodation upstairs, and storage and garaging for machinery on the ground floor. Of course we renewed the owl 'window' in the gable, and barn owls showed their gratitude by rearing a brood there in the first year and in every year since then!

At **Saltfleetby-Theddlethorpe Dunes** following the National Nature Reserve declaration in 1968, the Nature Conservancy Council gradually assumed main responsibility for management, but Trust volunteers continued to help with wardening and a Trust-NCC Working Group met regularly to discuss a whole range of management matters. This liaison was diluted, however, when the functions of the Group were absorbed in a new North-East Lincolnshire Coast Advisory Group which covers a much longer stretch of coast and on which a number of other bodies are represented.

The Trust had purchased the Sea View meadow – the old caravan camp site – from the County Council in 1965. We also leased from the County Council a smaller area further south in the reserve where for a number of years we maintained a wooden bungalow known as Journey's End to let to visiting naturalists. We also held a licence from the Ministry of Defence for two areas within the proposed National Nature Reserve, one of them comprising part of the main dune slack. At a high level meeting between the Trust and NCC officers, including the Director and Deputy Director England, in May 1995 it was agreed that when the MoD decided to release them the Trust would seek to acquire the freehold of the two areas which it had occupied since 1956, and that the NCC and the Trust should both acquire part of the foreshore probably on a 50:50 basis. That agreement, although freely entered into, was never ratified by the NCC – perhaps because of changes in personnel – and was eventually disowned by the successor body English Nature. When in 1997 the MoD decided to release one of the Trust occupied areas, English Nature asked if we would stand aside and allow them to acquire it on the grounds that they had funds available from a legacy. I had always taken the view that the Trust should retain a stake of real significance in the reserve and its management and that that could best be achieved by a substantial share of the ownership. There was strong historic justification for that as well as other reasons. Without the Trust's initiative in creating the reserve and its crucial part in defending it against development it is highly unlikely that there would have been an NNR at Saltfleetby-Theddlethorpe. Moreover, the Trust as the long-standing licencee and occupier of the area in question would have had a strong case for acquiring it. So it was with some reluctance that I agreed to English Nature's request, and I did so only on the understanding that we should seek a new deal with them on the joint management of the NNR, defining our participation and re-establishing regular consultation on management between us.

By the 1990s the Trust was already in a strong position at Saltfleetby. The most popular access to the reserve and car park from the main road at Rimac is by a track and a bridge over the river Great Eau. The bridge had originally been erected by the MoD to provide access to the Saltfleetby RAF range. When that closed the Department had no further use for it and no obligation to maintain it. In the 1980s its condition was giving rise to some concern, and in 1988, after a structural survey, East Lindsey District Council obtained a court order restricting access to pedestrian use only. No authority was prepared to take responsibility for its ownership, upkeep and insurance, but eventually after protracted negotiations, initiated largely by the Trust, it was agreed by all the parties concerned that the Trust should acquire the bridge and that the County and District Councils, the National Rivers Authority and the NCC would meet the capital costs of repair and contribute appropriately to future maintenance. The bridge was re-opened at a ceremony hosted by the Trust in May 1991.

Nature in Lincolnshire had highlighted the rapid disappearance of old Outmarsh pasture and the need to retain and restore this important winter habitat for the many thousands of lapwing and golden plover and smaller numbers of curlew and other waders that winter in the Lindsey Outmarsh. It was a theme taken up later in the Lincolnshire BAP. The Trust made a start on redressing this loss by the acquisition in 1999 of thirty-five acres of arable land for conversion to pasture close to Saltfleet Haven and adjoining the NNR and the Trust's existing Sea View field. Since then further acquisitions have extended the Trust's holdings to nearly 170 acres comprising most of the land on either side of the river from the Haven to south of Rimac. This has not only enabled us to restore permanent pasture and provide a flood plain for the river; it also forms a permanent buffer protection for the NNR.

The value of the Trust's holdings for the management and protection of the NNR is also demonstrated by our agreement to enable English Nature to establish a workshop and office on the Sea View site, and more recently to remove the Rimac car park from the NNR to the Trust's nearby property. These developments strengthened our case for a full partnership agreement for the management of the NNR, and thanks to Stuart Crooks' diligence and persistence, a Memorandum of Understanding to that effect was prepared and agreed by both parties in 2004. This sets out common objectives and joint working arrangements for the management of the NNR and the Trust's reserve, and the provision of facilities for use and access. It also consolidates the good working relationship which has always existed between the Trust and English Nature's reserve staff. It marks another important landmark in the somewhat turbulent history of this splendid coastline.

At **Donna Nook** to the north of Saltfleet Haven accretion of mud and sand has resulted in extensive flats and saltings backed by a dune system which has features similar to those of the Saltfleetby-Theddlethorpe NNR including slacks and lagoons with a rich flora. The area had long been known for its diversity of bird life of both breeding and migratory species. By the 1980s a breeding colony of grey seals was also well established and increasing year by year.

Assisted by a more active interest by the Ministry of Defence at national level – which included the appointment of a Wildlife Officer – in the conservation of the wildlife of their ranges and training areas, and by the willing cooperation of their local officers and staff, the Trust was able to secure a licence in 1978 to manage some five miles of coastland from just north of Saltfleet Haven to Grainthorpe Haven. This was extended three years later by a lease from the County Council of an area of saltmarsh adjoining Saltfleet Haven.

As at Saltfleetby in the 1950s, the first task of our band of volunteer wardens was to clear up the rubbish deposited on the dunes and in the lagoons. We were also concerned to protect from disturbance a little tern colony on the high sand and shingle banks out beyond the saltmarsh. It was primarily for that reason that in the 1980s we also began to employ a summer warden, although the rapid build up of the grey seal colony soon necessitated an extension of his duties until the end of the year. In 1996 a full-time North-East Coast warden's post was created. For a few years it was run jointly with the RSPB to assist with their reserve at Tetney, but with our growing management commitment on this coast we soon took full responsibility for the post. Not least of those commitments was the growing popularity of the seal colony and the need to manage the many thousands of people – up to 30,000 by the late 1990s – coming to see it. Fencing off a path along the dune edge allowed the seals to be viewed at close quarters without danger to the visitors or disruption to the colony. Voluntary wardens were recruited for what became a major exercise in November and December each year. Nowhere else in the British Isles can a breeding colony of grey seals be seen at such close quarters. Little wonder that it became so popular.

Our management of the reserve was clearly approved by the Ministry of Defence and the RAF locally, with the result that in 1998 our licence was converted into a lease for a large part of the area. That was followed in 2002 by its designation by English Nature as a National Nature Reserve, the first such in the country on MoD land, and the third NNR in Lincolnshire to be managed by the Trust.

Central Coast. I referred in Chapter XI 'The Expanding Estate' to the increasing recreational development pressures on the central Lindsey coast between Skegness and Mablethorpe and the consequent weakening of the Coastal Conservation Area provisions in the stretch from Ingoldmells to Chapel Point. It is a problem which I further described in an article 'Conserving our Coastline' in the January 2002 number of *Lapwings*. In the Coastal Conservation Area from Chapel Point to Anderby the Trust has sought to promote the designation of a coastal Nature Park or Local Nature Reserve through numerous discussions with County and District planners. Ownership and occupation of the five Sea Bank Clay Pits gives us some territorial status in the Area, but that could be significantly enhanced by the acquisition of further land for conversion to grazing pasture and wetland. Enquiries have shown that that might be possible and I hope that progress will be made to that end.

Moulton Marsh. The absorption of South Lincolnshire Nature Reserves in 1992 brought several new reserves into the care of the Trust, the largest of them being Moulton Marsh, a long strip of land of some ninety acres on the south bank of the River Welland below Fosdyke Bridge. It had been created by the realignment of the sea bank and consisted of a series of lagoons and areas of saltmarsh. Although small in relation to the adjoining vast areas of the Wash, it is strategically situated near the outfall of the Welland and is used by wildfowl and waders. In recent years the non-tidal saline lagoons have been recognised by English Nature as some of the best examples in the country of this rare habitat which supports some highly specialised animals such as the lagoon sand shrimp which is specially protected under the Wildlife and Countryside Act. The reserve was originally leased from the local Drainage Board, but the freehold was acquired by the Trust in 2001 partly with funds raised by an appeal.

1963   *Croft Marsh transformed.*   *2005*

Ruins of Sykes Farm cartsheds 1996
and after conversion to NNR office and management base 2000.

Marsh mallow
in the original
site at Gibraltar
Point, 1962.

Paradise Field, Saltfleetby, 2004.

Grey seal
breeding colony,
Donna Nook.

Woodlands

The Trust's nature reserves acquisition policies had always included representative examples of woods from the three main areas of ancient woodland in Lincolnshire: the Middle Marsh in the east; the oak-lime woods of the Central Vale, and the Kesteven uplands. Acquisition opportunities, however, were infrequent and the cost of woodland in the early days of the Trust was relatively high. It was indeed fifteen years before we acquired our first ancient wood, Hoplands at Claxby, and that was only possible because it was partly gifted.

By the early 1980s the Forestry Commission had withdrawn from their holdings in the Middle Marsh woods which were all left in private ownership, some being used for intensive softwood production, some sadly neglected. In this situation woods were more likely to come onto the market than in areas like the central limewoods where Forestry Commission ownership dominated. SSSI designation was never a particularly significant guide to acquisition targets. Only three in the Middle Marsh were so designated: Willoughby which the Trust had originally hoped to purchase, but which was deteriorating; Hoplands which was designated SSSI only after the Trust acquired it, and Muckton half of which the Trust purchased in 1983, the other half having been clear-felled and replanted with a mixture of broadleaves and conifers. Most of the Middle Marsh woods were ancient in origin, and we took the view that those which retained sufficient of the traditional coppice-with-standards structure and features could be restored and were worth acquiring if opportunities and resources permitted, taking account also of the fact that restoration measures were seldom as urgent as those pertaining, for example, to heath or grassland where vegetation succession was rapid. It was considerations of this kind that persuaded us to acquire Rigsby Wood in 1980 and more recently (in 2004) **Legbourne Wood**. At Hoplands, Rigsby and Muckton more than twenty years of management largely by volunteers has removed non-native trees, restored blocks of hazel and ash coppice and reinstated rides and glades. It has been a considerable achievement.

Like the other three, Legbourne lies at the base of the old degraded sea cliff at the eastern edge of the Wolds, and it is clear from our early investigations that there is a variety of soil types and vegetation including areas of bracken with skullcap and common cow-wheat, the latter recorded in the county in recent years only from three of the central limewoods. The ride system is still discernible and can readily be restored. Special measures will be taken to protect the important heronry from disturbance. If you travel now along the little road called the Barton Street – an ancient trackway in origin – along the edge of the Wolds from Little Cawthorpe to Claxby you are seldom out of sight of a Trust woodland reserve.

For reasons already mentioned, few woods have come onto the market in the Central Vale in recent years. **Goslings Corner**, acquired by the Trust in 1987, is our only holding in the area. We have subsequently enhanced the site by acquiring two adjoining grass fields to create the kind of woodland edge habitat which is now rare in Lincolnshire. We are also participating in a Forest Enterprise scheme with HLF funding to link the various Bardney Forest woods by creating ecological corridors. Acquisition of other representative samples of these nationally important oak-limewoods would be a high priority for the Trust should opportunities occur.

Representation of the Kesteven woods in our reserves is still confined to Tortoiseshell, Dole, and **Lawn Wood**. The latter, is an ancient wood of oak and ash with field maple, midland hawthorn and, as at Tortoiseshell, some fine wild service trees. The wood adjoins the two meadows of Bottleneck and Jacksons which were a memorial gift to the Trust. The reserve overlooks the earthworks of the motte and bailey castle and the attractive stone village of Castle Bytham. Possibilities of acquiring other Kesteven woods have been investigated but so far without success.

Whilst management of newly acquired woodland might not be so urgent as for some habitats, in the longer term it requires considerable input from volunteer workers and staff. It is highly unlikely that the sale of produce from woodland nature reserves will ever recover the full costs of management, but it can make a useful contribution to it. We already sell coppice wood for firewood, for use in thatching and other specialised purposes. We have also sponsored a small charcoal manufacturing business based at Moor Farm launched with the aid of European funding. The Trust receives £1 for every bag sold.

Chalk and Limestone Grassland
When the Trust came into being in 1948 species-rich chalk and limestone grassland was already a very scarce habitat in Lincolnshire, confined to a few remnants in steep valleys, on hillsides and in old quarries and road verges. By the 1970s we had acquired a few of the best of those: on the chalk at the Red Hill and the quarries at Claxby Mill Hill and Welton, and on the limestone at that time only at Rauceby Warren. Protection of limestone sites was given high priority in the 1980s and 90s. The result was the acquisition of the most important of them: the Ancaster Valley, Roberts Field rescued from a conifer plantation, **Duke's Covert**, and in the north Clapgate Pits which I have already described. Duke's Covert, a four-acre grassland site adjoining the roadside verge at Copper Hill on the Ermine Street above Ancaster, has a rich limestone flora which includes columbine in one of its few Lincolnshire localities. The nearby verges, now an SSSI, are a gem of limestone flora with such classic plants as purple milk vetch, thyme, rock rose, kidney and horseshoe vetches, the latter the food plant of the beautiful chalkhill blue butterfly which occurred here at the northern edge of its range and in its only Lincolnshire locality until 1974 when it was last seen. It had appeared in our film 'Nature in Lincolnshire' few years earlier. Another rarity, also at its northern extremity in Britain, which is happily still there, is the neat and comely man orchid. Copper Hill was a mandatory stopping-off place on our summer family journeys to the south or west, an opportunity to count the orchids and admire the well-loved limestone flowers. Traffic on the Ermine Street is much heavier than it was forty years ago and the Copper Hill verges have suffered in consequence. So too has another verge further south on the Ermine Street where the lovely perennial flax in one of its only three localities in Lincolnshire is threatened with extinction.

Further south again near the county boundary verges at South Witham are of such importance as to merit nature reserve status. More than 260 species of flowering plants, 28 of butterflies and 34 of breeding birds have been recorded. For fifteen years this reserve was managed with great skill and devotion by volunteer Wayside Warden Eric Simms, the well-known naturalist, writer and broadcaster.

On the chalk Wolds verges are just as important for wildlife including such localised plants as yellow-wort, autumn gentian and clustered bellflower. Verges on the Bluestone Heath road are particularly notable. At Tetford Hill, where the Protected Road Verge scheme between the Trust and the County Council originated in 1960, Mary and I had discovered in the early 1950s the rare, exotic looking lizard orchid which Mary subsequently drew for Butcher's *Illustrated British Flora*. Its distribution range had spread northwards over the previous fifty years, but by the 1960s it had retreated southwards again. There are other chalk plants on the roadside bank at Tetford Hill and in the ash wood on the hillside, and there are also old records of fly orchid and other rarities. Other rich verges occur at the south-eastern tip of the chalk Wolds at Calceby, Claxby and Welton where pyramidal and common spotted orchids are abundant. The verges on Dawber Lane in Welton parish show a striking transition in their flora as the lane descends from the chalk onto the Middlemarsh boulder clays below.

We had estimated in *Nature in Lincolnshire* that no more than 120 acres of chalk grassland remained in the County and that was in small and scattered remnants of the kind which the Trust was already managing. To restore larger areas of downland would require re-creation of the habitat, a process for which the techniques were constantly being improved by research and experimentation. So in 1998 we took the opportunity to purchase sixty acres of farmland adjoining the small Red Hill reserve on the Wolds above Goulceby. One of the two fields had been in set-aside for some time and had a cover of grass with some chalk flowers already appearing; the other we sowed with a grass mixture and cropped for a time to reduce the nutrient content of the soil. As at Roberts Field, bales of hay full of wildflower seed from the original reserve were then scattered over the fields which in due course were grazed by a flock of the Trust's Hebridean sheep. Enthusiastic volunteer manager Harry Turner also collected seed, some of which he sowed into the ground and some to raise plants in modules for setting out. Volunteers helped to control ragwort and thistles until a tight sward was well established. Now after five or six years almost all the plant species from the original reserve are spreading, and some of the rarer ones like pyramidal orchid have appeared. Butterflies, including a strong colony of common blue, are increasing and meadow pipits have colonised the area.

The success of the Red Hill experiment encouraged us to seek opportunities for similar re-creation projects elsewhere on the chalk and limestone hills. One such scheme which was included in the 2001 appeal was within a few miles of Red Hill. Unfortunately we were unable to complete negotiations successfully, but there will doubtless be other opportunities.

Other Grasslands
Snipe Dales, acquired as a nature reserve in 1972, was one of the few valleys in the Spilsby sandstone country to have remained as grassland. On the other side of the sandstone ridge to the south-east in the valley of **Sow Dale** the plough had already made considerable inroads, and one of the objectives of the Coast and Country Campaign in the mid-1980s was to purchase land there to retain the Dale in its traditional usages of meadow, rough pasture, ash wood and carr of alder and willow. Sow Dale is the most extensive of the 'Dales' of the southern Wolds. For centuries it formed an important access to the hills from the Fenland country to the south; the famous prehistoric site of Hall Hill overlooks the entrance to it, and by the Middle Ages it was guarded by John of Gaunt's great castle at Old Bolingbroke. It is a place of rare landscape beauty, historic association and variety

corridor between surrounding pine and birch woodland. Aerial photographs from different periods dramatically illustrate the change. It was not that we had not tried to control the spread of trees. Volunteer parties had worked tirelessly pulling up birch and pine seedlings and cutting back older trees, but it was a losing battle. Only a massive clearance of trees followed by grazing could save the heathland. With the timely assistance of English Nature's Reserves Enhancement Scheme and the strengthening of the Trust's own financial position, it was possible to fence both the Scotton and Linwood reserves and introduce grazing using the Trust's own Hebridean flock. Both reserves are gradually improving, and Scotton Common will benefit from the decision of Forest Enterprise to fell the central section of the adjoining Dallison's Plantation and leave it to revert to heath. Perhaps it is a good omen that the round-leaved sundew has been rediscovered at Scotton, but what is needed for that reserve in particular is a thorough hydrological and soil survey to provide a sound basis for further enlargement and improvement measures.

At Epworth and Haxey Turbaries scrub encroachment was already far advanced when they came into the possession of the Trust in the mid-1950s, and it was not until the formation of the Isle of Axholme Area Group in 1977 that we were able to make any real progress with restoration of open fen at Epworth. Under the enthusiastic and dedicated leadership of Geoff Trinder the Group embarked on a clearance programme, removing birch and selling logs to make a substantial contribution to management costs. In 1981 with the help of a supportive neighbouring farmer a series of ponds linked by channels were excavated on an area cleared of trees, and a hide was provided to overlook them. In the following years further substantial areas of woodland were cleared by using new sources of funding and Government training schemes, the reclaimed areas then being fenced and grazed by sheep and cattle. As a result by 2005 almost 50% of the Turbary had been cleared of scrub and woodland, and further clearance is planned.

Crowle Moors was an equally formidable task, but the Group began clearance around the site of the rare greater yellow rattle and, here too, as new funding became available contract labour was used to supplement voluntary work in clearing and fencing extensive areas to be grazed by the Hebridean sheep. The installation of dams at critical points helped to retain a high water table.

For reasons largely beyond its control, wet heath and bog reserves have presented the Trust with some of its most formidable management problems. More adequate resources and the dedication and ingenuity of volunteers and staff have enabled us to rescue these vulnerable places and their specialised plants and animals from virtual extinction. At the same time we have helped to create greater awareness of the unique wildlife interest and fragile beauty of these places. There is still much to be done in the restoration process and the effects of climate change are unpredictable, but for now we can find some satisfaction in what has been achieved.

Wetlands

At our premier wetland reserve **Far Ings** we have continued with considerable success our policy of expansion whenever opportunities arose. In 1996 we acquired the two lakes known as Westfield Lakes to the east of the Visitor Centre, and more recently we have taken a licence from the North Lincolnshire Council to occupy and manage the next lake, the former Outdoor Pursuits Pit, which in turn adjoins the existing Barton Reedbed reserve. Meantime in 2000 we purchased the two fields and the blow wells on the south side of Far Ings Lane. Clay from these fields was then sold to North Lincolnshire Council for the reclamation of a former industrial site in Barton. Carefully designed excavation created five new pits in which reedbeds have been planted. Finally in 2006 we have completed the purchase of Target Lake, the westernmost of the Far Ings pits. The reserve now extends for more than a mile along the Humber Bank and comprises some 200 acres. As well as reedbed and open water it includes the adjoining Humber foreshore, and there are meadows, hedgerows and areas of scrub.

The reserve has grown not only in size but also in quality of habitat. By controlling water levels, and by cutting and harvesting and occasionally burning, the reedbeds have been rejuvenated. New channels have been excavated and marginal habitats improved. As a result bird populations have flourished including a wide range of waterfowl and reedbed specialists such as water rail, sedge and reed warblers and reed bunting. Especially notable are scarce national species bearded tit, marsh harrier and bittern. For the latter the Barton area reedbeds are now second only in importance in the UK to the Suffolk coastal wetlands.

Access to the reserve has also been improved. There are waymarked paths and viewing hides at strategic points. Some 60,000 people visit the reserve and Visitor Centre each year, and school use of the facilities at the Centre has developed significantly in the last few years when the Trust has been able to provide teaching services through the Education and Community Action Project. That provision is now to be further extended through the South Humber Wildlife and People Project which will have a main base at the former Outdoor Pursuits Centre, for which further funding has been secured from Yorkshire Forward. The Heritage Lottery Fund, which contributed substantially to some of the land purchased at Far Ings, is a major funder of the Project which covers the Humber Bank from Burton-upon-Stather to North Killingholme. Within the area are two major coastal realignment schemes, one at Alkborough at the confluence of the Trent and the Humber; the other at Chowder Ness immediately adjoining the Far Ings reserve. The Trust has an interest in both schemes.

Far Ings was officially declared a National Nature Reserve by Environment Minister Elliot Morley on 15 August 2005, a fitting recognition of its outstanding quality. Many bodies have contributed to its development, but the day to day planning and management is the work of the Site Manager and North Lincolnshire Warden Lionel Grooby and his staff, and of many dedicated volunteers.

In the further complex of clay pits to the east of Barton and within the Humber SSSI the Trust has acquired Pasture Wharf, Barrow Haven, Fairfield Pit and Dawson City, a total of 150 acres.

With the virtually complete loss of natural wetlands in Lincolnshire the habitat is dependent on disused mineral workings and re-creation projects like those at Gibraltar Point and Far Ings. It has been the Trust's policy therefore to discover as much as possible about abandoned flooded quarries and to look for opportunities to make acquisitions or other means of safeguarding the best examples, those which have biodiversity value or seem likely to develop it. Since such places are often fairly robust, potential for education and public enjoyment use has also been a consideration. Competition for such places for fishing and sailing has increased and many have become municipal refuse tips. Apart from the Humber Bank Clay Pits those which the Trust has acquired in the last twenty years have been the result of excavation of sand and gravel deposited in the last glaciation. The most notable of these has been at **Whisby** in the Witham valley to the west of Lincoln. Extensive areas of flooded pits are now bisected by the A46 relief road. I was first introduced to this area with Barrie Wilkinson in the 1960s by Peter Prince, a young ornithologist who went on to become a leading researcher with the British Antarctic Survey for which his tragically early death was a great loss. His association with the Whisby nature reserve is commemorated by the Peter Prince Hide opened in 2001 which overlooks the northernmost of the lakes.

Mr William Feare, Managing Director of Robert Teal Ltd, the owners of a large area of the pits, was anxious that the flooded workings should remain as a sanctuary with minimum disturbance. After somewhat lengthy negotiations an agreement was reached in 1985 for the Trust to manage some fifty acres as a nature reserve. Further exploration revealed an area of equal interest immediately to the south, and as a result of negotiations with Lincolnshire County Council and North Kesteven District Council and financial assistance from the Countryside Commission, the Trust acquired a further 145 acres by lease and purchase to establish the Whisby Nature Park, so called to indicate that providing for education and public enjoyment would be a primary objective. A Project Officer was appointed to set up a management scheme, and a small information centre was provided. The venture was a great success, and in 1999 the partnership between the Trust and the County and District Councils made a successful bid to the Millennium Commission for a £3.3 million project to construct visitor and education centres and workshops on a new site overlooking another of the lakes, Thorpe Lake, for which a long lease was given to the Trust by a supportive sand and gravel company Lafarge Redland. With the addition of further areas of worked-out pits the Nature Park covers more than 375 acres. As a condition of the Millennium Commission grant the management agreement for the nature reserve was superseded by a long lease to the Trust.

The Natural World Centre is managed by the District Council; the Education Centre by the Trust which also manages the Nature Park, employing a teacher for the education service and a site manager and assistant. Whisby has been a major project for the Trust in working out financial and administrative arrangements with the partners, in administering the education service and in the management of a large reserve in which the conservation of wildlife and public use has been successfully reconciled. More than 50,000 people visit and use the facilities each year, and the number is steadily increasing.

Provisions for use have perhaps tended to overshadow the value of its rich and varied wildlife: over 180 species of birds recorded – wildfowl in winter, nesting common tern, great-crested grebe, kingfisher and nightingale in spring and summer; 20 species of dragonflies and 250 moths, and a great variety of wetland and waterside plants including a spectacular display of marsh orchids. There is still considerable potential for future expansion of the Whisby reserves.

Extraction of sand was one of the operations which damaged and destroyed some of the north-west Coversands heaths as I recounted in an earlier chapter. On the south-western fringe of the former Manton Common SSSI in **Messingham** parish sand quarrying has left a series of lagoons with marginal beds of reed and reedmace interspersed with patches of scrub and woodland and a few remnants of the original heathland with ling, broom and other heathland plants including the now rare petty whin. Damp areas have cottongrass, bog pimpernel, and an abundance of marsh orchids. The gradual removal of a conifer plantation is producing a similar marshy area where another rare Lincolnshire plant the round-leaved wintergreen has been discovered. This is also a site for pillwort, an aquatic fern rare not only in Britain but on a European scale.

The site which was acquired by British Industrial Sands in the early 1960s for further working became a focus of interest for Scunthorpe ornithologists and members of the Trust's Scunthorpe and Brigg Area Group. As a result of negotiations with BIS the Trust secured a lease of the site of 100 acres in 1981. With the help of Tarmac and other local firms the management group created paths, built hides and improved habitats. Its wealth of wildlife and excellent access facilities have made this one of the most popular Trust reserves.

In the lower Bain valley on the margins of the great Fen lake deltaic deposits of sand and gravel are being extensively excavated leaving a mosaic of flooded pits with fringing reedbeds and scrub. Abandoned pits are soon in demand for fishing, and a massive refuse tip is still accumulating within the area. In the early 1990s in considering the East Lindsey Local Plan we suggested to district and county planners that an after-use plan should be prepared for all the lower Bain sand and gravel workings. The suggestion was well received, but unfortunately one of the sand and gravel companies declined to cooperate and the proposal was not pursued. Meantime the Trust succeeded in acquiring one of the recently worked-out pits which was already known as an important bird site. The **Kirkby Pit** is a shallow thirty-six acre pit with wide beaches and islands where common terns, oystercatchers, ringed and little ringed plovers nest and where waders and wildfowl of many species occur on passage and in winter. The River Bain flows through the site which is bordered on the east by the disused Horncastle Canal. Cessation of pumping as adjoining areas were worked out raised the water level in the pit for several years and the wet margins and islands disappeared. Control of water levels was eventually effected by the installation of an ingenious tilting weir. A hide gives excellent views over the pit and the wide valley with a backdrop of the Tumby woods.

In the south at Witham-on-the-Hill another flooded sand pit – **Stanton's Pit** named after the donor – attracts a variety of migrant waders and is proving to be a notable site for scarce and localised beetles.

With continuing extension of sand and gravel working in the county there will doubtless be further opportunities for the Trust to acquire wetland sites should that accord with acquisition policy, and resources for purchase and management be available. One such opportunity occurred indeed in 2003 when with generous grant-aid the Trust was able to purchase **The Lake at Deeping St James**. The Lake, an SSSI, covering seventy-eight acres was excavated for sand and gravel in the last twenty-five years of the 19th century. It is an impressive stretch of water with a fringe of trees and a tree-covered island waiting for a nesting osprey! It is a winter wildfowl site of regional importance.

Adjoining The Lake is a recently excavated area of gravel pits – the **Welland Bank Pits** – on which the Trust has secured a long lease. There are two shallow lakes with islands, areas of grassland, scrub and woodland, all habitats which will become richer in wildlife as the site matures. Grant-aid for the purchase also provided for the employment of a Project Officer for an initial period, and in

Sow Dale in maytime.

Scotton Common after scrub clearing and introducing grazing.

Red Hill reserve extension in winter with Hebridean sheep.

Epworth Turbary 1985 (right) and after further clearance of scrub and woodland 1995 (below).

Teal's Lake, Whisby Nature Park

Deepings Lakes reserve.

that capacity Dave Vandome, our former South Lincolnshire Warden and long-time devoted Trust volunteer, has initiated habitat management, prepared access tracks, car park and interpretative boards as well as recruiting a new group of local volunteer helpers. I saw the place lately on an early autumn day of blue sky and scattered high cloud. A large flock of lapwings circled overhead wings flashing white in the sunlight. In the distance only the squat spire of Crowland Abbey pierced the flat fenland horizon.

The Urban Environment

The Trust has always encouraged its Area Groups to collect information about wildlife in towns and villages in their areas and to promote conservation measures wherever appropriate. Some have done so – there were surveys of various kinds in the 1990s in Grimsby, Spalding and Alford, for example – but there is much scope for further action which could involve many more members. Group members across the county were indeed involved in the Conservation in Churchyards project conducted jointly by the Trust and the Diocese of Lincoln in which more than 160 churchyards were surveyed for their natural history interest. Area meetings were held to discuss management methods, and plans were prepared for a selection of sites.

The most notable developments in an urban area have been in Lincoln. A survey conducted by Area Group members and others over three years from 1985 to 1988 revealed more than thirty sites of wildlife interest within the city boundary. Two of the main habitat types in those sites are represented in Trust reserves: the marsh and wetlands of the floor of the Lincoln Gap by Boultham Mere, a reed fringed 19th century ballast pit; and Greetwell Hollow a worked-out limestone quarry with a characteristic flora. Following up the findings and recommendations of the survey – which was published as a booklet – the Trust in association with the City Council launched a Lincoln Green Project to encourage community involvement in the management of green spaces and to foster interest in wildlife conservation issues. This developed in 1996 into a three-year project managed by the Trust, the Council and Groundwork Lincolnshire. Funds were found to employ a Project Officer, Phil Porter, who later became Manager of the Whisby Nature Park and Reserve. The Trust had no longer term involvement, but many of the aims and activities of the Project were continued by the Council and other agencies.

Gardens whether in town or village are of great importance for wildlife and a valuable avenue for promoting interest in and concern for the natural world. The Trust has been active for many years in promoting this interest and good gardening practice through the medium of leaflets, talks, day courses and demonstrations (including the Banovallum House gardens) and regular features in the *Lapwings* magazine. Open Days at some excellent wildlife gardens created by members feature in the Trust's annual programme of outdoor events.

The Future for Nature Reserves

What is the future for nature reserves? For forty years we were engaged in a kind of salvage operation to save the unspoilt coast from development and the best surviving examples of heath and downland, meadow and marsh and ancient woodland from intensive farming and forestry. Now the situation has changed dramatically. Not only has the intensity of production slackened, but the whole system of subsidy on which the agricultural industry depends is shifting from production to the promotion of sustainable land use and management. Diversity of wildlife should be restored to the wider countryside as a result. Special places, the Sites of Special Scientific Interest especially, which we fought to safeguard not only now enjoy real statutory protection which was missing in the past, but have to be managed positively by owners to achieve favourable conditions. In these circumstances one may well ask the question 'are more nature reserves needed?'.

For a variety of reasons the answer I believe must be emphatically yes. First, although more environmentally sensitive farming and forestry will be beneficial for wildlife, the process is likely to be accompanied by progressive relaxation of planning control which will mean more greenfield development for housing, industry and recreation, and greater demands on water resources. More and bigger nature reserves may well be needed to offset the effect of such developments, including replacement of sites which may be lost or damaged. Growing public interest in nature and the 'outdoor laboratory' needs of education will also require more reserves like Whisby Nature Park resilient enough to support such uses. And however enlightened agricultural practices may become, they are unlikely to re-create such special habitats as wet heath, herb-rich chalk grassland and traditionally managed hay meadows.

The Trust's existing reserves are already a crucial factor in the maintenance of Lincolnshire's biodiversity. The statistics we researched for *Nature in Lincolnshire* were conclusive evidence for this. For example, of 630 hectares of wet and dry heath left in the county 168 (32%) were in six nature reserves; of 247 hectares of peatland and raised bog 87% was in three reserves; of 142 hectares of hay meadows 40% was in thirteen reserves. For endangered species the figures are even more impressive. To quote just three examples: out of 113 plants 59 occurred in reserves, 24 of them being confined to reserves and a further 17 confined to reserves and only one other site. Of eleven molluscs seven occurred in reserves, four being confined to them and one other confined to reserves and one other site. Of 52 macro-moths 41 occurred on reserves, 27 confined to them and seven to reserves and one other site.

Those figures highlight another problem. Species which become confined to one or two sites can be lost to the county altogether if those sites are destroyed or seriously damaged, as the beautiful grass-of-Parnassus was lost with the destruction of Waddingham Common. Even on reserves, fragile habitats and their vulnerable species can be severely damaged or destroyed by processes like a falling water-table. The more and bigger reserves we have, therefore, the more likely it is that their endangered species will survive. Another way of ensuring this is to translocate species, which is what we did by the re-establishment of the natterjack toad at Gibraltar Point. Reintroduction raises other issues, but it highlights the 'reservoir' function of reserves as places from which plants and animals can recolonise newly restored or re-created habitat, as is now happening with the extension of chalk grassland at the Red Hill, of heath at Kirkby and reedbed at Far Ings.

Nature reserves are an indispensable means of conserving nature. They have other values too. Many of them represent landscapes and land usages such as downland, traditional hay meadow and coppiced woodland, which have otherwise largely disappeared. Many also have historic and archaeological interest and remains, like the little Mill Hill chalk pit at Claxby which I described in an earlier chapter. The Trust's reserves are indeed an essential part of the county's heritage. As long as we can find the essential management resources of staff, volunteers and cash we should continue to create more of them on a larger scale.

Education and Promotion

Promoting understanding and appreciation of the natural world has always been a principal purpose of the Trust, not only for the pleasure and interest it brings to people's lives but also as the surest means of arousing their concern for its wellbeing. I have described in earlier chapters how this purpose is achieved by talks, films, publications – *Lapwings* magazine in particular – guided walks, special events, interpretative boards and leaflets on reserves, the Watch organisation for young people, and the Area Groups' programmes of events.

Until the 1980s, however, opportunities to promote more formal educational courses for schools and further education establishments were confined largely to Gibraltar Point where the residential field station established in 1958 was put to full use especially after Lindsey County Council's appointment in 1967 of Derek Golicher as Field Studies Tutor. One of his responsibilities was to organise school courses at Gibraltar Point and elsewhere and to train teachers in field study methods applicable to the coast and other Lincolnshire habitats. By the 1980s, however, his duties in the Education Department had widened and he could no longer devote the same attention to Gibraltar Point.

From the mid 1980s the Trust was able to employ a seasonal Interpretative Officer at Gibraltar Point, for some years on a government training scheme. He or she assisted with school and other day visits and guided walks for the general public, but the need for a teacher to take charge of the Field Station became increasingly urgent, and in 1995 we found the means to make such an appointment. As a result, activity expanded on all fronts, and in 2002 the Gibraltar Point education post was included in the ambitious three-year HLF-funded 'Education and Community Action Project'. Today more than 1,300 students from schools and colleges use the residential facilities of the field station (now the Wash Study Centre), and a further 2,300 come on organised day visits. In addition to school, college and university use, the Nottingham University Department of Adult Education continued to provide weekend and summer courses, and for some twenty years after my retirement from the Department I was able to continue teaching on some of their weekend bird and general environmental study courses. In recent years, especially since David Robinson's retirement as resident tutor, the University has largely withdrawn from its extramural role in Lincolnshire and its links with Gibraltar Point are now very tenuous.

As soon as the Visitor Centre was opened in 1974 an enthusiastic group of volunteers took over the day-to-day manning of it, providing information for visitors and making sales from the shop. From that time onwards volunteers, largely from the Trust's Skegness Area Group, have manned the Centre seven days a week through the summer and at weekends in winter. It has been a remarkable achievement. 60 to 70 thousand people visit the Centre each year and many attend the full programme of events which are organised for people of all ages. An ambitious plan to rebuild the Centre and the Field Station in the late 1990s was unsuccessful in attracting funding from the Millennium Commission and the Heritage Lottery Fund, but an extension to the Centre, including a small café and a major renewal of displays, is now (2006) being undertaken.

The growth of field studies in the 1960s and 70s placed a considerable strain on the facilities available at Gibraltar Point, and there was a danger too that excessive use of the reserve might damage habitats and species. Alternative sites were needed, and Derek Golicher in consultation with the Trust produced a list of other places which might be used. One of them was Snipe Dales where the Country Park had been added to the Nature Reserve in 1987. This offered grassland, streamside, pond and woodland habitats, and as the Trust's management staff and eventually its teaching resources were strengthened there, it became a popular venue for schools.

On Humberside the conversion of the Far Ings farmhouse and buildings into a Visitor Centre provided a base for field studies, and a small classroom was incorporated to supplement the more spacious first floor meeting room. From the 1980s the field staff there organised visits by school parties and youth groups to study lake, reedbed and saltmarsh habitats. Nature trails, guided walks and other events also became a regular feature.

An important element in the development of the Whisby Nature Park and Reserve was the provision of a classroom which local schools were encouraged to use by the Trust's employment of a seasonal field studies teacher. As at Far Ings, nature trails, guided walks and other events were organised throughout the year. From 2001 the Whisby Millennium Project transformed the facilities there by the construction of the Natural World Centre with its interactive displays and special exhibitions, and by the Trust's Education Centre which is well equipped with classrooms and laboratory. It was recognised that to develop the full potential of the new education facilities a full-time teacher would be required, and that was one of the main features of the application to HLF in 2002 for funding a major expansion of the Trust's educational services.

That application prepared by the Director and Chairman with the help and advice of the Trust's Education Team under its Convenor Derek Golicher so impressed the HLF that they provided a generous grant of £365,000 over three years. That together with tax credit funding from Waste Recycling Environmental Group enabled the Trust to appoint an Education Development Officer at headquarters, Education Officers at Gibraltar Point and Whisby, and a Peripatetic Education Officer with special responsibility for developing work at Far Ings and Snipe Dales. The Education and Community Action Project was a great success in developing the Trust's relationship with schools and community groups and producing valuable interpretative material. As with all fixed-term grant-aided projects, however, the challenge is to find the necessary resources to sustain the momentum when the funding comes to an end. This has been achieved on Humberside in 2006 by the South Humber People and Wildlife Project, an integrated educational service provided by a consortium of the Trust, North Lincolnshire Council and the Environment Agency. As part of the project the Trust will convert the former Outdoor Pursuits Centre into a new Far Ings Education and Visitor Centre.

The Trust's general promotional work, including services to members, developed steadily in the 1980s and 90s aided by the appointment of a Promotions Officer from 1988 and by the strengthening of headquarters and field staff and the increasing input of volunteers in many aspects of the process. Waymarked routes in nature reserves, easy-access trails for the disabled where practicable, leaflets about particular reserves, information and interpretation boards on site, open days and events, the Trust's annual presence at the Lincolnshire Show: those are just some of the means of creating interest and awareness of the County's natural heritage. The presence of the Promotions Officer also helped to secure more media coverage for nature conservation issues and the work of the Trust. Press releases were issued regularly and, thanks to some supportive presenters at Radio Lincolnshire, Trust officers and staff were heard frequently on the radio including the long-running 'A Country Diary' programme. The Promotions Officer also had a slot for comment on current conservation issues. For four or five years I enjoyed reading my own version of A Country Diary.

More specifically, our thrice yearly *Lapwings* magazine for members has been progressively enlarged and improved. In 1988 the Ruby Anniversary issues appeared in full colour with a review of forty years of achievement and prospects. For the Golden Jubilee the three issues had cover paintings by wildlife artist Debbie Thorpe. In 2002 the magazine was enlarged from 24 to 28 (now 32) pages. The successful development of *Lapwings* over the years has been due in large measure to David Robinson's editorial skill and experience, to Geoff Trinder's articles and splendid photographs, and to many contributors on a wide variety of topics including regular news from reserves. Since 1995 the Director has edited an illustrated Annual Review, a publication designed particularly for partners and financial supporters and for media purposes.

The first Handbook to our reserves which I edited in 1974 was re-issued in revised form in 1981, 1989 and 1997, the last two editions edited by Stuart Crooks. The first edition described 36 nature reserves; by 1997 the number had risen to 104.

Financing the Organisation

In 1974, the 25th anniversary year, the Trust's revenue income had risen to £15,409. Expenditure was £15,800 giving a deficit of £391. That, according to the report of the Council, was a result of rapidly escalating costs of administration and management. The report went on to warn that 1975/6 was likely to be an even more difficult year, as indeed it proved to be. These results indicate quite clearly the constant need in every year to balance the costs of running the organisation against the available income. Some of the income of £6,143 in 1974 was a contribution from Local Authorities and other bodies specifically for costs of administration. Earmarked income of that kind has grown substantially since then as projects and programmes funded by bodies such as English Nature and the Heritage Lottery Fund have come on stream. As I have already indicated, funding of that kind can give a tremendous boost to the Trust's capacity to achieve its purposes, but it is almost always time limited and its termination presents a serious problem of how to sustain the higher level of activity which it has generated. Careful forward planning is necessary to manage short-term special funding without distorting priorities or becoming over-reliant on it.

Looking ahead another ten years to 1984 we find in increasingly complex accounts that income had risen to nearly £156,000, but expenditure had exceeded that by £7,000. By the Ruby Jubilee Year 1988, income was £334,663 and there was a healthy surplus over expenditure of £3,223. There had been some leaner years in between when deficits had been incurred. To some extent the Trust's financial position reflected fluctuations in the national economy, particularly in the income derived from members' subscriptions and donations. Growth from those and other sources took the total income to more than £1M in the Golden Jubilee year of 1998.

Meantime we had established a Conservation Fund to which we transferred legacies to provide a regular source of income from investments. This was followed later by a Nature Reserves Establishment and Development Fund intended for the purchase and setting up of reserves and to provide matching funding for external grant-aid.

The Trust's income is like a barometer of its health and progress, none more so than that derived from **members' subscriptions** which forms the bulk of its unrestricted income. The 4,500 membership of 1974 produced an income of £5,789 including £426 of income tax recoverable on Deeds of Covenant, a method of payment which we constantly urged members who were eligible to adopt. By 1988 the total income from membership had risen to almost £52,000, £6,500 of which was the result of covenanting. The ordinary subscription, which had started at 10 shillings a year in 1948 and was raised to £1 in 1965, had become £10.50 after a series of increases in the 1970s and 80s largely to compensate for the high inflation of the period, but reflecting also the Trust's increasing size and commitments.

By 1998 subscription and covenanted income was £139,746. In the next six years the dramatic increase in membership pushed that total to well over half a million. By then the more flexible tax concession of gift-aid had largely replaced covenanting. Subscriptions and recoverable tax have thus remained the Trust's largest source of income, representing over the years some 20 to 25% of its total unrestricted income. Maintaining that is clearly vital for sustaining the day-to-day operations including employment of staff. Any significant diminution of it would be a cause for concern.

Before the surge in subscription income after 2000 we had employed a Marketing Manager for an experimental four-year period from 1995 with the aim of increasing unrestricted income from various sources. Whilst the appointment helped to secure grants and donations for nature reserve acquisition and other projects, it was less successful in its primary aim. Its functions have since been largely absorbed by other staff and by special contracts.

Income from properties has steadily increased as the Trust's estate has grown. Apart from the rent from the Old Hall Farm property at Caenby, much of it is derived from grazing rents. Whilst much of our considerable acreage of grassland is now grazed by our own sheep and cattle, some of it is let to other graziers on appropriate management conditions. Some income also results from the sale of sheep as the flock is necessarily reduced for the winter period. Sale of woodland produce also figures from time-to-time and this could eventually increase modestly as management of our woods produces more saleable timber and small wood – always provided that there is a market for such produce. The substantial income already derived from agri-environment schemes and likely to increase significantly was described earlier in this chapter.

When **grants** from the three former County Councils were first made to the Trust in 1968 the £1,550 received in that year represented about 20% of its total income and was an important factor in enabling the Trust to employ its first administrative officer. Of all the Lincolnshire local authorities only Lincolnshire County Council have maintained their financial support for general administrative purposes (as distinct from the service payments for Gibraltar Point, Snipe Dales, Whisby and road verges). In contrast to the 1968 position, however, the £25,850 received from the County Council in 2003/4 represented less than 1½% of the Trust's total income. The support is nonetheless still highly valued and the County Council clearly feel that it is well used.

General donations is another element of income. Some of it is money raised by Area Groups although that has diminished somewhat in recent years perhaps because – as indicated earlier – Groups and members have gained the impression that the Trust no longer needs relatively small donations derived from local events like coffee mornings and plant sales. This is a misapprehension which should be dispelled. Every pound is needed especially when matching funding for grants can effectively double it. Local fundraising efforts also help members to feel involved, that they are doing their bit for the Trust and for nature conservation.

Another source of income which has appeared on the Trust's accounts for forty years is **profit on sales**. Sales began in a very small way in 1963 when the SPNR produced an attractive set of Christmas cards for Trusts to sell to their members. Other items of stationery and a Trust tie with the badger motif were added to the range over the next few years. Brochures advertising the items were produced by the Society for Trusts to send to their members. Orders were dispatched by post and items were also on sale at events and other outlets. In Lincolnshire volunteers were responsible for handling orders from the Trust's office initially at Willoughby and after 1968 at Alford. This was a new outlet for volunteer involvement and one which the newly formed Area Groups took up with enthusiasm from 1968 onwards. As the range of goods expanded there were items for sale at all seasons of the year. Sales stalls appeared at Area Group meetings, at public nature trails, village galas and shows, and individual members kept stocks for coffee mornings and other home events. One couple, for example, sold £1,300 of goods in one year 1974. In the following year the opening of the new Visitor Centre at Gibraltar Point provided our first permanent sales outlet. Public nature trails became a popular feature of the Trust's programme and the caravans which were adapted as a base also had sales stalls. By 1978 we were confident enough to rent a shop in Castle Square in Lincoln which promptly attracted a devoted group of members.

By that time we were also purchasing goods directly from suppliers, and the organisation of the sales business, which had been the responsibility of the Administrative Officer at headquarters, was taken over by a part-time officer, a post converted to full-time in 1986. A small shop was incorporated in the Far Ings Centre when it was opened in 1991, and in 1985 we opened a shop in Abbey Gate in Grimsby, again with enthusiastic support of local members. Turnover increased rapidly: £32,000 in 1978 became £60,000 in 1980 and a record £152,000 in 1990. That, however, was the high water mark of the sales business. The national downturn in business activity, increasing staff and rental costs and increasing sales competition from other charitable organisations – we had been relatively early in the charity sales market – all combined to depress turnover and profits. In 1992 we were forced to give up the Grimsby shop and, although in 1996 we opened a seasonal shop at Grimsthorpe Castle – again with strong support from local volunteers – it too had to close in 2002. Nevertheless the sales business, now incorporated in Lapwings Consultants, has survived with the shops at Gibraltar Point, Lincoln, Far Ings and Banovallum House. Turnover has picked up again

– thanks in considerable measure to sales of bird food – and the business yields a small but worthwhile profit for the Trust's funds. Its success owes much to the enthusiastic management of Sales Officer Helen Baker.

I have commented on the sales business under sources of income. There are, of course, other dimensions to it which were decisive when its future came under scrutiny in the difficult years of the 1990s. It is a valuable means of contact with the general public: many people first become aware of the Trust through visiting our shops, buying goods and meeting our volunteers. Even more important perhaps is the fact that it involves many of our members in Trust activity, giving them a sense of ownership of the organisation in the same way as nature reserve and other helpers.

By the 1990s several of the Wildlife Trusts had established consultancies using information and experience of wildlife and environmental management and problems to undertake surveys and assessments of the kind increasingly required for planning and other purposes. In 1992 we set up our own consultancy – **Lapwings Consultants** – as a subsidiary company with a part-time manager. There was growing competition in this field and our promotional resources were somewhat meagre. Progress was slow although the Consultancy gained a reputation for sound and reliable service. In 2002, however, the Board of the Company decided that only a full-time manager could give the business the impetus it required to be really worthwhile. After two years under Caroline Steel's experienced management the business was flourishing and in the financial year 2003/4 yielded a profit for the Trust of more than £27,000. On her appointment as the Trust's Assistant Director (Conservation) she was succeeded by Tim Smith who had long been associated with the Trust in volunteer capacities.

Finally under income there are **legacies** and In Memoriam gifts. The great majority of these have been unrestricted, but in two or three cases they have been left specifically for nature reserve acquisition. The first legacy, for £100, appears in the accounts for 1964, but it was another eight years before a second one was received. Then they began to come in regularly, one in most years of the 1970s and 80s. Some of the legators were members who had joined the Trust in its early years or been closely associated with it, like Irene Court whose husband had been the Trust's first President and whose bequest exceeded £27,000, the largest up to that time.

At the Lincolnshire Show in 1986 an elderly gentleman, Lewis Green, enquired of the Trust's Director if the Trust would like a redundant church. When Stuart Crooks explained that care of old buildings was not one of the Trust's purposes, Mr Green added that there would be 'a bit of land to go with it'. Lincolnshire people are given to understatement (you never say, for example, that you are very well, you are fair or fair to middlin) and 'a bit of land' turned out to be the 373 acre Old Hall farm at Caenby with a substantial house, cottages and the redundant church, all of which he had bequeathed to the Trust. Tom Twigg and I went to see Mr Green and for the rest of his years we visited him every few months, and in summer took him around the county to see the Trust's meadows and other reserves. His main wish was that the house and the farm should be kept together if possible, and after his death in 1986 we were fortunate to be able to let the farm and sell the house to the tenant. That immensely valuable legacy was an important factor in the Trust's development. It was followed closely afterwards by another of over £83,000 from Ted Mason, one of the partners in the Trust's firm of solicitors Andrew & Co. Mr Mason, a bachelor, was a naturalist from a family of naturalists. When I met him one day by chance at Kirkby Moor he told me what pleasure the Trust reserves had given him in retirement. The Hatton Meadows reserve are dedicated to his memory. Nurse Heath's legacy of £74,000 which I mentioned earlier was one of those restricted to reserve purchase and was honoured with the dedication of Heath's Meadows at Bratoft. George Jackson was a small farmer at Hogsthorpe who left his house and land to the Trust. The land was of little conservation interest so we sold it and the house and used the proceeds to purchase the new meadow and wetland area at Gibraltar Point now named Jackson's Marsh in his memory. These and other benefactions, some of which I have mentioned earlier, are recorded in a Book of Remembrance which is kept at Banovallum House. It includes not only legators but also donors of land and other property, and some who have given outstanding service to the Trust.

It became apparent in the 1970s that legacies had the potential to be a major source of income, and we began to draw attention regularly in the *Lapwings* magazine to their value. We also issued leaflets from time to time about bequests and how to make them. As Chairman I wrote, with the guidance of Philip Race the Trust's own solicitor, to the senior partners of all the law firms in Lincolnshire drawing their attention to the aims and achievements of the Trust, a practice continued from time to time by my successor.

The size and frequency of legacies have increased over the years. In the ten years from 1986 to 1997 we received 58 bequests ranging from £100 to £260,000. The rate accelerated in the new century. From 2000 to 2004 there were 35, again from £100 to more than £900,000, the latter from Mr J R Cook of Aylesby, one of the largest so far received by the Trust.

The reasons for the increase in legacies are, I suggest, not far to seek: growing awareness and concern about the natural world; the wish to be remembered by association with wild places or traditional land usage and to help save them for future generations, and the reputation and achievements of the Trust are all factors which have played a part. Some solicitors have undoubtedly helped by bringing the Trust to the attention of clients wishing to benefit wildlife and countryside in Lincolnshire. By investing the bulk of legacy money to produce a regular source of income we ensure that it will be of lasting benefit to the Trust and its purposes. We believe that that is what most benefactors would wish.

MARY PORTER

The Trust's Wildlife Gift Shop (white building on the left) in Castle Square, Lincoln.

BARRIE WILKINSON

Gibraltar Point Visitor Centre extended and refitted 2006.

Education and Community Action Project

PYEWIPES

The Smiths arrived at Pyewipes April 1957.

Alison and Helen in the orchard 1962.

Alison OBE 2006

Helen monitoring the fen raft spider at Redgrave and Lopham Fens 2006.

Part VI

Home at Pyewipes

– 18 –

Family, Home and Garden

Childrens' voices in the orchard
Between the blossom and the fruit-time Eliot

HOME is where I started this story. Home is where I end it. When we moved to Willoughby to the house we named Pyewipes in March 1957 Alison was not quite three and Helen only eight months. From an early age they were 'busy' children always fully occupied with imaginative games in house and garden, and listening eagerly to our readings of the stories of Beatrix Potter, Alison Utley, Racey Helps and others. The Paddington Bear stories by Michael Bond were introduced to us by my old Northumberland friend Tony Tynan inextricably associated thereafter by the children with marmalade sandwiches, Paddington's favourite food.

Both attended the village primary school conveniently situated on the opposite side of the road from Pyewipes. There were about seventy children at the school when Alison started there in 1959. Almost all the village children attended, although after two or three years some of the better-off parents – mainly large farmers – sent their offspring to boarding school.

The school buildings and accommodation at that time were still fairly basic. The loos for example were in an open building across the playground. There was one virtue in that: they provided a nest site for swallows! One day Mary received an urgent appeal for help from the Headmistress. A nest full of young swallows had fallen into the boys' urinal! The young were gathered up none the worse for the calamity. The nest was put into the children's teddy bear's picnic basket and fastened on top of a ladder, whereupon the agitated parents quickly resumed feeding!

Alison treated lessons as seriously as play. One day at lunchtime after a few weeks at school she solemnly announced that she was not going back in the afternoon. "Why?" we asked. "Not enough to do" was the answer. With such small numbers there was no great stimulus or competition, but it had all the virtues of a village school with a mix of children from a range of social background and ability.

Our orchard and little wood were the scene of many of their games and pastimes as they grew older. We installed a swing and acquired an old caravan which they could regard as their own place and where they could invite their friends. One ambitious scheme which they developed there was a dragon research project. Pictures of dragons were collected and displayed and references in literature copied out. We searched for dragon images in church carvings and windows. Friends were invited to exhibitions and treated to mysterious dragon noises from the wood! We still have the manual which they compiled.

Bikes from the age of eight or nine gave the two of them more freedom to explore the lanes and paths around the village and to develop a sense of discovery and observation. We fostered an interest in natural history with discretion, not wishing to appear to foist it on them. Frequent outings to the seaside aroused an interest in many of the objects found in the tide wrack and in the great variety of pebbles on the beach. The children were also influenced by our friends and contacts in the Trust, in the SPNR and in the Nature Conservancy many of whom who were frequent visitors to Pyewipes. They accompanied us to meetings in the field and on visits to reserves spending much time at the Gibraltar Point field station where in later school holidays they assisted with the catering and cleaning, absorbing in the process much natural history knowledge and experience. They have told me that all those influences were decisive in determining their choice of study in biological sciences and ultimate careers.

Their natural history interests are evident from their early diaries. Alison took a special interest in plants, even learning to identify mosses at quite an early age. Helen's first natural history interests were in butterflies and moths, stimulated during one of our visits to Dorset when Brian Pickess, the RSPB Warden at Arne, showed her how to mount the wings of moths found dead for identification purposes. In later years our old friend Rick Pilcher further encouraged her interest. Birds for Helen came a good deal later.

Foreign travel with children was not easy in the 1950s and 60s, and in any case we wanted to see more of our own country and to introduce the children to its great variety of landscapes and wildlife. We were drawn first to the south-west, staying for a time at a Cornish farmhouse where Mary had recuperated after a wartime illness. We went back in later years to explore the magnificent coastline of Devon and Cornwall: the cliffs, the sandy bays and the exciting wonders of rock pools. We also spent parts of several holidays in Dorset, staying with our friend Helen Brotherton to explore that wonderfully varied county. There were visits to Portland Bill and its bird observatory; to the heaths – the remnants of Hardy's Egdon – to see such specialities as Dartford warbler and smooth snake; to Lyme Regis and the Golden Cap searching for fossils along the cliffs, and to Brownsea Island with its tern colony and red squirrels. Shakespeare plays at the open-air theatre there were always a highlight of the holiday.

We also went westwards to the Welsh borders, to Ludlow and Offa's Dyke and the Black Mountains, and on to the Pembroke coast and the delightful little town of St David's. By that time visiting Skokholm was difficult, but we went to Skomer and gave the children their first experience of a sea bird island. We stayed too on Anglesey visiting castles and gardens in North Wales and the summit of Snowdon.

Nearer home we went back to the north Norfolk coast to see the tern colonies on Scolt Head and to listen to the bitterns booming in the marshes at Cley. We explored other Norfolk landscapes too: the Breckland and the Broads where Christopher Cadbury invited us to stay on occasions at Whiteslea Lodge on Hickling Broad, a rare treat. There was also that magical house at Blickling which I had first seen in the autumn of 1946 when I went for an interview for a teaching post at North Walsham. The unexpected sight of it beyond its great yew hedges in the fading light of an autumn afternoon is unforgettable.

In 1950 Mary and I had spent a holiday in the Cairngorms at Aviemore then a quiet village on the main road and railway to the north. We explored the ancient pine woods of Rothiemurcus with their crested tits and crossbills; we watched ptarmigan in the Lairig Ghru, and climbed to the plateau summit of Braeriach at 4,000 feet where snow was still lying. Discovering the birds and flowers of the mountains and northern forests was an exciting experience. I am looking as I write at Mary's little book of watercolour paintings of many of those flowers made during that holiday.

We took the children to Scotland as soon as they were old enough to travel longer distances, to the Cairngorms again and then on to the northern coast of Caithness where we listened to corncrakes at Bettyhill and sought out the little Scottish primrose on the coastal dunes. After the University adult summer course which I organised in 1959 at the Nature Conservancy's field station at Anancaun on Loch Maree in the magnificent Beinn Eighe reserve in Wester Ross, I took the family there a few years later to stay at Ullapool and at Poolewe from where we visited the famous 'Gulf Stream' gardens at Inverewe. We made contact also with Ray Collier with whom I had kept in touch since his earlier application for the Gibraltar Point warden's post and who had subsequently joined the Nature Conservancy and, after a spell at the Castor Hanglands National Nature Reserve, had become warden of the Inverpolly NNR. Ray showed us many features of the reserve including an occupied golden eagle's nest. Helen, always adventurous, climbed with him up a steep cliff to get a better view.

It was fortunate that my university duties usually enabled me to take time off to coincide with the children's half-term in late May and early June which we were able to extend by a few days whilst they were at primary and early secondary school. Travelling too was less demanding and more leisurely than it often is these days, especially since we tried to avoid the busiest roads and had the time to stop now and again to look at a National Trust house or garden, a nature reserve or church or attractive village. Going south-west we usually broke our journey in the Cotswolds; northwards we stopped in the Borders. Even popular areas like the south-west were not as crowded and congested as they are at holiday times today. Once the girls' education was at a more advanced secondary stage such late spring holidays came to an end. They were an important feature of our family life, a kind of bonding experience away from home. Both of them, Alison in particular, have travelled much more extensively abroad since then. But that those early holidays around Britain made a lasting impression is evident from the great detail in which they both remember them.

At the age of eleven Alison transferred to Alford Grammar School which by that time had become co-educational. The headmaster for her first two years was H J H Dyer who had been headmaster for my last three years! Alison was a good all-rounder academically and took a full part in games, in play productions and in music, playing the flute in the Lindsey Youth Orchestra. By then in a much larger school than in my time science teaching was greatly improved, and

Alison secured a place to study Natural Sciences at Girton College, Cambridge on which she had set her sights from visits to Cambridge to see our friends the Walters at the Botanic Garden. Once she had adapted to university life she made great progress, supplementing academic studies with vacational field work for the Nature Conservancy in various parts of the country. A first-class degree led to a PhD in the Botany School (now the Department of Plant Sciences) under the tutelage of outstanding plant biochemist Professor Tom ap Rees. A post-doc position took her to the University of Dusseldorf and there her career suffered a temporary setback. When she came home at the end of the first Christmas term she was clearly unwell and had been for several weeks. Our doctor and a consultant to whom she was referred diagnosed the viral infection glandular fever. A period of rest and recuperation was necessary and eventually the Dusseldorf post had to be abandoned. After six anxious months and further medical tests for possible leukaemia – which fortunately proved negative – Alison began to recover sufficient energy and motivation to apply for posts in the UK. An offer from Harold Woolhouse, Professor of Botany at Leeds, to become his research assistant was gladly accepted. Within a year he had been appointed Director of the John Innes Centre at Norwich and he took Alison there with him. That proved to be a critical turning point in her career and she went on to become the Head of the Department of Metabolic Biology, an Honorary Professor at the University of East Anglia, and a plant scientist of international distinction. She was appointed OBE for services to plant biochemistry in the Queen's Birthday Honours List in 2006. She is happily married to Mark Buttner, a fellow scientist at the John Innes Centre.

Helen's academic career was more chequered than Alison's. She followed Alison to Alford Grammar School in 1967 and made good progress. Anxiety to do well, however, led to periodic crises of confidence at examination times which became something of an ordeal. After excellent GCSE results she spent a gap year doing field work for the Nature Conservancy in the south-east and east Midlands, including a survey of sea buckthorn at the Saltfleetby-Theddlethorpe NNR and a vegetation survey at Gibraltar Point. She also had a spell assisting at the Preston Montford Field Study Centre. After a false start at Imperial College in London in 1975 she went to the University of Sussex where she secured a first-class degree in Natural Sciences in 1979. From there she moved to Aberdeen to obtain an MSc in ecology. Whilst at Aberdeen she met and eventually married Stephen Baillie who later became Director of Populations Research at the British Trust for Ornithology. Helen then returned south to the University of East Anglia to obtain a PhD by a study of glasswort (*Salicornia*) and seablite (*Suaeda*) as saltmarsh pioneering colonists. The BTO at that time was based at Tring and Helen set up house with Stephen at Whitchurch working first for the Berks, Bucks and Oxon Trust, and then at the Wildlife Conservation Research Unit at the University of Oxford. When the BTO moved its headquarters to Thetford in 1990 they bought a delightful cottage at South Lopham on the edge of Redgrave and Lopham Fens National Nature Reserve. Our grandchildren Alice and James were born in 1991 and 1994. Besides bringing up a family Helen now works as a consultant ecologist and has also become a leading authority on the fen raft spider (*Dolomedes plantarius*) which was first found in Britain in 1956 at Redgrave and Lopham Fens by our old friend Dr Eric Duffey. In addition she has played a leading role in setting up the Little Ouse Headwaters Project, an independent charity which by acquisition, lease and agreement is protecting and restoring the landscapes and habitats of the upper reaches of that river. The Project, a notable example of local community initiative in conservation, has received funding from Heritage Lottery Fund and European sources, and in 2006, only three years after it was founded, won the prestigious national Living Wetlands Award.

Alice and James are making their own marks. Both of them are making excellent progress at their local High School in Diss. Both have won national Rock Watch awards; both are musicians – Alice a very competent flautist, James a trumpeter. In 2006 Alice at the age of 14 campaigning largely on environmental issues was elected MP for South Norfolk in the UK Youth Parliament. Both share the family interest in natural history. Alice is a keen and knowledgeable bird watcher; James, an avid reader and a careful observer, has a more general interest in nature and the environment and a passion for history.

And Mary

When the children had both started school Mary briefly considered returning to teaching, but she decided instead to concentrate on home and family, supporting the Trust and my work for it, and maintaining a large garden, all of which she did with skill, devotion and enthusiasm. After the drawings she made for the Butcher *Flora* she regularly contributed artwork for Trust publications including illustrations for a *Flowers of the Wolds* brochure which was published for sale in association with East Lindsey District Council *(see page 384)*. Support for the Trust came in many other ways: housing the office for seventeen years; entertaining many visitors to the Trust; helping with botanical surveys; raising funds by selling plants, and opening the garden to the public.

In 1961 she was elected to Willoughby Parish Council topping the poll in a rare contested election. She was Chairman for several years and eventually retired from the Council in 1993 after a record thirty-two years service. She was a County Council appointee to the governing body of the village school, and regarded as the school's unofficial consultant on natural history matters.

She was a member of the Willoughby Women's Institute for thirty years and served two spells as President. Her involvement in the wider WI movement included the chairmanship of the North Lincolnshire Federation's Agriculture and Environment Committee. She was also an active member and a Controller of the Alford WI Market.

Mary's skills as a gardener were soon recognised in the village and beyond. In the early 1960s she brought together a group of gardeners to form the Willoughby Garden Club, and although that faded after fifteen years she re-formed it in 1988 and it has flourished ever since. She served as the Chairman from its inception until retirement in 1997. Elsewhere she chaired the Alford Horticultural Society from 1965 to 1971 and was awarded an honorary life membership for her service. She also qualified as a horticultural show judge and was much in demand for shows in the east Lincolnshire area.

In a busy life she still found time for art and craft work. In addition to plant drawings for the Trust she worked very skilfully in scraperboard, a medium capable of surprising delicacy. She also taught herself rush weaving and her work won awards in WI competitions.

She also continued to write. For several years she contributed a monthly column on wildlife and gardening matters for a local newspaper. Research into the history of the village produced the Willoughby Village Guide which was published by East Lindsey District Council. She entered WI essay competitions and won prizes and commendations. Privately her facility for composing comic verses was a constant source of family amusement. For most of the 1970s and 80s Mary kept a daily diary which provides a fascinating record of family and village life and activity, journeys and holidays, Trust events and my comings and goings, visitors and weather, wildlife and garden. It is well worthy of publication in some form.

Mary maintained much of this great variety of activity and output until well into her seventies, until advancing age and the onset of Parkinson's disease caused her gradually to reduce her commitments. The increasing limitation on mobility imposed by the disease has been especially disappointing for someone who had been so active and dexterous. However, with the devoted assistance of Iris Hardy, our domestic help over nearly forty years, of retired nursing friends and the County Council's Home Care Service, she has been able enjoy home and garden and greenhouse and contact with family and friends.

Garden and Wildlife

Like us the garden has changed over the years. The original design reached a kind of middle-aged maturity and then went into a slow decline needing increasing attention to retain its character. This applied especially to trees and shrubs. Short-lived ones needed replacing; the more vigorous sometimes overwhelmed their neighbours and required more drastic pruning. Some have improved with age, however, none more so than the magnolias, the Japanese maple, the rowan species, the ginkgo and the dawn redwood (*Metasequoia*) which is on its way to being the tallest tree in the village. Some weeds have become more prevalent in borders in spite of efforts to contain them. Some ground-cover plants, although suppressing weeds, have become rampant – like the periwinkle which we planted under shrubs. On the other hand some very desirable plants have multiplied and spread like the snowdrops and the colchicums and the cyclamen, both *hederifolium* and *coum*, which line the foot of the beech hedge and have even colonised the lawns.

Gradual adjustments have become necessary, sacrificing some parts of the design, prolonging the life of others and occasionally bringing in something quite new from the ever-increasing range of plants available. Milder winters due to climate change have enabled us to grow shrubs which would not have been considered hardy forty or fifty years ago. Californian *Carpenteria* and *Fremontia*, and the Moroccan Broom all flourish on the south-facing front of the house and outbuildings together with a variety of other shrubs including *Ceratostigma willmottianum* whose blue late summer flowers outside my study window are especially attractive to humming-bird hawk-moths. The main herbaceous border and the big pond with its marginal kingcups, primulas, irises and other plants are still attractive features. We have also retained a small vegetable garden which remains productive in spite of the depredations of wood pigeons, collared doves and cabbage white caterpillars. The garden was the subject of a full page feature in the *Weekend Telegraph* in March 1990.

We did not design the garden specifically for wildlife, but it has attracted a great variety of birds, insects and other creatures and they have been a constant source of interest and delight to us. Species changed as the garden developed.

The herbaceous border.

Beech hedge and Cyclamen hederifolium.

Snowdrops in the orchard.

The 'big' pond.

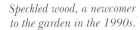

Speckled wood, a newcomer to the garden in the 1990s.

The swallows are back – on the weathervane.

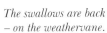

Roo and Tig on the greenhouse roof.

The last swallow out of the porch nest, 2005.

Mountain flowers from Mary's Cairngorms sketchbook 1950.

Initially there was little to attract birds in the rough paddock, but the buildings provided nest sites, especially the cart shed (now the garage) where old nests told of generations of swallows. For almost all the fifty years that we have been here swallows have nested there and at times in the house and office porches. We have always looked forward eagerly to their return, a real landmark of the spring. Their numbers have declined in the last twenty years as they have in eastern England generally. Perhaps the disappearance of cattle in the village in recent years has been a contributory factor in that. The trees, shrubs and hedges which we planted gradually provided habitat, food and nest sites for a variety of birds, all supplemented by nest boxes and by winter feeding. Changes in variety and numbers of species have also reflected national trends: the arrival of the collared dove, for example, and the sad disappearance of the turtle dove; the appearance of the blackcap as a regular summer resident delighting us with his virtuoso song; the decline of willow warbler, willow tit and cuckoo now seldom heard from the garden.

Badger is now a nightly visitor, but we have had no hedgehogs for a number of years. Any connection between the two I wonder? We have pipistrelle and long-eared bats and the occasional grass snake. The ponds have been particularly attractive: frogs, toads and smooth newts all flourish; there are three breeding species of damselfly, and two dragonflies as well as other occasional visitors.

Butterflies have increased in variety as the garden has grown up. Like birds they have also reflected national population trends. The holly blue, for example, having been a rarity for the first thirty years of the garden has become regular and frequent in both spring and summer broods. Perhaps the most notable newcomer in the last twenty years, however, has been the delightful speckled wood, now to be found regularly in shady places in the garden where sunlight is filtered through leaves matching its creamy spots.

From the winter jasmine, the witch hazel and the orchard snowdrops to the autumn cyclamen and the colchicums and the rowan berries, the garden is a source of endless pleasure and interest to us throughout the year, an integral element of our lives. It is pleasing too that both our daughters are keen and knowledgeable gardeners.

As For Me

As for me, the years of 'retirement' (from paid employment that is!) have passed all too quickly. As described in earlier chapters, they were years of rapid growth and development in the Lincolnshire Trust in which my position as Chairman kept me constantly occupied. I continued to be involved throughout the 1980s in the affairs of the RSNC as a member of the Council and Executive Committee and of the Nature Reserves Committee. Chairmanship of the Advisory Committees for the Breckland and Woodwalton Fen provided another pleasant and rewarding piece of service to conservation. Five years on the National Trust's Conservation Panel from 1985 to 1990 involved advisory visits to several of the Trust's properties of high conservation interest including the Lake District, the Farne Islands, the Cotswolds and the North Downs. I also continued into my seventies to teach for my old University Department on weekend and summer courses at Gibraltar Point.

Domestically there was more time for home and garden and visiting our daughters; time too to begin to set down my recollections and experiences in what has gradually evolved into the present *Memoir*. Mary and I were able to take more extended holidays and to see places, people and wildlife – flowers, birds and butterflies in particular – in other parts of Europe: in Switzerland, France, Spain, Portugal, Italy, mainland Greece, Crete, and Norway. We also revisited some of our favourite places in Britain – The Lakes, the Yorkshire Dales, the Northumberland coast, the Welsh Borders, the Cotswolds, Kent and Sussex and for the first time south-west Scotland, Galloway. Landscapes, gardens, houses leave a rich tapestry of memory. My only regret was that we could not see more at home and abroad before age and infirmity constrained our mobility.

I had received the OBE in 1963 for services to nature conservation, and this was advanced to CBE in 1998. By that time Mary was unable to travel to London for an award ceremony so I elected to have the presentation in Lincolnshire by the Lord Lieutenant Mrs Bridget Cracroft-Eley. It took place on a fine April day (April 23rd St George's Day and Shakespeare's birthday) in 1999 at Banovallum House in the presence of family, friends and colleagues in the Lincolnshire Trust, a memorable occasion. There were two other equally unexpected awards at that time. The first was the conferment of an Honorary Doctorate of Science by the then University of Lincolnshire and Humberside (now Lincoln) which was made at a degree ceremony in Hull where I also presented degrees to graduates and addressed the congregation. The following year I was invited to the Netherlands to be installed as an Officer of the Order of the Golden Ark. Alison and her husband Mark accompanied me to the ceremony at the Soestdijk Palace for the presentation by Prince Bernhard. That too was a memorable and friendly occasion and I felt particularly honoured to receive the international recognition which it implied. All these awards – including earlier the first Christopher Cadbury Medal – were extremely gratifying and I was delighted to receive them, but my real reward in all that I have done is the achievements which I have helped to promote in the conservation of wildlife, and the dedicated support which I have constantly received from family and from many colleagues and friends.

With Max Walters (centre) and Franklyn Perring at the 40th anniversary celebration of the founding of the Cambridgeshire and Isle of Ely Trust, 1996.

Conferment of Honorary Doctorate of Science by the Chancellor of the University of Lincolnshire and Humberside, 1998.

With Helen Brotherton and Christopher Cadbury against the record of Cadbury Medal recipients, 1992.

Presentation of CBE at Banovallum House by the Lord Lieutenant of Lincolnshire (1998) with family, colleagues and friends (below).

Installation as an Officer of the Order of the Golden Ark by Prince Bernhard of the Netherlands, 1999.

With speakers at the 40th anniversary celebration of the Lincolnshire Trust 1988.
L-R: Dunstan Adams, Chairman RSNC, Sir William Wilkinson, Chairman NCC and
Christopher Cadbury, President RSNC.

Sir David Attenborough at the 50th anniversary
celebrations at Banovallum House 1998 with
young Wildlife Watch members (upper left), The
Lincolnshire Poacher (John Lill, left) and speaking
to the press (above).

At the Trust's 50th anniversary
dinner 1998 with principal
guest Baroness Young,
Chairman of English Nature.

Epilogue

So many worlds, so much to do,
So little done, such things to be Tennyson

THE TRUST'S 40th anniversary in 1988 was celebrated by a reception in Lincoln for members and representatives of associated bodies. Special guests and speakers were Sir William Wilkinson, Chairman of the Nature Conservancy Council, Christopher Cadbury, President of the RSNC, and Dunstan Adams, Chairman of the RSNC. All of them praised the Trust's pioneering role in the development of the national nature conservation movement. I was greatly honoured by the unveiling of my portrait commissioned by the Trust Council and painted by Lincolnshire artist Bill Bates. It now hangs in the conference room at Banovallum House. Area Groups also celebrated the anniversary by events, and there were three special issues of *Lapwings*.

Ten years passed all too quickly and in 1998 we celebrated an even more significant anniversary, the 50th. The whole of the year was treated as a Jubilee Year with events and exhibitions in many parts of the county. In September we welcomed more than 300 delegates to the Wildlife Trusts' national conference which was held appropriately in Lincoln on the University Campus, thirty-eight years after the first such conference – a landmark in the early development of the Trusts' movement – took place in Lincolnshire at Skegness in 1960. Another highlight of the year was a visit by Sir David Attenborough who returned to Gibraltar Point twenty-four years after he opened the Visitor Centre there. Later that day he spoke to more than 300 members in a marquee in the grounds of Banovallum House. On the exact birthday 2 December we held a dinner for invited members and guests who were addressed by Baroness Young of Old Scone, Chairman of English Nature. The Lord Lieutenant of Lincolnshire Mrs Bridget Cracroft-Eley was present, and Helen Brotherton from Dorset and several other old friends of the Trust from other counties were among the invited guests. It was another enjoyable and memorable event.

Anniversaries are inevitably nostalgic occasions, but they are also opportunities to take stock of the present and look to the future. This Memoir has been largely concerned with past events and achievements and how they have shaped the present. I have described from time to time my own impressions of the changing circumstances in which the Trust has operated over the years and the ways in which it has adapted its policies and its organisation. Outstanding among those impressions are first the efforts of the early pioneering years to build the organisation, to secure recognition and support for the cause, and to save precious places. Protecting the unspoilt stretches of the coast from development was an urgent priority from the start, and our success in establishing with Lindsey County Council the nature reserves at Gibraltar Point and at Saltfleetby was an achievement of lasting value and significance. Then, the 1960s and 1970s were dominated by the effects of intensive agricultural production fuelled by a government policy of subsidy long after it was justifiable. The consequent transformation of great swathes of the Lincolnshire countryside into arable prairies presented a formidable challenge to the Trust to salvage the remnants of heath and downland, of meadow, woodland and wetland, and that at a time when land prices were high and the SSSI provisions which should have protected many of the sites were lamentably ineffective. We were not always successful, there were serious losses, but without our action many of our existing reserves would also have been destroyed.

Now after thirty years agricultural policies and practices have been put into reverse. Farmers are supported financially by government not for production but for sound land management and conservation. A similar change is taking place in forestry where native trees are once again coming back into favour after years of intensive conifer cultivation. Add to all this the quite stringent legal protection now afforded to SSSIs and you have an almost bewildering transformation of the land use and conservation scene. Meantime on the credit side also, re-creation of habitats like wetlands, heaths and calcareous grasslands is enabling rare and threatened species to survive and flourish and lost ones to recolonise.

Agricultural pressures have eased, but the demand for land and resources for housing, for industry, for new and bigger roads and for recreation is constantly increasing, often posing new problems for conservation. Windfarms, the latest development, sometimes present a real dilemma. The Trust of course supports generation of power by renewable, non-polluting methods, but on some sites wind turbines could be seriously damaging to wildlife and will certainly impair the landscape character of areas like the Lindsey Outmarsh. And an even more ominous threat to the whole of the natural world, mankind included, now looms ahead in the form of climate change which is indeed already beginning to affect the distribution and behaviour of plants and animals. To mitigate its effects may require radical measures affecting our lifestyle which to be universally acceptable and effective in this country – and we should be setting an example to others – will need political consensus. The voluntary conservation movement has always sought to arouse awareness of man's dependence on the natural world and of our responsibilities for its wellbeing. That message now assumes a more urgent significance and we must redouble our efforts to help to get it across. We can also urge the adoption of measures to relieve pressures on wildlife, such as a continuing ban on sand-eel fishery in the North Sea. We can expand our nature reserves to enable wildlife to adapt more readily to changing conditions, and we can re-create habitats threatened by rising sea levels and other consequences of climate change.

The changes in the land use situation in which the Trust has operated have already been accompanied by changes in attitude towards conservation on the part of official bodies and the general public. When we started fifty-eight years ago few people knew what we were on about and even fewer cared. Even the word 'conservation' as applied to wildlife and environment was virtually unknown. Whilst there is still much to be done in influencing attitudes, the changes that have taken place have been dramatic and we operate now in a totally different atmosphere from that of 1948.

The great strength of the Wildlife Trusts is their local voluntary basis responsive to local needs and circumstances. To sustain that strength and character requires volunteer involvement at all levels of governance and activity. It has been one of the great challenges therefore to reconcile that involvement with the role of the increasing numbers of staff inevitably required to administer and manage the Trust's expanding activities and commitments. That we have been able to do that successfully in Lincolnshire has been due to carefully planned adjustments of the respective roles of staff and volunteers, and above all to sensitive and understanding attitudes on both sides. Although inevitably the number of active members has shrunk in recent years as a proportion of the vastly increased total membership, there are still at the last count more than 1,250 of them involved in almost every activity at all levels from the Board of Trustees, the joint volunteer-member Teams, the Area Groups, the sales business, fund-raising and other projects. Minor differences no doubt arise from time to time, but the success of the Trust over the years has been due in no small measure to the harmonious and productive working relationships that exist between volunteers and staff.

It has been a long journey from the spare bedroom office in Alford to Banovallum House; from the 129 members of the first year to the 26,000 of today; from the £82 income of 1949 to over £1 million; from the first five or six nature reserves of the 1950s to the present hundred; from the handful of pioneering volunteers who launched the Trust to the present forty or more staff. The Trust has earned its recognition as the leading environmental body in the historic county which is all the richer for its achievements.

The development of the Wildlife Trusts' movement country-wide has been equally impressive. The example of the early pioneers and the rejuvenation of the SPNR led to that remarkable surge in the early 1960s which saw the whole country covered by a Trust within five years. Since then they have grown steadily in strength and influence individually and corporately, and with a total membership of more than 600,000 have become a major force in conservation action and planning at local and national level.

I was exceptionally fortunate to be involved at the beginning of a new movement in conservation and to have been able to exercise some small influence over its development. I have been fortunate too in my family, in my friends and colleagues past and present in the Trust, in the national movement, in the former NC/NCC and in my old University department. Their support and encouragement have been the mainstay of my aspirations and endeavours.

Shorelarks by Steve Message

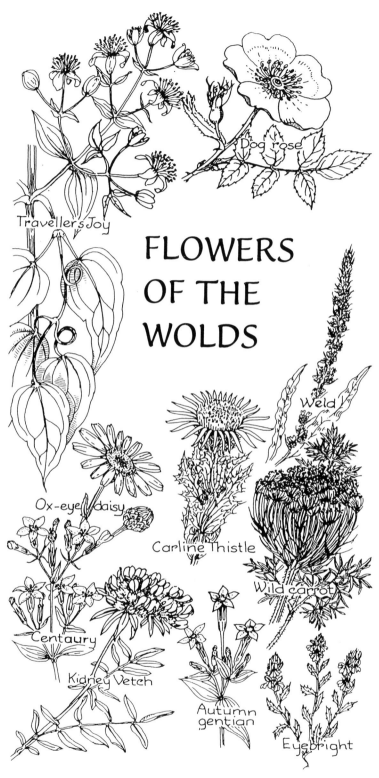

Travellers Joy

Dog rose

FLOWERS OF THE WOLDS

Weld

Ox-eye daisy

Carline Thistle

Wild carrot

Centaury

Kidney Vetch

Autumn gentian

Eyebright

Drawn by Mary Smith